INTEGRATED SERVICES DIGITAL NETWORKS

Architectures, Protocols, Standards

INTEGRATED SERVICES DIGITAL NETWORKS

Architectures, Protocols, Standards

Hermann J. Helgert

The George Washington University, Washington, D.C.

Addison-Wesley Publishing Company
Reading, Massachusetts • Menlo Park, California
New York • Don Mills, Ontario • Wokingham, England
Amsterdam • Bonn • Sydney • Singapore • Tokyo • Madrid • San Juan

To my wife, Janet

Library of Congress Cataloging-in-Publication Data

Helgert, Hermann J.
   Integrated services digital networks : architectures,
protocols, standards / Hermann J. Helgert.
      p.   cm.
   Includes bibliographical references and index.
   ISBN 0-201-52501-1
   1. Integrated services digital networks. I. Title.
TK5103.7.H46   1991
621.382—dc20   90-47659
                                                     CIP

ABCDEFGHIJ-MA-943210

Preface

In recent years the technical evolution of the telecommunications industry has largely been driven by three key factors: the introduction of digital transmission circuits, stored program controlled switches, and common channel signaling techniques in the interexchange networks of the public carriers. These developments have resulted in a considerable simplification of the integration of voice and data over the same network facilities, a generally higher quality of service at a reduced cost, and fast and sophisticated call control. In parallel with the changes in the interexchange network and as a direct result, new and innovative uses of the telecommunications infrastructure have emerged. The network has also gradually been expanded into an intelligent facility.

Integrated services digital networks (ISDN) are the logical culmination of these developments. They extend the benefits of digital communications to the subscribers, make the voice and nonvoice services of a network available over an integrated network access arrangement, and have the potential of providing the subscribers with a high level of control over network services and facilities.

This book offers the reader a description of the ISDN from the technical point of view. Most of its features are embodied in a series of standards that have been developed by the CCITT, ANSI, and other standards bodies over the last decade. Although most of the specifications in these standards are substantially complete and enjoy the consensus of the major telecommunications organizations of the

v

world, the reader is nevertheless advised that several important aspects of ISDN are still under active discussion within the standards organizations and subject to future revision. This is particularly true of the so-called broadband ISDN (BISDN), whose specification has at the time of this writing not reached a high degree of maturity. From the point of view of implementation, ISDN is still in its early stages and may evolve in unforeseen directions. Consequently, certain parts of the book must be considered to be tentative.

The book is an outgrowth of lecture notes that the author has used over a period of several years in a graduate course on telecommunications networks at the George Washington University. Portions of these notes also formed the basis for an intensive short course offered by the Continuing Engineering Education Program at GWU.

The book is divided into three areas that cover the user-to-network interface, the technology of common channel signaling, and the definition of telecommunications services. The early portions of the book and its last chapter can profitably be read by individuals with a general understanding of telecommunications technology, including computer scientists and the users of telecommunications services. The remaining parts, however, require some background in telecommunications engineering and are therefore directed toward graduate students in communications, telecommunications and information networking programs, communications researchers, practicing telecommunications engineers, consultants, and telecommunications managers. Except in a few instances, the book consciously avoids the use of mathematical analysis in order to make as much of the material as possible accessible to the nonspecialist.

As do all authors of technical works, I wish to acknowledge the vast array of contributors on whose work my own presentation is based. I have benefited immensely from numerous discussions with my colleagues and students at GWU. I am also grateful to reviewers Fred Goldstein, Eric L. Scace of US Sprint, and Gottried W. R. Luderer of Arizona State University. Thanks to all for their many contributions.

H. J. Helgert
Washington, D.C.

Contents

CHAPTER 8 The Digital Section   273

CHAPTER 9 Common Channel Signaling   307

CHAPTER 10   ISDN Telecommunications Services   **371**

CHAPTER 1

Introduction

In recent years the world's telecommunications networks have gone through a number of dramatic evolutionary changes that have been largely prompted by two basic factors.

The first is the expanding nature of the user requirements. From the early emphasis on voice communications, the needs of the commercial user—and to some extent of the residential user as well—gradually came to include communication of text, graphics, facsimile, and audio and video, largely in step with the development of the digital computer and the technology of imaging.

The demand for these telecommunications services is especially pronounced in today's offices and factories. Functions such as word processing, document transmission, data storage and retrieval, electronic mail, teleconferencing, accounting and payroll, production control, inventory control, and computer-aided design and manufacturing have become integral and indispensable parts of the enterprise, requiring increasingly sophisticated means for the transmission of information between computers, workstations, file servers, process controllers, and other intelligent machines.

Within the home, the telecommunications industry is attempting to create a similar demand through the development of videotex services that allow access to diverse sources of commercial information, the evolution of television into a high-resolution interactive entertainment medium, and the gradual introduction of electronic text communication services based on the personal computer.

Along with this expansion of user applications has come a need for greater flexibility and simplicity in the use of the available communications options, and for higher levels of integration and standardization of the communication services, equipment, access procedures, and tariffs.

The second factor in the evolution of telecommunications derives from the technological changes brought about by the microelectronics industry. The increasing digitization of telecommunications switching and transmission hardware, the development of inexpensive and highly reliable wideband communications media, and the parallel development of software-driven intelligent networks have allowed the implementation of a multitude of new network-based services for the efficient and cost-effective transmission, storage, and processing of an unlimited variety of user information.

It is in this environment of changing user needs, intelligent digital communication technologies, and declining costs that many of the world's telecommunications networks have begun to deploy the Integrated Services Digital Network, or ISDN.

1.1 The ISDN Concept

By general and commonly accepted definition, an *ISDN* is a telecommunications network evolving from the present telephone system that provides a limited set of standard end-to-end digital connection types and network facilities. These support a wide range of information transmission, storage, and processing services—including voice and nonvoice services—to which the end-users have access through a limited set of standard and multipurpose user-to-network interfaces. As shown in Figure 1.1, this concept of the ISDN incorporates several major innovations in the structure of today's telecommunications networks, in the subscribers or end-users, and in the relationship between the networks and the end-users. These innovations in turn require a number of important technical and operational changes in the entire telecommunications environment:

- The deployment of digital interoffice transmission facilities— initiated by the world's telecommunications networks more than two decades ago—must be completed and extended to the local-access level, in order to create the possibility of end-to-end digital connections whose characteristics are independent of the type of

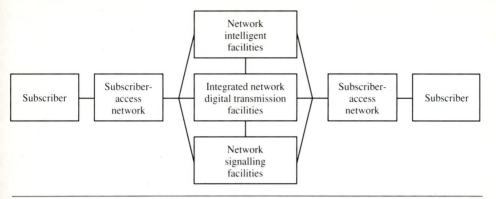

Figure 1.1 *The ISDN concept*

information carried on them. Furthermore, the available channel capacities on these connections must be increased to accommodate the needs of high–data rate information sources.

- The existing network switching systems and inband signaling techniques, still largely based on analog methods, must be replaced with digital stored program controlled exchanges and digital common channel signaling systems, through which the users can access and control the network transmission facilities and services.

- Today's multiple and largely independent network structures and connection types must in the long term be combined into an integrated network transmission facility, whose service characteristics can be dynamically configured to the requirements of the end-users.

- The numerous physical access arrangements and logical procedures by which the users currently interact with the different networks for the purpose of establishing and controlling connections must be replaced by a small number of simple, standardized, and universally agreed on user-to-network interface structures.

- The networks, in cooperation and competition with private service providers, must develop and market a wide range of intelligent telecommunications services that are attractive to the end-users in terms of their usefulness, availability, and cost and offer an economic incentive to the networks and service providers.

Let us examine these issues in some detail.

Beginning in the 1960s, and as a result of the development of digital signal processing and transmission technology during the preceding decade, most of the telecommunications administrations of the world initiated the process of converting from analog to digital methods for the transmission of voice inside the network. The reasons for this massive undertaking are to be found in the improved transmission quality, higher reliability, decreased power consumption, and lower cost offered by digital equipment. This process, encouraged by the efforts of AT&T and CCITT in the development of standardized transmission formats and electrical signaling conventions, continues today and provides the basis for an all-digital network transport backbone of the future.

More recently, the technology of optical fiber transmission has created the potential for a major increase in the available transmission capacity of the physical medium, and offers the possibility of carrying digital signals at data rates commensurate with the requirements of high-speed data and wideband video applications. The large-scale deployment of these optical cables as part of the ISDN development can also represent a substantial contribution to the improvement of the performance-cost relationship of a network connection.

Although the digitization of the internal network transmission plant is thus well underway and nearly complete in some networks, the provision of an end-to-end digital connection also presupposes digital transmission capability between the network exchange and the customer premises. Given the large infrastructure of twisted metallic pairs in the local-access plant of the world's telecommunications networks, it is clear that in the near term the digital subscriber loops will be mostly provided over these existing pairs by converting the data transmission technology from analog carrier modulation methods to baseband signaling, thereby eliminating the need for a modem. For certain applications, however, the limitations on transmission distance, quality, and data rate of the existing twisted pairs will necessitate the deployment of new media such as optical fiber in the local-access plant. In any case, the major challenge here is to develop and implement simple and efficient subscriber line transmission schemes for the two-way transfer of digital information over a broad range of data rates and at high levels of reliability.

We turn now to a consideration of the changes in the network switching technology demanded by the ISDN. From the applications point of view the switching system must offer fast setup and clearing of point-to-point, multipoint, and broadcast connections, and accommodate a broad range of data rates, message sizes, call holding times, and other traffic characteristics. The switch must also integrate the handling of digital voice and data at high throughput rates and low throughput delay.

These requirements imply the replacement of today's analog switches with modern stored program controlled switches based on time division multiplexing and time slot interchange principles. In the short run the required high throughput and calling volume are achieved through the use of data compression and synchronous assignment of fixed-size time slots to the connections. In the long run even faster switching technologies employing asynchronous packet switching or variable time slot multiplexing must be developed and deployed.

To obtain the required fast call setup times and sophisticated call control features envisioned for ISDN, call control must be carried out over intelligent and highly reliable dedicated signaling networks operating at high data rates.

As far as the network is concerned, in today's environment we can identify three distinct types that are based on circuit switching, message switching, and packet switching. Within these categories, a number of specialized structures have emerged, designed to serve the needs of specific applications. The most important of these is the *circuit switched analog voice network,* which for some time has also been employed in the transmission of data. In fact, because of their universal availability and low cost, analog voice circuits on either a dial-up or leased basis support the majority of today's low rate data communications. Their limited bandwidth and quality, however, make them unsuitable for many if not most high–data rate applications.

More recently, specialized data networks employing fast circuit switching and access protocols based on CCITT Recommendation X.21 have been implemented in a number of countries. Some of these offer end-to-end digital connections at data rates substantially in excess of those available in the voice network.

The common attribute of all these circuit switched networks is the provision of a dedicated connection between end-user pairs on a dial-up or permanent basis, through which voice or data can be transferred transparently at a given bandwidth, data rate, and error rate and with minimum end-to-end delay.

Among the existing networks using the technology of message or packet switching, the most prominent are the packet switching networks based on CCITT Recommendation X.25 and the Telex or Teletex networks for the transmission of textual information. Their distinguishing characteristics are the store-and-forward method of transmission over circuits that are under contention from more than one connection, and the existence of data storage and processing facilities within the network.

Whereas most of the above networks share a common internal transmission plant that is largely derived from the voice network, they exhibit major differences in the characteristics of the connections that may be established. The initial objective of the ISDN development is to provide the user with a relatively small number of standardized connection types and network facilities that are available on a global basis and can accommodate the user's short-term requirements. The long-term evolution of the ISDN, however, foresees the merger of the various connection types into a single universal end-to-end digital transmission capability that can be dynamically configured to the needs of the application in terms of its transmission characteristics, performance, and cost.

Let us examine next the user-to-network interface. In today's environment, the physical and logical signaling structures between user and network—by means of which the user gains access to the network facilities—depend almost totally on the particular network to which the user is attached. Thus, for example, the dialing procedure for establishing a voice call over the Public Switched Telephone Network bears little resemblance to the network-level protocol used to set up a connection over an X.25 packet switched network. Moreover, the user-to-network procedures are often carried out over separate physical circuits with distinct characteristics such as cable type, plug design, and signal levels.

A major aim of the ISDN development is to limit the number of different user-to-network interface arrangements by defining a small set of standard access protocols and physical media between the user and the network, so as to reduce the inefficiencies inherent in the current practice. In the long term the objective is to create a single integrated interface structure of sufficient generality and flexibility to accommodate all anticipated requirements.

Up to this point we have concerned ourselves with the engineering aspects of the ISDN transmission plant and user-to-network interface. Along with the developments outlined earlier, however, it is necessary to consider the equally important issue of the telecommunications services an ISDN will offer to the user. Here we distinguish between two broad categories of services, which are referred to as bearer services and teleservices. An ISDN *bearer service* provides a transmission facility to the end-user for the purpose of carrying information to another end-user. Its definition therefore involves the specification of transmission capacity, the level of performance, the type of information that may be carried, and the procedures by which connections are established and controlled. *Teleservices,* on the other hand, also involve capabilities beyond the transmission of information between end-users. They provide the end-user with access to the network's higher-level functions such as data processing and database facilities.

It is clear that the range of such telecommunications services offered by an ISDN must be carefully selected so as to assure the current and future usefulness of the ISDN to the user community, provide the economic basis for its existence, and stimulate the development of telecommunications in general. The spectrum of services offered must also be restricted, and standardized specifications of particular services must be developed, in order to guarantee that the service will be available in a global sense and to assure international compatibility.

1.2   ISDN Evolution

The considerations in the previous section show that the global deployment of the ISDN requires a substantial and continuing investment in research and development, manufacturing, management, and marketing. Its progress will therefore be gradual and will no doubt involve a time frame extending well into the next century. Given the large infrastructure of current telecommunications installations, it is also evident that during its evolutionary period the ISDN must be at least partly built on the existing network facilities and interwork with today's telecommunications networks. It must also allow the use of the existing subscriber equipment and offer today's services at today's cost.

For these reasons the ISDN is being deployed in stages, with the initial emphasis on the so-called *narrowband ISDN*. The latter is designed to provide facilities for the transmission of information requiring bit rates of less than several megabits per second. With relatively minor changes and additions to the existing circuit and packet switched network transmission circuits and switches, narrowband ISDN can be implemented to share these facilities with the traditional voice and data services during a period of transition. In contrast, the so-called *broadband ISDN,* which is intended to offer services at bit rates extending to several hundred megabits per second, depends on the large-scale availability of wideband transmission media such as optical fiber cables in both the interexchange and local exchange plant and the deployment of very high speed switching fabrics. Its full-scale implementation is therefore likely to require a much larger time frame than for narrowband ISDN. Current expectations are that no significant broadband impact will occur before the mid-1990s.

1.3   Benefits of the ISDN

The development and evolution of the ISDN, as outlined in the previous sections, involve the interaction and cooperation of the four major participants in the telecommunications enterprise, namely the network operator, the independent service provider, the equipment manufacturer, and the end-user. Each of them will derive important benefits from the ISDN technology, although the extent of these is not yet entirely clear.

From the point of view of the network, we note three key advantages. First, a network configuration based entirely on digital transmission and switching offers the reduced cost, lower power consumption, and easier maintainability that are general characteristics of digital equipment.

Second, the high level of functionality of an ISDN and the integration of multiple connection types, services, and user applications on a single network are expected to result in a higher utilization of the network's resources, with a corresponding increase in revenues. The eventual development of new services as well as the enhancement of existing services by the network operator is likely to have a similar effect. It is also reasonable to expect a reduction in the difference between peak and average traffic levels due to the different traffic characteristics of the various applications, with the resulting beneficial effects on future network provisioning. Finally, service integration offers the possibility of integrated network management, maintenance, and billing, leading to important reductions in cost and complexity.

A third major benefit to the network lies in its ability to provide a variety of data communications services over a single digital subscriber line. As far as these services can be supported by an existing subscriber line, the latter's normally low utilization factor is likely to increase substantially. This consideration is, however, somewhat affected by the fact that subscriber lines currently used for data communications services already tend to have a higher utilization than those used exclusively for voice.

The major business opportunity for the independent service vendor lies in the ability to provide access via an ISDN to external sources of information such as databases, as well as to data processing and storage facilities. Although many of the services envisioned here strictly speaking do not depend on the availability of an ISDN, the latter will likely act as a stimulus to their further development. Other potential offerings of interest to the independent service vendor include the wide variety of software products designed for the control and manipulation of the ISDN by the end-user.

From the end-user's perspective, one important benefit derives from the specification of standardized interfaces to the facilities of the ISDN. This feature, if implemented on a worldwide basis, would allow the design and manufacture of end-user equipment by multiple manufacturers on a large scale, leading to important reductions in the cost of such equipment. Furthermore, it would create a global interconnectivity and portability of the equipment. At the level of physical interconnection the standardization of the interface would also result in a substantial reduction of customer-premises wiring, although the cost of the wiring may increase somewhat.

The end-to-end digital connections offered by the ISDN eliminate the need for modems and are likely to provide a higher level of performance at a smaller cost than the currently available alternatives. Performance and cost will be largely independent of the type of information being transferred across the connection and may also be independent of the location of the end-users. The creation of unified tariff structures based on individual service parameters such as transmission bit rate will also simplify cost control and cost accounting, although the emergence of such tariffs is currently not apparent.

In the long term the end-users of an ISDN may also derive major benefits from the evolution of the network into an intelligent facility that can be configured to the user's precise needs, making possible such service features as "bandwidth on demand." In addition, the ISDN may evolve to provide a large variety of new information transmission services as well as substantially enhanced forms of traditional services, and may offer access to a multitude of information sources, both within and outside of the network. Finally, the integration of services and access procedures will no doubt result in important simplifications in the ordering, installation, and maintenance of the customer-premises facilities.

As far as the equipment manufacturer is concerned, the benefit of the ISDN lies primarily in the potentially large market for standardized and service-integrated user terminals and network termination equipment. In the short run, the need for terminal adapters to convert existing end-user devices to the ISDN standards offers additional opportunities. The evolution of the network into a totally digital facility will also accelerate the replacement of analog switching devices with stored program controlled switches, at least in some networks.

1.4 ISDN Applications

Although the engineering features of an ISDN represent a significant advance in the capabilities and performance of telecommunications networks, the commercial success of the ISDN will depend in large measure on the development of useful applications that are currently either unavailable, available in only a limited geographic area, or not cost effective. Consequently, substantial consideration is being given by various groups of potential ISDN users, network implementers, manufacturers, and other interested parties to the development and standardization of new and innovative uses of the network's transmission capabilities and intelligent services (IFFL89). Among the most important of these groups are the North American ISDN Users' Forum (NIUF), sponsored by the U.S. National Institute of Standards and Technology (NIST); the TriVista Project of AT&T; and the Information Technology User's Standards Association (ITUSA) in the United Kingdom.

Most of the emerging applications being developed by these organizations involve the use of one or more of the following major features of the ISDN.

From a transmission point of view, an ISDN is designed to offer the worldwide availability of end-to-end connections over digital circuits at bit rates and qualities far in excess of those generally obtainable from the existing analog voice network or even from networks with a significant infrastructure of digital circuits such as T1 carriers.

End-users also have the ability to establish several simultaneous connections between themselves in either a point-to-point or a multipoint arrangement. These can be configured to different bit rates, may be established over the network's circuit switched or packet switched facilities, and may involve a dynamically varying set of end-users.

By means of simultaneous and multipoint digital connections the users have access to a large amount of information concerning various aspects of existing connections and the identity and characteristics of other users. This information is provided by the users themselves or by specialized databases and is conveyed via the network's internal signaling system. The users may also be connected to special-feature nodes provided by independent vendors or by the ISDN itself to obtain various data processing and storage services.

Perhaps the most important applications of the ISDN relate to the traditional voice communications services, augmented with certain enhanced service features. Included here are the transfer of standard digital voice at 64 kbit/s, compressed digital voice at various submultiples of 64 kbit/s, high-fidelity voice, and a host of new and traditional supporting call control procedures. Among these are calling party identification, multilocation ringing, call waiting, call forwarding, and call charging indication, to mention just a few. Additional applications in this category are the provision of secure voice transmission, personal and private voice mail services, and other existing and planned voice store and forward services such as prerecorded announcements.

An important example of the use of these features is to be found in telemarketing. Figure 1.2 shows the components of a typical installation.

A voice call from a customer to a service provider is conveyed over an ISDN voice channel, while the customer's telephone number

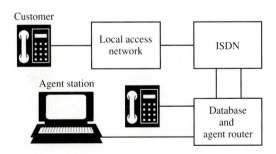

Figure 1.2 *ISDN telemarketing application*

is simultaneously made available to the service provider's customer database over a separate signaling channel. The relevant customer information can then be extracted from the database and presented to a particular agent's terminal, along with the voice call. Agent selection can be based on customer-related criteria such as geographic location and previous activity, or on agent workload and area of expertise.

Applications of this type generally result in shorter call holding times and a decrease in agent errors. Note also that as long as the calling party's telephone number is available to the network, the ISDN capability is only required at the service provider's end of a connection, even if the customer is connected to a non-ISDN facility. This application is therefore suitable during a time of limited ISDN availability.

The second major category of applications involves the transmission of programming material such as high-fidelity audio, existing broadcast-quality audio and television, high-definition television, and other video material for entertainment and business use. Further examples are provided by videotelephony and other multimedia communications involving simultaneous voice and video. Because of the high data rates characteristic of video, many of these applications require the availability of broadband ISDN, unless the data are highly compressed.

In a typical scenario a high–data rate one-way connection carries the video part of a movie from a service provider to the end-user, whereas a second one-way connection of much lower data rate conveys the sound track in one of a number of different languages. In addition, a low–data rate two-way connection is used to request a specific movie and the language of its sound track, verify the identity of the end-user, and convey security codes and billing information.

As another example, the transmission of still pictures or documents over one connection could be accompanied by a voice commentary transmitted simultaneously over a separate connection. A particular form of this application is shown in Figure 1.3. Here two users simultaneously obtain the same database information over individual high-speed forward channels and manipulate this information via individual reverse data channels. Their respective activities regarding the database information can be discussed and coordinated via a separate voice connection between themselves. This arrangement would allow, for example, the interactive design of a product by design teams whose members are geographically remote from each other.

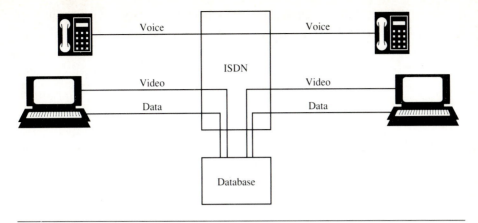

Figure 1.3 *ISDN interactive design application*

The data communications requirements of the modern office lead to a third category of applications, the most important of which are text and graphics message communications, including telex, teletex, videotex, electronic mail, facsimile, and videoconferencing. Other uses such as PC-to-PC communications, local-area network (LAN) interconnection, and remote-access to LANs, document storage and retrieval, database management, and word processing are also readily supported by the ISDN.

A fourth potential source of applications is to be found in the intelligent building. Important functions benefiting from the availability of ISDN transmission services here include smoke detection, temperature sensing and climate control, energy management, building access control, and security monitoring.

Many other applications of the ISDN are actively being discussed and proposed within the user and vendor communities or are being implemented in parallel with the development of the network and its functional capabilities. Prominent among these are examples in the automated factory of the future, the financial services industry, and travel- and entertainment-related services.

It is important to point out that most if not all of the envisioned service offerings of an ISDN can in principle be provided in a limited sense by the existing telecommunications networks, using either analog or digital transmission technology, possibly in conjunction with a digital PABX. The advantage of an ISDN must therefore lie in the pervasiveness of these services, the global connectivity, and a more favorable cost-benefit ratio.

1.5 ISDN Standardization

The fundamental concept of a public telecommunications network based on digital transmission of information and offering an integrated access to multiple network connections and services has evolved over a period of about 12 years, largely through the work of the CCITT. Starting in the late 1970s, Study Group XVIII, in close cooperation with Study Groups VII and XI, was given the task of developing the recommendations that define the concepts and principles of the ISDN and specify its service capabilities, network features, user-to-network interfaces, internetworking interfaces, and maintenance aspects. The current state of this effort is contained in the I-series recommendations approved by the IXth Plenary Assembly of the CCITT in November 1988 and published in Volume III of the *Blue Book*.

These recommendations are divided into six series, as shown in Figure 1.4, and concern themselves mainly with the interface between the user and the network and the interface between networks. Although the disposition of a number of issues is still tentative, especially in regard to supplementary services and the broadside version of ISDN, the recommendations in existence today are substantially complete and form the basis for the worldwide deployment of the ISDN.

Appendix A includes a complete list of all currently published recommendations of the I series. Following is a brief description of their content.

The I.100 series provides a general introduction to ISDN, its terminology, design principles, and evolutionary development. It also contains a set of recommendations introducing the concept of attributes in defining the specific services offered by the ISDN and the principles on which these services will be tariffed.

The I.200-series recommendations contain a methodology by means of which the services offered by the ISDN may be classified and described. Generally, a service is classified as either a bearer service, a teleservice, or a supplementary service. Bearer services provide the means of conveying information between end-users in a

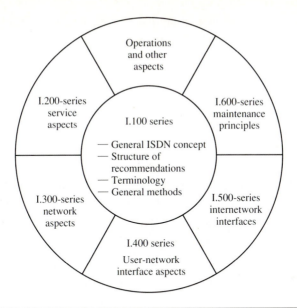

Figure 1.4 CCITT I-series recommendations for ISDN
© Reprinted from CCITT Blue Book, vol. III.7, 1988.

transparent fashion—that is, without alteration of the message content by the network. Teleservices, in contrast, imply the involvement of the network for purposes above and beyond the transmission function. Supplementary services are always associated with a bearer service or teleservice and provide additional service features to the end-user. In addition to recommendations describing the methodology for defining services, the I.200 series also contains several recommendations in which a number of specific bearer services, teleservices, and supplementary services are defined.

The recommendations of the I.300 series define the attributes and topologies of the network connections that may be established over the ISDN, the performance objectives for these connections, and the structure of the numbering and addressing plan. The I.300 series also introduces the ISDN protocol reference model. The latter is in part based on the *open systems interconnection reference model (OSI)*, but extends and modifies the OSI principles by separating the signaling and management operations from the user application and creating independent instances of communication between user and network, between network components, and between network management resources. Each such instance is individually modeled and is supported by an independent set of protocols.

The major I.400-series recommendations concern themselves with a detailed description of the interface between the end-user equipment and the network. Of primary importance here are the definitions of channel structures, interface points, and reference configurations, and the specification of the user-to-network protocols corresponding to the lower three layers of the OSI model. Other recommendations deal with the problem of resolving incompatibilities in data rates between end-user equipment and network, and ISDN support of existing terminals based on X.21-, X.25-, and V-series interface structures.

The recommendations of the I.500 series concern themselves with the problem of interworking between ISDNs and other network structures. The purpose here is to develop a set of standard interworking functions to ensure that users on existing public or private networks can be incorporated into a global communications environment during the evolutionary phase of the ISDN. The recommendations contain reference configurations for interworking, detail the functional requirements for the network interfaces, and specify the protocols of interaction between the network entities. Primary consideration is given to interworking between two different ISDNs, between an ISDN and the telephone network, between an ISDN and the circuit or packet switched data networks, and between an ISDN and the public Telex service.

The I.600-series recommendations provide for a maintenance service for the interface between the subscriber and the network, as well as for the subscriber installation insofar as it is the responsibility of the network. Included are a general maintenance architectural model, reference configurations of loopback points within the subscriber installation, and procedures for supervision, internal testing, failure detection, and failure location.

In addition to the I-series recommendations, several other CCITT standards play an important role in the definition of the ISDN. These include the parts of the G.700-, G.800-, and G.900-series recommendations governing digital transmission systems, the Q.500 and Q.600 series on digital switching and interworking of signaling systems, the work of Study Group XI in the development of Signaling System #7 as described in the Q.700-series recommendations, and the X-series recommendations of Study Group VII that define the user-to-network aspects of public data networks. A number of I-series recommendations also appear in other series of the *Blue Book,* as shown in Appendix A.

Various other organizations have made major contributions to the standardization of the ISDN. Among the most important of these are the International Organization for Standardization (ISO) through its Technical Committee 97, Subcommittee 6; the European Conference of Post and Telecommunications Administrations (CEPT); Technical Committee 32 of the European Computer Manufacturers' Association (ECMA); and the recently formed European Telecommunications Standards Institute (ETSI). The latter, through its European Telecommunications Standards program (ETS/NET), is developing standard versions of two types of user-to-network interface known as *basic rate interface (NET3)* and *primary rate interface (NET5).*

In the United States, the most important forum for this work is the T1D1 subcommittee of the Exchange Carriers Standards Association (ECSA), which operates under the auspices and procedures of the American National Standards Institute (ANSI). Its activities closely parallel those of the CCITT, and many of its contributions are submitted to Study Group XVIII via the U.S. National Committee.

Major contributions are also made by Bellcore, the research arm of the Regional Bell Operating Companies (RBOC). Bellcore is concentrating its efforts in the development and publication of so-called *technical references (TR),* which define the form of the ISDN that will be implemented by the RBOCs. Its current activities center around the standardization of ISDN service capabilities and features, call control, network signaling, interworking, user-to-network interfaces, ISDN terminals, and ISDN numbering plans. Most of this work is in conformity with the corresponding recommendations of the CCITT.

Technical references containing specifications of the ISDN user-to-network interface structures have also been published by AT&T. These are intended as guides for the designers and manufacturers of components that must meet AT&T's ISDN implementation standard. Although minor deviations exist, for the most part the content of these documents also conforms to the CCITT recommendations.

In view of the large number of organizations involved in the specification of the ISDN, the numerous options incorporated into those specifications, and the divergent economic and technical interests of public and private network providers, it is not surprising that today no single globally compatible version of ISDN exists. Consequently a great deal of effort is currently directed toward achieving worldwide agreement by at least the public carriers on a basic subset of services and user-to-network interface functions. An important step in this direction is the recent agreement among the European public networks under the auspices of CEPT to harmonize their versions of the ISDN in accordance with the ETSI specifications.

1.6   Outline of the Book

The intent of this book is to offer an exposition of the most important engineering and service aspects of the ISDN, as far as they have been worked out today. As such, it emphasizes the narrowband version of the ISDN, since its definition is nearly complete and various implementations are presently available or will be deployed in the near future. Certain aspects of broadband ISDN concerning the user-to-network interface that appear to be reasonably stable at the time of this writing are also covered. The reader is nevertheless advised that much of the broadband material is still somewhat tentative and has not been agreed on by the standards organizations.

Chapter 2 presents a detailed discussion of an abstract ISDN system model—known as a reference configuration—that divides the set of functions of the ISDN into a number of subsets, with well-defined interface points between them. Such reference configurations are developed for the subscriber-access network, the interexchange network, and interconnections to other networks.

The next five chapters concentrate primarily on the user-to-network interface, which governs the relationship between the ISDN and the end-users. Its definition by the CCITT for narrowband ISDN is nearly complete, and thus it constitutes the most mature part of the ISDN technology.

Chapter 3 describes the ISDN from the architectural point of view. It derives a reference model that serves as the basic conceptual framework for the development of the protocols governing the exchange of information across the user-to-network interface and within the interexchange network.

Chapter 4 concentrates primarily on the physical layer specifications for the narrowband user-to-network interface. It includes a complete discussion of the services provided by the physical layer and the protocols by which they are carried out. Also included is a section dealing with the physical layer aspects of the broadband user-to-network interface, as far as they are known today.

Chapter 5 focuses on the services provided by the data link layer across the user-to-network interface. It describes the layer 2 service model and offers a tutorial treatment of the link layer protocol known as LAPD.

Chapter 6 discusses the service and protocol aspects of the network layer, again as they pertain to the user-to-network interface. Here the emphasis is on the functional and stimulus call control procedures for establishing, operating, and terminating circuit switched connections through the ISDN, for controlling supplementary services, and for transferring data over user-to-user signaling connections.

Chapter 7 covers various aspects of the problem of adapting non-ISDN user terminals to ISDN user-to-network interfaces. Included are discussions of data rate adaption and protocol conversion for terminals operating in the packet or circuit mode according to the procedures of CCITT Recommendation X.25 or X.21, and for terminals with V-series interfaces.

In the next two chapters we extend our view of the ISDN by including the network transmission plant.

Chapter 8 focuses on the digital section, which includes the subscriber loop between the customer premises and the local exchange. It offers a general discussion of the engineering aspects of data transmission over existing twisted pairs and describes the details of two transmission schemes that are emerging as de facto standards.

Chapter 9 contains a tutorial treatment of CCITT Signaling System #7, a common channel signaling system that provides the capability for call control in the interexchange part of the ISDN.

Chapter 10 is devoted to a discussion of the telecommunications services provided by the ISDN. It contains the definitions of the various bearer services, teleservices, and supplementary services that have been identified to date and provides a characterization of each service in terms of its service attributes.

Appendix A is a listing of CCITT recommendations pertinent to ISDN, and Appendix B describes the CCITT Specification and Description Language (SDL).

The book concludes with a glossary of ISDN terminology, a table of acronyms, and an up-to-date list of references.

1.7 Summary and Recommended Reading

This chapter introduced the concept of the ISDN as an extension and elaboration of the present global telephone network. It reviewed the technological developments in which the ISDN is embedded and discussed the worldwide activities of the national and international standards organizations in producing the technical specifications of the ISDN. It also illustrated several major areas of application, gave the economic motivation for the deployment of the ISDN, and speculated on its implementation and evolution.

The majority of the technical papers on ISDN appear in four IEEE publications. Two of these, the *IEEE Journal on Selected Areas in Communications* and the *IEEE Transactions on Communications,* contain many highly technical and original contributions on ISDN research and development. The other two, the *IEEE Communications Magazine* and *IEEE Network,* concentrate mostly on tutorial material of a technical nature, but also publish articles and special issues on the legal, regulatory, economic, and standards issues affecting the ISDN.

An excellent summary of the features and commercial applications of the ISDN is provided by the December 1987 issue of the *IEEE Communications Magazine* entitled "ISDN: A Means Towards a Global Information Society" and by the September 1989 issue of the *IEEE Network Magazine* devoted to "ISDN—An Applications Perspective." Telecommunications deregulation is covered in the December 1985, January 1987, and January 1989 issues of the *IEEE Communications Magazine*. A good treatment of the activities of the various standards organizations can be found in the January 1985 issue of the *IEEE Communications Magazine*.

Other articles of general interest in connection with ISDN are [STIN88], [CARE89], [GEES89], [DUNN89], and [WOLF87].

Much important work is also contained in the proceedings of the IEEE GLOBECOM conferences from 1985 to the present, the proceedings of the IEEE INFOCOM '88 and INFOCOM '89 conferences, and the journal *Computer Networks and ISDN Systems*.

CHAPTER 2

The ISDN Reference Configuration

Although the topology of an ISDN depends to a considerable extent on the nature of the users and network providers, for the purpose of specifying its architectural properties in a generic sense it is convenient to divide it into three major parts. These are shown in Figure 2.1.

Central to any ISDN is the so-called *interexchange network (IEN)*, which consists of the physical and logical components of the backbone transmission network, including a number of network transit exchanges and the transmission trunks connecting these exchanges. As far as the end-user is concerned, the IEN's main purpose is to provide physical and logical transmission and switching facilities across which user information flows may be conveyed. There are two types of IEN, those providing circuit switched connections (CSIEN) and those based on the store-and-forward principle, of which packet switching (PSIEN) is an example.

Superimposed on the IEN and interacting with it is the *common channel signaling network (CCSN),* which combines the functions required for the control, management, and maintenance of the ISDN. It provides the physical and logical transmission capacity for the transfer of connection control signals between the components of the IEN, for the management and allocation of network resources, and for the performance of maintenance functions.

The last major part of the ISDN— the *subscriber-access network (SAN)*—consists of the part of the ISDN between the end-user or subscriber and the IEN and CCSN. It can be divided in turn into three components, namely the *customer-premises installation (CPI)*, the *digital section (DS),* and the *logical exchange termination (LET)*. The CPI combines those aspects of the SAN that are directly under

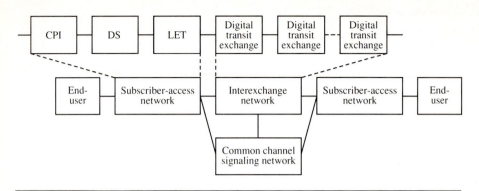

Figure 2.1 *ISDN decomposition*

the control of the subscriber. The DS consists of the local loop or subscriber-access line—also known in CCITT parlance as the *digital transmission system (DTS)*—and the physical line termination equipment. It provides the transmission capacity for carrying information between the local exchange and the customer premises. The purpose of the LET is to terminate these transmissions in a logical sense.

To specify the physical and logical properties of the IEN, CCSN, and SAN, and to aid in the development of standard ISDN implementations, it is useful to define a decomposition of the ISDN's total capability. This is accomplished by dividing it into an abstract topological arrangement of groups of functions that interact with each other across so-called *reference points*. Such a decomposition is known as a *reference configuration*.

The functional groups consist of certain combinations of physical and logical functions that are required for the transmission and control of the signals across the IEN, CCSN, and SAN. They do not necessarily correspond in a one-to-one manner to specific physical devices. In particular, individual functions in a group may be implemented in one or several pieces of equipment, and one piece of equipment may perform functions from more than one group.

The reference points define conceptual points of demarcation between pairs of functional groups. They may correspond to physical interfaces between separate pieces of equipment implementing the two functional groups, or virtual interfaces in cases where both functional groups are found in the same equipment.

This chapter discusses the ISDN reference configuration in detail as it applies to the SAN and IEN and presents a decomposition of an

ISDN connection. For the most part the discussion follows the material contained in CCITT Recommendations I.411, Q.502, and Q.512 for the SAN and IEN and Recommendations I.324, I.325, and I.340 for ISDN connections. The consideration of the CCSN is deferred to Chapter 9.

2.1 The Subscriber-Access Network Reference Configuration

In defining a decomposition of the subscriber-access network into functional groups and reference points, several objectives must be considered.

Both from a regulatory and an economic point of view, it is desirable to have a clearly defined line of demarcation between the responsibilities of the end-user and those of the network provider, so as to create a certain level of independence between the two. This assures that the customer-premises part of the ISDN can evolve in a way that is not constrained by the network provider, as long as a basic adherence to the structure of the interface between the two is maintained. The networking aspects of the customer-premises devices and their end-user functions also need to be clearly delimited to permit flexibility in the design of the end-user equipment. For the local exchange termination equipment it is also desirable to separate the purely physical aspects of terminating the subscriber line from its logical switching and routing functions.

These considerations result in the particular form of the reference configuration for the SAN shown in Figure 2.2.

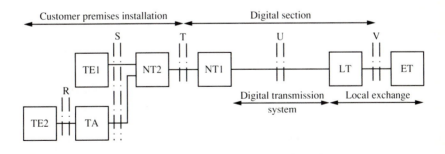

Figure 2.2 *Subscriber-access network reference configuration*
© Reprinted from CCITT Blue Book, vol. III.8, 1988.

2.1.1 Functional Groups

According to Figure 2.2, the ISDN subscriber-access network reference configuration is decomposed into six general groups of functions
that collectively describe the capability of the SAN to carry information between the end-user and the interexchange network. In an actual
implementation of the SAN these groups of functions usually, but not
always, correspond to specific pieces of equipment.

The *exchange termination (ET)* is the logical part of the subscriber's central office and provides the functions necessary for the logical
attachment of the SAN to the IEN. It performs signaling insertion and
extraction, the conversion of information exchange codes, frame
alignment, the generation of alarms, and fault indications.

The physical aspects of terminating the digital transmission system on the network premises are contained in the *line termination
(LT)*. Specific functions include the feeding of power across the DTS
to the customer installation, fault location through the transmission of
loopback signals, the generation and regeneration of baseband signals,
and the conversion from one baseband code to another.

Together, the ET and LT are that part of a central office that is
dedicated to a set of subscribers accessing the network over a single
subscriber line.

The *network termination 1 (NT1)* forms the intermediary between
the network and the equipment on the customer premises in a physical
sense. Its main purpose is the termination of the DTS on the customer-
premises side. It also performs conversion between the electromagnetic signals generated and received by the customer equipment and
those transmitted over the subscriber line, transmission timing, and
the feeding of power to the customer-premises equipment. Another
important function is the protection of the network and terminal
equipment against disturbances and physical damage. The NT1 also
cooperates with the ET in providing fault diagnosis, performance
monitoring, and maintenance of the SAN.

The functions of the *network termination 2 (NT2)* usually correspond to those of a switching device located on the customer premises; they extend over the physical, link, and network layers of the
OSI architecture. The key features here are multiplexing, concentration, and switching of multiple information streams, and protocol handling at layers 2 and 3. In actual implementations the entire capability
of an NT2, or certain subsets of functions, may be incorporated in
various types of equipment such as a *private automatic branch ex-*

change (PABX), local-area network (LAN), terminal cluster controller, or time division multiplexer.

The *terminal equipment (TE)* typically corresponds to customer terminals such as digital telephones, integrated voice/data terminals, personal computers, and work stations. It incorporates the functions required for protocol handling, physical connection to the equipment associated with the NT1 or NT2 functions, and maintenance. Two types of TEs are identified. The *terminal equipment 1 (TE1)* functions completely in conformity with the ISDN specifications. Given the early state of ISDN hardware development, only a limited variety of equipment containing this capability is currently available. A *terminal equipment 2 (TE2)* corresponds to the capabilities of existing data communications equipment that does not adhere to the ISDN conventions. Thus it includes devices with such interface characteristics as RS-232C, RS-232D, X.21, and X.25, as well as various nonstandard or proprietary protocols.

The *terminal adapter (TA)* provides the functional capability of converting the layer 1, 2, and 3 protocol functions of a TE2 into those of a TE1, so that the combination of TE2 and TA appears as a TE1. TAs are intended to allow the attachment of conventional data communications equipment to an ISDN and may therefore eliminate the need for modems.

With reference to Figure 2.2, we note that the customer-premises installation consists of the functional groups TE1, TE2, TA, and NT2, whereas the digital section includes NT1, LT, and the digital transmission system between them. The *local exchange* is defined as the combination of LT and ET, with the latter corresponding to the logical exchange termination in Figure 2.1.

2.1.2   Reference Points

The functional groups defined in the subscriber-access network reference configuration interact with each other across five distinct reference points that correspond to physical or virtual interfaces between the groups. These are also shown in Figure 2.2.

The *S reference point* defines the demarcation between the TE1 or TA on one side and the NT2 on the other. If we consider the functions of NT2 to be primarily network related, S provides a separation of the logical and possibly physical functions of the end-user and the network and thus corresponds to a boundary between the two.

The *T reference point* marks the interface between NT1 and NT2 and allows the separation of these functions into different groups. This creates the possibility that the NT1 and NT2 functions are provided by different entities. As in the case of the S reference point, T may mark the separation between user and network, but only in the physical sense.

The *R reference point* between the TE2 and TA accommodates existing non-ISDN terminal equipment designed to other CCITT standards such as X.25 or X.21, as well as interface standards not conforming to CCITT recommendations. It thus allows the connection of an existing TE2-type terminal device to the ISDN without modification of the TE2 itself.

The *U reference point* defines the interface between the DTS and the NT1. In some implementations of the ISDN it serves as the boundary between the network provider and the subscriber.

The *V reference point* separates the physical and logical aspects of terminating the subscriber-access network on the network premises. Four versions—denoted V1, V2, V3, and V4—have been defined. V1 and V3 mark the interface between the physical termination of the digital transmission system in the LT and its logical termination within the ET. They are applicable when the digital section provides individual user-to-network access capabilities known as *basic access* and *primary access* (their characteristics are defined in Chapters 3 and 4). V2 is located on the network side of a concentrator that serves as a remote line termination unit and terminates several basic-access or primary-access DTs. In a similar manner, V4 corresponds to the interface on the network side of a remote multiplexer that combines several basic-access DTs.

2.1.3   Examples of Reference Configurations

Within the scope of the general subscriber-access network reference configuration of Figure 2.2, many different physical arrangements of the functional groups and reference points are possible. Let us consider some of the most important cases. Figures 2.3 and 2.4 identify several arrangements of the functional groups involving the part of the architecture on the subscriber side of the U reference point. The simplest of these, shown in Figure 2.3(a), is one in which the NT2 is absent, so that the terminal equipment connects directly to the physical network termination NT1 and the S reference point disappears or coalesces into the T reference point. For this arrangement to be possible, the physical and electromagnetic characteristics of the interfaces at S and T have to be identical. Conversely, their common physical design

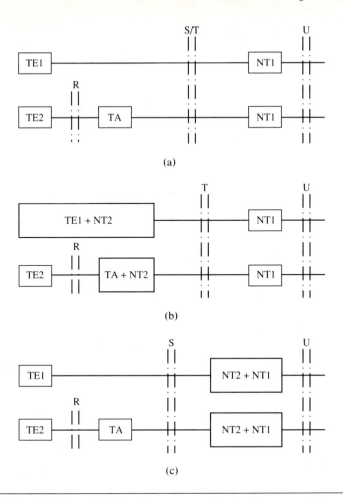

Figure 2.3 *Point-to-point subscriber-access network reference configurations (CPI side)* © Reprinted from CCITT Blue Book, vol. III.8, 1988.

ensures that a terminal can be physically connected to either an NT2 or an NT1. Similarly, a private branch exchange, local-area network, terminal controller, or any other device incorporating the NT2 functions then has the same physical interface to the NT1 as a terminal, for example.

The arrangements of Figure 2.3(b) and (c) correspond to situations in which two adjacent functional groups are combined into a single functional group—possibly in the same physical equipment—thus

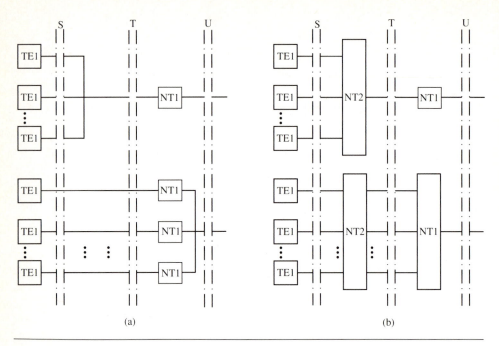

Figure 2.4 *Multipoint subscriber-access network reference configurations (CPI side)* © Reprinted from CCITT Blue Book, vol. III.8, 1988.

eliminating one or the other of the explicit reference points between them. Note, however, that in a virtual sense the reference points may still be present within the combined functional group.

Figure 2.4 concerns itself with various multipoint configurations involving the connection of several terminals to a shared NT2 or NT1. In Figure 2.4(a) the TE functional groups are connected directly via a single T reference point to a shared NT1 by means of a multidrop arrangement, or via separate T reference points in a star topology. In these cases the NT2 functional group degenerates to providing only the physical multidrop or point-to-point connection to the NT1, but performs no multiplexing, concentration, switching, or any other higher-layer functions. All the physical and electromagnetic characteristics of the interface at the S and T reference points must be identical.

Figure 2.4(b) depicts a somewhat similar case. Several terminals— connected through separate S reference points to a shared NT2—are concentrated through a single T reference point and connected in a

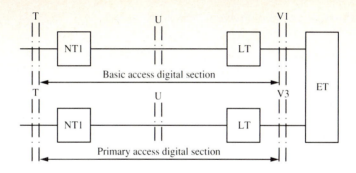

Figure 2.5a *Subscriber-access network reference configuration (local exchange side)* © Reprinted from CCITT Blue Book, vol. III.8, 1988.

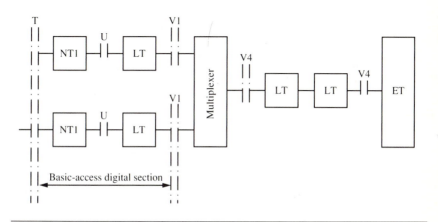

Figure 2.5b *Subscriber-access network reference configuration (local exchange side)* © Reprinted from CCITT Blue Book, vol. III.8, 1988.

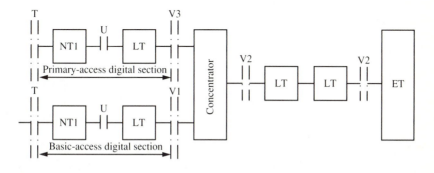

Figure 2.5c *Subscriber-access network reference configuration (local exchange side)* © Reprinted from CCITT Blue Book, vol. III.8, 1988.

bus arrangement or via separate T reference points in a star arrangement to a shared NT1. Unlike the previous example, however, the NT2 in this case provides multiplexing and switching functions, in addition to the physical connectivity, and the interfaces at the S and T reference points may differ at the physical level. Configurations of this type are representative of terminal attachments to private branch exchanges that accommodate multiple terminals at the input and connect them to a single network termination point.

Turning now to the network side of the U reference point, the various versions of the V reference point defined earlier give rise to many possible reference configurations. Several of these are shown in Figure 2.5.

Figure 2.5(a) depicts the termination of two variants of a single digital section, one corresponding to a basic-access interface and the other configured to a primary-access interface. In these two cases the LT and ET functional groups are separated by the real reference points V1 or V3, respectively.

Figure 2.5(b) shows a multiplexer that is remote from the ET at the local exchange and acts as a remote ET that combines the inputs from several basic-access digital sections. The latter are attached to the multiplexer across V1 reference points. The multiplexer itself is connected to the local ET via a V4 reference point and a separate digital section.

A similar arrangement involving a remote concentrator in place of a multiplexer is shown in Figure 2.5(c). Here the concentrator terminates a combination of basic-access and primary-access digital sections.

2.1.4   User-to-Network Interfaces

The components of the subscriber-access network reference configuration described in the previous sections can be divided into two classes, depending on whether they are considered to be the responsibility of the end-user or of the network. Currently, the regulatory authorities in most countries consider the T and S reference points to mark the dividing line between the end-user and the network, so that the functional groups TE1, TE2, and TA are under the control of the end-user. In this view NT1 and NT2 collectively represent the physical and logical termination of the network and the S and T reference points are associated with the interface between the user and the network—the so-called *user-to-network interface (UNI)*. In North America, the Federal Communications Commission and other regulatory agencies consider the functional group NT1 to also be a part of the user side, so that the physical boundary between user and network corresponds to the U reference point. This arrangement somewhat complicates the network provider's ability to perform tests of the digital transmission system, since the termination of the DTS is under the control of the subscriber. On the positive side, it opens the manufacture and marketing of the NT1 equipment to the free enterprise environment.

2.2   The ISDN Interexchange Network Reference Configuration

We now turn to a consideration of the ISDN interexchange network that provides the backbone of an ISDN connection.

As shown in Figure 2.6, the IEN consists of a number of switching exchanges called *digital transit exchanges* and a series of transmission

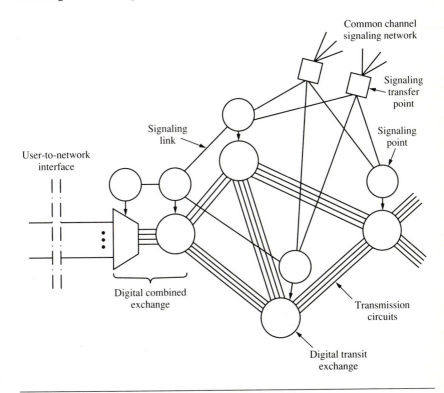

Figure 2.6   *The ISDN interexchange network*

media that interconnect the exchanges in a distributed network topology. The exchanges provide the physical terminations of the interexchange transmission media, select and allocate transmission and storage facilities for the end-user connections, and carry out the switching and relaying of the end-user information. In addition to these functions, certain switches may also have a local function for the termination of the subscriber-access network, in which case they are referred to as *digital combined exchanges*. Since the end-user connections can be circuit switched or packet switched in an ISDN, both circuit and packet switching exchanges are normally present. In principle, they may be integrated into the same physical device.

The digital transmission channels that connect the digital transit exchanges and digital combined exchanges are designed to handle standard CCITT pulse code modulation frames at the primary, secondary, and tertiary multiplex transmission rates of 2048/1544 kbit/s, 8448/6312 kbit/s, and 34368/44736 kbit/s, respectively, as specified in CCITT Recommendation G.702. Higher rates are also sometimes used. Here the lower rate for a given level is implemented mainly in North America and to some extent in Japan.

The actions of the switching and transmission facilities of the IEN are governed by certain connection control messages that are exchanged among the switches over a distinct network referred to as a *common channel signaling network*. This network, which operates in packet switching mode, consists of two types of network nodes— *signaling transfer points* and *signaling points*—that are connected by transmission media known as *signaling links*. Although the common channel signaling network may be entirely separate, certain parts of the IEN facilities are usually dedicated to the transmission and switching of control information. In this case the distinction between an end-user connection and a signaling connection exists only at the logical level.

2.2.1 The Digital Transit Exchange Reference Configuration

Figure 2.7 shows the reference configuration for the type of exchange that has only a relay function within the IEN. The exchange is divided into a switching block and a transmission block.

Within the switching block, the switching function provides a path for transmission of the information received on one transmission line over the same or a different line to another exchange. It may consist of several stages of time division switching and/or space division switching and is capable of switching individual time slots in a PCM

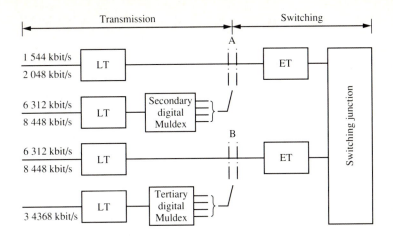

Figure 2.7 *Digital transit exchange reference configuration*
© Adapted from CCITT Blue Book, vol. VI. 5, 1988.

frame or a series of slots, which collectively correspond to a user information stream. The exchange termination functional group provides the capability for signaling insertion and extraction, code conversion, frame alignment, alarms, and fault indication.

The transmission block consists of a series of digital transmission lines operating in PCM mode, which are terminated in a line termination functional group that performs the functions of power feeding, fault location, signal regeneration, and baseband code conversion. A multiplexer/demultiplexer converts frames and data rates from the formats and values used at the secondary PCM multiplex level to the primary PCM multiplex level or from tertiary to secondary PCM level.

Reference point A is associated with the digital interface between the exchange termination and the digital transmission line operating in primary PCM mode at either 1544 kbit/s or 2048 kbit/s.

Reference point B, on the other hand, is associated with the digital interface between the exchange termination and the digital transmission line operating in secondary PCM mode at either 6312 kbit/s or 8448 kbit/s.

2.2.2 The Digital Combined Exchange Reference Configuration

Figure 2.8 shows the structure of the type of exchange that combines the transit function with a local subscriber-access network termination. On the subscriber side this reference configuration conforms to

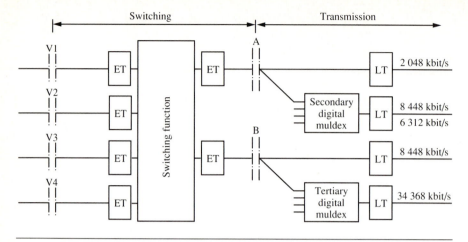

Figure 2.8 *Digital combined exchange reference configuration*

the one described in Section 2.1. Since the function of the transit exchange part of a digital combined exchange is identical to that of a digital transit exchange, the reference configuration of that part of the exchange is the same as in Figure 2.7.

2.3   Reference Configurations for ISDN Connections

As noted, the reference configurations for the subscriber-access network and the interexchange network described in the previous sections provide a convenient decomposition of the ISDN into groups of functions and points of demarcation between them. This decomposition in turn allows the independent development of the various parts of the ISDN in a well-defined manner.

For purposes of describing the networking capabilities that an ISDN makes available to an end-user, it is convenient to decompose the ISDN into a set of so-called *connection types* that collectively represent the service capabilities of the network to the end-user. Each connection type is characterized by a set of telecommunications attributes that describe its essential properties. Among these attributes are transmission mode, information transfer rate, connection establishment mode, connection performance, and interworking interfaces to other networks.

Each ISDN connection may be decomposed into a corresponding

reference configuration that represents the connection in abstract terms. This section discusses the details of these decompositions for the various connection types.

2.3.1 ISDN Connection Types

In general, an ISDN connection exists between a pair of reference points that are external to the network's transmission facilities. It is necessary to distinguish between a number of different cases, as shown in Figure 2.9.

In the first case, Figure 2.9(a), the ISDN provides a complete and direct connection between a pair of ISDN subscribers, which are attached to the network at the S or T reference points. This connection may be completely provided by the ISDN, or the ISDN may rely on one or more intermediate networks, which may or may not conform to the ISDN structure. From the end-user's point of view, however, any intermediate networks are invisible.

As a second possibility, the ISDN connection may exist between

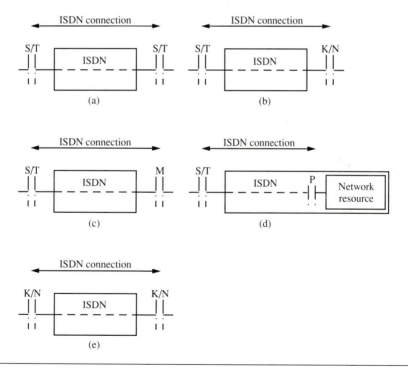

Figure 2.9 *ISDN connection types*
© Reprinted from CCITT Blue Book, vol. III.8, 1988.

an ISDN end-user and an access point to a non-ISDN telecommunications network or another ISDN. Such connections may only be relevant for a period of time in the evolution of the ISDN toward a single, globally integrated facility that provides all types of telecommunications services.

Two different scenarios must be considered. In the first, the ISDN provides access to the existing public telephone network, the packet and circuit switched data networks, the telex network, and other public or private facilities dedicated to a particular telecommunications application. In the second, the ISDN is used as a connection to another ISDN.

The boundary between an ISDN and these other non-ISDN or ISDN facilities is marked by reference points, as indicated in Figure 2.10. The *K reference point* is associated with the interface to one of the public telecommunications networks. Two types have been identified. K1 requires that the interworking function between the two networks be contained within the ISDN, whereas K2 refers to a situation where the interworking function is a part of the non-ISDN facility. Depending on the type of telecommunications network, different versions of K may be defined.

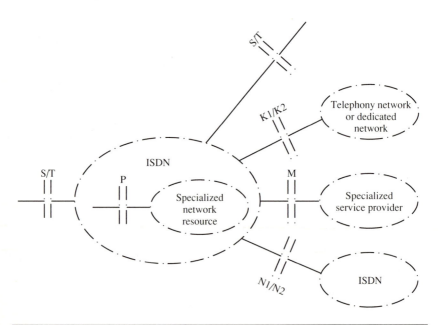

Figure 2.10 *External reference points for ISDN connections*
© Reprinted from CCITT Blue Book, vol. III.8, 1988.

The connection between two ISDNs of possibly different characteristics is provided across reference points N1 or N2. For N1, the
interworking function is split between the two ISDNs, whereas for N2
it is entirely contained within one of them. Figure 2.9(b) depicts the
corresponding ISDN connection type.

The third type of ISDN connection provides access to specialized
services available externally to the ISDN. Examples of such services
are message handling, data processing, and videotex services. As
shown in Figures 2.9(c) and 2.10, these are attached to the ISDN via
reference point M.

In the fourth case the ISDN connection involves access of an
ISDN end-user to specialized information storage and processing centers internal to the ISDN, such as a network-provided database, an
operations center, or a network management center. These facilities
interface with the ISDN through the *internal reference point P,* as
shown in Figure 2.10. The corresponding ISDN connection is shown
in Figure 2.9(d).

Finally, we can envision an ISDN that provides a connection between two non-ISDN facilities—that is, between pairs of K reference
points—or acts as an intermediate network between two ISDNs that are
attached at *N reference points*. This situation is shown in Figure 2.9(e).

2.3.2 The ISDN Connection-Type Reference Configuration

A general reference configuration that applies to any of the connection
types mentioned earlier is shown in Figure 2.11. It consists of a set of
connection elements (CE) that are interconnected at *internal reference
points (IRP)* and together constitute a connection between a pair
of *external reference points (ERP)* of the various types discussed

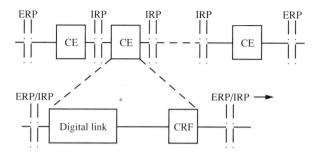

Figure 2.11   *Reference configuration for ISDN connections*
© Reprinted from CCITT Blue Book, vol. III.8, 1988.

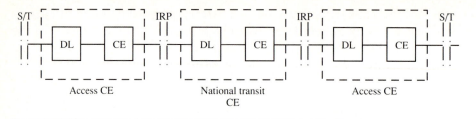

Figure 2.12 *Reference configuration for national connection between ISDN end-users* © Reprinted from CCITT Blue Book, vol. III.8, 1988.

previously. This reference configuration forms a first level of decomposition of the connection.

Each CE is composed of two parts, a so-called *connection-related function (CRF)* and a *digital link (DL)*. The CRF of a particular CE contains all the functions involved in the control of a given connection within that CE. Thus it may include facilities for exchange terminations, routing and relaying, network management, maintenance, and operations. The DL provides the transmission facility between CEs.

Five types of CEs—known as *access CE, national transit CE, international transit CE, interworking CE,* and *specialized resource CE*—are defined. The access CE is the part of the ISDN subscriber-access network between the T reference point and the boundary of the ISDN interexchange network. The national transit CE corresponds to the part of the ISDN interexchange network between the access CE and the first international exchange. The international transit CE covers the part of the ISDN interexchange network between the first and last international exchanges and may include one or more transit in-

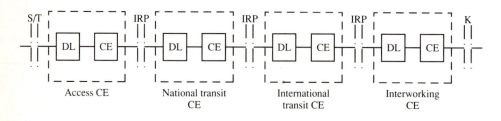

Figure 2.13 *Reference configuration for international connection to interworking reference point* © Reprinted from CCITT Blue Book, vol. III.8, 1988.

ternational exchanges. The interworking CE provides access to other ISDN or non-ISDN telecommunications networks. Finally, the specialized resource CE allows a connection to a specialized service provider.

As examples of the application of this reference model to specific connection types, Figure 2.12 shows the arrangement of CEs for a national connection between a pair of S or T reference points, and Figure 2.13 depicts the reference configuration for an international ISDN connection to a non-ISDN facility.

2.4 Summary and Recommended Reading

This chapter defined an ISDN in terms of an abstract reference configuration that divides the network's total capability into a set of interconnected components. At the highest level of decomposition an ISDN is divided into an interexchange network, a subscriber-access network, and a common channel signaling network. The functions of each of these parts are contained in one or more functional groups that interact with each other across reference points. The latter act as conceptual points of demarcation between the functional groups.

The chapter also defined the concept of an ISDN connection and specified its reference configuration in terms of functional groups and reference points.

Additional information on reference configurations can be found in [DECI82], [WABE82], [ROBI84], and [GIFF86]. Connection types are considered in [LUET86]. See also [GRIF82] for a discussion of the functions of the network termination functional group.

CHAPTER 3

The ISDN Communications Architecture

The previous chapter described the integrated services digital network in terms of reference configurations—that is, abstract decompositions of its overall structure into a number of functional groups and a set of reference points that serve as points of demarcation between the groups.

This representation of the ISDN is extremely useful in that it allows us to partition the network into a set of components that may be specified individually and that interact with each other at well-defined interfaces. In addition, the reference configurations provide a clear distinction between the responsibilities of the user and those of the network.

In this chapter we turn our attention to the development of an abstract model that describes the overall structural aspects of the ISDN's communications capabilities. Such a communications architecture serves three primary purposes. First, it imposes a logical structure on the communications-related aspects of a functional group. Second, it provides a convenient framework within which we may define the physical and logical relationships between communicating functional groups, the types of information flows they exchange with each other, and the protocols that govern their interaction. Third, the architecture allows us to describe the characteristics of the services that an ISDN makes available to the end-users.

Although in many ways the communications aspects of an ISDN are unique and different from those of other telecommunications networks, we base our architectural model on the open systems interconnection (OSI) protocol reference model ISO 7498 developed by the International Organization for Standardization for communications between general open data communications systems. The reader should already be familiar with the key concepts of this architecture, including the notions of layering, layer service, service primitive, peer entity, and peer protocol [HALS88].

Much of the material discussed in this chapter is based on CCITT Recommendations I.121, I.320, I.412, and Q.940, which represent the current view of the ISDN's communications architecture within the CCITT.

3.1   User-to-Network Interface Types

With respect to the relationship between an end-user and a network, an ISDN manifests itself essentially at the boundary between the user and the network, corresponding to the S, T, or U reference points. The part of the ISDN that is relevant to this relationship is therefore completely defined by specifying the characteristics of the UNI.

Such a specification involves two important general considerations. The first concerns the services made available to the end-user across the S, T, or U reference points by the network or by independent service suppliers. Generally, these services are specified to the end-user by describing their information transfer characteristics, their associated costs, and the procedure by which the user gains access to a particular service. It has already been mentioned that services are classified into bearer services, teleservices, and supplementary services, but a detailed examination of these issues is postponed until Chapter 10. The second aspect of the ISDN relevant to the end-user—and the one of interest here—concerns the physical interconnections and logical relationships of the functional groups TE, NT1, NT2, LT, and ET on the two sides of the S, T, or U reference points. In this respect the ISDN is completely described to the end-user by specifying the following characteristics:

- The mechanical and electromagnetic properties of the devices in which the functional groups are implemented and the interconnecting media by means of which these devices are attached to each other.
- The signaling structures and logical protocols of interaction employed by the functional groups in communicating with each other across the S, T, or U reference points.

- The operational, performance, and maintenance properties of the functional groups and interconnecting media.

One of the most important objectives of the ISDN development is to standardize these characteristics of the user-to-network interface in order to obtain several major benefits. First, individual ISDN components can be designed and produced to well-known and universally accepted specifications by multiple suppliers, resulting in economical implementations and widespread availability. Second, end-user devices can evolve independently of the network equipment and network configuration. Finally, end-user devices may be relocated from one interface point to another on either the same network or a different network, without any concerns for compatibility.

Although it would appear from these considerations that a single, standard user-to-network interface should be defined and implemented, in practice the multitude of sometimes drastically different user applications precludes this approach. Consider, for example, the issue of transmission capacity across the S or T reference points. A UNI designed to accommodate both low–bit rate information such as digital voice and the much higher bit rates associated with video would involve a level of complexity in the transmission and receiving equipment unwarranted in voice-only installations. Similarly, for various reasons such as cost, size, and power consumption a simple data terminal or digital telephone cannot be designed to incorporate the same level of protocol complexity in its interaction with an ISDN as, say, a private branch exchange, even allowing for possible economies of scale and future progress in microelectronics. Another factor in conflict with the idea of a single standardized interface is the likelihood that the design of an interface matched to the requirements of today's applications may be entirely inappropriate for applications still in the evolutionary stage or not yet conceived.

It follows from these considerations that in order to balance the requirements of efficiency, universality, flexibility, low complexity, and low cost on the one hand, and the wide variety of existing and evolving devices and applications on the other, several distinct standard user-to-network interfaces should be defined. These should offer the potential of matching the user application to the network capabilities in an optimum fashion. Three of these—with increasingly higher levels of capability—are identified in Figure 3.1, together with examples of the intended applications. They are known as *basic-access UNI, primary-access UNI,* and *broadband-access UNI.*

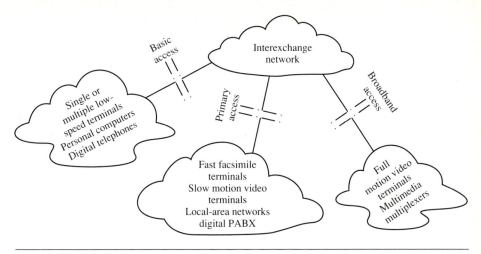

Figure 3.1 *ISDN applications and user-to-network interface types*

The basic-access UNI is primarily designed for the kinds of devices typical of the residential or small-business user. Specific examples are the digital telephone, synchronous or asynchronous data terminals, personal computers, facsimile machines, and printers. Various types of low–data rate telemetry devices such as security alarms and remote metering and control equipment are also included. The peak data rates generated in applications involving these devices typically are below 100 kbit/s.

The primary-access UNI is designed to accommodate slow scan or freeze frame video terminals, high-quality audio devices, high-speed graphics terminals, and digital facsimile machines. More complex data communications components such as communications controllers, terminal cluster controllers, and local-area networks are also appropriate. Perhaps its most important application, however, is in the connection of a digital PABX to the terminals on the one side and to the network on the other. Data rates for the devices utilizing the primary-access UNI range up to 2 Mbit/s.

The broadband-access UNI provides the capability required for the transmission of moving pictures, standard- and high-definition television, videoconferencing, and video surveillance data. Other applications include very high speed file transfer, document retrieval, and multimedia multiplexers that combine data from a variety of high-speed sources. Here the aggregate data rates may extend up to several hundred Mbit/s.

In addition to their differences in data rates, the three types of UNI just described vary substantially in the level of physical and logical complexity of the functional groups, the degree of end user control over the network connections, and the types of connections required. As a result, they are designed to distinct electrical specifications, may utilize different user-to-network signaling protocols, and rely on various types of interconnecting media to carry the electrical signals across the interface.

We defer a complete treatment of these issues to subsequent chapters, but concentrate next on the problem of defining a set of standard data rates for the transmission of information across the basic-access, primary-access, and broadband-access UNIs.

3.2 Channel Structures and Component Channels

The selection of the rates at which information is carried across the UNI is influenced by several important considerations. First, the rates must be appropriate for the present and future needs of the end-user applications and must take into account the statistical fluctuations of the information generated by a given application. Second, they must be compatible with the channel capacity limitations imposed by the subscriber-access network, and in particular the digital transmission system. Third, the data rates over the UNI must correspond to the available transmission rates on the circuits of the interexchange network. Finally, the choice of data rates is constrained by the desire to limit the cost and complexity of the interface, which implies a limit on the number of different data rates made available across the UNI.

Concerning the first point, we noted earlier that the end-user data rate requirements can roughly be divided into three broad classes, with data rates below 100 kbit/s, up to several Mbit/s, and up to several 100 Mbit/s, respectively. Some applications generate information at a constant rate and so require a dedicated transmission capacity at the appropriate rate. In other applications the amount of information that must be transmitted varies with time in a random manner. In such cases the allocated transmission capacity may be related to either the average rate or the peak rate. In the former case, of course, the information transfer process is potentially subject to delays and blocking problems.

Across the UNI the possible data rates are determined primarily by the characteristics of the transmission medium between the NT1 and LT functional groups. Chapter 8 takes up these issues. Here we note that, given the planned evolution of the ISDN from the telephone network, the existing infrastructure of twisted pairs in the local-access plant will provide the most important means of communication across the subscriber-access network of the ISDN for some time. With modern digital transmission technology, twisted pairs can support data rates of up to several 100 kbit/s over distances of 10 miles or more without repeatering, while the larger data rates required for primary access usually require repeatering every 1 to 2 miles. Broadband access, of course, can only be achieved over wider bandwidth media such as fiber optic cables. These exist today only in very limited quantities.

From the point of view of the interexchange network, the main limitations on data rates result from the digital transmission and switching standards developed by CEPT, CCITT, and AT&T, which generally specify data rates in multiples of 64 kbit/s.

In North America the existing digital multiplex structures are based on the primary PCM multiplex format DS1, which combines 24 channels at 64 kbit/s each, together with certain control information, into a first-level multiplex arrangement operating at a transmission rate of 1.544 Mbit/s. Second, third, and fourth levels of the multiplex hierarchy, known as DS2, DS3, and DS4, are obtained by iteratively combining 4 first-level arrangements at 6.312 Mbit/s, 7 second-level arrangements at 44.736 Mbit/s, and 6 third-level arrangements at 274.176 Mbit/s. Multiples of 2, 6, and 8 times the first level and 2 times the second level also exist, but to a lesser extent.

The CEPT standards are based on a multiplex arrangement of 32 channels at 64 kbit/s each, for a first-level transmission rate of 2.048 Mbit/s. Successive multiples of 4 extend this rate to 8.448 Mbit/s for level 2, 34.368 Mbit/s for level 3, and 139.264 Mbit/s for level 4.

These considerations, and the desire to restrain the complexity of the signaling structures across the UNI through standardization and the limiting of choices, lead to the concept of channel structure (see Figure 3.2). By definition, a channel structure consists of the total information-carrying capacity of the UNI. The value of this capacity is constant but depends on whether the UNI supports basic access,

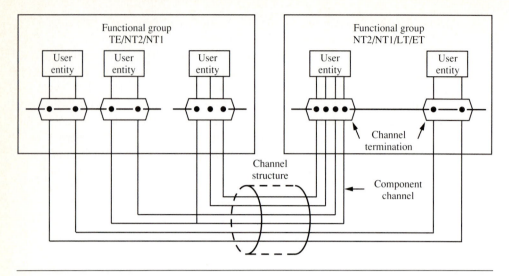

Figure 3.2   *User-to-network interface channel structure*

primary access, or broadband access. The channel structure is divided into one or more component channels, each with a specified data rate, that represent logically independent portions of the total capacity. The entire channel structure is transmitted synchronously over a single physical medium across the S, T, or U reference points. Alternatively, the transmission of the information in the individual component channels may be distributed over several media.

As shown in Figure 3.2, the component channels are terminated at both ends in functional groups. They exist between any pair of functional groups in the UNI. A component channel may either be dedicated to a particular user application or be shared among several applications.

Although formally a channel structure and its component channels exist only over the subscriber-access network, two component channels can be connected across the interexchange network to create a component channel between a pair of end-users. In this sense the concept of channel structure and component channels is also valid between end-users.

Generally, two types of channel structures—known as *synchronous* and *asynchronous channel structures*—are defined. In a synchronous channel structure, the transmission rate of a component channel is constant but may vary from one component channel to another.

Furthermore, the combination of component channels in a channel structure is fixed, at least in the short term.

Three types of synchronous channel structures—termed *basic rate channel structure, primary rate channel structure,* and *broadband channel structure*—are defined. They contain various combinations of component channels called *B channel, D channel,* and *H channel.*

By contrast, in the asynchronous channel structure a component channel is dynamically created by the instantaneous transmission requirements of the application. Its capacity may therefore be constant or vary with time, depending on whether the information is generated at a constant or variable rate. However, the maximum value of the capacity of any one component channel is limited by taking into consideration the requirements of the application, the available transmission capacity of the interexchange network, and, of course, the total capacity of the channel structure. Asynchronous channel structures, by virtue of their "bandwidth-on-demand" feature, allow an essentially unlimited variety of component channels. At present they are only intended for the broadband-access UNI.

3.3   Synchronous Channel Structures

Let us turn now to a detailed examination of the three types of synchronous channel structures introduced in the previous section.

Although other arrangements are possible, the combining of the component channels into a synchronous channel structure is normally accomplished by synchronous time division multiplexing. As shown in Figure 3.3, the channel structure consists of a continuous and periodic sequence of frames that are separated by framing channels and synchronously transmitted across the S, T, or U reference points of the UNI at a certain transmission rate. Each frame is divided into a certain number of time slots. A component channel is then formed by the permanent assignment of one or more specific and not necessarily contiguous time slots in every frame. The resulting capacity of the component channel is determined by the duration of the frame and the time slot, by the number of data bits carried in a time slot, and by the number of time slots.

As an example, a frame of 125 µs duration divided into 32 time slots and carrying 256 bits of information yields a component channel capacity of $m \times 64$ kbit/s if m time slots per frame are assigned to the

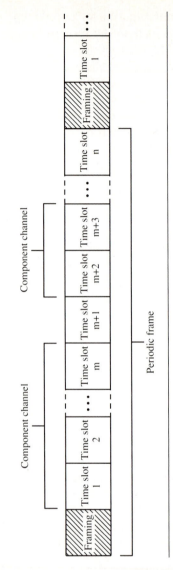

Figure 3.3 *Synchronous channel structure*

channel. As is discussed later, the values of $m = 1$, $m = 6$, $m = 24$, and $m = 30$ give rise to four types of component channels of particular interest.

Several options for accommodating the transmission of frames in the two directions across the UNI exist. The usual arrangement between TE and NT2 or between NT2 and NT1 is to provide separate physical media. On the other hand, the DTS between NT1 and LT that carries the data stream across the U reference point may be constrained by the availability of only a single physical medium. In this case, some type of hybrid or burst mode transmission is normally employed. Alternatively, full duplex transmission can be achieved through a separation of the two directions in the frequency domain. The reader should refer to Chapter 8 for a full consideration of these issues.

As mentioned earlier, it is useful to specify three particular synchronous channel structures, which are associated with the basic-access, primary-access, and broadband-access interface structures. In general, the channel structures implemented across each of the various S, T, or U reference points of a particular UNI do not have to be identical with each other.

Each channel structure consists of a specific combination of three basic types of component channels. The properties of these channels are specified next.

3.3.1 The B Channel

The B channel operates at a synchronous data rate of 64 kbit/s in full duplex mode. Its primary purpose is to carry information between a specific pair of end-users across the S, T, or U reference points of the UNI, without imposing any restrictions on the binary representation of the data.

Three classes of end-user information are generally considered appropriate for transmission over the B channel, although no strict adherence to these classes is required:

1. Digital voice encoded at 64 kbit/s, using pulse code modulation techniques according to CCITT Recommendation G.711.

2. Data streams corresponding to the synchronous user classes of service 3–12 and 30, as defined in CCITT Recommendation X.1, with data rates of 0.6, 1.2, 2.4, 4.8, 9.6, 48, and 64 kbit/s. These streams may exist in the B channel either individually or in combination with other data streams at the X.1 rates.

3. Digital voice encoded at bit rates less than 64 kbit/s, either alone or in combination with other voice or data streams.

In the second and third class the aggregate data rate of the combined bit streams must be adapted to equal 64 kbit/s.

Two B channels at separate UNIs may be attached to each other via network-provided circuit switched or packet switched connections, or by permanent or semipermanent connections based on circuit switching or packet switching. For circuit switched connections, the entire B channel, possibly consisting of multiple data streams, is delivered to a single UNI in transparent mode and no signaling information for the control of the connection is permitted on the B channel. For packet switched connections, the individual data streams of the B channel may be switched over different virtual circuits to separate destinations and the B channel may also carry the signaling information for the control of the virtual circuits.

3.3.2   The D Channel

Two types of D channels, operating at synchronous data rates of either 16 kbit/s or 64 kbit/s in full duplex mode, have been defined. Their major function is to carry the signaling information for the control of circuit switched connections involving one or more B channels between the user and the network. During periods of time when it is not needed for this purpose, a D channel may also be used for the transmission of user-to-user signaling information, low–bit rate packet switched data, and telemetry signals, using statistical multiplexing techniques and priority access for call control signals to resolve any contention.

3.3.3   The H Channel

H channels are designed to carry the types of user information requiring data rates in excess of 64 kbit/s and up to several 100 Mbit/s. Examples of specific applications are high-resolution digital video and audio for the distribution of television, teleconferencing and surveillance, high-speed file transfer, high-resolution graphics, and fast facsimile. Four types of H channels, with successively higher data rates, have been defined. They are summarized in Table 3.1.

The H0 channel operates at a full duplex synchronous data rate of six times the B-channel rate, or 384 kbit/s, which is a submultiple of both the 1.544 Mbit/s and 2.048 Mbit/s CCITT multiplex structures.

TABLE 3.1   H channel data rates

COMPONENT CHANNEL	DATA RATE kbit/s	MULTIPLE OF B-CHANNEL RATE	MULTIPLE OF H0-CHANNEL RATE
H0	384	6	1
H11	1536	24	4
H12	1920	30	5
H21	32768	512	—
H22	44160	690	115
H4	135168	2112	352

These two transmission systems are therefore rate-compatible at the H0 level. Since the data rate is matched to the requirements of standard broadcast quality digital audio programs, H0 can be expected to be used for signals of that type.

The H1 channel exists in two versions—H11 and H12—that correspond to the two CCITT first-level digital multiplex hierarchies. H11 operates at 24 times the B-channel rate for a total of 1536 kbit/s, whereas H12 corresponds to 30 B channels with a data rate of 1920 kbit/s. These channels are mainly intended to carry standard compressed videoconferencing signals with reduced spatial resolution and movement and very high speed digital facsimile signals. Another important application involves the provision of transmission capacity for private network trunks.

Similarly, two versions of the H2 channel—denoted H21 and H22—have been defined, with data rates of 32.768 Mbit/s and 44.160 Mbit/s, respectively. These are primarily chosen to satisfy the requirements of certain fast scan compressed video sources. Note that within the network the H21 channel can be carried over the existing level 3 of the PCM hierarchy, whereas the H22-channel rate is matched to the DS3 level.

Finally, a single H4 channel with a data rate of approximately 135 Mbit/s is currently under consideration. Its major application is the conveyance of standard PCM color television signals, various forms of enhanced video, and compressed high-definition television (HDTV). In at least one implementation the rate of H4 is set at 135.168

Mbit/s, which can be supported by level 4 of the PCM hierarchy [DOMA88].

For circuit switched connections none of the H channels carries signaling information.

3.3.4 The Basic Rate Channel Structure

The first of the synchronous channel structures, corresponding to basic access, is referred to as the basic rate channel structure and consists of two B channels and one 16 kbit/s D channel, for an aggregate data rate of 144 kbit/s. The B channels are used simultaneously and independently of each other, in either different connections or in the same connection, and carry the end-user data. Call control information for both B channels is transmitted on the logically separate D channel, creating an "out-of-band" signaling arrangement and allowing the entire B-channel capacity to be used for the transmission of user information.

The primary intent in defining this particular arrangement of channels is to create the possibility of two simultaneous and independent voice or data calls, either by the same or by different terminals, over a single UNI. Alternately, one B channel may be used to carry a voice call, while the other is engaged in the transmission of data, facsimile, low-speed video, or any other signal with a data rate that does not exceed 64 kbit/s.

In addition to carrying the call control information for the B channels, the independent D channel creates the possibility of a third connection for the transmission of low-speed data and control information between end-users.

As will become apparent in Chapter 8, the aggregate data rate of 144 kbit/s of the basic rate channel structure can be reliably supported over a large percentage of the existing subscriber lines of the world's telephone networks. For situations in which this is not the case, or where the network's internal switching and transmission capacities are inadequate, two alternate versions of the basic rate channel structure have been defined. The first consists of one B channel and the 16 kbit/s D channel, for an aggregate data rate of 80 kbit/s. The second uses only the 16 kbit/s D channel without any B channel.

This downgrading of the complete basic rate channel structure may also be effected in a virtual sense by blocking access to one or both of the B channels in situations where the full capacity is not needed or desired.

3.3.5 The Primary Rate Channel Structure

The second type of synchronous channel structure—the primary state channel structure—is associated with the primary-access interface. It is designed to accommodate applications requiring more than two simultaneous connections and/or data rates in excess of 64 kbit/s. Two distinct configurations, based on the two CCITT primary PCM transmission standards, have been defined.

Generally, in the 1544 kbit/s version any combination of B and H0 channels, with or without a 64-kbit/s D channel, is permitted, as long as the aggregate data rate does not exceed 1536 kbit/s. Thus, the primary rate channel structure can be specified as either

$$n\text{H0} + m\text{B} + \text{D}$$

where the integers n and m range over the values

$$0 \leqslant n \leqslant 3 \qquad 0 \leqslant m \leqslant 23 \qquad 6n + m \leqslant 23$$

or in the form

$$n\text{HO} + m\text{B}$$

where

$$0 \leqslant n \leqslant 4 \qquad 0 \leqslant m \leqslant 24 \qquad 6n + m \leqslant 24$$

The most common of these possible arrangements combines 23 independent B channels and one 64-kbit/s D channel into a data stream with an aggregate data rate of 1536 kbit/s. Again, the B channels carry the user information, whereas the call control signals are transmitted on the D channel.

In some situations the network may not support or the user may not require the complete channel structure of 23 B channels and one D channel, in which case the number of B channels may be reduced to any nonzero value.

Another important version of the 1544-kbit/s primary rate channel structure combines three H0 channels and one 64-kbit/s D channel, for an aggregate data rate of 1216 kbit/s. The remaining capacity of 320 kbit/s can be allocated to as many as five B channels.

For a UNI supporting more than one primary rate channel structure, the absence of a D channel in one of the channel structures may be justified by assigning the call control information for the B channels and H channels to the D channel of another channel structure. The capacity of the D channel can then be assigned to an additional B channel.

Specific examples of this arrangement are twenty-four B channels, four H0 channels, or the combination of three H0 channels and six B channels, all for a total capacity of 1536 kbit/s.

The entire capacity of 1536 kbit/s of the primary rate channel structure can also be dedicated to a single H11 channel, without the presence of a D channel. Although H11 channels are only likely to be used over permanent connections, any required signaling for this H11 channel must again be provided by the D channel of another channel structure over the same UNI.

Table 3.2 summarizes the various options of the 1544-kbit/s primary rate channel structure.

In the 2048-kbit/s version of the primary rate channel structure, the general arrangement is given by

$$n\text{H0} + m\text{B} + \text{D}$$

where the integers n and m are constrained by the relations

$$0 \leqslant n \leqslant 5 \qquad 0 \leqslant m \leqslant 30 \qquad 6n + m \leqslant 30$$

The most important of these arrangements combines thirty B channels and one 64-kbit/s D channel into one data stream at an aggregate rate of 1984 kbit/s. For the same reasons as in basic access, one or more

TABLE 3.2 Synchronous primary rate channel structures

1544 kbit/s PRIMARY RATE CHANNEL STRUCTURES	2048 kbit/s PRIMARY RATE CHANNEL STRUCTURES
23B + D	30B + D
	nB + D $(1 \leqslant n \leqslant 29)$
3H0 + 5B + D	
3H0 + D	5H0 + D
3H0 + 6B	
24B	31B
4H0	5H0
H11	H12 + D

of the B channels may not be supported by the network. Consequently, the number of B channels may in general vary between one and thirty.

Another important channel structure combines five H0 channels and one D channel, for the same aggregate data rate of 1984 kbit/s as before.

Various other specific combinations of B, H0, and D channels, up to the maximum data rate of 1984 kbit/s, have also been defined. The 2048-kbit/s version also allows the arrangement of one H12 channel and one D channel, for 1984 kbit/s.

Table 3.2 shows the different options of the 2048-kbit/s primary rate channel structure.

In North American implementations of ISDN the primary rate channel structure is based on the 1544-kbit/s transmission standard, whereas in most other parts of the world the 2048-kbit/s version is used. Evidently, the differences in these formats result in important incompatibilities, especially between the H11 channel and H12 channel.

3.3.6 The Broadband Channel Structure

The specification of synchronous channel structures for the broadband-access interface is still somewhat tentative, and considerable uncertainty exists as to whether such channel structures are even appropriate in the broadband environment. Nevertheless, several options are under active consideration. These are based in part on the formats of the so-called *synchronous optical network (SONET)* recently defined by the T1 committee of the American National Standards Institute. SONET, which is discussed in more detail in Chapter 4, combines channel structures corresponding to the primary PCM multiplex arrangements into higher–bit rate structures by a hierarchical multiplexing technique.

The bit rates and channel combinations for the synchronous broadband channel structure are chosen to match the data rates of standard television signals that have been digitized in either linear pulse code modulation or some form of rate reduction coding such as adaptive differential pulse code modulation. Channel structures designed for the transmission of digital high-definition television signals have also been proposed.

To date, two specific synchronous channel structures have been identified. The first combines the equivalent of 2016 B channels for a total rate of 129.024 Mbit/s. The second operates at four times that rate, combining the equivalent of 8064 B channels for a rate of 516.096 Mbit/s. These combinations are shown in Table 3.3.

Other combinations of channels have been considered [DOMA88], several of which are also given in Table 3.3. In one of these a single H4 channel is combined with four H12 channels and a basic rate channel structure. The H4 channel is intended to carry television signals of present-day quality, highly compressed HDTV, moving image videotext, and very high resolution images and documents. The four H12 channels provide the capacity to convey high-resolution color facsimile and allow fast data transfer. The remaining channel capacity of 2B+D can be used in various supporting ways for the transmission of voice, audio programs, or other low–data rate information.

For the transmission of multiple television signals, four H4 channels can be combined with either a basic rate or a primary rate channel structure. Here each of the H4 channels can carry a single standard television signal. Alternatively, the combination of two H4 channels provides the capacity for moderately compressed HDTV or all four H4 channels can be used for a single uncompressed HDTV signal.

Videoconferencing applications that do not require the high bit rates of television can be supported by an H21 channel. Several options for combining three H21 channels with basic rate or primary rate channel structures and a number of H12 channels have also been proposed.

Given the current emphasis of the CCITT and other standards bodies on asynchronous methods of transmission in broadband networks, it is likely that none of the proposed synchronous broadband channel structures will be incorporated in the emerging broadband standards. Their use will therefore be confined to private implementations of broadband ISDN.

TABLE 3.3   Synchronous broadband channel structures

2016B
8064B
H4 + 4H12 + 2B + D(16)
4H4 + 16H12 + 30B + D(64)
4H4 + 2B + D(16 or 64)
3H21 + nH12 + mB + D(16 or 64)

3.4 Asynchronous Channel Structures

For certain applications in which the information flows are not constant, it is desirable to base the design of a channel structure on the concept of the virtual component channel. By definition, the capacity of a virtual component channel is derived from the channel structure in competition with the capacity demands of other virtual component channels. It varies with time in accordance with the fluctuations of the information flow carried by it.

There are two major reasons for this approach. First, since the virtual component channel provides a data rate matched to the requirements of the application, rather than being fixed as in the case of a synchronous component channel, an information flow carried by the virtual component channel consumes only the fraction of the total capacity of the channel structure required by it. In particular, it consumes no capacity during idle periods. Second, a channel structure based on the statistical time division multiplexing of virtual component channels offers the flexibility to support a wide and dynamically varying spectrum of applications with different data rates and usage patterns in an efficient manner.

There are also several disadvantages. Since the capacity of the channel structure is shared among a number of applications whose instantaneous demands on this capacity are generally unpredictable, the total instantaneous demand may at times exceed the capacity of the channel structure. This implies that the information flows must be buffered and will encounter variable delays in accessing the channel structure. Parts of the information flows may also be lost due to buffer overflow conditions, unless mechanisms for restricting admission to the channel structure and controlling the fluctuations of the admitted information flows are implemented. A further problem involves the need to allocate the total capacity of the channel structure in a fair and equitable manner among the competing applications throughout the network and to enforce this allocation. Finally, certain types of applications such as speech cannot tolerate a variable delay, whereas others such as file transfer may be sensitive to information loss. In these cases mechanisms for priority access or a reservation system must be implemented.

The design of the virtual component channels and the asynchronous channel structures is based on the concept of a transfer cell, which provides an elementary unit of capacity. A cell is an information frame containing a fixed and integral number of octets of information.

A channel structure is created by transmitting a continuous sequence of cells synchronously across the UNI at a constant rate. The cells may be packaged into larger frames or they may be transmitted individually without reference to any such structure. In either case, the use of certain of these cells in a sequence on a periodic or irregular basis in accordance with the needs of an information flow then constitutes a virtual component channel. Figure 3.4 shows an example.

Since a particular transfer cell may generally be associated with any of the virtual component channels, it must carry within it a header that among other things identifies the virtual component channel. Thus, only a portion of its capacity is available to carry the information flows. The data rate of a virtual component channel and the time between successive cells occupied by a virtual component channel depend on the usage pattern of the cells, their size, the number of octets of overhead, and the rate at which the cells are transmitted. Let L be the number of octets in a cell, of which H are overhead, and let the transmission rate of the channel structure be R bit/s. If a virtual channel uses on average one out of every K cells, its average data rate R_v is given by

$$R_v = R(L - H)/KL \text{ bit/s}$$

and the average time T_v between successive cells of a virtual channel is given by

$$T_v = 8 \, KL/R \text{ seconds}$$

These relationships make clear that for a given average data rate the average time between available cells of a virtual component channel

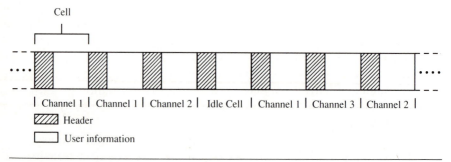

| Channel 1 | Channel 1 | Channel 2 | Idle Cell | Channel 1 | Channel 3 | Channel 2 |

▨ Header

☐ User information

Figure 3.4 *Asynchronous channel structure*

is determined by the size of the cell. Thus, in order to limit the time delay, L must be kept small. On the other hand, to achieve high efficiency L must be large compared to H. In the past various cell sizes ranging from 30 to 120 octets (of which 2 to 5 octets are reserved for the header) have been proposed. Within the CCITT a consensus has recently been reached that specifies a cell of 53 octets with 5 octets of header information.

The total capacity of the channel structure must be sufficient to at least accommodate the application with the highest data rate that must be supported over the UNI. For broadband access, where video applications require data rates up to several hundred Mbit/s, two channel structures are currently under consideration. The first operates at a transmission rate of 150.336 Mbit/s and the other at four times that rate, or 601.344 Mbit/s.

As a specific numerical example of data rates and time delays, consider the case of transmitting digital voice coded at 64 kbit/s, using a cell size of 36 octets, of which 4 octets are overhead. Since this application cannot tolerate variable delays, 250 cells per second are required to support the peak demand of 64 kbit/s and these cells must be dedicated to the application. For a rate of 150.336 Mbit/s and assuming that the entire transmission capacity is available for cell transport, a total of 522,000 cells are transmitted every second, of which 1 of every 2088 cells is dedicated to the application. The time between successive cells then equals 4 ms. Since voice octets are generated at the rate of 8000 per second, the 32 octets generated in the 4 ms between available cells must be buffered.

The sharing of the available cells in a channel structure among multiple applications requires a limit on either the number of virtual channels simultaneously present on the channel structure, the data rate of each virtual channel, or a combination of both. Several allocation schemes can be considered. It is for example possible to limit an application's peak data rate and allocate a sufficient number of cells to the corresponding virtual channel. The maximum number of virtual channels that can be supported is then just the ratio of the capacity of the channel structure to the sum of the peak application data rates. As an alternative, one may take into account any random or deterministic fluctuations of the information flows and limit an application's average data rate or the ratio of peak rate to average rate. Limits on other statistical measures such as burst size and time between successive bursts can also be imposed.

3.5 The Subscriber-Access Network Protocol Reference Model

The channel structures defined in the previous sections provide the transmission capacity for the exchange of information between the functional groups on the two sides of the UNI. We turn now to a consideration of the functional groups themselves and develop a model by which their logical structure and their interactions with other functional groups can be described. Our model uses the concepts and terminology of the open systems interconnection reference model, although many of its structural properties deviate significantly from the latter. We restrict our attention in this section to the SAN.

3.5.1 Information Flows

From the point of view of an end-user, the information transmitted over an ISDN can be classified into four types of flows known as *user information flow, control information flow, user-to-user signaling information flow,* and *network management information flow.* They are exchanged bidirectionally across the SAN, IEN, and CCSN between the end-users, between an end-user and the CCSN, and between an end-user and a network management facility. Of course, in the context of a complete ISDN many other flows can be identified—for example, flows between internal network management or signaling elements. None of these, however, directly involve the end-user.

Each of the above defined flows manifests itself in two ways. Physically, the flows are represented by digital signals that are transmitted across the physical media between all adjacent pairs of functional groups of the SAN and between functional groups in the IEN or CCSN. Logically, the flows represent information that is conveyed only between the particular functional groups to which the information is relevant.

User information flows consist primarily of data not of a control nature, which is relevant to the end-users only. Examples are digital voice, data, text, graphics, and image. They also include end-to-end control information used to convey the end-user data, such as acknowledgments, sequence numbers, and flow control quantities. Physically, these flows exist between all adjacent functional groups in the SANs of the end-users and between those functional groups in the IEN involved in a connection between the end-users. In a logical sense they exist between TE functional groups and are also relevant to those functional groups in the SAN and IEN where the information is processed.

Control information flows contain signaling information for the establishment, operation, and termination of connections between end-users. They are also associated with the modification of the service characteristics of an established connection, the indication of its status, and the control of the supplementary services offered by the network.

Physically these flows exist between all adjacent functional groups in the SAN and between the functional groups in the CCSN involved in connection control. Logically, the flows are relevant to a subset of the SAN functional groups and the components of the CCSN. In some cases they may also have end-to-end significance.

User-to-user signaling information flows contain control information that is transparent to the network but relevant to the end-users. Thus, in a logical sense they exist only between TEs. Physically they are again carried between adjacent functional groups in the SAN and between functional groups within the IEN or CCSN.

The network management information flows convey data in support of various management activities such as network configuration control, resource allocation, maintenance, accounting, and performance monitoring. They are used to carry indications of the occurrence of certain events such as faults, convey requests from one functional group for management functions to be performed by another functional group, and distribute management information such as performance and accounting data among various functional groups.

Physically, the network management information flows exist between adjacent functional groups in the SAN and may be conveyed across the circuit switched or packet switched facilities of the IEN or the CCSN. Logically, they could be relevant to a pair of TEs, a TE and a remote management center external to the ISDN, or a TE and a network management functional group within the ISDN.

Figure 3.5 summarizes these concepts by means of a specific example. Physically, the user information flow is conveyed between a pair of end-users via the SAN and the circuit switched IEN and is logically relevant only between the end-users. The network management information flow is assigned physically to the packet switched IEN and exists logically between an end-user and a network internal management center. The control information flow and user-to-user

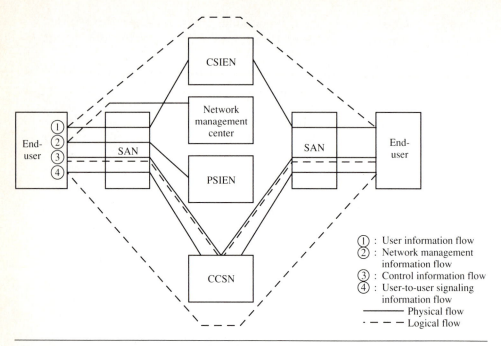

Figure 3.5 *Information flows*

signaling flow are both transmitted over the CCSN. Logically, the first are relevant to the SAN and CCSN, as well as the end-users, whereas the second exist only between the end-users.

3.5.2 *Information Flows and Channel Structures*

The information flows just discussed are transmitted across the SAN over specific component channels of the existing channel structure. Although in principle any association of information flows to channels is possible, arrangements in which the B channels or H channels are used exclusively for user information flows are preferred. By way of an example, Figure 3.6 illustrates a particular arrangement for the case of a 2B+D basic rate channel structure on both ends of a connection. Similar associations may be established between two primary rate channel structures or between basic and primary rate channel structures.

In our example, the D channel is used to convey all four classes of information flows. First, in conjunction with the CCSN it carries

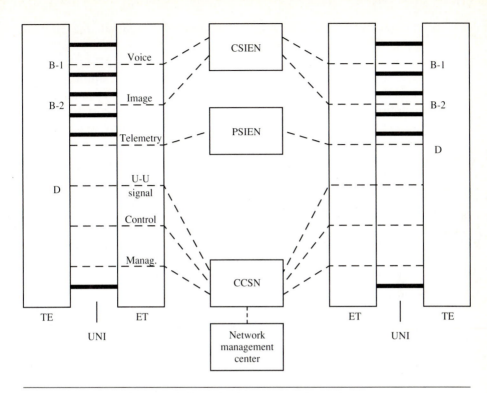

Figure 3.6 *Information flows for basic-access channel structure*

the control information flows necessary to establish two independent circuit switched connections between two ISDN terminals over the two available B channels B1 and B2. While these connections over the B channels are in place, the D channel, again in conjunction with the CCSN, also carries the control information flow used by the ISDN terminals to effect a change in the transmission characteristics of one or both connections or to invoke supplementary services.

Second, the D channel, in conjunction with a packet switched IEN, carries low–data rate user information flows such as telemetry and alarm signals between end-users on a time-sharing basis with the control information flows.

Third, the user-to-user signaling flows between the terminals are also carried on the D channel, but in conjunction with the CCSN. The control information flows to establish the corresponding connections are also conveyed over the D channel and the CCSN. The ISDN terminals can employ this user-to-user connection to exchange control data that are relevant to the end-users only. Examples are the negotiation or declaration of terminal communications capabilities or a change in visual information mode from graphics to facsimile.

Finally, the D channel is shared to carry the network management information flows between the terminals and the network management center via the CCSN. The terminals may use this facility to report the occurrence of an unacceptably high rate of error to the network management function, along with a request for rerouting of the connection. Or the network management center may notify the terminals that it will carry out tests of the subscriber access network, and convey the test signals across the SAN over the D channel.

The connections over the B channels are dedicated to the transfer of the user information flows. They may exist independently of each other and either simultaneously or sequentially in time. In our example, one of the B channels carries a voice conversation, while the other is engaged in the transmission of visual information such as graphs or charts pertinent to the voice conversation, in either graphic or facsimile mode. Both transmissions take place over the circuit switched IEN facilities.

3.5.3 Out-of-Band Signaling

The existence of a channel structure and the association of information flows to specific component channels leads to some important properties of the communications capabilities across the user-to-network interface.

Clearly, the logical division of the total UNI channel capacity into individual component channels allows the UNI to support several simultaneous and independent connections for the transfer of information flows. The connections can exist in a variety of modes, using the circuit switched and packet switched transmission facilities of the IEN and the CCSN. The number of available connections depends, of course, on the type of interface and channel structure implemented. One result of this arrangement is the possibility to convey the signaling required for the control of the connections and the user information flows over logically separate and independent connections across the UNI.

The channel used for connection control, in conjunction with the CCSN or the IEN's packet switched facilities, can also serve as an additional connection between end-users for the transfer of user-to-user signaling information flows. Such a connection can exist with or without an established connection over the user information channels and may involve the same or a different user pair. Furthermore, the management information flows between end-users and network management facilities may be conveyed over the connection control channel or another independent channel.

This logical separation of the control flows, management flows and user-to-user signaling flows on the one hand and the user information flows on the other is known as *out-of-band signaling*. If this separation is supported by separate and independent protocols, several advantages are realized.

One of these relates to the fact that the protocols for connection control, network management, and user-to-user signaling may then be defined in step with the evolution of the capabilities of the ISDN and be designed with the degree of flexibility and logical sophistication required to support the multiple information flows mentioned above. In a similar manner, the development of the user information transfer protocol may be related to the present and future needs of the end-users and service providers, without any concern about its impact on the protocols governing the other information flows. Perhaps most important, however, the control, management, and user-to-user signaling flows may be transmitted concurrently with the user information flows. This creates the possibility of providing the user with such features as detailed call progress information, access to supplementary and other specialized connection-related services, and sophisticated network management capabilities during the life of the connection, without any interruption of the user information transfer process.

3.5.4   The General Protocol Reference Block

The decomposition of the information transfer process into separate and independent flows, as discussed previously, and the principle of functional layering inherent in the open systems interconnection reference model lead to the representation of the total communications capability of a functional group shown in Figure 3.7. Horizontally, a functional group is decomposed into three planes of communications functions, the *user plane (U plane)*, the *control plane (C plane)*, and the *layer management plane (LM plane)*.

The U plane controls the transfer of the user information flows, as well as any user-to-user signaling flows and those management information flows that are exchanged between the end-users. It is generally incapable of altering the state of the connection itself. From the

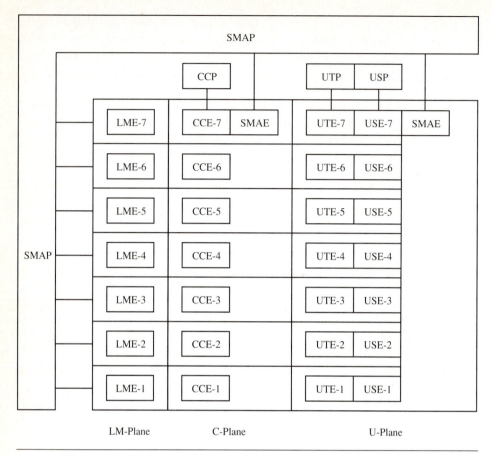

Figure 3.7 *Protocol reference model for a functional group*

point of view of the channel structure, the U plane is normally associated with the B channels or H channels, but may also involve the D channels.

The primary purpose of the C plane is to convey the control information flows. Thus it provides the functions for establishing and terminating network connections between end-users, controlling the use and characteristics of already-established connections and allowing access to supplementary connection-related network services. It is also used for the transmission of management information flows exchanged between an end user and a network management center. The C plane is normally associated with the D channels.

The set of functions of the U plane and C plane is further decomposed by defining a hierarchical partition into seven layers, as shown in Figure 3.7. The general principles on which this vertical decomposition is based are those of the open systems interconnection reference model. Formally, the layers in the U plane and C plane are numbered from U-1 to U-7 and C-1 to C-7, respectively. Names such as *network layer* or *data link layer,* which are descriptive of a layer's function, are also sometimes used to identify them.

Each of the layers in the U plane and C plane contains one or more entities that communicate with their peer entities in another functional group across the UNI for the purpose of transferring the various information flows. Thus, the *user information transfer entities (UTE)* correspond to the user information flows, the *user-to-user signaling entities (USE)* are associated with the user-to-user signaling flows, and the *connection control entities (CCE)* govern the transfer of the control information flows. Layer 7 of the U plane and C plane also contains the *system management application entity (SMAE),* corresponding to the management information flow.

Associated with both the U plane and C plane is the LM plane, which is also divided into seven layers, labeled LM-1 to LM-7. Each of these layers contains a *layer management entity (LME),* which manages the resources of its corresponding U-plane and C-plane entities and exchanges information regarding these resources with a peer layer management entity in the same layer of another functional group.

For the U plane and C plane, an entity in layers 2 to 6 of a specific plane offers services to an entity in its superior layer within the same plane and obtains services from an entity in its inferior layer within the same plane. Layer 7 only obtains services and layer 1 only offers services. In contrast, an entity in any of the 7 layers in the LM plane obtains services from its adjacent U-plane or C-plane entity in the same layer. It offers no services to the LME at any higher layer and obtains no services from an LME at any lower layer.

These services are requested and offered through the exchange of U-plane, C-plane, or LM-plane service primitives across the appropriate boundaries between adjacent entities. In specific applications some entities in the U plane, C plane, or LM plane may be null, so that the boundaries between adjacent entities exist only in a conceptual sense. In such cases the primitives of a given U-plane or C-plane entity are mapped directly onto those of the adjacent entity and the primitives of the LM-plane entity do not exist.

At layer 1 the entities in the U plane and C plane are supported by physical media that carry the physical signals representing the information flows between functional groups. Usually all flows are transmitted in time division multiplexed form over a single medium, although separate media are, of course, also possible.

At layer 7 the entities in the U plane and C plane interface with the ultimate users of the communications architecture, the applications processes. Generally, four types of application processes are defined. The UTE-7 or USE-7 located in the U-7 interface with a *user information transfer process (UTP)* or a *user-to-user signaling process (USP)* for the purpose of conveying user information flows or user-to-user signaling information flows, respectively. The CCE-7 in the C-7 interacts with a *connection control process (CCP)* and allows the latter to establish, manipulate, and terminate connections. The SMAE interfaces with the *system management application process (SMAP)* for the purpose of conveying system management information to another SMAP.

The interactions between the layer 7 entities and the application processes take place across the human-machine interface and are governed by a protocol that is outside the context of the communications architecture.

As far as the LM plane is concerned, each of its entities interacts with the SMAP for the purpose of managing the resources of the layers in the U plane and C plane.

Although not shown in Figure 3.7, it is necessary to provide a function that coordinates the various activities in the U plane, C plane, and LM plane. This so-called *plane management function (PMF)* performs the task of distributing incoming information to either the U plane or C plane according to its relevancy and allows communication between the three planes in a given functional unit for the purpose of synchronizing their activities. The PMF is a purely local matter associated with a particular functional group and does not communicate with the PMF of another functional group.

3.5.5 The Subscriber-Access Network Protocol Reference Model

From the representation of a functional group shown in Figure 3.7, we now derive a reference model for the subscriber-access network.

As we discussed earlier, the decomposition of the functional groups into planes and layers induces a corresponding decomposition of the information flows between the functional groups. Thus, the U plane serves the purpose of conveying user information flows, user-to-user signaling information flows, and end-user management information flows, whereas the C plane is restricted to control information flows and management information flows between a user and a network management facility. Each of these flows is divided into seven logical subflows. These are conveyed in a logical sense between peer entities in the appropriate plane of the communicating functional groups. Physically, however, these subflows are transmitted as a single flow over the physical transmission medium interconnecting the functional groups.

As far as an entity in a given layer of the LM plane is concerned, it relies on the entities in the associated U-plane or C-plane layer to transmit the management information flow to a peer entity in another functional group.

The logical transfer of the subflows between functional groups is governed by peer-to-peer protocols between pairs of U-plane entities or pairs of C-plane entities. The protocol at each layer of a given plane is independent of the protocol at another layer, and the protocols in one plane are independent of those in the other plane. The transfer of management information flows between peer LMEs is controlled by the protocols of the associated U-plane or C-plane entities.

A specific version of the SAN reference model, in which the SMAE is located in the U plane and the LM plane is associated with the C plane, is shown in Figure 3.8.

Figure 3.8(a) depicts the structure of the U plane and its associated logical and physical user information flows, assuming that the connection carrying the U-plane flows across the IEN is circuit switched. We note that the logical subflows at layers U-2 to U-7 exist only between TEs, whereas at layer U-1 the subflow also exists between all adjacent functional groups of the SAN.

The case of a management information flow between two U-plane SMAEs in originating and receiving TEs would be similar to Figure 3.8(a). Logically, the subflows at layers U-2 to U-7 are only relevant between a pair of TEs. Across the SAN they are therefore end-to-end. The subflow at layer U-1 is again conveyed between all adjacent functional groups.

In Figure 3.8(b) we show the interactions in the C plane for the transfer of control information flows.

The logical control information subflows at layers C-2 to C-7 exist between the TE and the NT2, as well as between the NT2 and the ET.

contain all planes. Similarly, one or more layers within a plane may be empty.

Physically, the various information flows that are exchanged between the peer planes and peer entities in different functional groups are usually carried over the same physical medium. Logically, they may either be carried over the separate component channels of the existing channel structure or be multiplexed onto a single component channel.

A number of specific connection types and information flows are of particular interest. Among these are the simple circuit switched connection over a basic-access interface structure, a packet switched connection, and the case of a user-to-user signaling connection. These are discussed in the following sections.

3.6.1 Circuit Switched Connections for Basic Access

A somewhat simplified version of the reference model for the case of a connection over the circuit switched IEN between a pair of end-users is shown in Figure 3.9. For greater clarity we have omitted the LM plane and depicted the U plane and C plane in separate diagrams.

We assume the existence of a basic-access channel structure across the T and U reference points on both sides of the connection between two TEs and the absence of the NT2 functional group, so that the S and T reference points are merged. This very simple configuration corresponds to many practical applications, including the single point-to-point voice call.

The user information subflows are carried across the SAN over a B channel and between SANs by a circuit switched IEN. Over the SAN they are controlled by the protocols of the U plane. Since a circuit switched connection is normally logically transparent to the nature of the user information, the relationship between the functional groups in the SAN extends only to layer U-1. All user information subflows at layers U-2 to U-7 are therefore between U-plane entities in TE functional units and thus have end-to-end significance only. Figure 3.9(a) shows these interactions. Note that an interworking function may be required for the conversion of layer 1 protocols between the SAN and CSIEN.

In the C plane, which corresponds to the connection control signaling between the functional groups on the two sides of the UNI, normally only the entities in layers C-1, C-2, and C-3 are involved. This is in particular the case for dialing up a voice connection between a pair of subscribers. The subflow associated with C-1 is relevant be-

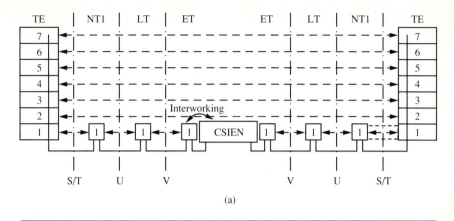

Figure 3.9a *Circuit switched connection over the B channel (U plane)*

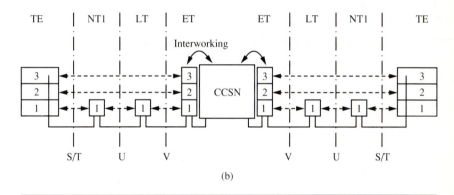

Figure 3.9b *Circuit switched connection over the B channel (C plane)*

tween the TE and NT1 functional groups, between the NT1 and LT functional groups and between LT and ET. The other two subflows associated with layers C-2 and C-3 exist only between the TE and ET functional groups. Across the SAN all three subflows are transmitted over the D channel.

Since the control information flows are also relevant to the CCSN, an interworking function between the SAN and the CCSN is provided which converts the physical and logical flows to a form appropriate for the CCSN. Specifically, what is required here is the conversion of the D-channel connection control protocol to the signaling system

used by the CCSN. We refer the reader to Chapter 9 for a consideration of this issue.

The reference model for the C plane is shown in Figure 3.9(b).

3.6.2 Packet Switched Connections over the B Channel

In this example involving a packet switched connection between a pair
of end-users we assume that the packet switched IEN is accessed via
a basic-access channel structure between a TE and a *packet handler
(PH)*. The latter performs the functions of the ET and interfaces the
SAN with the packet switched IEN. Figures 3.10(a) and 3.10(b) show

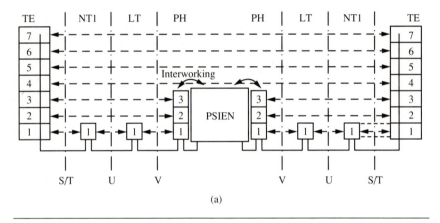

(a)

Figure 3.10a   *Packet switched connection over the B channel (U plane)*

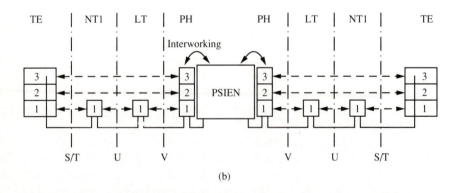

(b)

Figure 3.10b   *Packet switched connection over the B channel (C plane)*

the corresponding protocol reference model for the U plane and C plane, respectively. As in the previous case, we have omitted the LM plane.

User information transfer over the virtual circuits between TEs is accomplished according to the procedures of the U plane. At layer 1 the user information flows exist between the U-1 entities in all components of the SAN, whereas layers 2 and 3 are relevant only between the TE and the PH. All relationships above layer 3 are end-to-end. Note that an interworking function for conversion between the SAN and PSIEN protocols may be required.

In special types of packet switched connections, as for example frame relaying, the U-plane procedures across the SAN between the TE and PH encompass only layers U-1 and U-2, so that the U-3 functions such as error control, flow control, and sequence numbering of the user information packets over the virtual circuit are relegated to the end-users. The reader is referred to Chapter 10 for more information concerning frame relaying and other modes of packet switching.

The connection control information subflows are conveyed between the TE and the PH over the D channel and internally over the packet switched IEN. Their function is to establish and terminate virtual circuits over one of the B channels between the end-users via the PH and the packet switched IEN. At layer 1 the control information subflow exists between the C-1 entities in the TE and NT1, the NT1 and LT, and the LT and the PH. At layers 2 and 3, on the other hand, the subflows exist only between the entities in C-2 and C-3 of the TE and the PH.

3.6.3 *User-to-User Signaling over the D Channel*

The protocol reference model for the case of user-to-user signaling over a D channel in conjunction with the CCSN is essentially similar to Figure 3.9, with the exception that the CSIEN is replaced by a CCSN in the U plane.

Both the user-to-user signaling information flows as well as the control information flows are carried over the D channel. The first is under the control of the U plane, whereas the second is governed by the C plane. The upper four layers of the C plane have end-to-end significance only and are therefore contained only in the communicating TEs. The entities in layers C-1 to C-3, on the other hand, provide the control function for the user-to-user signaling information flows. C-1 is relevant between TE and NT1, between NT1 and LT, and between LT and ET. C-2 and C-3 provide the functions for a TE to interact with the ET for the purpose of accessing the resources of the CCSN. The latter conveys the user-to-user signaling information flows between the ETs on the sending and receiving sides.

We point out that user-to-user signaling is essentially independent of any other activities. In particular, it may be carried out with or without the existence of a connection over the B channels. In cases where the D channel is required for the control of a B-channel connection, the user-to-user signaling flow shares the capacity of the D channel and the CCSN with the control information flow for the connection. It may then be appropriate to impose priorities on the two types of use and to preempt one of the flows when the higher priority flow is present. Care must, of course, be taken to assure that this preemption does not result in a loss of data.

Mainly for reasons of security and network integrity, most existing networks do not allow at the present time the use of their signaling facilities for the transfer of user-to-user signaling information flows. In this case a packet switched IEN could take the place of the CCSN. Except for the replacement of the CSIEN by a PSIEN, the protocol reference model of Figure 3.9 would apply unchanged.

3.7   Summary and Recommended Reading

Our main concern in this chapter has been the development of an architecture for the description of the structural aspects of an ISDN's communications capabilities. We defined three types of user-to-network interfaces labeled basic access, primary access, and broadband access and characterized their transmission capacity in terms of a set of component channels and their aggregation into synchronous and asynchronous channel structures. We then developed a protocol reference model for the functional groups of the subscriber-access network that divides the communications capability of a functional group into a user plane, a control plane, and a layer management plane. Each of these planes is further divided into seven layers. We also illustrated these concepts by applying the reference model to several specific types of connections.

[DU C85] offers a review of the ISDN protocol reference model and its application to packet switched, circuit switched, and user-to-user signaling connections. Further information on this subject can also be obtained from [POTT85]

CHAPTER 4

The ISDN User-to-Network Layer 1

In the general context of the ISDN subscriber-access network protocol reference model developed in the previous chapter, layer 1—the physical layer—is responsible for the bidirectional transmission across the R, S, T, U, and V reference points of the electromagnetic signals that represent the logical quantities in the B, D, and H channels. Accomplishing this task requires the implementation of a physical signaling and control structure in the devices that incorporate the various functional groups of the SAN. In addition, an electromagnetic medium between these devices is needed. The detailed specification of layer 1 therefore involves at least the following features:

- The electrical or optical characteristics of the signal generators and receivers

- The design of the signals in terms of their line codes, amplitudes, waveforms, time durations, and spectral composition

- The electrical and physical characteristics of the interconnecting medium, as well as its topological and mechanical configuration

- The provision of power to the components corresponding to TE1, TE2, TA, NT1, NT2, LT, and ET

- The organization of the user information flows, control information flows, user-to-user signaling flows, and network management flows, including the adaption of data rates and the assignment of component channels to the flows

- The multiplexing of the B, D, and H channels and the provision of timing and synchronization

- Access control to the D channel in multipoint configurations where the channel is used by more than one functional group or more than one information flow, to provide for the orderly sharing of its capacity

- Activation and deactivation of the subscriber equipment and network equipment
- Procedures for maintenance and performance monitoring

Considering the fact that the TE2 corresponds to existing, non-ISDN equipment, it is clear that the specification of layer 1 at the R reference point must conform to the public and proprietary interface standards that currently govern the design of such devices as analog telephones, data terminals, facsimile machines, and telex terminals. For data communications equipment, the most important of these standards is RS-232D, developed by EIA within the United States and adapted internationally by the CCITT as Recommendations V.24/V.28 and X.21 bis. Other significant designs include the more recent EIA standards RS-422/423/449 and the physical layer of CCITT Recommendation X.21. We will consider these interfaces within the framework of the ISDN in Chapter 7.

In contrast to the situation at the R reference point, the design of the interface at the S, T, U, and V reference points is not constrained by prior practice. The structure of layer 1 may therefore be chosen in keeping with simplicity, efficiency, and cost considerations. As noted previously, however, given the wide range of current and future applications and their corresponding data rates and equipment complexity, it is necessary to develop several distinct versions of layer 1 to correspond to the basic-access, primary-access, and broadband-access interface structures.

In this chapter we limit ourselves to a discussion of layer 1 as it pertains to the S and T reference points—that is, to the relationship between a TE1 or TA and an NT2, or an NT2 and an NT1. Layer 1 for the U reference point is treated in Chapter 8. We use the term *NT* to identify the NT1 functional group, as well as the layer 1 aspects of the NT2, considered as a network terminating functional group. Similarly, the term *TE* identifies the layer 1 aspects of the TE1 and TA functional groups and the layer 1 terminal aspects of the NT2.

4.1 Layer 1 Specifications for Basic Access

For the basic-access interface structure, the responsibility of layer 1—whether it is implemented at the S or T reference points—is the bidirectional transmission of the information flows contained in any of the basic rate channel structures 2B+D, B+D, or D over an interconnecting medium between terminal equipment and network termination. A standard implementation of this interface for the 2B+D version has been defined by CCITT in Recommendation I.430. This section examines its most important aspects.

4.1.1 Layer 1 Services and Protocol Tasks

With respect to the protocol reference model for the SAN, as described in the previous chapter, most of the functions of the U-plane and C-plane entities of layer 1 for basic access are merged into a single common entity that offers services to the layer 2 entities of the U plane and C plane and to its layer management entity LME-1. In turn this common layer 1 entity receives services from the underlying transmission medium for the transport of electromagnetic signals.

To support these services, a pair of cooperating layer 1 entities on the two sides of an S or T reference point interact with each other by means of a peer-to-peer protocol. The purpose of this interaction is to carry out certain tasks, of which these are the most important:

- A procedure for the activation and deactivation of the physical customer and network equipment containing the communicating functional groups

- A procedure for regulating access to the resource of the D channel, in cases where the latter must be shared by multiple TEs

- The performance of diagnostic and maintenance functions across the S and T reference points, including the indication of equipment status

- The coding, multiplexing, synchronization, and timing of the peer-to-peer protocol information and the B- and D-channel information flows obtained from the layer 2 U-plane and C-plane entities and the LME-1

- The transmission and reception of these information flows over the physical medium between TE and NT

The services supported by these tasks are requested and provided through the exchange of five service primitives between layers 1 and 2 and five additional primitives between layer 1 and its LME-1. Figure 4.1, which applies to both the U plane and C plane, shows these interactions.

The information flows between the layer 1 and 2 entities are passed across the *service-access point (SAP)* by means of the

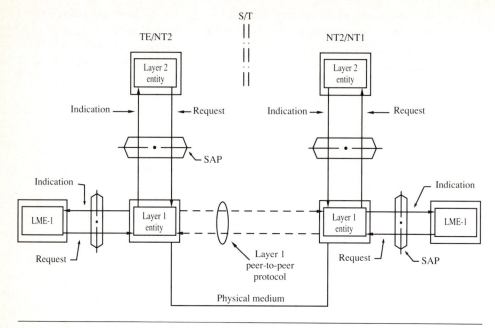

Figure 4.1 *Physical layer interactions (U plane and C plane)*

PH-DATA Request and PH-DATA Indication primitives. Activation of layer 1 is requested by a layer 2 U-plane or C-plane entity through the PH-ACTIVATE Request primitive and activation or deactivation of layer 1 are indicated to the requesting layer 2 entity by means of the PH-ACTIVATE Indication and PH-DEACTIVATE Indication primitives.

The layer 1 entity provides an indication to its LME-1 of whether the equipment is activated or deactivated by means of MPH-ACTIVATE Indication and MPH-DEACTIVATE Indication primitives. It also transfers to its LME-1 error information and information regarding its condition by means of the MPH-ERROR Indication and MPH-INFORMATION Indication primitives, respectively. Finally, the LME-1 may request deactivation by transferring to the layer 1 entity the MPH-DEACTIVATE Request primitive.

4.1.2 Wiring Configurations

To carry out the tasks just listed, the devices containing the communicating TE and NT functional groups must be interconnected across an S or T reference point by an electromagnetic medium. In selecting a particular type of medium several criteria must be kept in mind.

From the point of view of performance, the most important factors are the signaling rate and transmission distances that can be supported, given the permissible limits on error rates, propagation delay, and signal attenuation. With respect to the 2B+D basic-access channel structure, the medium must accommodate an aggregate data rate of 144 kbit/s, together with a certain amount of overhead incurred by the peer-to-peer protocol. For customer installations in large office buildings—which may involve the connection of many terminals to a PBX, multiplexer, or remote concentrator, for example—distances of several hundred meters to perhaps one kilometer are frequently encountered. In other situations, where terminals are connected to a local-area network or directly to the physical network termination, the distances may be somewhat shorter.

The extent to which existing customer-premises wiring such as telephone circuits or coaxial cable and their associated plugs and jacks can be used is another important criterion. Clearly, the selection of such wiring may have a major effect on the cost and complexity of the installation. A similar comment applies to the use of existing transmission and receiving equipment.

Given these and other considerations, the CCITT chose to specify the use of two unshielded metallic pairs, one for each direction of transmission, to physically carry the information flows in the channel structure across the S and T reference points. In typical installations the wires have a diameter of 0.4 to 0.6 mm and are covered with polyvinyl chloride or teflon insulation. Typical values for propagation delay, characteristic impedance, and attenuation at 100 kHz are 7 μs/km, 100 Ω, and 8 dB/km, respectively.

The pairs are passive conductors in the sense that they perform no signal amplification or other processing. They may be arranged in either a point-to-point configuration, connecting one active transmitter to one active receiver at each end of the cable, or a point-to-multipoint topology, which allows the connection of several simultaneously active devices at one end to one active device at the other.

Two configurations, shown in Figures 4.2 and 4.3, are defined in Recommendation I.430.

For the point-to-point arrangement of Figure 4.2, the cable between a pair of interconnected devices—that is, between a TE and NT2, TE and NT1, or NT2 and NT1—is restricted to a length of 1000 m in order to limit the attenuation and propagation delay of the

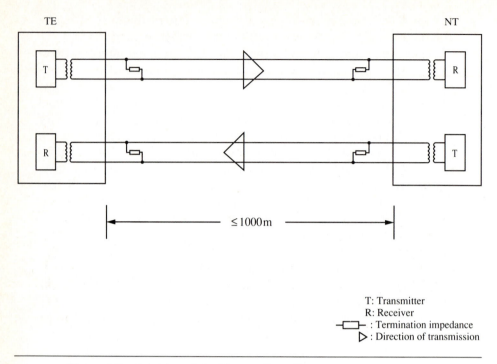

TE   NT

≤1000m

T: Transmitter
R: Receiver
: Termination impedance
▷ : Direction of transmission

Figure 4.2 *Point-to-point wiring configuration*

signals. Each pair is terminated at both ends in an impedance of 100 Ω and transformer coupled to the transmitting and receiving circuitry in the equipment.

The first of the two point-to-multipoint options—the so-called *short passive bus*—is shown in Figure 4.3. It allows the connection of up to eight devices, here indicated as TEs, at random points along the cable. In order to restrict the total attenuation, as well as the dispersion of signals due to the varying propagation delays between the TEs and an NT, the cable is limited to between 100 and 200 m, depending on its characteristic impedance. Furthermore, the devices must be attached via stubs of no more than 10 m in length to control the impact of reflections from stubs with no attached TEs. The *extended passive bus* option extends the distance between the bus termination and the NT to 500 m by clustering the terminal connection points near the terminal side of the bus termination. As in Figure 4.3, up to 8 terminals may be attached via 10 meter stubs, but the distance between the con-

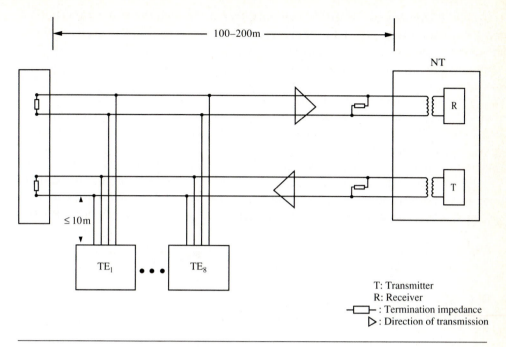

Figure 4.3 *Short passive bus wiring configuration*

nection points of adjacent terminals is limited to a range of 25 to 50 m. Both the short and extended passive bus must be terminated at both ends in a 100-Ω impedance.

4.1.3 Power Feeding

The provision of electrical power to the TE, NT1, and NT2 equipment may be accomplished in various ways, depending on the application.

   The simplest and ultimately the only arrangement that assures the portability of the equipment from one SAN to another is one in which each device supplies its own power drawn from a standardized local source such as a battery. The equipment can also be powered from the public power mains, provided that the power source variations in frequency, voltage, and mechanical attachment from one country to another can be accommodated. In some installations, locally powered equipment such as an NT2 or NT1 may be called on to provide power to the terminal; in the reverse situation, the locally powered terminal supplies power to the network termination equipment or another TE in direct TE-to-TE connections. In most cases, however, it is advantageous for the network to remotely power the TE, NT1, and NT2 equipment via the U reference point. (One important reason for this is the maintenance of the physical signal transmission capability during a local power failure.)

These various remote power feeding arrangements across the S and T reference points can be implemented either through the transmission of power as a phantom signal on the metallic pairs that carry the information flows, or via a separate power circuit in one or the other direction. The latter approach, of course, requires the modification of the wiring configuration between the devices to handle the additional circuitry. Such an enlarged wiring arrangement with two additional metallic pairs is specified in Recommendation I.430 and shown in Figure 4.4. Power source 1 is intended to supply power to the terminal side in phantom mode over the two information carrying

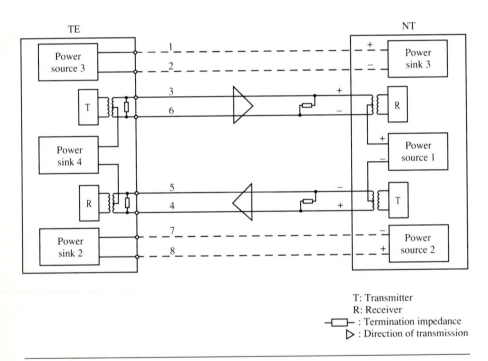

Figure 4.4 *Extended wiring configuration for signal transmission and power feeding*

circuits. Under normal operating conditions, it derives its power locally at the NT. The level of power supplied depends on a number of factors—for example, the expected power consumption of the terminals and the power transfer loss—and so is a function of the specific installation and the state of activation of the devices. The voltage level at the NT, however, is specified as 40 V DC; the maximum power available at the TE is limited to 1 W in the activated state and to 100 mW in the deactivated state. The polarity of the DC voltage is negative at the transmitting end of the NT.

Under certain emergency situations such as a local power failure, power source 1 may derive a limited level of power from the network across the U reference point and provide it to those terminals that must maintain a basic communications capability. In such a case only a reduced capability of the terminals may be supplied with power, and the level of power consumption is limited to 380 mW at 40 V for terminals in the active state and 25 mW at 40 V for inactive terminals. The change from normal to restricted powering is indicated to the terminal side by a polarity reversal of the feeding voltage, so that the polarity of the DC voltage is then positive at the transmitting end of the NT.

Figure 4.4 indicates two other methods of power feeding that are considered optional. In the first, power source 2 in the NT obtains its power locally and provides it to the terminal side at levels similar to power source 1. In the second case, power source 3 provides locally derived power to the NT side or to another TE. In the latter situation a reversal of the two optional power feeding circuits across the interface is necessary since a TE accepts and provides power on different circuits. Again, the power levels are the same as in the previous cases.

4.1.4 Interface Cabling Arrangements

As shown in Figure 4.5, the complete cabling arrangement across the S and T reference points for basic access consists of three distinct parts, identified as connecting cords, extension cords, and interface cable.

Connecting cords are normally permanently attached to the TE and NT equipment and provide a plug for connection to an extension cord or directly to the interface cable. The maximum allowable length is limited by the total permissible attenuation across the interface.

Extension cords connect to the connecting cords through a jack

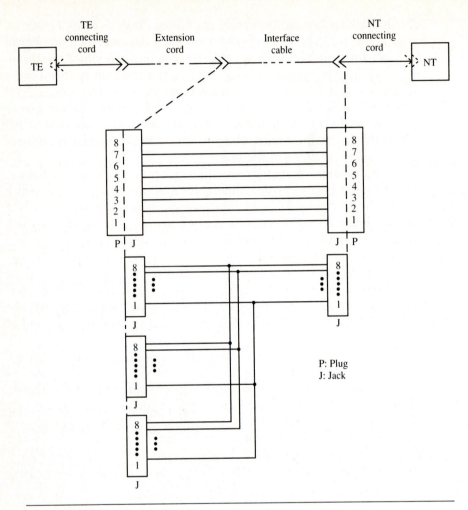

Figure 4.5 *Cabling and connector arrangements*
© Reprinted from ISO IS 8877.

and to the interface cable through a plug. They may only be used in point-to-point configurations and are limited to a length of 25 m.

The *interface cable* is normally terminated at both ends in a jack, but may also be attached directly to the NT.

Each of the component cables contains the four mandatory wires that constitute the information carrying circuits. In addition, the wires for one or both of the optional power feeding circuits may also be incorporated. The total length of the cabling arrangement is determined by the wiring configuration and is subject to the limitations discussed earlier.

The terminating plugs and jacks for the cables, as well as the arrangement of the contacts in the plugs and jacks, have been standardized by the International Organization for Standardization and are described in ISO 8877. This standard specifies the design and dimensions of 8-pole plugs and jacks, based on the RJ plastic plugs and sockets in widespread use in the United States for telephone connections.

The assignment of the four mandatory wires and the four optional wires to the contacts, together with the corresponding voltage polarities, is shown in Table 4.1. The transmit and receive circuits are assigned to contacts 3,6 and 5,4. The polarities indicated for these correspond to the polarity of a framing pulse. For the power feeding circuits 1,2 and 7,8 the indicated polarity is that of the DC voltage provided by the power source. For applications not requiring one or both of the optional power feeding circuits, the appropriate contacts in the plug and jack may be omitted.

For TE-to-NT connections the contacts for the transmit and receive pair at the TE are also the contacts for the receive and transmit pair at the NT. Thus, a given wire is connected to the same contact at both ends of the cable. Since the interface cable is terminated at both ends in a jack, the TEs and NTs may be connected at either end of the cable if the wiring configuration is point-to-point.

TABLE 4.1   Contact assignments for plugs and jacks

CONTACT NUMBER	TE	NT	POLARITY
1	Power source 3	Power sink 3	+
2	Power source 3	Power sink 3	−
3	Transmit	Receive	+
4	Receive	Transmit	+
5	Receive	Transmit	−
6	Transmit	Receive	−
7	Power sink 2	Power source 2	−
8	Power sink 2	Power source 2	+

© Reprinted from ISO IS 8877.

For connections between two TEs, a crossover arrangement for the transmit and receive pairs, as well as for the optional power feeding circuits, is required.

4.1.5 Frame Structure

As noted earlier, at layer 1 of the basic-access interface structure, most of the U-plane and C-plane functions are merged into a single entity that provides the bidirectional transmission across the S and T reference points of the flows obtained from the layer 2 entities and the LME-1. These flows are organized into recurring frames of 48 bits, with each frame transmitted synchronously in 250 µs, for an effective transmission rate of 4000 frames per second, or 192 kbit/s. Of this total bit rate, 144 kbit/s correspond to the information obtained from the higher layers of the protocol architecture, with the remaining 48 kbit/s constituting layer 1 peer-to-peer protocol overhead and control information.

The binary structure of the frame is shown in Figure 4.6. The structure is the same for both point-to-point or point-to-multipoint wiring configurations, but depends on the direction of transmission. In the direction from terminal to network—that is, TE to NT or NT2 to NT1—the frames are organized into 10 groups of bits, indicated by dots. These are individually DC balanced by appending to each group a L bit whose logical value is chosen in such a way as to create a line signal with a zero average voltage over the balanced group. This balancing is required by the fact that the transmit and receive circuits are transformer coupled to the transmitters and receivers.

The two groups of bits labeled B1 in positions 3–10 and 27–34 form one of the B channels, while the bits of the second B channel labeled B2 are located in positions 16–23 and 38–45. Thus, two times 16 bits of B-channel data are carried in each frame, for a total of 64 kbit/s per B channel. Normally, the B-channel bits carry the user information flows obtained from U-2 entities across the S or T reference points.

The four D bits in positions 12, 25, 36, and 47 form the D channel, for an effective rate of 16 kbit/s. In general, any of the information flows from U-2, C-2, and LME-1 may be associated with these bits.

The remaining two bits F and F_A in positions 1 and 14 are used to provide frame synchronization, so that the data contained in the frame may be properly demultiplexed at the receiver.

In the direction from network to terminal—that is, NT1 to NT2 or NT2 to TE—the frame structure differs from the previous one in sev-

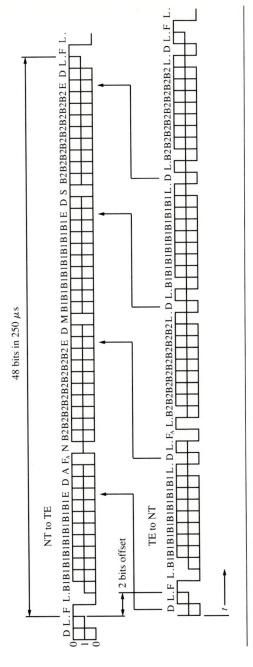

Figure 4.6 *Structure of S/T basic-access frame*
© Reprinted from CCITT Blue Book, vol. III.8, 1988.

eral respects. First, DC balancing is applied only to the first framing bit F and the overall frame. Second, the E-bit position immediately following each of the four B-channel groups contains a copy or echo of the D-channel bit most recently received from the other side. Thus, as shown in Figure 4.6, the D-channel bits arriving in positions 12, 25, 36, and 47 of a terminal-to-network frame are echoed in positions 24, 35, and 46 of one network-to-terminal frame and position 11 of the following network-to-terminal frame, respectively.

Of the remaining bits in positions 13, 15, 26, and 37, the use of the S bit is currently unspecified and its value is set to binary 0. The N bit is used as part of the framing procedure and the A bit plays a role in the activation and deactivation procedure of the interface. The M bit, known as the *multiframe bit*, allows the identification of a group of frames that form a multiframe. The use of these three bits is described in Section 4.1.7.

Table 4.2 summarizes the group structure of these frames.

4.1.6   Line Code

A *pseudoternary line code*–also known as *bipolar* or *modified alternate mark invert (MAMI)*–whose nominal pulse width equals the duration of a bit (5.21 μs) and whose nominal pulse amplitude has a value of 750 mV is used to physically represent the bits contained in a frame. The permissible tolerances on the pulse waveform are shown in Figure 4.7. The pulses are chosen so that a logical 1 corresponds to a zero voltage condition on the transmission circuit. Successive logical 0s are represented by alternating positive and negative pulses, with the polarity of the first logical 0 of each frame section always opposite to that of the framing bit F. Special conditions are also imposed on the framing bits F, F_A, and N. These are discussed in the next section.

An example of the pseudoternary line code is shown in Figure 4.8.

4.1.7   Timing and Frame Synchronization

The timing of the transmissions by the terminal side at the frame, octet, and bit levels is extracted from the frames received from the network side, which in turn derives its timing from the network clock. Thus, all transmissions from the terminal side are synchronized to the reception of a frame from the network side. At the frame level, the terminal side initiates transmission of a frame to the network side two bit transmission times after it has received the leading edge of the

TABLE 4.2   Group structure of S/T basic-access frame

TE TO NT

BIT POSITION	GROUP
1 and 2	framing signal with balance bit
3–11	B1 channel (first octet) with balance bit
12 and 13	D-channel bit with balance bit
14 and 15	F_A auxiliary framing bit or Q bit with balance bit
16–24	B2 channel (first octet) with balance bit
25 and 26	D-channel bit with balance bit
27–35	B1 channel (second octet) with balance bit
36 and 37	D-channel bit with balance bit
38–46	B2 channel (second octet) with balance bit
47 and 48	D-channel bit with balance bit

NT TO TE

BIT POSITION	GROUP
1 and 2	framing signal with balance bit
3–10	B1 channel (first octet)
11	E, D–echo channel bit
12	D-channel bit
13	bit A used for activation
14	F_A auxiliary framing bit
15	N bit
16–23	B2 channel (first octet)
24	E, D–echo channel bit
25	D-channel bit
26	M multiframing bit
27–34	B1 channel (second octet)
35	E, D–echo channel bit
36	D-channel bit
37	S: the use of this bit is for further study
38–45	B2 channel (second octet)
46	E, D–echo channel bit
47	D-channel bit
48	frame balance bit

© Reprinted from CCITT Blue Book. vol. III.8. 1988.

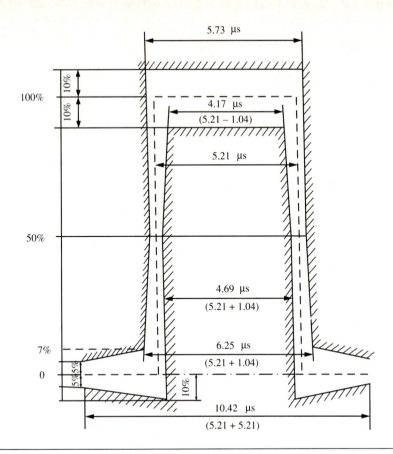

Figure 4.7 *Transmitter output pulse mask for S/T basic access*
© Reprinted from CCITT Blue Book, vol. III.8, 1988.

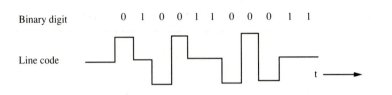

Figure 4.8 *Example of pseudoternary line code*

frame synchronization bit F from the network side (see Figure 4.6). This delay allows the terminal side to properly synchronize the received frame and provides the flexibility to align the transmissions from multiple TEs on a passive bus to a common bit clock. At the bit level, the terminal side derives its timing from the received pseudoternary signal by locking onto the transition from one pulse amplitude to another. Octet timing for the information in the B channels can be obtained by locating the beginning of the received frame and counting an appropriate number of bit clock cycles.

Let us define the round-trip delay T_d across the S or T reference points as the time difference between the transmission of a frame by the network side and its reception of the frame synchronized to it, measured at points in time that correspond to the zero crossings of the voltage between the framing bit F and its associated balance bit L, as shown in Figure 4.9. T_d is given by

$$T_d = T_o + 2T_p + T_e$$

where T_o is the frame offset delay, T_p is the one-way propagation delay, and T_e is the timing error at the terminal side. T_o corresponds to the two-bit delay at the terminal side between received and transmitted frames and is equal to 10.42 μs. T_p is a function of the specific wiring configuration, the electrical characteristics of the interface circuit, and its length. T_e measures the error incurred by the terminal side in establishing the timing of the frame received from the network side and initiating its own transmission. The value of T_e is limited by the electrical specifications of the transmitters and receivers to the range between -7 and $+15$ percent of the bit duration, or -0.36 to $+0.78$ μs.

A lower bound for T_d may be obtained by assuming a negative timing error and zero propagation delay, corresponding to the case where the terminal-side and network-side equipment is collocated. In this case we have

$$T_d > 10.42 - 0.36 = 10.06 \text{ μs}$$

At the other extreme the maximum value of T_d is limited by the requirement that a D-channel bit transmitted in a TE-to-NT frame must reappear as an echo in the NT-to-TE frame synchronized to it. Figure 4.6 shows this time interval to equal 10 or 8 bit transmission times, depending on the bit's location in the frame. If we assume the worst-case timing error of $+0.78$ μs, we have

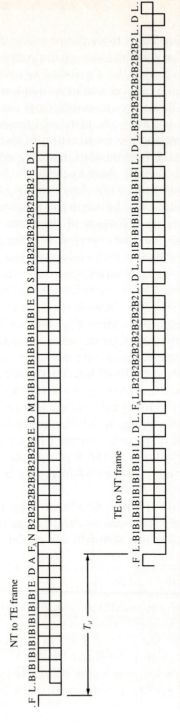

Figure 4.9 *Round-trip delay time*

$$T_d < 8 \times 5.21 + 0.78 = 42.4 \ \mu s$$

The fraction of the round-trip delay due to the one-way propagation delay is then upper-bounded by

$$T_p < 15.62 \ \mu s$$

which is well within the approximately 5–7 μs typically required for propagation over a metallic pair of 1 km length.

The alignment of the received frames by the terminal and network sides is accomplished through the technique of creating violations of the pseudoternary coding rule among the primary and auxiliary framing bits F, F_A and N. Logically, the first bit of each frame, the F bit, is always equal to 0. For network-to-terminal frames, F_A and N are logically complementary, whereas in the direction terminal-to-network F_A is always 0 and equal to its corresponding balance bit L.

In a given frame, the polarity of the pulses representing F, F_A, and N and the first logical 0 following the frame balance bit is always the same as the polarity of the most recent logical 0. Consequently, at the sending end each frame contains a violation of the pseudoternary coding rule at either 13 or 14 bits from the framing bit F, depending on the frame direction. At the receiver, a loss-of-framing condition exists when no such violation is detected over a two-frame interval. Frame realignment is assumed after the detection of three consecutive pairs of violations within the 13- or 14-bit intervals. Note that this technique is independent of the polarity of the framing pulses and thus functions even with a reversal of the wires.

A multiframe, consisting of 20 consecutive single frames, may be established by setting the M bit in position 26 of NT-to-TE frames to binary 1 in every twentieth frame and to binary zero in all other frames. By allowing the use of the F_A bit in frames 1, 6, 11, and 16 of a multiframe from TE to NT for purposes other than framing, a separate 800-bit/s signaling channel, known as the *Q channel,* is created. The use of this capacity is currently unspecified.

4.1.8 *Activation and Deactivation Procedures*

In order to control the power consumption of terminals and network termination equipment during periods of inactivity, the physical layer of basic access provides a service to layer 2 by which the terminal and network side equipment can be activated and deactivated through the exchange of certain signals across the S or T reference points. This service permits the activation and deactivation of a TE from NT1 or NT2, and NT2 from NT1. In the opposite direction, TE may activate NT2 or NT1 and NT2 may activate NT1. Deactivation in the direction terminal to network, however, is not allowed, because other terminals attached to a common NT2 or NT1 may require this equipment to remain active.

Activation and deactivation services involve the exchange across the layer 1/2 boundary of the service primitives PH-ACTIVATE Request (PH-AR), PH-ACTIVATE Indication (PH-AI), and PH-DEACTIVATE Indication (PH-DI). In addition, the primitives MPH-ACTIVATE Indication (MPH-DI), MPH-DEACTIVATE Request (MPH-DR), MPH-DEACTIVATE Indication (MPH-DI), MPH-ERROR Indication (MPH-EI), and MPH-INFORMATION Indication (MPH-II) are exchanged between layer 1 and the LME-1.

The actions implied by these primitives are carried out by a protocol between peer physical layer entities across S or T. The corresponding protocol data units consist of five signals, labeled Info 0 (I0) to Info 4 (I4), that are defined as follows:

- I0 denotes the absence of any signal on the interface circuits and signifies a deactivation request from NT to TE and a deactivation indication from TE to NT.

- I1 is a continuous signal with repetitive pattern 0 0 1 1 1 1 1 1, represented by a pseudoternary line code, with the first 0 always coded as a positive pulse, the second 0 as a negative pulse, and the 1's as the absence of a pulse. This signal is transmitted from TE to NT to request activation of the NT and is not synchronized to any network side timing.

- I2 consists of a normal layer 1 frame of 48 bits in the direction NT to TE, in which all bits in the B, D, and echo locations are set to logical 0. Bit A is also set to 0, and bits N and L follow the normal coding rules for layer 1 frames discussed in Sections 4.1.6 and 4.1.7. I2 is transmitted from NT to TE to request the activation of the TE or to indicate the activation of NT as a consequence of a request from the TE. Its high density of logical 0's allows rapid bit timing at the TE.

- I3 is a properly synchronized layer 1 frame with operational data in the B and D locations and transmitted from TE to NT.

- I4 also contains operational data in the B, D, and echo locations, but flows in the direction NT to TE. The A bit is set to logical 1.

The transmission of one of the signals between peer physical layer entities causes a change of state in the equipment on the two sides of the interface. At any one time the terminal side exists in one of eight states, F1 to F8, whereas at the network side four states, G1 to G4, are specified. The terminal states are defined as follows:

- F1 (Inactive) corresponds to downpowered terminal equipment and is entered whenever the TE detects the loss of power from either the remote power feeding circuits or the local power supply.

- F2 (Sensing) corresponds to terminal equipment that has been powered on, but has either not received any of the signals from the network side or has not reacted to such a signal.

- F3 (Deactivated) defines the deactivated state of the physical layer protocol, where neither side is transmitting any of the signals.

- F4 (Awaiting Signal) corresponds to the situation where the terminal side has responded to an activation request and is waiting for a response from the network side.

- F5 (Identifying Input) corresponds to the state where the terminal side has received a signal from the network side and is awaiting its identification.

- F6 (Synchronized) corresponds to the state in which the terminal side has received an activation signal from the network side and is now waiting for normal frames from the network side.

- F7 (Activated) is the normal active state where both terminal and network sides are transmitting normal frames.

- F8 (Lost Framing) corresponds to a situation where the terminal side has lost frame synchronization and is awaiting resynchronization or deactivation.

The four states on the network side correspond to the following situations:

- G1 (Deactivated) is the state where the network side is deactivated and not transmitting any signal.

- G2 (Pending Activation) is a partially active state entered on request from a higher layer.

- G3 (Active) is the normal active state where the network-to-terminal direction is active.

- G4 (Pending Deactivation) corresponds to the state where the network side is waiting for a return to the deactivated state.

The protocol of interaction between the peer physical layer entities in the terminal and network equipment carries out the instructions conveyed by the exchange of primitives between layer 1 and layer 2 and between layer 1 and the layer management entity. This protocol governs the relationship between the current state of the TE and NT equipment, the transmission of a signal, and the state of the equipment that results from this exchange. Given the many possible conditions that may arise in the relationship between the two sides, the interactions between the peer physical layers are quite complex. Since a complete discussion is beyond the scope of this book, the following paragraphs provide only a somewhat simplified description of several procedures. Further details can be found in CCITT Recommendation I.430.

In our examples we describe the interactions by means of a flow diagram constructed according to the formats and conventions of the *Specification and Description Language (SDL),* as defined in CCITT Recommendations Z.100 to Z.104. For a brief introduction to this language the reader is referred to Appendix B.

We start with the example of activation of an NT by the terminal side. The SDL flow diagram describing this procedure is given in Figure 4.10. Let us assume that the NT and TE exist initially in states G1 and F3, respectively. Thus, the equipment is powered on, but the interface is deactivated and both sides are indicating the I0 signal to each other. The activation process in the TE—which may, for example, be triggered by the desire to establish a connection—is initiated by the reception of a PH-AR primitive from its layer 2 entity. This causes the start of a timer T3, the transmission of the activation request signal I1 to NT, and a change of state to F4. As a consequence of the reception of I1, the network side transmits within 1 second the terminal synchronization signal I2, initiates timer T1, and enters the pending activation state G2.

The timers T1 and T3 are set to the maximum amount of time allowed by the respective sides for the completion of the activation process. Since the activation of NT usually also involves the local exchange, the activation times depend to a degree on the length of the subscriber loop and the transmission technology used. They may therefore vary considerably from one implementation to another and are not standardized. This means the terminal and network equipments must be designed with adjustable timers T1 and T3 to assure equipment portability.

The terminal side, on sensing the signal from NT, stops the transmission of I1 and within 5 ms indicates I0 to the NT. It then enters

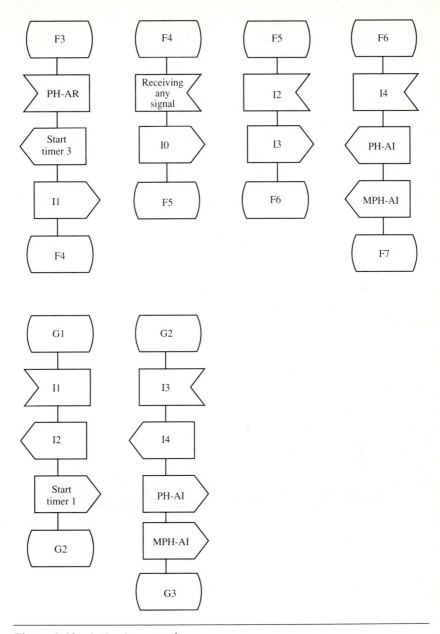

Figure 4.10 *Activation procedure*
© Reprinted from CCITT Blue Book, vol. III.8, 1988.

state F5 for the purpose of identifying the received signal. Within 100 ms after it has recognized the signal as I2, it transmits a normal layer 1 frame I3 and enters the synchronized state F6.

In response to the reception of I3, within 500 ms the network side transmits its own normal layer 1 frame I4, provides the PH-AI and MPH-AI primitives to its layer 2 and management entities, and enters the activated state G3.

In the final step of the activation procedure, the terminal responds to the reception of I4 by transferring the PH-AI and MPH-AI primitives to its own layer 2 and management entities. It then enters its own activated state F7 and is ready to transmit additional I3 signals.

The maximum times within which the various actions just described must normally take place have been standardized by the CCITT, although considerably larger values are permissible under certain abnormal conditions.

As a second example we consider the deactivation of a terminal by the network, assuming the two sides are currently in their respective activated states F7 and G3. The SDL diagram of the procedure is

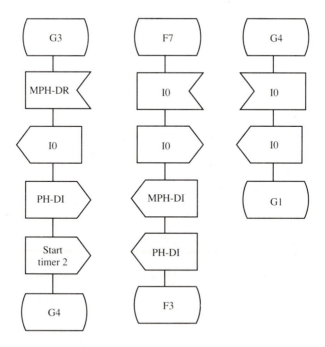

Figure 4.11 *Deactivation procedure*
© Reprinted from CCITT Blue Book, vol. III.8, 1988.

shown in Figure 4.11. Deactivation of the TE is initiated by the NT as a result of various conditions such as the absence of a signal from the TE for a period of time or the release of an existing connection. The management entity in the NT passes the MPH-DR primitive to its layer 1 entity, which in turn indicates the no-signal condition I0 to the TE, passes a PH-DI primitive to its layer 2, and sets timer T2 to control the deactivation time. T2 may vary from 25 to 100 ms. The NT then enters the pending deactivation state G4.

Within 25 ms of receiving I0, layer 1 at the terminal side also reacts by indicating I0, passing the MPH-DI and PH-DI primitives to its management entity and layer 2 entity, respectively, and entering the deactivated state F3.

The sensing of I0 by the network side then causes a state change to G1, which completes the procedure.

Figure 4.12 offers another view of the interactions between TE and NT during the activation and deactivation procedures.

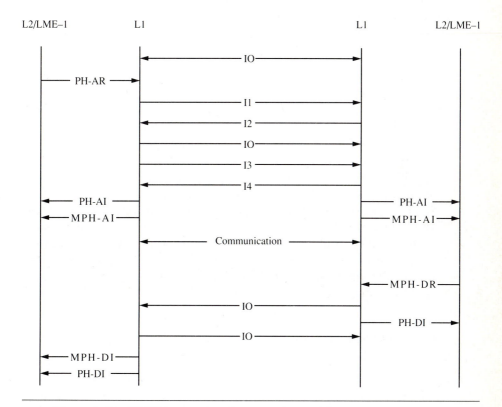

Figure 4.12   *TE-NT interactions for activation and deactivation*

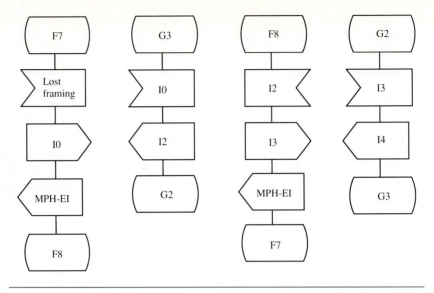

Figure 4.13 *Recovery of lost frame synchronization*
© Reprinted from CCITT Blue Book, vol. III.8, 1988.

In our last example we discuss the sequence of events following a loss of framing at the TE at a time when both sides are in the activated state. As shown in Figure 4.13, on loss of synchronization of a received I4, the terminal indicates the no-signal condition I0 to the NT and notifies its management entity of the loss of synchronization by conveying the error indication primitive MPH-EI. It then enters state F8. The reception of I0 by the NT causes the transmission of the synchronization signal I2 and a transition to the pending activation state G2. The TE, on receiving I2, recovers synchronization and responds with a normal frame I3. It also issues a MPH-EI primitive to its management entity to indicate the recovery from the previously reported loss of synchronization and enters state F7. At the NT side the receipt of I3 results in the transmission of I4 and a transition to G3, to complete the procedure.

4.1.9 D-Channel Access Control

In multipoint wiring configurations, where several terminals share a common NT, two or more activated TEs can attempt to access the B- and D-channel sections of a layer 1 frame in order to transmit layer 2 or management information to the NT. Since the resulting overlap of the line signals would destroy all information in the B-channel or D-channel locations, there needs to be some way of resolving the contention and allowing the terminals to gain orderly access to the shared resource. The B channels are normally assigned to specific terminals for the duration of a connection by a procedure carried out over the D channel. Once an assignment has been made, contention for that B channel is not permitted. On the other hand, the D channel—which serves multiple purposes—is under contention at all times, whether the B channels have been assigned or not.

To differentiate between the various uses, the control of the D channel is based on a dual priority scheme. First, control information flows for acquiring and releasing B channels are given priority over all other information flows. Second, after a terminal has obtained control of the D channel for the transmission of either control or noncontrol information, it may send a predetermined amount of information. Then it assumes a lower level of priority relative to the terminals still awaiting access to the D channel. The terminal reverts to its normal level of priority after all other terminals have had a chance to send information at the normal priority level.

A terminal in the active state, which does not currently control the D channel, transmits logical 1's in the D-channel locations of its I3 signal to the NT. According to the pseudoternary coding rule, this corresponds to the absence of a line signal. These transmissions therefore present no interference to the D-channel line signal from any other terminal. The TE also monitors the echo bits in frames from the NT, keeping a count C of the number of consecutive logical 1's and resetting C to zero on detection of a logical 0.

If the terminal wants to transmit control information and is currently in normal priority, it may initiate the transmission as soon as the count C reaches the value 8, whereas in lower priority it must accumulate a count of $C = 9$. For all other types of information flows such as user data, for example, the counts must reach 10 and 11, respectively.

Once transmission has been initiated, the terminal monitors the received echo channel bits and compares the corresponding transmitted and echoed D-channel bits. As long as the bits agree, the transmission continues; when the end of the information frame is reached it releases the D channel by sending logical 1's. A disagreement, on the other hand, indicates either the presence of line signals from more than one terminal or a transmission error. In either case the terminal ceases transmission immediately and returns to the monitoring state, while maintaining its present level of priority.

4.2 Layer 1 Specifications for Primary Access

The previous section covered the salient characteristics of layer 1 for the basic-access interface structure, and considered the properties of the underlying medium across which the information flows are transmitted.

We turn now to layer 1 of the primary-access interface structure, whose purpose is the bidirectional transmission of the various versions of the primary rate channel structure across the S or T reference points.

The characteristics of layer 1 are largely derived from the two existing and incompatible specifications for PCM transmission systems that have evolved over the last three decades. In particular, the electrical characteristics of the transmitters and receivers, the layer 1 frame structures, and the electrical signaling schemes conform either to the T-1 carrier system developed by AT&T and ANSI for use in North America and Japan, or the 2048-Mbit/s primary PCM standards developed by CCITT and CEPT and used in most other parts of the world.

This technology is well known because of its use in digital telephone and data transmission, and so we limit ourselves to a discussion of those aspects of the primary rate layer 1 design that are unique to the ISDN. For a complete treatment, see AT&T Publications 41449 and 54016 and CCITT Recommendations I.431, G.703, G.704, and G.706.

4.2.1 *Wiring, Power Feeding, and Activation*

There are several important differences in design between basic access and primary access.

Due to the difficulty of providing common timing to multiple terminals on a bus, only a point-to-point wiring configuration between the TE and NT is provided. The cabling consists of two symmetric metallic pairs with a characteristic impedance of 120 Ω, one pair for each direction of transmission. In order to limit signal attenuation to 6 dB at 772 kHz, a length limit of approximately 150 m is imposed on the cables.

Under normal circumstances no power is supplied across the interface, so that each piece of equipment must be powered from a local source. Optionally, however, the NT1 may be powered across the T reference point from either the NT2 or the TE over a separate circuit.

The interface is maintained in a constant active state, eliminating the need for the activation and deactivation procedures. Because of the restriction to point-to-point configurations, the need for multiple access control over the D channel also disappears.

4.2.2 Frame Structure

As in the case of basic access, the layer 2 and management information flows in the U plane and C plane are conveyed over the same physical medium, using a common layer 1 transmission format. The flows are organized into two distinct frame formats, according to the two versions of the primary-access interface.

In the 1544-kbit/s interface the frame structure is based on AT&T's well known Digital Signal Type 1 (DS1) channel arrangement in the extended superframe format, which has also been standardized by the CCITT in Recommendation G.704. In this arrangement, 24 groups of 8 bits each are combined with one additional bit into a frame of 193 bits. The frame structure is the same in both directions of transmission and is shown in Figure 4.14(a).

Each frame is transmitted in 125 µs, at the rate of 8000 frames per second, for an overall transmission rate of 1544 kbit/s. Each 8-bit group is transmitted in a time slot of 5.18 µs, yielding a rate of 64 kbit/s per 8-bit group. All component channels for the primary rate channel structure occupy an integral number of time slots. If the interface supports a D channel, it is contained in time slot 24. An H0 channel, if present, may generally occupy any six not necessarily consecutive time slots in the frame. This flexibility can be used to minimize congestion due to multiple demands for time slots. Four fixed assignments have also been specified. In these the H0 channels are allocated to time slots 1–6, 7–12, 13–18, and 19–24, as shown in Figure 4.15(a). The last of these assignments is, of course possible only in the absence of a D channel. The H11 channel, if present, occupies time slots 1–24. Again, no D channel is possible in this arrangement. In general, all available time slots can be used for B-channel information, and any feasible mixture of D, B, and H0 channels is permitted.

In any of the preceding assignments, all 8 bits of each group are always available to the user for signaling or data transmission

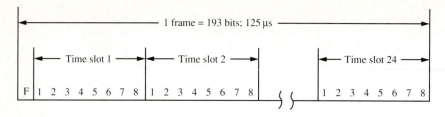

a) 1544 kbit/s Primary – access interface

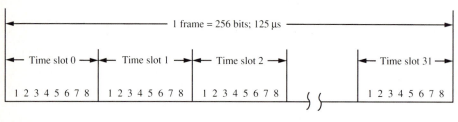

b) 2048 kbit/s Primary – access interface

Figure 4.14 *Structure of S/T primary-access frames*

H$_0$ channel	a	b	c	d
Time slots used	1 to 6	7 to 12	13 to 18	19 to 24

H$_0$ channel	a	b	c	d	e
Time slots used	1-2-3 17-18-19	4-5-6 20-21-22	7-8-9 23-24-25	10-11-12 26-27-28	13-14-15 29-30-31

H$_0$ channel	a	b	c	d	e
Time slots used	1-2-3 4-5-6	7-8-9 10-11-12	13-14-15 17-18-19	20-21-22 23-24-25	26-27-28 29-30-31

Figure 4.15 *Time slot assignments for H0 channels*
© Reprinted from CCITT Blue Book, vol. III.8, 1988.

purposes and no internal network use of the bits is permitted. The effective user data rate is therefore equal to 64 kbit/s per time slot and 1536 kbit/s per frame.

The function of the first bit in each frame, the F bit, depends on the frame's position in a 24-frame multiframe known as an *extended superframe*. The latter's structure is shown in Figure 4.16.

For frames 4, 8, 12, 16, 20, and 24 the F bits form the repetitive multiframe synchronization pattern 0 0 1 0 1 1, which is transmitted at the rate of 2 kbit/s.

For frames 2, 6, 10, 14, 18, and 22, on the other hand, the F bits are a *cyclic redundancy check (CRC)*. This 6-bit pattern is identified in Figure 4.16 as e1, e2, e3, e4, e5, e6. For a given multiframe it is

Multiframe frame number	F-bits			
	Multiframe bit number	Assignments		
		Framing	Maintenance channel	CRC
1	0	-	m	-
2	193	-	-	e_1
3	386	-	m	-
4	579	0	-	-
5	772	-	m	-
6	965	-	-	e_2
7	1158	-	m	-
8	1351	0	-	-
9	1544	-	m	-
10	1737	-	-	e_3
11	1930	-	m	-
12	2123	1	-	-
13	2316	-	m	-
14	2509	-	-	e_4
15	2702	-	m	-
16	2895	0	-	-
17	3011	-	m	-
18	3281	-	-	e_5
19	3474	-	m	-
20	3667	1	-	-
21	3860	-	m	-
22	4053	-	-	e_6
23	4246	-	m	-
24	4439	1	-	-

Figure 4.16 *Primary-access multiframe structure (1544-Mbit/s format)*

equal to the remainder obtained by the modulo-2 division of all the bits in the previous multiframe by the binary polynomial

$$g(x) = x^6 + x + 1$$

For the purpose of this division all F bits in the previous multiframe are set to binary 1. For additional details concerning the CRC computation, see Section 5.2.4.

The F bits labeled *m* in the 12 odd-numbered frames of the multiframe are used to convey certain maintenance, diagnostic, and status information, at the rate of 4 kbit/s. Their use and values are currently not specified.

The frame structure for the 2048-kbit/s version of the primary-access interface is shown in Figure 4.14(b). It consists of 32 groups of 8 bits each, numbered from 0 to 31. As before, the frames are transmitted in 125 µs, for a transmission rate of 8000 frames per second or 2048 kbit/s. Each 8-bit group is transmitted in a time slot of 3.91 µs, yielding a data rate of 64 kbit/s per time slot.

The D-channel information, if present, is assigned to time slot 16. Any of the time slots 1–15 and 17–31 may be allocated to the B channels. An H0 channel may occupy any six time slots in various combinations; the time slots do not have to be consecutive. Two particular arrangements of H0 channels have been defined, with the second one being the preferred implementation. They are shown in Figure 4.15(b) and (c). An H11 channel occupying time slots 1–15 and 17–25 and an H12 channel assigned to time slots 1–15 and 17–31 have also been specified.

The use of the bits in time slot 0 is organized around a 16-frame multiframe consisting of two 8-frame submultiframes, as shown in Figure 4.17. Bits 2 to 8 in even-numbered frames are always set to the pattern 0 0 1 1 0 1 1, which forms the frame synchronization signal. In these same frames the bits in position 1 labeled c1, c2, c3, and c4, considered over a submultiframe, form a 4-bit cyclic redundancy check over all bits of the previous submultiframe. These bits are generated by the binary polynomial

$$g(x) = x^4 + x + 1$$

In the odd-numbered frames bit 2 is always set to 1 to inhibit the unintended creation of the frame synchronization signal and bit A in position 3 serves as a so-called *remote alarm indication (RAI)*. The RAI bit is conveyed in TE-to-NT frames as a result of the loss of layer 1 capability in the direction of the TE and vice versa.

	Submultiframe	Frame number	Bits 1 to 8 of the frame							
			1	2	3	4	5	6	7	8
Multiframe	I	0	C1	0	0	1	1	0	1	1
		1	0	1	A	Sa4	Sa5	Sa6	Sa7	Sa8
		2	C2	0	0	1	1	0	1	1
		3	0	1	A	Sa4	Sa5	Sa6	Sa7	Sa8
		4	C3	0	0	1	1	0	1	1
		5	1	1	A	Sa4	Sa5	Sa6	Sa7	Sa8
		6	C4	0	0	1	1	0	1	1
		7	0	1	A	Sa4	Sa5	Sa6	Sa7	Sa8
	II	8	C1	0	0	1	1	0	1	1
		9	1	1	A	Sa4	Sa5	Sa6	Sa7	Sa8
		10	C2	0	0	1	1	0	1	1
		11	1	1	A	Sa4	Sa5	Sa6	Sa7	Sa8
		12	C3	0	0	1	1	0	1	1
		13	E	1	A	Sa4	Sa5	Sa6	Sa7	Sa8
		14	C4	0	0	1	1	0	1	1
		15	E	1	A	Sa4	Sa5	Sa6	Sa7	Sa8

Figure 4.17 *Primary-access multiframe structure (2048-Mbit/s format)*

Bit 1 in the first six odd-numbered frames forms the multiframe alignment pattern 0 0 1 0 1 1. The E bits in the last two odd-numbered frames are individually set to 0 to indicate that the CRC procedure detected an error in one or the other of the previously received sub-multiframes and are otherwise set to 1. The use of the five remaining bits Sa4 to Sa8 in time slot 0 is presently undefined by the CCITT. Sa4 and Sa8 are reserved and may be the subject of future international standardization, whereas Sa5, Sa6, and Sa7 are available for national use.

4.2.3 Line Code

The line code, which represents the logical information contained in the frames discussed in the previous section, differs substantially for the two types of primary-access interface. For the 1544-kbit/s interface the line code is a bipolar signal with a 50 percent duty factor. Successive logical ones are represented by voltages of alternating polarity during the first half of the bit duration and by a zero voltage condition during the second half. Logical zeros are always coded as a zero voltage condition. The nominal magnitude of the pulse is 3 V, and its nominal time duration is 324 ns. The detailed pulse characteristics are shown in Figure 4.18.

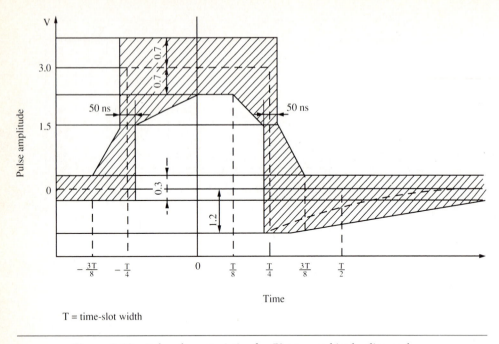

Figure 4.18 *Pulse characteristics for 50 percent bipolar line code*

To ensure timing recovery at the receiver, the maximum time interval during which the transmitted line code voltage is zero must be limited. This implies either a restriction on the bit patterns of the user data contained in the B, D, or H channels of the frame, or some type of line code conversion when unacceptable bit patterns are present. Accordingly, we identify the individual channels as either restricted channels or clear channels.

Restricted channels are subject to the following requirements:

- No group of 8 bits corresponding to a B, D, H0, or H11 channel is allowed to contain the all-zero octet.

- Alternatively, the H11 channel only may satisfy the less stringent condition that any section of $8(n + 1)$ consecutive bits in the channel contain at least n ones, for every $n = 1, 2, 3, \ldots, 23$.

The suppression of strings of zeros in the user data that violate the preceding conditions can be accomplished in many ways and is usually only an end-user concern, although in some cases the potential impact on network equipment must be taken into account. One scheme already in widespread use as part of certain layer 2 protocols such as the *high-level data link control (HDLC)* is the method of bit stuffing and bit inversion that is intended to avoid the occurrence of false synchronization flags in the data stream. At the transmitter the data stream in the B, D, or H channels is monitored for the presence of 5 ones in sequence and a logical zero is inserted after each such run. The resulting data stream is then inverted prior to transmission. At the receiver the process is reversed by first inverting the received data stream and then discarding any zero that may occur after 5 consecutive ones.

Although this arrangement provides a higher density of pulses in the line code than is implied by the previously stated conditions, it has the advantage that the data may already have been bit stuffed as part of the layer 2 control procedure, in which case only the sequence inversion would be required at layer 1.

For a full discussion of this issue, see AT&T Publication 41449.

The implementation of a clear channel interface, with no restriction on the bit patterns of the user data stream, requires that the line code be modified to create the necessary density of bipolar pulses for timing extraction. In the 1544-kbit/s interface this is accomplished by means of the so-called *bipolar with 8 zeros substitution (B8ZS)* code, which represents any eight consecutive logical zeros by a bipolar line code with certain violations of the coding rule. Two specific sequences are used, depending on the polarity of the pulse in the line code immediately preceding the sequence of eight logical zeros. If that pulse is of positive polarity, the line code chosen for the sequence of eight logical zeros is 0 0 0 + − 0 − +. Otherwise the pattern 0 0 0 − + 0 + − is selected. In either case, the code contains a violation of the bipolar coding rule in positions 4 and 7, since the pulse polarities in these locations are the same as the polarity of the immediately preceding pulse.

Figure 4.19 shows the line code for the two cases.

Let us consider the 2048-kbit/s interface next. As in the previous case, the line code is bipolar with a 50 percent duty factor and a 3-V nominal pulse amplitude. The nominal pulse duration, however, equals 244 ns. Figure 4.18 shows the pulse characteristics.

Bit sequence independence is assured through the use of the *high-density bipolar code of order 3 (HD3B)*, in which each block of four consecutive 0s is replaced by either the sequence 0 0 0 V or by the sequence 1 0 0 V. Here V represents a violation of the bipolar coding rule, and the choice of the particular sequence is determined by the

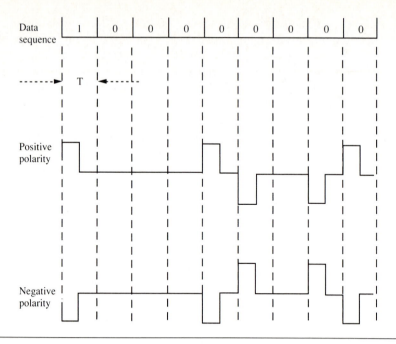

Figure 4.19 *B8ZS code*

requirement that successive V pulses alternate in polarity. Figure 4.20 shows a typical example.

4.2.4 Timing and Frame Synchronization

As in the case of basic access, timing for the terminal side equipment is obtained from the network side equipment, which in turn derives its timing from a network clock. The terminal clock at the bit, octet, and frame level is extracted from the frames received from the network side and is used to time the transmission of the frames to the network side. Thus all transmissions toward the network are ultimately synchronized to a network clock.

For the 1544-kbit/s interface, synchronization of a received frame is accomplished by locking onto the F-bit framing pattern 0 0 1 0 1 1 contained in the first position of frames 4, 8, 12, 16, and 24 of the 24-frame extended superframe. The CRC procedure may be applied to assure that the frame alignment pattern is detected in the right position and was not falsely created by channel errors occurring during frame

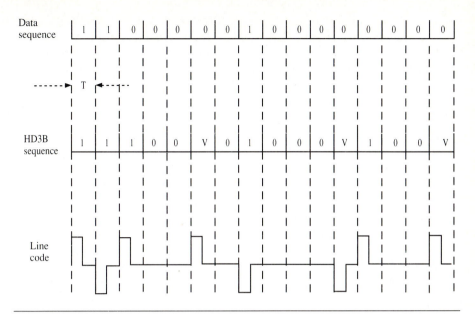

Figure 4.20 *HD3B code*

transmission. Because of these kinds of errors, or procedural errors at the transmitter such as the omission of a framing pattern, the receiver may not always be able to locate this pattern and will consequently enter into an out-of-frame condition. By definition, such a condition is detected and declared whenever 2 out of 4 or 2 out of 5 consecutive frame bits are missing for a period of 2 to 3 seconds. As a result, the receiver transmits a special signal known as a *remote alarm indication (RAI)* or yellow alarm, which consists of the 16-bit pattern 1 1 1 1 1 1 1 1 0 0 0 0 0 0 0 0, to inform the other side that frame synchronization has been lost. The pattern is transmitted in the m-bit locations of the extended superframe—that is, in the first position of the odd-numbered frames—and continues until the receiver reacquires frame synchronization for 10 to 20 s.

For the 2048-kbit/s interface, individual frames are considered synchronized by the receiver as long as the framing pattern 0 0 1 1 0 1 1 is observed in positions 2 to 8 of time slot 0 in every other frame. Multiframing is achieved by the correct detection of the multiframe alignment pattern 0 0 1 0 1 1 E E in position 1 of frames not containing the individual framing pattern.

Frame alignment is lost when three consecutive framing patterns are received in error. This state is indicated by setting the remote alarm indication bit A to 1. It is assumed reacquired as soon as the correct framing pattern has been obtained in two frames spaced one frame apart and a 1 is contained in position 2 of time slot 0 in the intermediate frame.

4.2.5   Layer 1 Procedures

As mentioned earlier, the primary rate interface is permanently active, so that no activation or deactivation procedures are required. Nonetheless, the occurrence of certain faults will at times cause the loss of layer 1 capabilities and necessitate an interaction between the user side and the network side for the purpose of recovering from the fault.

Four types of fault conditions are generally encountered on either side of the interface. The TE or NT equipment may experience a loss of power, the loss of an incoming frame may be detected, one or the other side may be unable to achieve proper frame synchronization, and a received frame may contain transmission errors, as indicated by a failed CRC.

To report the actual state of the interface, the layer 1 entities on the user and network sides convey to their respective layer 2 entity the activation and deactivation indication primitives PH-AI and PH-DI. These indicate whether or not the layer 1 capabilities are available for the transfer of frames. The layer 1 entities also transmit to their management entity the activation indication primitive MPH-AI and the error indication primitive MPH-EIn. The parameter n in the last primitive specifies the different fault conditions.

The layer 1 peer-to-peer procedures between the user side and network side are carried out through the exchange of three types of signals. The first of these, the normal operational frame, is a frame that conforms to the formats described previously, but carries no defect indication. For the 2048-kbit/s interface only it may, however, include an indication that a previously received frame contained transmission errors. Such errors are detected by the presence of an invalid CRC pattern and are indicated by setting the E bit to 0. Either side may send normal operational frames as long as the interface capability to carry such frames exists. The remote alarm indication (RAI) frame is an operational frame that conveys the loss of layer 1 capability. It is normally sent by either the user side or the network side as a result of a lost signal or an inability to properly synchronize a received frame. For the 1544-kbit/s interface it contains the sequence

1 1 1 1 1 1 1 1 0 0 0 0 0 0 0 0

in the m-bit locations of the extended multiframe, whereas in the 2048-kbit/s interface it is coded by setting bit A to 1. RAIs may also contain an indication of a transmission error in a previously received frame.

In addition to these frames, an *alarm indication signal (AIS)* is also defined. AIS is coded as a continuous stream of 1's and is transmitted by the network side to indicate a loss of network timing.

4.3 Layer 1 Specifications for Broadband Access

For several reasons, the emerging layer 1 specifications for the transmission of information across the broadband-access S or T reference points are different from the two other ISDN user-to-network interface structures discussed earlier.

First, since broadband access specifies transmission rates far in excess of the narrowband interface structures, certain wideband media such as coaxial cables and optical fibers are logical choices for the interconnecting cable between TE and NT. The physical and optical properties of these media, as well as the characteristics of the transmitters and receivers, present many unique design problems not encountered in narrowband interfaces. Second, the wide variety of data rates expected in a broadband environment, the intermittent or bursty nature of many information sources, and the different levels of tolerance to delay demand a certain flexibility in the allocation of the available channel capacity. This creates the need for two types of transmission service, one in which channel capacity is allocated dynamically to a data source according to the fluctuations in its data rate and another that allocates a fixed amount of channel capacity sufficient to satisfy the peak data rate of the source.

Practically all aspects of layer 1 for broadband access are still in the evolutionary stage and subject to major changes as their development proceeds. The current status within the CCITT is summarized in Recommendation I.121, and certain related issues are covered in Recommendations G.707, G.708, and G.709. In the following paragraphs we briefly discuss the issues in selecting a wiring configuration, the way that information flows are conveyed across the interface, and the layer 1 protocol reference model.

4.3.1 Transmission Media and Wiring Configurations

There are many factors that influence the choice of a medium and wiring configuration for the interconnection of the TE and NT functional groups in a broadband-access interface structure.

Perhaps the most important consideration is that of the total required transmission rate, which is determined by the data rates of the individual applications and the combination of applications that are to be supported over the interface. Taking into account the bit rates of services likely to be of interest to residential and commercial subscribers and likely to be offered by a broadband ISDN, studies have indicated that in the near future maximum bit rate requirements on the order of 600 Mbit/s are to be expected.

Two types of media suggest themselves to support these rates. The simplest in terms of existing technology is the coaxial cable, which offers a transmission capacity of 600 Mbit/s over distances of up to 150 m. This range of transmission can be increased to 300 m by the use of single mode or graded index optical fibers without reducing the transmission rate.

Another important concern relates to the topology of the interconnection between TE and NT. As shown in Figure 4.21, three versions can be considered.

In the star configuration of Figure 4.21(a) the entire capacity of the medium is available to one TE, and no complex multiple-access control scheme is required. As a disadvantage, the amount of cabling in the installation grows directly with the number of TEs. In addition, each TE requires a separate physical termination and a separate transmitter and receiver in the NT.

The amount of wiring and the complexity of the NT can be reduced by the use of a ring configuration, shown in Figure 4.21(b). Here, a penalty is incurred by the fact that the capacity of the medium is shared among multiple TEs and each TE must be actively engaged in relaying transmissions from other TEs or from the NT. As a third alternative, the bus configuration shown in Figure 4.21(c) requires only one cable and one termination in the NT, but incurs the complexity of multiaccess control and a reduction in the available channel capacity per TE.

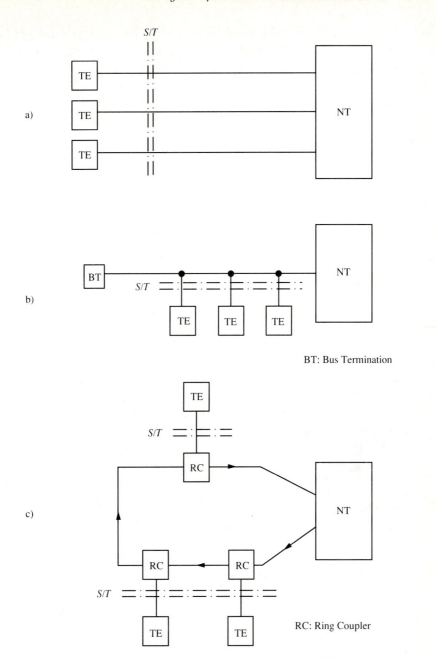

Figure 4.21 *Topologies for broadband S/T interface*

To date no decision as to the type of wiring configuration has been reached, although several experimental systems have used the bus structure.

4.3.2 Packet Structure

As we pointed out in Chapter 3, in the preferred mode of operation for broadband ISDN the information flows that are to be transmitted across the S or T reference point are divided into relatively short and fixed-size packets that are carried in transfer cells. Each such packet consists of a payload carrying the user information and a header. Figure 4.22 shows the packet structure, as currently conceived by the CCITT [LIN 89].

The size of the payload, which has been set to 48 octets, represents a compromise between the desire for a low-overhead transmission system and the need to limit the packetization delay. The latter issue is especially important in the context of digital voice transmission. Interworking considerations with existing services also play a major role in the selection of payload size.

The header contains the information necessary to transport the payload across the S or T reference point in a reliable manner. It consists of five subfields.

The first of these is a 4-bit *generic flow control field (GFC)* used to control the volume of information from a particular source across the UNI.

The second field contains an explicit label that identifies the logical connection to which the payload of the packet belongs. It is composed of a 12-bit or 16-bit *virtual channel identifier (VCI)* and an 8-bit or 12-bit *virtual path identifier (VPI),* for a total of 24 bits. The VCI identifies a virtual channel to which the packet belongs, and the VPI is used to multiplex several different virtual channels into a virtual path that may be transmitted and switched as a unit. These two identifiers—which have local significance only—allow the packets associated with a given connection to be located anywhere in a sequence of transfer cells; any given packet may be associated with any connection.

The third field contains a 2-bit *packet type (PT),* which identifies the packet payload as being either user information or network information.

The 8-bit *header error check field (HEC)* contains error control information that optionally provides for the correction of single errors

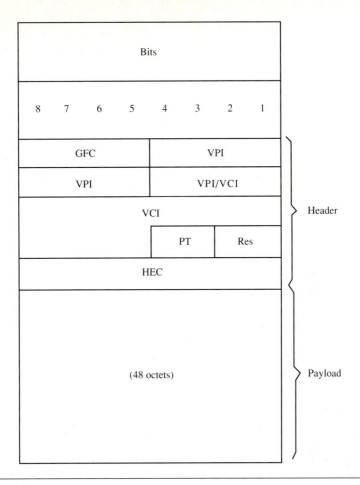

Figure 4.22 *ATM packet structure*

or the detection of multiple errors anywhere in the header. No error checking for the payload is included.

The remaining part of the header is currently reserved. It could be used for cell-access control, priority, detection of cell loss, cell sequence numbering, and quality-of-service indication.

4.3.3 Transfer Modes

For broadband access two modes of transferring the packets described in the previous section across the S or T reference points are currently being considered. These are known as *cell-based asynchronous transfer mode (CATM)* and *frame-based asynchronous transfer mode (FATM)*.

In CATM a continuous sequence of transfer cells matched to the size of the packets is synchronously transmitted across the interface. To aid in the demultiplexing of the cells at the receiver, the sender periodically inserts a cell containing a synchronization pattern. Alternatively, synchronization cells may be inserted irregularly during idle periods. The size of the cells and the rate at which they are transmitted are generally constant but may differ in the two directions of transmission. Figure 4.23 shows a typical sequence of packets contained within a sequence of cells.

The information flows to be transmitted over a given logical connection between two layer 1 entities may be assigned to available cells in several ways. In one method, specific cells in the sequence are associated with one of the D, B, or H channels in a permanent manner, with the component channel being dedicated to a connection during a connection establishment phase. The cells could also be assigned individually to connections, independently of any association with one of the synchronous component channels. For constant rate sources producing continuous streams of information, the number of dedicated cells would be selected to accommodate the actual data rate, so that cells are always available to the source when needed and no cells are wasted. A similar arrangement would be appropriate for variable rate sources that are delay-sensitive, with the number of assigned cells matched to the peak data rate. In all these cases, since specific cells in a sequence are always associated with specific sources and the cells are transferred synchronously across the interface, the transfer scheme is substantially equivalent to synchronous time division multiplexing, although the amount of overhead is generally somewhat larger.

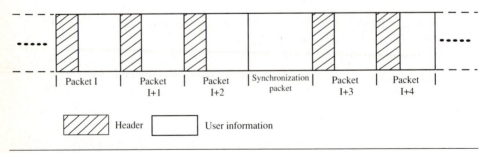

Figure 4.23 *Packet sequence in cell-based asynchronous transfer mode*

For sources with bursty traffic that can tolerate some delay, the assignment of specific cells in a sequence could be matched to a level somewhere between the maximum and average expected data rates. This arrangement would require buffers to store the information packets during times when the actual demand for cells exceeds the supply. The packets carried across the interface would then be subject to variable queuing delays whose magnitude depends on the difference between the number of allocated cells and the average demand for cells. Assignment of cells in this manner is equivalent to asynchronous or statistical time division multiplexing.

As an alternative to the dedicated assignment of cells to a logical connection, the available cells could be assigned to the existing connections on a random basis, using certain criteria such as priority and required quality of service as the factors that determine the probability distribution of allocation to a given data source. We can also envision a sharing of the cells among a number of sources in a purely first come, first served manner. In either case, the part of the capacity associated with a particular source would vary randomly with time and a given source may not always be able to satisfy its demand for cells. As a result, sections of data may experience queuing delays or be blocked from accessing the transmission capacity.

As we discussed in Chapter 3, each transfer cell corresponds to a basic level of transmission capacity whose value is determined by the size of the cell, the portion of the cell used for overhead transmission, and the number of cells transferred per second. A component channel is associated with the selection of a specific subset of the transfer cells. If this subset is preassigned, a synchronous component channel with a constant data rate results. If, on the other hand, the cells are under contention from multiple information flows, are randomly assigned, or are used on a first come, first served basis, a virtual component channel with variable data rate is created. For examples of such component channels, see Chapter 3.

The complete channel structure that exists across the S or T reference points can in general be envisioned as a combination of synchronous and virtual component channels, with the actual arrangement likely to vary from one interface to another and to change dynamically with time over a given interface.

In the second transfer mode, the frame-based asynchronous transfer mode, a number of transfer cells are combined at the sending side into a transport frame that is then synchronously transmitted across the interface. Several transfer frame structures are currently under

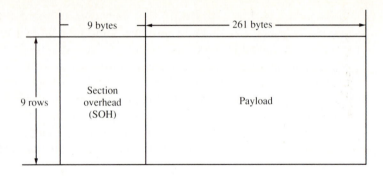

Figure 4.24 *STM-1 frame structure*

consideration. Their formats are based on the so-called *synchronous optical network (SONET)* specifications developed by the T1 committee of the American National Standards Institute during the last several years and published in ANSI T1.105 and T1.106. The CCITT has defined similar frame structures based on its version of SONET known as the *synchronous digital hierarchy (SDH)*. These are specified in CCITT Recommendations G.707, G.708, and G.709.

All frames are constructed from a basic transfer frame known as a *synchronous transport module level 1 (STM-1)*. Its structure is shown in Figure 4.24. The STM-1 contains a total of 2430 bytes of information, organized in a rectangular array of 9 rows and 270 columns. The first 9 columns of each array contain the *section overhead (SOH)*, which consists mostly of information needed to synchronize and demultiplex the frame, perform error checking, and carry out certain maintenance activities. The remaining 261 columns—referred to as the *payload*—carry the information flows and certain additional overhead. Each frame is transmitted in 125 μs, resulting in 8000 frames per second, a bit rate of 155.520 Mbit/s, and a payload rate of 150.336 Mbit/s.

By combining the bytes contained in *N* STM-1s, a higher-level frame labeled STM-N is obtained that consists of a rectangular array of *N* × 270 columns and 9 rows. As indicated in Figure 4.25, the frame is constructed by sequentially interleaving the bytes of the STM-1s taken along a row of the STM-1 frame, with the last byte of one row followed by the first byte of the next row. Thus, for example, the first *N* bytes in row 1 of the STM-N are the first bytes A1, A2, . . . , AN in row 1 from each of the *N* STM-1s, the second *N* bytes in row 1 of

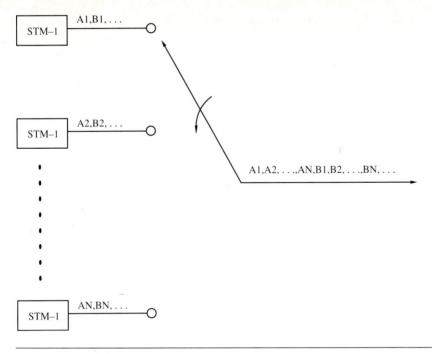

Figure 4.25 *Byte interleaving of STM-1 to STM-N*

the STM-N are the second bytes B1, B2, . . . , BN in row 1 from each of the N STM-1s, and so on. As a result, the first $N \times 9$ columns of the STM-N contain the composite section overhead of the N STM-1s and the remaining $N \times 261$ columns carry the composite payload. Figure 4.26 shows this arrangement. Again, each STM-N frame is transmitted in 125 µs at the rate of 8000 frames per second.

Of the higher-level frames, only the STM-4 is currently under consideration by the CCITT. It consists of an array of 9 rows and 1080 columns, with 1044 columns of payload and 36 columns of section overhead. The bit transmission rate is 622.080 Mbit/s and the payload rate equals 601.344 Mbit/s.

To create component channels within such a transfer frame, the payload section is divided into transfer cells, with each cell occupying successive bytes along the rows of the frame. The number of cells that can be packed into a frame depends of course on the size of the cell. As an example, the cell size of 53 bytes currently specified by the CCITT leads to a total of 44 cells, with 17 bytes remaining. Note that

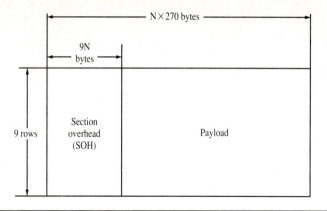

Figure 4.26 *STM-N frame structure*

in general a cell does not necessarily fit entirely within a row, nor is a frame necessarily completely filled with cells. By using certain pointers contained in the section overhead and payload of the transfer frame that identify the beginning of a cell in the frame, it is possible to allow cells to overlap successive frames.

An arrangement of cells carrying packets consisting of a header and a payload is shown in Figure 4.27 for the STM-1.

Let us now consider the construction of specific component channels and channel structures within a transfer frame. Each cell in a frame corresponds to $L - H$ bytes of information, where L is the size of the cell and H is the size of the header. Thus, the permanent assignment of N cells in every set of K successive frames creates a synchronous component channel whose capacity is given by

$$C = N(L-H) \times 64/K \text{ kbit/s}$$

With the proper choice of the parameters L, H, N, and K, any of the synchronous component channels defined in Chapter 3 can be obtained.

As an example, assume the STM-1 frame and a cell size of 30 octets of information and 3 octets of header. The payload of a single STM-1 frame can then accommodate 71 cells, with 6 spare cells. By setting $N = K$—that is, selecting one cell in every frame—we obtain the H12 channel with a capacity of 1920 kbit/s. The value $N = 23K$

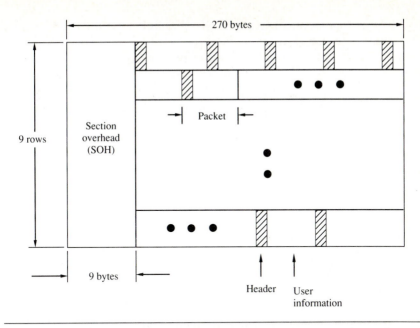

Figure 4.27 *Packet sequence in frame-based asynchronous transfer mode*

yields the H22-channel rate of 44.160 Mbit/s, and using the same single cell in every 30th frame ($N = K/30$) results in the B channel or the 64-kbit/s D channel.

The synchronous component channels can be combined in various ways to create a large number of synchronous broadband channel structures. In the preceding example, we can combine three H22 channels with two H12 channels by assigning in each frame cells 1–23, 24–46, and 47–69 to the H22 channels, cell 70 to one of the H12 channels, and cell 71 to the other. Alternatively, the channel structure H4 + 3H0 results from the assignment of all 71 available cells in 9 out of 10 frames and cells 1–65 in every tenth frame to the H4 channel, and cells 66–67, 68–69, and 69–70 to the three H0 channels.

The transfer cells in a transfer frame can also be accessed on a contention basis, in which case virtual component channels are created. Depending on the demand for cells and the allocation strategy, any instantaneous or average data rate up to the full cell capacity of the transfer frame can be obtained.

By assigning some of the cells to synchronous component channels and placing others under contention, a combination of synchronous and asynchronous channel structures can also be supported by the transfer frame.

As an alternative to the two asynchronous transfer modes just discussed, a third scheme—known as *synchronous transfer mode (STM)* and also based on the synchronous transport module—has been considered. In this case, however, the information flows are not segmented into constant-size packets that are transferred in cells but are transmitted at the byte level in synchronous time division form.

In STM only synchronous component channels are present in the channel structure, with each component channel assigned to a specific section of the frame in a manner similar to the 2B+D layer 1 frame structure for basic access. Since 8000 STM-N frames are transmitted across the interface every second, a single byte in every frame is equivalent to a capacity of 64 kbit/s. Thus, for example, a B channel or a 64-kbit/s D channel occupies one byte per frame, whereas a 16-kbit/s D channel occupies only one byte in every fourth frame. From Table 3.1 we also note that the H12 channel and H4 channel require 30 bytes per frame and 2112 bytes per frame, respectively. The complete synchronous broadband channel structure H4 + 4H12 + 2B + D(16) listed in Table 3.3 is therefore easily accommodated.

Although a number of specific assignments of D, B, and H channels to the frame have been proposed, the precise nature of the STM broadband channel structure remains to be defined. See CCITT Recommendations G.707, G.708, and G.709 for further information on this subject.

We mention in passing that for an interim period in the evolution of broadband ISDN, synchronous and asynchronous transfer modes will necessarily coexist on the same user-to-network interface. For the long term, however, the CCITT has expressed its intention to develop specifications for only the cell-based and frame-based asynchronous transfer modes [MINZ89], and it is likely that only the FATM will ultimately be implemented in broadband UNIs.

4.3.4   The Layer 1 Protocol Architecture

As in the basic- and primary-access interface structures, layer 1 of the broadband-access interface structure is common to both the U plane and the C plane, but is divided into three sublayers, as shown in Figure 4.28.

The physical medium dependent sublayer is mainly responsible for the generation, transmission, and reception of the optical or electrical signals that represent the information flows and associated overhead.

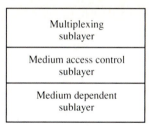

Figure 4.28 *Broadband layer 1 protocol reference model*

Its specification therefore includes the optical, electrical, and mechanical characteristics of the transmission medium between the TE and NT functional groups, as well as the optical or electrical characteristics of the transmitters and receivers. This sublayer is also concerned with the generation of the line codes, the organization of the transmission capacity into recurring cells or frames, and their timing and synchronization. In addition, it provides the functions for activation and deactivation of the physical devices containing the TE and NT functional groups.

For ring or bus wiring configurations, where the capacity of the medium is shared by multiple TEs, the *medium-access control sublayer (MAC)* offers the capability to regulate access to the medium. It also performs the function of monitoring the quality of the transmissions and provides for an orderly recovery in case of collisions or other anomalies.

The multiplexing sublayer controls the transmission of the component channels and channel structures across the S or T reference points. As such, it performs multiplexing and demultiplexing of the component channels and effects their synchronization.

Aside from these general structural aspects, the layer 1 protocol architecture for broadband ISDN, including the sublayer interactions and the peer-to-peer protocol, remains to be specified.

4.4 Summary and Recommended Reading

In Chapter 4 we have concentrated on the specification of the protocols for layer 1 of the ISDN user-to-network interface. We offered a thorough treatment for layer 1 of the basic and primary-access UNIs, based on the relevant CCITT standards. Due to the early stage of the development of the broadband UNI our discussion of this topic was incomplete and tentative. We described the current CCITT specification for the packetization of information and three modes of information transfer—the synchronous transfer mode, the cell-based asynchronous transfer mode, and the frame-based asynchronous transfer mode. In the context of the latter we also introduced the concept of the synchronous optical network. Finally we gave a brief introduction to layer 1 of the protocol reference model for broadband ISDN.

[JULI86] contains a discussion of layer 1 for basic and primary access. The current state of development of broadband ISDN is summarized in the special January 1989 issue on broadband networks of the *IEEE Network Magazine*. Additional material on the asynchronous mode of information transfer is given in [MINZ89]. [DOMA88] discusses synchronous alternatives for channel structures and possible wiring configurations for the broadband UNI. [BALL89] offers a tutorial description of SONET, and [LIN89] and [VORS88] provide information on the ATM packet structure.

CHAPTER 5

The ISDN User-to-Network Layer 2

Within the framework of the open systems interconnection reference model, layer 2—commonly referred to as the data link layer—provides a reliable and efficient information transfer service over one or more logical channels between peer layer 3 entities and between peer management entities in different functional groups. In carrying out its task, it relies on the services provided by the physical layer 1 for the actual transmission of the information carrying signals. It also uses a peer-to-peer protocol between peer layer 2 entities to control the transmissions in a logical sense, and exchanges primitives to provide the services to its layer 3 and management entities and to invoke the services of its layer 1.

Relative to the ISDN user-to-network interface, the transfer taking place across the S or T reference point is either between a TE on one side and the NT2 or ET on the other or between the NT2 and ET. Note that the NT1 is not involved in this exchange, since its functions extend only to layer 1.

In principle, the information flows conveyed across the S or T reference point by the data link layer are not restricted in any way and may be associated with either the U plane or the C plane of layer 3 or the layer management entity. They may also be carried by any of the component D, B, or H channels of the basic, primary, or broadband synchronous channel structures or any asynchronous channel structure.

Recently the CCITT has issued the specifications for a set of services and procedures known as the *Digital Subscriber Signaling System No. 1 (DSS 1)* that govern many of the interactions across the subscriber-access network of the ISDN. In this chapter we offer a discussion of the data link layer of this system and its application to the D channel.

In the first section we focus on the definition of the services offered by the data link layer to its layer 3 and layer management entities. These specifications are in close conformity with the OSI reference model and are described in Recommendation I.440 (Q.920). The subsequent parts of the chapter contain a tutorial treatment of the major aspects of the peer-to-peer interactions by which the data link layer carries out its tasks. The protocol is based on the *asynchronous balanced mode (ABM)* of the *high-level data link control (HDLC)* procedures developed by the International Organization for Standardization. The parts applicable to the information flows carried on the D channel—whether they are associated with the U plane or C plane of layer 3 or with the layer management entity—are known as *LAPD* and are described in CCITT Recommendation I.441 (Q.921). A specific version of LAPD used on the D channel of a primary-access interface structure as implemented by AT&T is contained in AT&T Publication 41449. See these documents for a complete and rigorous treatment of the subject.

Since the LAPD procedures are largely independent of the specific information flow and the particular channel carrying the flow, they may in principle be applied to any of the transmissions across the S or T reference points. Consequently a number of organizations, including the European Telecommunications Standards Institute (ETSI), are drafting specifications to adapt LAPD to the B channel. As far as the current ISDN recommendations are concerned, however, the use of LAPD on channels other than the D channel has not been formally decided.

The LAPD protocol is designed for either point-to-point, multipoint, or broadcast operations between the TEs, NT2, and ET. The last two are normally carried out only across the S reference point between a number of TEs and a single NT2 or ET. In our discussion of LAPD we concentrate on this specific configuration, with the understanding that a somewhat reduced set of LAPD procedures is also applicable to the connection between NT2 and ET, which is normally point-to-point.

5.1 Layer 2 Service Definition

We recall that the purpose of the ISDN data link layer is to convey in a reliable and efficient manner the layer 3 U-plane and C-plane information flows and the layer management information flows between

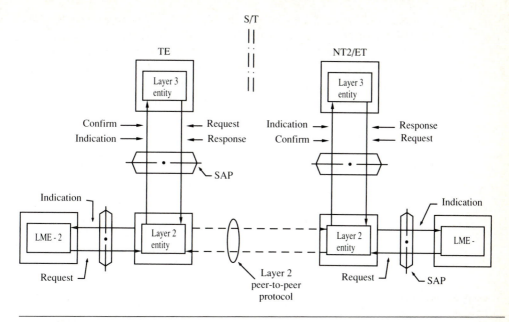

Figure 5.1 *Data link layer interactions*

peer entities. As shown in Figure 5.1, these entities reside in a TE on one side of the S or T reference point and an NT2 or ET on the other side.

We begin our study of the data link layer with an abstract description of how its services to the layer 3 entities are carried out.

5.1.1 Services and Service Primitives

In accordance with the OSI architecture, services offered by the data link layer entity to the layer 3 and layer management entities are requested and provided through the exchange of service primitives across the appropriate service-access points. These exchanges represent in abstract fashion the logical interactions between the data link layer entities, the layer management entities, and the entities in layer 3, all in the same system. We have already encountered these ideas in Chapter 4 in connection with the physical layer.

Figure 5.1 illustrates the relationships between a pair of correspondent peer entities and their adjacent entities. Generally the four primitive types Request, Indication, Response, and Confirm are used. The Request primitive is transferred by a service user to request a service from its data link layer, and the Indication primitive notifies the correspondent service user that a service request has been invoked. The Response primitive carries the acknowledgment of an Indication primitive from the correspondent service user to its data link layer, and the Confirm primitive notifies the initial service requester that the service has been performed. A given service does not necessarily use all four types of primitives.

The primitives exchanged between the data link layer on one side and layer 3 or the layer management entity on the other are listed in Table 5.1. They are identified by the label *DL* or *MDL*, depending on whether the associated services are offered to layer 3 or the layer management entity. Some of the primitives include parameters containing message units that are to be transferred between adjacent layers or between peer layers.

The three DL-ESTABLISH primitives are used to create a logical

TABLE 5.1   Data link layer primitives

PRIMITIVE NAME	TYPE				PARAM- ETERS MESSAGE UNIT	MESSAGE UNIT CONTENTS
	REQUEST	INDICATION	RESPONSE	CONFIRM		
DL-ESTABLISH	X	X	—	X	—	
DL-RELEASE	X	X	—	X	—	
DL-DATA	X	X	—	—	X	Layer 3 peer-to-peer message
DL-UNIT DATA	X	X	—	—	X	Layer 3 peer-to-peer message
MDL-ASSIGN	X	X	—	—	X	TEI value, CES
MDL-REMOVE	X	—	—	—	X	TEI value, CES
MDL-ERROR	—	X	X	—	X	Reason for error message
MDL-UNIT DATA	X	X	—	—	X	Management function peer-to-peer message
MDL-XID	X	X	X	X	X	Connection management information

© Adapted from CCITT Blue Book, vol VI. 10, 1988

association known as a *data link connection* between peer layer 2 entities across the S or T reference point for the transmission of multiple messages between layer 3 peer entities. The connection is terminated by the exchange of the three DL-RELEASE primitives. None of these six primitives contains any parameter information.

The actual transfer of a message unit between peer layer 3 entities may be accomplished in two modes: *acknowledged operation* and *unacknowledged operation*. The associated primitives are DL-DATA and DL-UNIT DATA, respectively, with the message unit being contained in the parameter field.

The exchange of the DL primitives between layer 2 and layer 3 is governed by certain rules, which are indicated in Figure 5.2. As viewed by layer 3, at any one time the data link connection is in one of four states, known as *Link Connection Released, Awaiting Establishment, Link Connection Established,* and *Awaiting Release.* In a particular state only selected primitives, shown by arrows labeled with the name of the primitive, may properly be issued by a given layer. On receipt of a primitive, the data link connection either remains in the same state or changes to a new state as indicated by the direction of the arrow.

The data link layer also carries out a number of services in support of the layer management entity LME-2. This entity manages the resources of a data link connection, provides and receives notification of the occurrence of errors, and is responsible for the management of identifiers associated with a data link connection.

The primitives associated with the data link layer management services are also shown in Table 5.1. The MDL-ASSIGN and MDL-REMOVE primitives are used respectively to assign and remove an identifier known as a terminal endpoint identifier (TEI). The latter is carried as a parameter, together with another identifier called a connection endpoint suffix (CES). (The use of the TEI and CES is discussed in the next section.) The MDL-ERROR primitive indicates to the management entity that an error has occurred that cannot be recovered by the data link layer entity. The MDL-UNIT DATA primitive is used to pass LME-2 messages to and from the data link layer. Finally, the MDL-XID primitive requests and indicates certain communication parameters—such as frame size and flow control window—that are applicable to the data link connection.

The data link layer carries out the services for its layer 3 and layer management entities by invoking the services of the physical layer. See Section 4.1.1 for a discussion of the layer 1 services and the associated primitives.

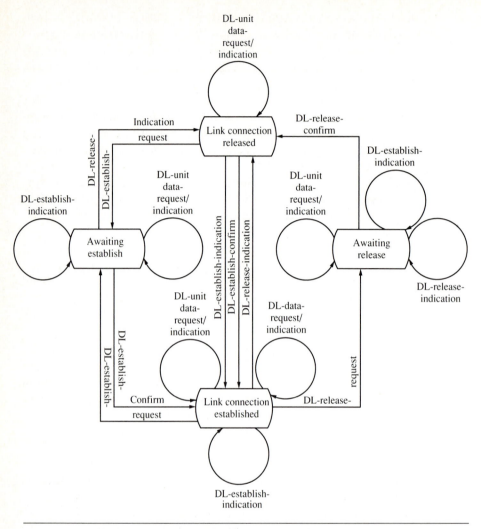

Figure 5.2   *State transition diagram for sequences of primitives*
© Reprinted from CCITT Blue Book, vol VI. 10, 1988

5.1.2   Service-Access Points, Connection Endpoints, and Connection Identifiers

The services of the data link layer are performed over a data link layer connection between a pair of data link layer *service-access points (SAP)*. As shown in Figure 5.1, these SAPs are located at the boundary between layer 2 and layer 3 and between layer 2 and the LME-2 in the TE, NT2, or ET. They are the logical points at which the data link layer provides its services and at which these services are accessed by the service user. SAPs are identified by their *service-access-point identifier (SAPI)*.

Since layer 2 may offer different services (either simultaneously or at different times) that are accessible by the layer 3 entity and the LME-2, several types of SAPs may exist within the same system. For example, a layer 3 call control procedure and a layer 2 management procedure would acquire data link layer services through different SAPs. Any particular data link connection, however, always exists between similar SAPs.

Associated with each data link layer SAP are a number of so-called *connection endpoints* that mark the actual termination of the data link connection within the SAP. From the point of view of the service user, a connection endpoint is specified by its *connection end-point suffix (CES)*. The connection itself is identified by the combination of SAPI and CES, referred to as the *connection endpoint identifier (CEI)*. The CEI is used to label messages that pass between the layer 3 and management entities on the one hand and the data link layer on the other. It also addresses the peer layer 3 and management entities. From the point of view of the data link layer, the connection endpoint is defined by the so-called *terminal endpoint identifier (TEI)* and the connection is known by its *data link connection identifier (DLCI)*. The latter consists of the combination of SAPI and TEI.

A data link connection is established when an association between the CEI and the DLCI exists. Connections between a pair of connection endpoints—one in the TE and the other in the NT2 or ET—that are associated with a given SAP are termed point-to-point. Those involving two or more endpoints (either in the same TE or in different TEs with the same SAP) and a single endpoint in the NT2 or ET are known as multipoint or broadcast connections.

A summary of these concepts is shown in Figure 5.3. In this example two TEs are connected to an NT2 or ET in a layer 1 multipoint arrangement. The TE on the left contains two layer 2 entities with SAPI 0 and 16, and the TE on the right contains one layer 2 entity with SAPI 0. Each TE layer 2 entity is engaged in two types of logical connections with a peer entity in the NT2 or ET. Broadcast connections are identified by a CES of value B and a TEI of 127 and are indicated by dotted lines. Logical point-to-point connections, on the other hand, are identified by various integer CES and TEI values and are indicated by a solid line. As a general rule the connections are

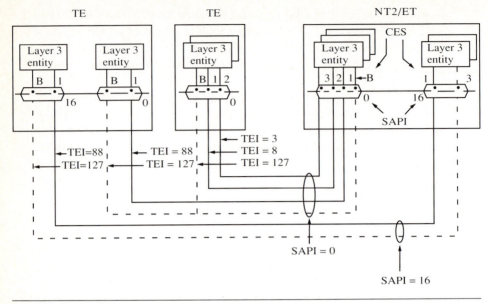

Figure 5.3 *Example of data link connections over a D channel*
© Adapted from CCITT Blue Book, vol VI. 10, 1988

always between entities with the same SAPI. On the network side an entity can at any one time be engaged in only one connection with a given SAPI. On the user side, however, an entity may also operate a simultaneous broadcast connection.

Since the connections between the SAPs exist only in a logical sense, the actual transmission of the information is the responsibility of layer 1, which provides this service to the data link layer at the layer 1 service-access point. These SAPs also contain endpoints that are identified in a similar manner to the data link layer endpoints.

5.2   Protocol Messages

To carry out its information transfer and control tasks, a data link layer entity on one side of the S reference point cooperates with its peer entity on the other side of the connection through the exchange of certain structured messages known as *frames*. These frames, which are to be distinguished from the physical layer 1 frames discussed in the previous chapter, generally contain three types of information:

- U-plane or C-plane information flows obtained from a layer 3 entity and intended for a peer layer 3 entity
- Information flows originating in a layer management entity and intended for a peer layer management entity
- Control information flows generated by a data link layer entity and intended for a peer data link layer entity, whose purpose is to manage the transfer of the information flows from the layer 3 and LME-2 in a reliable and efficient manner

This section describes the structural details of these frames.

5.2.1 General Frame Structure

The messages or frames exchanged between the peer data link layer entities on the two sides of a data link connection conform to the format shown in Figure 5.4. The frames contain an integral number of

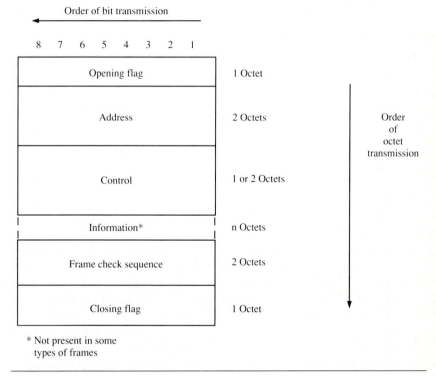

Figure 5.4 *General frame format*
© Reprinted from CCITT Blue Book, vol VI. 10, 1988

octets that are transmitted in increasing order from top to bottom. Within each octet the bits are labeled from 1 to 8, with bit 1 being the first transmitted bit.

Every frame contains at least five fields, labeled *opening flag, closing flag, address, control,* and *frame check sequence.* Certain frames contain an additional field labeled *information.*

The flags consist of one octet each and the address and frame check fields both contain two octets. The size of the control field may be one or two octets, depending on the specific type of frame. The information field must contain an integral number of octets, but is otherwise variable in length with a system-dependent upper bound whose default value is set at 260 octets.

Frames not bounded by two flags, not containing an integral number of octets, or not containing the corresponding minimum number of octets between flags are considered invalid. In addition, frames containing an address not supported by the data link layer and frames whose bits have been altered during transmission are also invalid. All such frames are discarded by the receiving entity without notification of the sending entity.

According to the rules of the protocol, frames are classified as command frames or response frames.

5.2.2 Flag Format, Transparency, and Frame Abort

The opening and closing flags of a frame serve as a unique marker to delimit its beginning and end and consist of the symmetric bit pattern

0 1 1 1 1 1 1 0

The closing flag of one frame may also serve as the beginning flag of the next frame.

For these flags to exist only in their proper location, it is necessary to avoid their occurrence in the remaining fields of the frame. This is accomplished through the technique of bit stuffing. Prior to or during transmission, the data link layer entity at the sending side examines the content of the frame between the opening and closing flags and inserts a 0 bit after every sequence of five consecutive 1 bits. The data link layer entity at the receiving side inverts this process by discarding any 0 bit that directly follows five 1 bits in a sequence. This simple procedure—together with the fixed lengths and locations of the address, control, and frame check sequence fields—allows the receiving entity to distinguish the information field of the frame from the address, control, and frame check sequence fields. Thus it provides the necessary transparency.

Since bit stuffing avoids the presence of seven or more contiguous 1s anywhere in a frame, the latter condition may be used to signal an extraordinary event. One application occurs when a frame whose transmission has been initiated must be aborted. The transmitting data link layer entity will signal this event by terminating transmission of the frame and sending a pattern of at least seven contiguous 1s. The receiving entity will then ignore the aborted frame and take no further action.

5.2.3 Addressing

The opening flag of a frame is followed in octets 2 and 3 by an address field that contains the DLCI, an identifier of the particular data link connection on which the frame is transmitted. The format of this field is shown in Figure 5.5. As noted in Section 5.1.2, the DLCI is identical on both ends of a connection and is used only by the communicating data link layer entities to identify the connection. It consists of two parts, the service-access-point identifier (SAPI) and the terminal endpoint identifier (TEI). The SAPI refers to the peer data link layer entities that process the data link layer frames and the type of layer 3 or management entities that generate and receive the information contained in these frames. The TEI is associated with the user side of the user-to-network interface. It identifies a particular endpoint of the connection within the TE for a point-to-point connection or a group of endpoints within the same TE or different TEs for a broadcast connection.

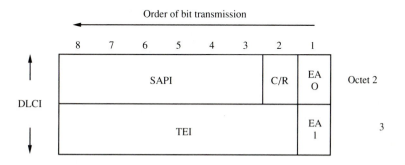

Figure 5.5   *Address field format*
© Reprinted from CCITT Blue Book, vol VI. 10, 1988

TABLE 5.2   C/R field digit assignment

COMMAND RESPONSE	DIRECTION	C/R VALUE
Command	network side → user side	1
	user side → network side	0
Response	network side → user side	0
	user side → network side	1

The six bits allocated to the SAPI allow the specification of up to 64 distinct service-access points. Currently the value 0 is used for the control of circuit switched network connections, and the values 1 and 16 are associated with packet switched connections. The SAP between the LME-2 and the layer 2 entity is identified by the value 63. All other SAPI values are reserved for future assignment.

Of the possible TEI values, the value 127 is used to specify the set of all terminal endpoints within a given service-access point. Therefore it is always a part of a broadcast data link connection.

The remainder of the address field consists of a single bit that identifies the frame as a command or response frame, according to the convention illustrated in Table 5.2, and the two address extension bits (EA). The EA in the first address octet indicates that the next octet also contains addressing information, and the second EA marks the end of the address field.

5.2.4   The Frame Check Sequence

The purpose of the *frame check sequence (FCS)* is to allow the detection by the receiver of any errors that may have occurred during the transmission of a frame. It consists of 16 bits of parity checking information that is computed at the sending side prior to bit stuffing from the bits contained in the address, control, and information fields, if present.

The computational procedure is derived from the well-known theory of cyclic codes. It proceeds as follows: Let the k binary bits contained in the address, control, and information fields of the frame be denoted by

$$a_{k-1}, a_{k-2}, \ldots, a_1, a_0$$

and represented algebraically by the binary polynomial

$$G(x) = a_{k-1} x^{k-1} + a_{k-2} x^{k-2} + \cdots + a_1 x^1 + a_0$$

where a_{k-1} is the first bit following the opening flag. Also define an auxiliary polynomial

$$L(x) = x^{15} + x^{14} + \cdots + x^1 + 1$$

and the generator polynomial

$$P(x) = x^{16} + x^{12} + x^5 + 1$$

$P(x)$ has been standardized by the CCITT in Recommendation V.41 for use on general user-to-network interfaces.

Compute the remainder polynomial of the modulo-2 division of the polynomial

$$x^{16}G(x) + x^k L(x)$$

by $P(x)$ and denote this remainder by

$$R(x) = r_{15}x^{15} + r_{14}x^{14} + \cdots + r_1 x^1 + r_0$$

The frame check sequence is the ones complement of the coefficients of $R(x)$ and is represented by the polynomial

$$FCS = R(x) + L(x)$$

The complete frame of $n = k + 16$ bits exclusive of the beginning and ending flags then takes the form

$$M(x) = x^{16}G(x) + R(x) + L(x)$$

The division by the generator polynomial is performed on the data sequence that has been modified in two ways. First, the multiplication of $G(x)$ by the factor x^{16} is equivalent to appending 16 zeros to the sequence and creates the space for the FCS in the frame. Second, the addition of $x^k L(x)$ to $x^{16}G(x)$ corresponds to the inversion of the first 16 bits of the data sequence and provides protection against the obliteration of the opening flag.

During transmission, the message $M(x)$ may incur errors through the deletion or addition of bits or a change in their logical value. The latter type of error can be represented by the addition of the polynomial

$$E(x) = e_{n-1}x^{n-1} + e_{n-2}x^{n-2} + \cdots + e_1 x^1 + e_0$$

to the message, so that the received message is given by

$$M_r(x) = M(x) + E(x)$$

The receiver calculates the remainder $R_r(x)$ obtained by dividing the polynomial

$$x^{16}M_r(x) + x^nL(x) = x^{16}[x^{16}G(x) + x^kL(x) + R(x)] + x^{16}E(x) + x^{16}L(x)$$

by the generator polynomial $P(x)$.

Given the relationship between $G(x)$, $R(x)$, and $L(x)$ imposed at the sending end, the term in square brackets is evenly divisible by $P(x)$. The desired remainder is therefore equal to the remainder that would be obtained from the division of

$$x^{16}E(x) + x^{16}L(x)$$

by $P(x)$. This shows that $R_r(x)$ does not depend on the particular data sequence but is a function of the error pattern alone.

Let us now suppose that the message is received without errors of any kind. Then $E(x) = 0$, and the preceding division results in the remainder

$$R_r(x) = x^{12} + x^{11} + x^{10} + x^8 + x^3 + x^2 + x^1 + 1$$

Any other value of $R_r(x)$ therefore indicates the presence of errors in the received message.

A shift register implementation of the FCS calculation at the transmitter and receiver is shown in Figure 5.6.

The addition of $x^kL(x)$ to $x^{16}G(x)$ is accomplished by presetting the

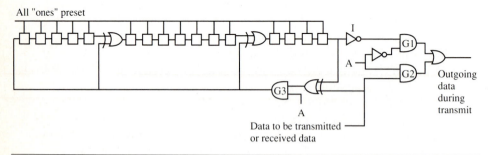

Figure 5.6 *Shift register implementation of frame check sequence calculation*

storage elements to binary 1. The register calculates $R(x)$ by enabling gates G2 and G3, disabling gate G1, and cycling the k coefficients of $G(x)$ through the register via the feedback path through G3. At the same time the data are shifted into the channel. After k shifts the register contains the 16 coefficients of $R(x)$, which are then shifted into the channel by enabling gate G1 and disabling gates G2 and G3. The inversion of the coefficients takes place in I1.

The register at the receiver, which is almost identical to the one at the transmitter, is again preset to binary 1. The entire received message $M_r(x)$ is then shifted through the register by enabling gates G2 and G3 and disabling gate G1. If the message contained no errors, the content of the register after n shifts will be the pattern

0 0 0 1 1 1 0 1 0 0 0 0 1 1 1 1

Any other error pattern would, of course, indicate the presence of one or more errors in $M_r(x)$.

As an example of these procedures, Table 5.3 shows the sequence of outputs from the transmitting register and the contents of the transmitting and receiving registers for the particular sequence of 19 data bits

0 1 1 1 1 0 0 1 1 0 0 1 1 0 0 0 1 1 1

assuming that they are received without error.

It can be shown theoretically that this error checking procedure is guaranteed to detect the presence of all odd numbers of errors anywhere in the address, control, information, and FCS fields of the frame, as long as this portion of the frame does not exceed 32767 bits. It also detects the presence of any pattern of errors confined to a maximum of 16 consecutive bits. In addition, empirical studies have shown that a large percentage of all other error patterns are also detected.

5.2.5 Control Field Formats

The structure of the control field, which occupies either octet 4 or octets 4 and 5, depending on the type of frame, is shown in Figure 5.7. Three types of control fields are specified, corresponding to three types of frames. The *information transfer format (I format)* of the control field is used in so-called *information frames (I frame)*, whose purpose is to carry messages between peer layer 3 entities and between

TABLE 5.3 Frame check sequence calculation

INPUT TO TRANSMIT REGISTER	STATE OF TRANSMIT REGISTER	INPUT TO RECEIVE REGISTER	STATE OF RECEIVE REGISTER
	1 1 1 1 1 1 1 1 1 1 1 1 1 1 1 1		1 1 1 1 1 1 1 1 1 1 1 1 1 1 1 1
a_{18} 0	1 1 1 1 1 0 1 1 1 1 1 1 0 1 1 1	0	1 1 1 1 1 0 1 1 1 1 1 1 0 1 1 1
a_{17} 1	0 1 1 1 1 1 0 1 1 1 1 1 1 0 1 1	1	0 1 1 1 1 1 0 1 1 1 1 1 1 0 1 1
. 1	0 0 1 1 1 1 1 0 1 1 1 1 1 1 0 1	1	0 0 1 1 1 1 1 0 1 1 1 1 1 1 0 1
. 1	0 0 0 1 1 1 1 1 0 1 1 1 1 1 1 0	1	0 0 0 1 1 1 1 1 0 1 1 1 1 1 1 0
. 1	1 0 0 0 1 0 1 1 0 1 1 0 1 1 1 1	1	1 0 0 0 1 0 1 1 0 1 1 0 1 1 1 1
0	1 1 0 0 0 0 0 1 1 1 0 1 0 0 1 1	0	1 1 0 0 0 0 0 1 1 1 0 1 0 0 1 1
0	1 1 1 0 0 1 0 0 1 1 1 0 0 0 0 1	0	1 1 1 0 0 1 0 0 1 1 1 0 0 0 0 1
1	0 1 1 1 0 0 1 0 0 1 1 1 0 0 0 0	1	0 1 1 1 0 0 1 0 0 1 1 1 0 0 0 0
1	1 0 1 1 1 1 0 1 0 0 1 1 0 0 0 0	1	1 0 1 1 1 1 0 1 0 0 1 1 0 0 0 0
0	0 1 0 1 1 1 0 1 0 0 1 1 0 0 0	0	0 1 0 1 1 1 0 1 0 0 1 1 0 0 0
0	0 0 1 0 1 1 1 1 0 1 0 0 1 1 0 0	0	0 0 1 0 1 1 1 1 0 1 0 0 1 1 0 0
1	1 0 0 1 0 0 1 1 1 0 1 0 1 1 1 0	1	1 0 0 1 0 0 1 1 1 0 1 0 1 1 1 0
1	1 1 0 0 1 1 0 1 1 1 0 1 1 1 1 1	1	1 1 0 0 1 1 0 1 1 1 0 1 1 1 1 1
0	1 1 1 0 0 0 1 0 1 1 1 0 0 1 1 1	0	1 1 1 0 0 0 1 0 1 1 1 0 0 1 1 1
0	1 1 1 1 0 1 0 1 0 1 1 1 1 0 1 1	0	1 1 1 1 0 1 0 1 0 1 1 1 1 0 1 1
0	1 1 1 1 1 1 1 0 1 0 1 1 0 1 0 1	0	1 1 1 1 1 1 1 0 1 0 1 1 0 1 0 1
1	0 1 1 1 1 1 1 1 0 1 0 1 1 0 1 0	1	0 1 1 1 1 1 1 1 0 1 0 1 1 0 1 0
1	1 0 1 1 1 0 1 1 1 0 1 0 0 1 0 1	1	1 0 1 1 1 0 1 1 1 0 1 0 0 1 0 1
a_0 1	0 1 0 1 1 0 1 1 1 0 1 0 0 0 1 0	1	0 1 0 1 1 0 1 1 1 0 1 0 0 0 1 0
	0 0 1 0 1 1 1 0 1 1 1 0 1 0 0 1	1	1 0 1 0 1 0 1 0 1 1 1 0 0 0 0 1
	0 0 0 1 0 1 1 1 0 1 1 1 0 1 0 0	0	1 1 0 1 0 0 0 1 0 1 1 1 1 0 0 0
	0 0 0 0 1 0 1 1 1 0 1 1 1 0 1 0	1	1 1 1 0 1 1 0 0 1 0 1 1 0 1 0 0
	0 0 0 0 0 1 0 1 1 1 0 1 1 1 0 1	1	1 1 1 1 0 0 1 0 0 1 0 1 0 0 1 0
	0 0 0 0 0 0 1 0 1 1 1 0 1 1 1 0 F	0	0 1 1 1 1 0 0 1 0 0 1 0 1 0 0 1
	0 0 0 0 0 0 0 1 0 1 1 1 0 1 1 1	1	0 0 1 1 1 1 0 0 1 0 0 1 0 1 0 0
	0 0 0 0 0 0 0 0 1 0 1 1 1 0 1 1 C	0	0 0 0 1 1 1 0 0 1 0 0 1 0 1 0
	0 0 0 0 0 0 0 0 0 1 0 1 1 1 0 1	0	0 0 0 0 1 1 1 1 0 0 1 0 0 1 0 1
	0 0 0 0 0 0 0 0 0 0 1 0 1 1 1 0 S	0	1 0 0 0 0 0 1 1 1 0 0 1 1 0 1 0
	0 0 0 0 0 0 0 0 0 0 0 1 0 1 1 1	1	1 1 0 0 0 1 0 1 1 1 0 0 0 1 0 1
	0 0 0 0 0 0 0 0 0 0 0 0 1 0 1 1	0	1 1 1 0 0 1 1 0 1 1 1 0 1 0 1 0
	0 0 0 0 0 0 0 0 0 0 0 0 0 1 0 1	0	0 1 1 1 0 0 1 1 0 1 1 1 0 1 0 1
	0 0 0 0 0 0 0 0 0 0 0 0 0 0 1 0	0	1 0 1 1 1 1 0 1 1 0 1 1 0 0 1 0
	0 0 0 0 0 0 0 0 0 0 0 0 0 0 0 1	1	1 1 0 1 1 0 1 0 1 1 0 1 0 0 0 1
	0 0 0 0 0 0 0 0 0 0 0 0 0 0 0 0	0	1 1 1 0 1 0 0 1 0 1 1 0 0 0 0 0
	0 0 0 0 0 0 0 0 0 0 0 0 0 0 0 0	1	1 1 1 1 0 0 0 0 1 0 1 1 1 0 0 0
	X_0 X_{15}		X_0 X_{15}

Order of bit transmission

Control field bits	8	7	6	5	4	3	2	1	
I Format				N(S)				0	Octet 4
				N(R)				P	5
S Format	X	X	X	X	S	S	0	1	Octet 4
				N(R)			P/F		5
U Format	M	M	M	P/F	M	M	1	1	Octet 4

Figure 5.7 *Control field format*

peer layer management entities. The *supervisory format (S format)* and *unnumbered format (U format)* are contained in *supervisory frames (S frame)* and *unnumbered frames (U frame),* respectively. These frames convey primarily data link layer control information between data link layer entities and between layer management entities. Certain U frames, however, may also contain layer 3 and layer management messages.

In the I format, the control field contains two counters, the *send sequence number N(S)* and the *receive sequence number N(R).* The latter is also a part of the control field in the S format, but neither N(S) nor N(R) are present in the U format. These counters derive their values from three state variables V(S), V(R), and V(A) that are associated with each endpoint of a data link connection.

The *send state variable V(S)* denotes the number of the next in-sequence I frame to be transmitted and is incremented by 1 with each complete or nonaborted transmission of an I frame. The send sequence number N(S) for a particular I frame is set equal to the value of V(S) at the time the frame is transmitted.

The *receive state variable V(R)* denotes the number of the next in-sequence I frame expected to be received. It is incremented by 1 on receipt of an error-free I frame whose send sequence number N(S) is equal to V(R). The receive sequence number N(R) for a particular I frame or S frame is set equal to the value of V(R) at the time of transmission. N(R) indicates that the data link layer entity transmitting the N(R) has correctly received all I frames up to and including N(R) − 1 from the other side and expects I frame number N(R) next.

The *acknowledge state variable V(A)* identifies the last I frame that has been acknowledged by the data link layer entity on the other side of the connection. It is updated on receipt of an I frame or S frame with a valid $N(R)$ count that must be in the range $V(A) < N(R) < V(S)$.

The $N(S)$ and $N(R)$ counters occupy seven bits in the control field and hence vary over the range 0 to 127. The same range applies to the three state variables.

The single bit identified as P or F in the control field formats is referred to as the *poll bit* in command frames and the *final bit* in response frames. P is set to 1 by a data link layer entity to elicit or poll a response frame from its peer entity on the other side of the connection. F must be set to 1 in the response frame resulting from the poll command frame. Note that I frames do not contain the F bit and are therefore never used as a response to command frames with P set to 1.

The two bits labeled S in the supervisory format represent three supervisory frames known as *Receive Ready (RR)*, *Receive Not Ready (RNR)*, and *Reject (REJ)*. The $N(R)$ counter in all three frames acknowledges the receipt from the other side of I frames numbered up to and including $N(R) - 1$. In addition, the RR frame indicates a readiness to receive additional I frames, starting with sequence number $N(R)$, the RNR frame indicates a temporary inability to accept additional I frames, and the REJ frame requests retransmission of I frames starting with sequence number $N(R)$.

The *M* or *modifier bits* in the U format are used to define seven additional frames. Only one of them, the *Unnumbered Information (UI)* command frame, contains layer 3 information and in addition may contain layer management entity information. It is used to convey this information between data link layer entities in an unacknowledged and unnumbered fashion. All other U frames serve the purpose of establishing, maintaining, and releasing a data link connection between peer data link layer entities for the exchange of multiple I frames with acknowledgments and sequence numbering. No layer 3 information is allowed in these U frames.

The *Set Asynchronous Balanced Mode Extended (SABME)* command frame is used to signal the establishment of a data link layer connection for the acknowledged transfer of multiple frames. The acknowledgment and acceptance of this command is contained in the *Unnumbered Acknowledgment (UA)* response frame, whereas a refusal of the connection is indicated by the *Disconnect Mode (DM)* response frame.

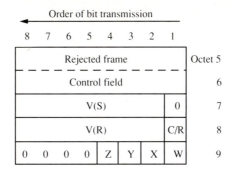

Figure 5.8 *Information field format of FRMR frame*

A connection is terminated by the transmission of the *Disconnect (DISC)* command frame, which is likewise acknowledged and accepted by the UA response frame.

The *Frame Reject (FRMR)* response frame may be used by a data link layer entity to report an error condition in a received frame that is not recoverable by the retransmission of an identical frame. Examples of such errors are the receipt of an invalid control field, the receipt of a frame containing an information field that is not permitted, the receipt of a frame of improper length, and the receipt of a frame with an invalid sequence counter N(R). A five-octet information field, whose format is shown in Figure 5.8, follows the control field. Octets 5 and 6 contain the control field of the rejected frame and octets 7 and 8 contain the current values of the send and receive state variable at the data link layer entity reporting the rejection. The bits W, X, Y, and Z are used to indicate the type of error in the received frame causing the reject. W = 1 implies an undefined control field, X = 1 reports that the received frame contained an impermissible information field, Y = 1 denotes that the frame was too long, and Z = 1 indicates that the control field contained an invalid N(R).

The *Exchange Identification (XID)* frame can be used as both a command and a response and serves to convey information regarding the parameters of the connection between layer management entities. These parameters are contained in the information field of the frame.

The binary encoding of the control field for the various I, S, and U formats discussed earlier is given in Table 5.4.

TABLE 5.4 Binary encoding of control field

APPLICATION	FORMAT	COMMANDS	RESPONSES	8	7	6	5	4	3	2	1	OCTET
	Information Transfer	I (information)					N(S)				0	4
							N(R)				P	5
	Supervisory	RR (receive ready)	RR (receive ready)	0	0	0	0	0	0	0	1	4
							N(R)				P/F	5
		RNR (receive not ready)	RNR (receive not ready)	0	0	0	0	0	1	0	1	4
							N(R)				P/F	5
		REJ (reject)	REJ (reject)	0	0	0	0	1	0	0	1	4
							N(R)				P/F	5
Unacknowledged and Multiple Frame Acknowledged Information Transfer	Unnumbered	SABME (set asynchronous balanced mode extended)		0	1	1	P	1	1	1	1	4
		UI (unnumbered information)		0	0	0	P	0	0	1	1	4
			DM (disconnected mode)	0	0	0	F	1	1	1	1	4
		DISC (disconnect)		0	1	0	P	0	0	1	1	4
			UA (unnumbered acknowledgment)	0	1	1	F	0	0	1	1	4
			FRMR (frame reject)	1	0	0	F	0	1	1	1	4
Connection Management		XIC (Exchange Identification)	XID (Exchange Identification)	1	0	1	P/F	1	1	1	1	4

5.3 Data Link Control Procedures

As we pointed out earlier, the purpose of the data link layer of a functional group is to provide a reliable and efficient transmission service to its layer 3 and management entities, so that the latter can convey information to their peer layers in functional groups on the other side of the user-to-network interface. Two types of relationships are possible. On the user side the data link layer entity may be contained in the TE functional group, whereas the peer data link layer entity on the network side may exist in either the NT2 or the ET. Figure 5.1 is a model of this arrangement. The peer data link layer entities may also be contained in an NT2 on the user side and an ET on the network side.

The service of the data link layer is carried out through the logical transfer of protocol frames across a peer-to-peer data link connection between the SAPs of peer data link layer entities. The type of frame that may be transmitted at a particular time, and the reaction to the reception of a frame by the peer entity, are controlled by a set of rules known as the *data link control*. Of course, as far as the data link layer is concerned, the transfer of layer 2 protocol frames is in response to the exchange of service primitives between the data link layer and layer 3 or between the data link layer and the LME-2 across the corresponding SAPs, as discussed earlier in this chapter. The transfer of the layer 2 protocol frames is accomplished by the exchange of service primitives with its physical layer, with the frames being contained in the parameter field of these primitives. The actual transmission of the frames is then carried out by the physical layer between peer physical layer entities and is controlled by the physical layer protocol.

The procedures of the data link control that govern its activities may be divided into a number of specific functional categories:

- Procedures for the control of terminal endpoint identifiers that may be assigned by a management entity to a particular data link layer entity for a time or on a permanent basis

- Procedures for the establishment and termination of information transfer modes over a data link connection between data link layer SAPs

- Procedures for the transmission of properly formatted individual frames over a data link connection, without control over the sequence in which the frames are received by the peer entity, without acknowledgment of receipt, and without control on the number of such frames that may be transmitted during a particular time

- Procedures for the transmission of frames with sequence control, flow control, and acknowledgment of receipt
- Procedures for the detection of format errors, procedure errors, and errors occurring during frame transmission
- Procedures for recovery from certain format, procedure, and transmission errors, and the reporting of unrecoverable errors to a management authority

Formally, the data link layer entities on each side of a data link connection exist at a particular time in one of eight states. Each of these is identified by a state number and a state name:

1 TEI Unassigned

2 Assign Awaiting TEI

3 Establish Awaiting TEI

4 TEI Assigned

5 Awaiting Establishment

6 Awaiting Release

7 Multiple Frame Established

8 Timer Recovery

A change from one state to another, as well as the operations within a state, requires the exchange of specific protocol frames in a particular order, according to the procedures of the data link control. These procedures are the subject of the following sections.

5.4 TEI Assignment, Checking, and Removal

We recall that from the point of view of the data link layer, the identifier of a data link connection consists of two parts—the SAPI and the TEI. The latter is associated with the equipment on the user side of the user-to-network interface and identifies a particular endpoint that is part of the SAPs within the TE.

The TEI to be used in a particular connection is assigned by the NT2 or ET prior to the transfer of information and normally applies to all the SAPs within a given TE. Its validity may also be restricted to a single SAP or a specified subset of SAPs, so that a TE may contain more than one TEI.

TEIs may be assigned on a per-connection basis by means of an automatic assignment procedure. This capability avoids the need to permanently associate specific TEI values with a particular TE and thus permits terminal equipment to be disconnected from one interface and reconnected to another during inactive periods without the need to notify the network side. It also creates the possibility of dynamically sharing the available TEI values among multiple data link connections and TEs operating across the same S or T reference point.

TEI values for a data link connection may also be established permanently at subscription time, as may be desirable for the point-to-point wiring arrangement of primary access.

In either case, the existence and validity of a TEI value may have to be checked by the NT2 or ET on initiation of a connection, or at other times for inventory or audit purposes. To carry out these assignment and checking tasks, or to remove a temporary assignment, the data link protocol contains a set of procedures that serve three purposes:

- A TE may request that the NT2 or ET assign a TEI value to be used in the identification of a subsequent data link connection.

- An NT2 or ET may check the set of currently assigned TEIs in connection with an assignment procedure, or to update its list of available TEIs.

- An NT2 or ET may remove a previously assigned TEI from the TE on termination of a data link connection, or at other times for administrative reasons.

Conceptually, these procedures exist in the layer management entities within the TE on the user side and NT2 or ET on the network side of the UNI. On the network side these management entities are known as the *assignment source point (ASP)*. The procedures are invoked and carried out through the exchange of the service primitives MDL-ASSIGN, MDL-REMOVE, and MDL-UNIT DATA between the LME-2 and the data link layer entity in the same functional group and the transfer of unnumbered information (UI) frames in broadcast mode between peer data link layer entities across the UNI. As indicated in Table 5.1, the primitives contain message units as parameters. Their structure is shown in Figure 5.9.

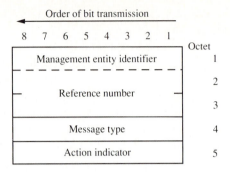

Figure 5.9 *Message format for TEI management*

Each message unit contains a one-octet field identifying it as a management message, a two-octet reference number, a one-octet message-type field, and a one-octet action indicator. Their binary coding is shown in Table 5.5 and their functions are discussed below.

Prior to the assignment of a TEI, the data link layer entities are in the TEI Unassigned state. Once a TEI has been assigned, verified, and checked, the entities enter the TEI Assigned state. Simultaneously, an association between the TEI and a connection endpoint suffix in each SAP is established, which creates a relationship between the data link connection identifier and the connection endpoint identifier. At that point a connection between peer layer 3 entities or between peer LME-2s has been established.

5.4.1 TEI Assignment Procedure

A permanent TEI that has been preassigned to a data link layer entity in a TE is considered to be under the control of the layer management entity of the TE. Assuming the data link layer entity to be in the TEI Unassigned state, the change to the TEI Assigned state is accomplished when the TE layer management entity transmits the MDL-ASSIGN Request primitive containing the preassigned TEI to its data link layer entity.

For a dynamically assigned TEI, the initiation of the TEI assignment procedure normally occurs when the data link layer entity in the TE, as a result of receiving a DL-ESTABLISH Request primitive or a DL-UNIT DATA Request primitive from its layer 3 entity, passes a MDL-ASSIGN Indication primitive to its layer management entity.

TABLE 5.5   Binary coding of TEI management messages

MESSAGE NAME	MANAGE-MENT ENTITY IDEN-TIFIER	REFERENCE NUMBER Ri	MESSAGE TYPE	ACTION INDICATOR Ai	
Identity request (user to network)	0000 1111	0-65535	0000 0001	Ai = 127,	Any TEI value acceptable
Identity assigned (network to user)	0000 1111	0-65535	0000 0010	Ai = 64–126,	Assigned TEI value
Identity denied (network to user)	0000 1111	0-65535	0000 0011	Ai = 64–126,	Denied TEI value
				Ai = 127,	No TEI value available
Identity check request (network to user)	0000 1111	Not used (coded 0)	0000 0100	Ai = 127,	Check all TEI values
				Ai = 0–126,	TEI value to be checked
Identity check response (user to network)	0000 1111	0-65535	0000 0101	Ai = 0–126,	TEI value in use
Identity remove (network to user)	0000 1111	Not used (coded 0)	0000 0110	Ai = 127,	Request for removal of all TEI values
				Ai = 0–126,	TEI value to be removed
Identity verify (user to network)	0000 1111	Not used (coded 0)	0000 0111	Ai = 0–126,	TEI value to be checked

Alternatively, the layer management entity may initiate the procedure on its own. In either case, the layer management entity in the TE transmits to its data link layer the Identity Request message in the parameter field of the MDL-UNIT DATA Request primitive. As shown in Figure 5.9 and Table 5.5, this message contains a reference number Ri and an action indicator Ai. Ri distinguishes between different TEs that may be simultaneously requesting the assignment of a TEI. Its length is two octets and its value is randomly selected from the range 0 to 65535. The single-octet action indicator Ai is used to request that any available TEI be assigned to the data link layer entity in the TE. Ai is set to the value TEI = 127.

At the same time that the MDL-UNIT DATA Request primitive is passed to the data link layer entity, the layer management entity sets a timer T202. If it receives no response to its Identity Request message prior to the expiration of T202, the timer is restarted and another Identity Request message with a different value of Ri is transmitted. After N202 unsuccessful attempts the TEI assignment is assumed to have failed. The management entity then informs its data link layer entity via a MDL-ERROR Response primitive and the data link layer entity informs its layer 3 entity by transmitting the DL-RELEASE Indication primitive.

The notation for the timers T202 and N202 follows standard CCITT usage. These timers are system parameters whose values are implementation dependent.

On receipt of the Identity Request message from its management entity, the data link layer entity in the TE transmits an Unnumbered Information command to its peer layer in the NT2 or ET. The Identity Request message is contained in the information field of the UI, the SAPI is set to the value 63, and the TEI is set to 127. The data link layer entity then enters the Awaiting TEI Assignment state.

When the peer data link layer entity in the NT2 or ET receives the UI frame, it passes the Identity Request message part to its ASP in the parameter field of the MDL-UNIT DATA Indication primitive. As a consequence the ASP will either select a TEI value or ignore the message if it is judged to be a duplicate of a previous message. The selection of a TEI is accomplished by reference to a database of currently assigned or available TEI values, which is maintained by the ASP.

After having selected the TEI, the ASP creates the Identity Assigned message, which contains the original reference number Ri and an Ai equal to the actually assigned TEI value. Its binary coding format is also shown in Table 5.5. This message is transmitted by the ASP to its data link layer entity in the parameter field of a MDL-UNIT DATA Request primitive. The data link layer in turn transmits it to every active user-side data link layer entity inside of a UI frame with SAPI = 63 and TEI = 127, and then enters the Awaiting TEI Assignment state.

The data link layer entities in the TEs on the originating side refer the message to their management entities as a parameter of the MDL-UNIT DATA Indication primitive. The particular management entity that recognizes the received Identity Assigned message by the fact that the Ri value in the message agrees with its previously selected Ri then transmits the MDL-ASSIGN Request primitive containing the assigned TEI to its data link layer entity. The latter then stores the received TEI and enters the TEI Assigned state. The TEI value remains valid for the duration of the data link connection.

If no TEI is available the ASP will transmit the Identity Denied message, in which the Ai contains the value 127, to indicate that no TEI is available. The relevant management entity in the TE receiving this message may reinvoke the assignment procedure or inform its data link layer entity via the **MDL-ERROR** Response primitive that no TEI is available. In the latter case the data link layer entity notifies its layer 3 entity by transmitting the **DL-RELEASE** Indication primitive.

An example of a successful procedure is shown in Figure 5.10.

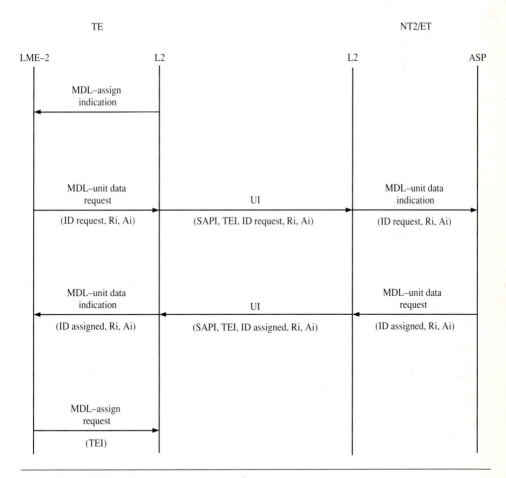

Figure 5.10   *TEI assignment procedure*

5.4.2 TEI Check Procedure

The layer management entity on the network side may use the TEI check routine to ascertain whether a particular TEI value is currently assigned to a TE or to determine the set of all values currently assigned.

The ASP in the ET, or in the NT2 if the latter is on the network side, initiates the procedure by transmitting the Identity Check Request message in the parameter field of a MDL-UNIT DATA Request primitive to its data link layer entity. The format of this message is shown in Figure 5.9 and Table 5.5. Ai is either set to a specific TEI value to be checked, or to 127 if all currently assigned values are to be determined. Ri is not used and is set to 0. Simultaneously with the transmission of the message the ASP starts a timer T201, whose value is a system parameter.

The Identity Check Request message is carried across the data link connection to every peer data link layer entity on the user side in the information field of a UI frame with SAPI = 63 and TEI = 127. These entities forward the message to their layer management entities via the MDL-UNIT DATA Indication primitive.

If the Ai field contains a specific TEI that is assigned to one of the TEs, only the corresponding management entity responds to its data link layer entity with a MDL-UNIT DATA Request primitive, which contains the Identity Check Response message. The latter includes the relevant TEI in the Ai field and a randomly selected reference number in the Ri field. If, on the other hand, Ai equals the value 127, all active layer management entities with assigned TEIs respond with the values of their assigned TEIs and individual randomly selected reference numbers Ri. The Ris allow the network side to eliminate duplicate responses that may occur as a result of a layer 1 contention.

When it receives these messages via UI frames with SAPI = 63 and TEI = 127, the data link layer in the NT2 or ET informs its ASP by means of a MDL-UNIT DATA Indication primitive containing Ri and Ai that the TEIs defined in the Ai field have been assigned. A diagram of the procedure for checking a single TEI is shown in Figure 5.11.

If no identity check response is received by the management entity in the NT2 or ET within the amount of time specified by T201, the entire procedure is repeated once. If no response is received after the second try, the appropriate TEIs are assumed to be unassigned and available for assignment to data link connections. Evidently, in order to prevent the assignment of a TEI already in use, the value of T201 must be at least as large as the response time of the slowest TE.

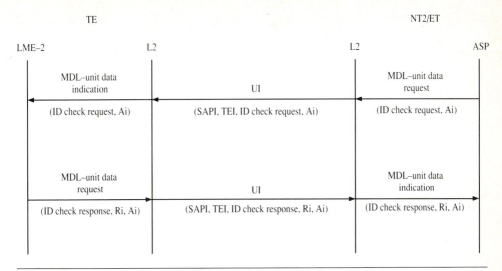

Figure 5.11   *TEI check procedure*

5.4.3   TEI Removal Procedure

For various reasons, such as when an assigned TEI has not been in use for a period of time or when a duplicate assignment has been detected, the layer management entity in the NT2 or ET may find it necessary and desirable to remove an assigned TEI value from the user side. This is accomplished by the following procedure:

The ASP transmits the Identity Remove message, whose Ai field contains the value of the specific TEI to be removed, to its data link layer in the parameter field of the MDL-REMOVE Request primitive. A value of Ai = 127 indicates that all LMEs should remove their assigned TEIs. The Ri field in the message is set to 0.

This message is transmitted to the peer data link layer in every TE in the information field of a UI frame, with SAPI = 63 and TEI = 127. To counteract the possibility of a lost frame, the message is sent twice in succession.

The layer management entities on the TE side obtain the Identity Remove message via MDL-UNIT DATA Indication primitives from their data link layer entities and instruct the latter to delete the TEI value, using the MDL-REMOVE Request primitive. The data link layer entities then enter the TEI Unassigned state.

Figure 5.12 shows an example of the procedure in diagram form.

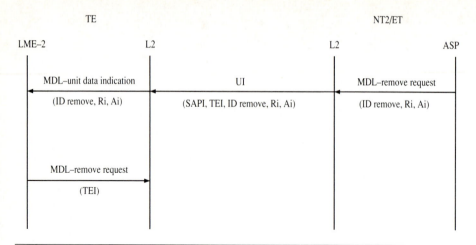

Figure 5.12 *TEI removal procedure*

5.5 Information Transfer

The data link control for the ISDN user-to-network interface conveys the frames containing the messages obtained from a layer 3 or management entity and the layer 2 control information in two modes of operation.

The first, known as *unacknowledged information transfer*, offers the functions required for a simple, generally unreliable frame transmission service without any capability for controlling the order in which the frames are received or the number of frames that are transmitted during a particular interval of time. The protocol also does not provide the receiver with the ability to acknowledge the reception of a frame, relying instead on a higher layer recovery procedure for lost frames or frames received in error.

The second mode of operation, known as *multiple frame acknowledged information transfer*, incorporates a procedure that allows the establishment of a logical relationship between the data link layer entities that is based on the sequence numbers N(S) and N(R) contained in I frames and S frames. This association makes it possible to control the flow of information and correct certain transmission errors, sequence errors, and procedural errors through timed and numbered acknowledgments and the retransmission of missing or incorrect frames.

In this section we describe the most important features of these procedures in somewhat simplified terms.

5.5.1 Procedure for Unacknowledged Information Transfer

Unacknowledged information transfer is normally carried out while the communicating data link layer entities are in the TEI Unassigned state and provides a broadcast transmission capability between an NT2 or ET and multiple endpoints in the TEs that are associated with a given service-access point. Its major application is the transfer of link management messages between peer layer management entities for the assignment, checking, and removal of terminal endpoint identifiers and the transmission of incoming call signals to the TEs prior to the existence of a TEI value in the intended TE.

Unacknowledged information transfer may also operate in point-to-point mode between a specific pair of endpoints, in which case the peer data link layer entities must be in the TEI Assigned state. It may then be used for the independent transfer of individual layer 3 messages.

An unacknowledged information transfer is initiated when a layer 3 entity or a layer management entity passes a DL-UNIT DATA Request primitive or a MDL-UNIT DATA Request primitive, containing the message to be transferred, across the service-access point to its data link layer entity. This message is mapped by the data link layer entity into the information field of a UI command frame. For broadcast transmission, the TEI value in the address field is set to 127. For point-to-point operation TEI assumes the value of the specific endpoint to which the transmission is directed or from which the transmission originates, depending on whether the frame is conveyed in the direction user to network or vice versa. The P/F bit is not used and always equals 0.

The UI frame is then referred to the physical layer entity via a PH-DATA Request primitive where it is transmitted to the remote physical layer entity. There it is conveyed by the physical layer entity to the data link layer entity in the parameter field of the PH-DATA Indication primitive.

Although the receiving data link layer entity uses the frame check sequence to detect the presence of any transmission errors, no error recovery mechanisms are defined within the data link layer. In addition, the receiver is unable to control when a frame is transmitted to it or acknowledge its reception to the sender.

On receiving a correct frame with a SAPI that corresponds to a SAP supported by the receiver data link layer entity, the information field in the UI frame is passed to the layer 3 entity or the layer management entity via DL-UNIT DATA Indication or MDL-UNIT DATA Indication primitives, respectively. If the SAPI is not supported, the frame is discarded without notification to the sender. Received frames that fail the error checking procedure are similarly discarded by the data link layer entity.

5.5.2 Procedure for Establishment of Multiple Frame Acknowledged Operation

Multiple frame acknowledged operation can only be used over point-to-point data link connections. Its establishment requires that the connection exist in the TEI Assigned state.

The layer 3 entity on the side initiating the establishment procedure transfers the DL-ESTABLISH Request primitive to its data link layer entity, at which time the latter transmits the Set Asynchronous Balanced Mode Extended (SABME) command to its peer layer. The P bit is set to 1.

At the same time, the originating data link layer entity clears all exception conditions that may exist from a previous connection. It also starts a timer T200 and resets a retransmission counter RC to value 0. T200 equals the amount of time allowed for a response from the peer layer, and RC—whose maximum value is N200—determines whether the transmission of a particular frame may be repeated. Both T200 and N200 are system dependent parameters with default values of 1 second and 3, respectively.

The originating data link layer entity then enters the Awaiting Establishment state.

If the receiving peer data link layer entity is able to enter into multiple frame acknowledged operation, it will, on receiving the SABME command, respond with the Unnumbered Acknowledgment (UA) response with the F bit set to 1, the same value as the P bit in the received command. Simultaneously it clears all of its exception conditions, resets its own retransmission counter, and sets the send, receive, and acknowledge state variables V(S), V(R), and V(A) to 0. It then informs its layer 3 entity by means of the DL-ESTABLISH Indication primitive that multiple frame operation with a peer layer 3 entity is being established and enters the Multiple Frame Established state.

If multiple frame acknowledged operation is not possible, the receiving data link layer entity responds instead with the Disconnect Mode (DM) response, again with the F bit equal to the received P bit, and remains in the TEI Assigned state.

When it gets a UA response, the originator of the SABME command stops timer T200, sets V(S), V(R), and V(A) to 0, and enters the Multiple Frame Established state. At the same time it transmits to its layer 3 entity the DL-ESTABLISH Confirm primitive to notify it of the fact that the multiple frame data link connection is in the operational state.

If, on the other hand, the originator receives the DM response, it transmits to its layer 3 the DL-RELEASE Indication primitive, stops T200, and reverts to the TEI Assigned state.

In case T200 expires prior to the reception of either a UA or DM response, the originating data link layer entity will repeat the transmission of the SABME command, increment the retransmission counter RC by 1, and reset T200. After N200 unsuccessful attempts it notifies its layer 3 and management entities of the failure to establish multiple frame acknowledged operation by means of the DL-RELEASE Indication and MDL-ERROR Indication primitives, respectively. It then enters the TEI Assigned state.

Figures 5.13 and 5.14 contain the SDL diagrams for these procedures at the originating and responding sides, respectively.

5.5.3 Procedure for Termination of Multiple Frame Acknowledged Operation

A request for the termination of multiple frame acknowledged operation may originate in either the network equipment or the user equipment of the user-to-network interface.

A request for termination is indicated by the corresponding layer 3 entity through the transfer of the DL-RELEASE Request primitive to its data link layer entity. The latter then initiates the release by transmitting the Disconnect (DISC) command with P = 1 to its peer entity, starting timer T200, and resetting the retransmission counter RC to 0. It then enters the Awaiting Release state.

The reaction of the data link layer entity receiving the DISC command depends on its current state. If it exists in the Multiple Frame Established state or the Timer Recovery state, it transmits the UA response with F set to the value of P in the DISC command, passes the DL-RELEASE Indication primitive to its layer 3 entity, and enters

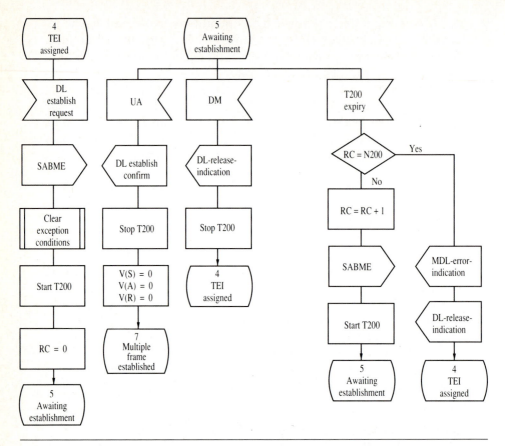

Figure 5.13 *Establishment of multiple frame acknowledged operation (originating side)* © Adapted from CCITT Blue Book, vol VI. 10, 1988

the TEI Assigned state. In the TEI Assigned, Awaiting Establishment, and Awaiting Release states it returns the DM response, again with F set to P, and remains in its state. In all other states the reception of the DISC command is ignored.

On receiving either the UA or DM response, the originating data link layer stops T200, transfers the DL-RELEASE Confirm primitive to its layer 3 entity, and enters the TEI Assigned state to complete the procedure.

If timer T200 expires before receiving the UA response, the originating data link layer retransmits the DISC command, resets T200, and increments RC by 1. After N200 attempts, it notifies its manage-

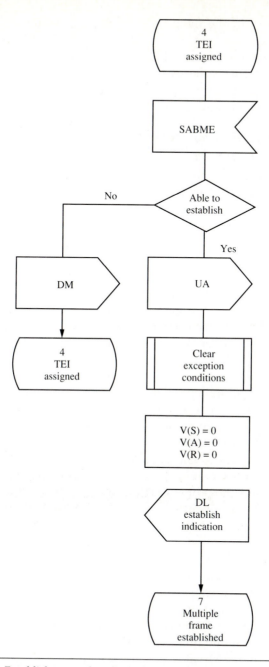

Figure 5.14 *Establishment of multiple frame acknowledged operation (responding side)* © Adapted from CCITT Blue Book, vol VI. 10, 1988

ment entity of the failure to terminate the multiple frame acknowledged operation by means of the MDL-ERROR Indication primitive
and transfers the DL-RELEASE Confirm primitive to its layer 3 entity. It then enters the TEI Assigned state.

These termination procedures are diagrammed in Figures 5.15 and
5.16 for the originating and responding sides, respectively.

5.5.4 Procedure for Multiple Frame Acknowledged Information Transfer

The information a data link layer entity receives from its layer 3 entity
as part of a DL-DATA Request primitive is transmitted to the peer
data link layer entity in the information field of an I command frame.
The sequence counters $N(S)$ and $N(R)$ are set to the current values of
the send and receive state variables $V(S)$ and $V(R)$, respectively, and
the value of the P bit determines the type of desired response.

The transmission of an I frame is subject to several controls.
Clearly, the data link connection must first be in the Multiple Frame
Established state. I frames may also not be transmitted if the peer
entity on the receiving side has signaled an inability to accept I frames
or is awaiting the recovery from an anomaly. Finally, the current value
of $V(S)$ must be less than $V(A) + k$, where $V(A)$ is the $N(S)$ value of
the last I frame whose reception has been acknowledged by the peer
entity and k is the maximum allowable number of sequentially numbered I frames whose acknowledgments are outstanding. The value of
k, which is a system parameter that may not exceed 127, is chosen in
accordance with the transmission time of a frame, the propagation delay between sender and receiver, and the frame error rate. It determines to a considerable extent the throughput of the connection.

Assuming the proper conditions exist, the sending entity transmits
an *I* frame, increments its $V(S)$ value by 1, and starts timer T200.
These actions are shown in Figure 5.17.

A peer entity that is prepared to accept an I frame will react as
follows on receiving it:

If the I frame exhibits transmission errors, as determined by the
frame check sequence, is not bounded by proper flags, or does not
contain an integral and minimum number of octets, it is discarded
without acknowledgment of receipt to the sender. A similar action follows when a frame that is not the next one in sequence—that is, one
in which the $N(S)$ value disagrees with the receiver's state variable
$V(R)$—is received. In all other cases the peer entity accepts the frame
and increments $V(R)$ by 1, which then represents the number of the

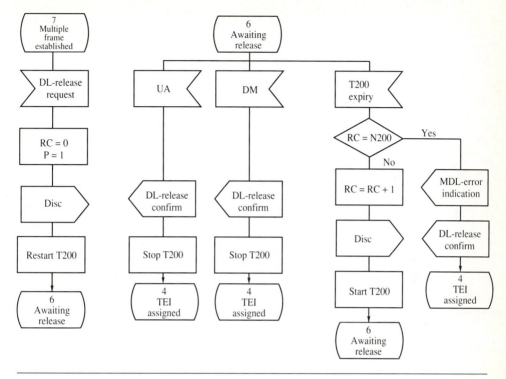

Figure 5.15 *Termination of multiple frame acknowledged operation (originating side)* © Adapted from CCITT Blue Book, vol VI. 10, 1988

next expected frame. It then transfers the information field of the I frame to its layer 3 entity, using the DL-DATA Indication primitive. At the same time, the data link layer entity also responds to the sending peer data link layer entity in one of several ways, depending on the value of the P bit in the received I frame.

If P = 1, it sends either the Receive Ready (RR) or the Receive Not Ready (RNR) supervisory frame. The first indicates the acceptance of the frame and a readiness to receive additional I frames, whereas the second implies the acceptance and temporary inability to receive additional I frames. The latter condition could occur as a result of buffer congestion, processor failure, and a host of other causes. N(R) is set to one larger than the value of N(S) in the received frame and F is set to 1.

If, on the other hand, the P bit in the received I frame equals 0, the peer entity may respond with an I frame if one is available and the

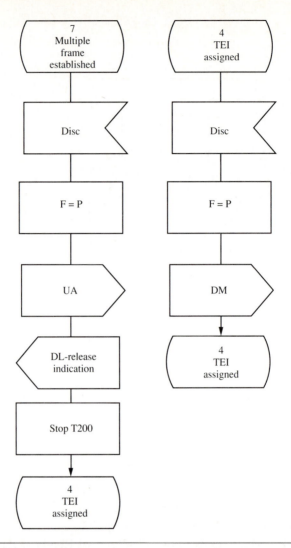

Figure 5.16 *Termination of multiple frame acknowledged operation (responding side)* © Adapted from CCITT Blue Book, vol VI. 10, 1988

other side is able to receive additional I frames. Alternatively, the response may be in the form of an RR or RNR frame. RR is appropriate if no I frame is available or the entity sending the original I frame cannot accept I frames, whereas the RNR frame would be used if the peer entity is itself unable to accept I frames. In both cases the F bit

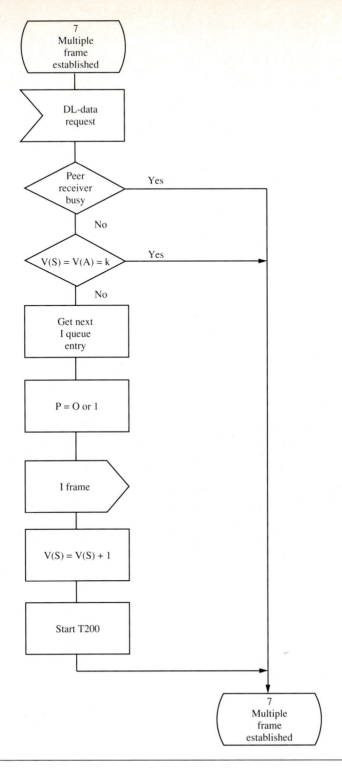

Figure 5.17 *I-frame transmission (originating side)*
© Adapted from CCITT Blue Book, vol VI. 10, 1988

is set to 0 and N(R) is set to V(R), which equals 1 plus the value of N(S) in the received I frame.

These procedures are shown in Figure 5.18.

On receiving a valid I, RR, or RNR frame prior to the expiration of T200, the original sending entity considers a value of N(R) greater than its current value of V(A) an acknowledgment of all transmitted I frames with sequence numbers N(S) less than N(R) and sets V(A) to N(R). It is then ready to transmit additional I frames, subject to the conditions stated earlier. If, however, T200 expired prior to receiving any response, the sending entity restarts T200, resets the retransmission counter RC to 0, and retransmits the last I frame, setting P = 1. It then enters the Timer Recovery state.

This procedure may be repeated until a valid response is obtained within the allowed time or until RC, which is incremented by 1 at each repetition, reaches the value N200. In the latter case the data link layer entity issues the MDL-ERROR Indication primitive to its management entity and initiates a reestablishment of the multiple frame acknowledged operation. This event is usually accompanied by a loss of information.

As an alternative, as long as RC is less than N200, the sending entity may transmit an inquiry in the form of an RR or RNR command with P set to 1, again under the control of T200 and RC. Such an action would be appropriate if the receiving peer entity is in a busy condition, for example, but may also be employed in other circumstances.

Figure 5.19 shows the acknowledgment and timer recovery procedures just outlined.

5.5.5 *Flow Control Procedures*

A data link layer entity that finds itself unable to accept transmissions from its peer entity signals a receiver busy condition by transmitting a RNR frame. This frame may be a response frame with F = 0, a command frame with P = 0, or a command frame with P = 1. N(R) is set to the current value of V(R).

As long as this flow control condition exists, the data link layer entity will discard all received I frames after updating its V(A) variable to the values of N(R) contained in the frames and, if P = 1, will respond with a RNR response frame in which F is set to 1. Received supervisory frames, on the other hand, will be processed as usual and, if P = 1, a RNR response frame with F = 1 will again be returned.

The receiver of a flow control indication is prevented from transmitting any further I frames. It updates its V(A) variable to the value

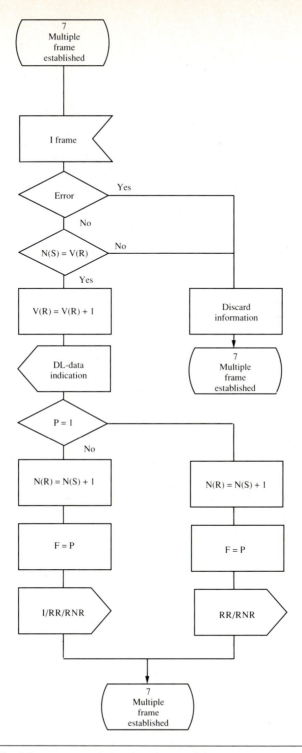

Figure 5.18 *I-frame transmission (receiving side)*
© Adapted from CCITT Blue Book, vol VI. 10, 1988

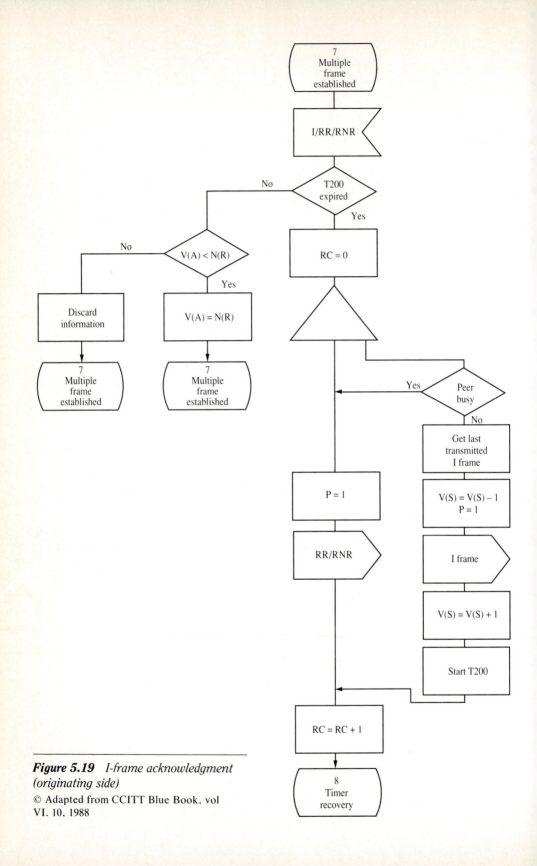

Figure 5.19 *I-frame acknowledgment
(originating side)*
© Adapted from CCITT Blue Book, vol
VI. 10, 1988

of N(R) contained in the received RNR frame and, if requested by P = 1, transmits an acknowledgment of the busy condition by means of RNR if it is itself in a busy condition or RR if it is not.

Busy conditions are cleared by the transmission of a RR frame or I frame with the appropriate value of N(R). Alternatively, the link may be reset.

5.5.6 Procedures for Recovery from Exception Conditions

A receiver enters an exception condition from the normal operation of the protocol when it receives an invalid frame or an otherwise valid frame that contains a procedural error. Three particular exception conditions are defined:

- An N(S) sequence error exception condition occurs when an otherwise valid I frame, whose N(S) value does not agree with the receiver's V(R) value, is received. This, of course, occurs when the I frame is not the one expected to be received next in sequence.

- An invalid frame exception condition occurs when a frame is received that contains transmission errors or does not conform to the structural requirements of a frame.

- A frame rejection exception condition occurs when the receiver obtains either an undefined frame, a frame with a value of N(R) outside the range V(A) < N(R) < V(S), or a frame containing an information field that is not allowed or that exceeds the maximum allowable length.

A data link layer entity receiving an I frame with an incorrect N(S) value will discard the information field and initiate a recovery by transmitting to its peer layer the Reject (REJ) frame with N(R) set to its current value of V(R). As a response, the data link layer entity receiving the REJ sets its V(A) and V(S) state variables to the value of N(R) contained in the REJ frame and repeats the transmission of all outstanding and unacknowledged I frames, starting with the I frame whose send sequence number equals the received value of N(R). These transmissions are again subject to acknowledgments within a time defined by the value of timer T200.

When an I frame with the proper N(S) value is received by the data link layer entity in the exception condition, it is acknowledged in the usual way and the exception condition is cleared.

An invalid frame condition is cleared by discarding the frame. No further action on the part of the receiver is taken.

The frame rejection condition is indicated by the transmission of a Frame Reject (FRMR) frame from one data link layer entity to the other and the transfer of the MDL-ERROR Indication primitive to their respective management entities. Recovery is then accomplished by a reestablishment of the data link.

5.6   Summary and Recommended Reading

This chapter contains a detailed description of the services provided by layer 2 of the ISDN protocol hierarchy and the protocol by means of which these services are carried out. The protocol, known as LAPD, is common to all three planes of the reference model and to both the basic- and the primary-access UNI. It can in principle be used to control the layer 2 interactions over any of the component channels, but currently applies only to the D channel.

A brief summary of LAPD is contained in [KANO86]. For an analysis of its performance in the presence of errors on the transmission circuit see [BRAD85].

CHAPTER 6

The ISDN User-to-Network Layer 3

In the last two chapters we examined the structure of the user-to-network interface as it pertains to the services offered by the physical and data link layers of the ISDN protocol architecture. Collectively, these two layers provide a reliable information transfer service by means of which the functional groups on the two sides of an S or T reference point can exchange messages. The physical layer protocols for basic access and primary access described in Chapter 4 and specified in CCITT Recommendations I.430 and I.431 are common to both the U plane and C plane. They manage the physical transmission of the bit streams representing the user information flows, control information flows, user-to-user signaling information flows, and network management information flows. The LAPD data link layer protocol discussed in Chapter 5 and specified in Recommendations I.440 (Q.920) and I.441 (Q.921), which forms layer 2 of the Digital Subscriber Signaling System No.1 (DSS 1), controls the logical transfer of the information flows carried on the individual component channels of the channel structure. LAPD must be used for the information flows carried on the D channel; it may also be employed for other flows over other component channels.

In the present chapter we continue the specification of the UNI by studying the characteristics of layer 3 of the ISDN communications architecture, whose function is to establish, operate, and terminate network connections, transfer information flows across them, and control the invocation of supplementary services.

As we saw in Chapter 3, an ISDN connection between a pair of users involves two types of component channels across the UNI, as well as two types of internal network facilities.

For the transfer of the user information flows in the U plane, a connection usually consists of an association between pairs of B channels or H channels, one on each side of the connection, and either a circuit switched or a packet switched connection over the interexchange network. Across the UNI the transfer of these flows between the functional groups on the user and network sides over the B channel or H channel is governed by a protocol between peer layer 3 user information transfer entities (UTE-3) associated with the U plane. Although a number of existing protocols such as the data transfer part of CCITT Recommendation X.25 can be adapted to the control of these flows, to date no single unified ISDN protocol serving this purpose has been defined. In fact, above the physical layer many types of user information flows are carried transparently between end-users and therefore do not require any layer 3 protocol across the UNI.

The control information flows of the C plane needed to establish, maintain, and terminate circuit switched or packet switched connections between the users and to provide control over supplementary services are conveyed across the UNI over the D channel. They require a packet switched connection through the common channel signaling network. They are exchanged between peer layer 3 connection control entities (CCE-3) associated with the C plane.

The D channel, in conjunction with a packet switched connection over the CCSN, also provides for the transfer of the user-to-user signaling information flows. Across the UNI these flows are conveyed between peer layer 3 user-to-user signaling entities (USE-3) in the U plane.

Finally, the D channel, in conjunction with either a packet switched connection over the CCSN or the packet switched interexchange network, may carry packet switched user information flows between peer UTE-3s in the U plane.

The exchange of these three types of flows over the D channel is governed by layer 3 of the Digital Subscriber Signaling System No. 1 (DSS 1) which has partly been specified by the CCITT. It is this protocol that is of concern to us in the present chapter. Some of its procedural and structural details are still under active consideration and therefore subject to future modifications and enhancements. Also, except for the adoption of CCITT Recommendation X.25 discussed in Chapter 7, no definition of an ISDN-specific protocol for packet switched connections has been given. Consequently, our approach will be tutorial in nature and will concentrate on the most important aspects of the protocol for the control of circuit switched connections, the transfer of user-to-user signaling information, and the invocation of supplementary services. See AT&T Publication 41449 and CCITT Recommendations I.450 (Q.930), I.451 (Q.931), and I.452 (Q.932) for a more complete and precise treatment of this topic.

6.1 Layer 3 Specifications for the C Plane and U Plane

In this section we begin our consideration of the layer 3 D-channel protocol by specifying the services carried out by the layer 3 C-plane and U-plane entities and the functions of the protocol.

6.1.1 Layer 3 C-Plane and U-Plane Services

As noted earlier, layer 3 of the C plane has the responsibility to establish, operate, and terminate circuit switched or packet switched connections over the interexchange network of the ISDN and to provide control over supplementary services. Layer 3 of the U plane conveys user-to-user signaling information flows and user information flows between pairs of users. To carry out these tasks the CCE-3, USE-3, and UTE-3 in the C plane and U plane in the functional groups of the UNI communicate with each other across the S or T reference point by means of a peer-to-peer protocol. Depending on the particular reference configuration implemented and the type of connection, this communication may be between the entities in the TE and NT2, the TE and ET, or the NT2 and ET. For simplicity we will speak of communication between a functional group on the user side and a functional group on the network side of the UNI, with the understanding that it applies to any of the pairs of functional groups mentioned earlier. Note that since the capability of the NT1 functional group extends only to layer 1, it is not involved in these layer 3 relationships.

In general the CCE-3, USE-3, and UTE-3 perform their services for the layer 4 entities CCE-4, USE-4, and UTE-4 and in turn rely on the services offered by the layer 2 entities CCE-2, USE-2, and UTE-2. The interactions between these various entities are carried out through the exchange of appropriate service primitives.

Figure 6.1(a) depicts the relationships between the peer layer 3 entities in different functional groups across the UNI and the adjacent layer 4 entities within a functional group.

In certain situations—such as the control of a circuit switched connection shown in Figure 3.9(b)—the functions of the C plane or U

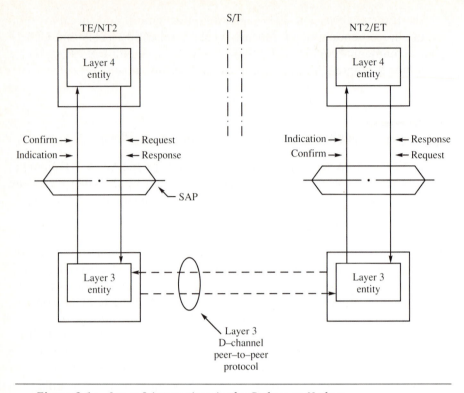

Figure 6.1a *Layer 3 interactions in the C plane or U plane*

plane extend only to layer 3. In terms of the protocol reference model for a functional group shown in Figure 3.7, the CCE-3, USE-3, or UTE-3 then interact directly with the connection control process (CCP), the user-to-user signaling process (USP), or the user information transfer process (UTP) through the exchange of signals across the human-machine interface. This relationship is shown in Figure 6.1(b).

6.1.2 Functions of the D-Channel Protocol

The CCE-3, USE-3, and UTE-3 in the functional groups of the UNI that communicate with each other over the D channel carry out their tasks of connection control, supplementary services control, user-to-user signaling, and user information transfer by performing a number

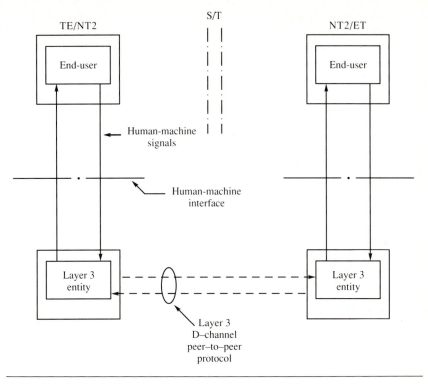

Figure 6.1b *Layer 3 interactions in the C plane or U plane*

of specific functions. The most important of these are described in the following paragraphs.

All information—whether it relates to connection control, supplementary services control, user-to-user signaling, or user information transfer—is conveyed across the UNI by means of *protocol messages.* These must be generated, transmitted, received, and interpreted by the communicating entities over a signaling connection in proper sequence according to the specifications of the D-channel protocol.

The transmission of these protocol messages is accomplished over an underlying data link connection operated in accordance with the LAPD protocol. For point-to-point configurations, the messages are contained in the information field of layer 2 I frames and are transmitted in the Multiple Frame Acknowledged mode of operation. In multipoint connections involving a group of user entities and a single network entity, a layer 3 message from the network side is contained in the information field of a UI frame and is transmitted in Unacknowledged mode.

In order to utilize this connection in an efficient manner the layer 3 entities must adapt the size of a layer 3 message to the structure of the LAPD frame. This requires the ability to multiplex several layer 3 D-channel messages pertaining to multiple connections onto a single data link connection and the capability to segment and reassemble the messages when their length exceeds the LAPD frame size limit. In addition, the entities must control the sequence in which the segments are transmitted and received.

The CCE-3, USE-3, and UTE-3 also need to be able to detect any procedural errors in the operation of the protocol or other anomalies and institute orderly recovery procedures.

Finally, the entities must be able to avoid network congestion by exercising control over the number of simultaneous connections allowed to exist and the amount of user-to-user signaling information or user information that may be conveyed across the UNI.

All of these tasks are accomplished by the two-way logical exchange of sequences of layer 3 protocol messages over the D channel across the S or T reference point. This exchange is governed by the layer 3 D-channel protocol that determines which messages may or must be transmitted, given the state of the connection. The transmissions are supervised by a set of timers that specify the maximum amount of time allowed for a response to a transmission.

6.1.3   *Functional Protocol and Stimulus Protocol*

As far as the implementation of the layer 3 D-channel protocol is concerned, it is necessary to consider two ways in which the interaction between the user and network is structured.

In the so-called *functional protocol implementation* the user and network sides cooperate as equal partners. The layer 3 entities on each side are able to interpret any received protocol messages, construct appropriate messages in response, and transmit these to the network in the proper order. The entities are also able to map layer 4 service primitives into layer 3 protocol messages and vice versa. If a layer 3 entity interacts directly with an applications process rather than with its layer 4 entity, it provides a conversion function between the signals generated and received by the applications process across the human-machine interface and the corresponding protocol messages exchanged between the user entities and network entities. It also translates the procedures governing the relationship between the applications processes in the user and network equipments into corresponding procedures between the layer 3 user entities and network entities.

This approach requires a substantial level of intelligence in both the user and network equipments that contain the functional groups TE, NT2, and ET. If it exists, it can be utilized to create a protocol structure that is configurable to almost any requirements and is essentially limitless in its capability. Also, the applications process in the user equipment may employ almost any procedure in interacting with the network, whether it exists above layer 3 or layer 7. Whatever signals are exchanged across the human-machine interface and whatever procedure is followed by the applications process can be mapped by the TE into the equivalent service primitives, functional protocol messages, and procedures, making the protocol independent of the structure of the human-machine interface. As a result, the many different dial-up procedures, physical signals, and displays employed in today's telecommunications terminals may be mapped into a single standard protocol structure governing the exchange of information between the layer 3 entities across the UNI. The inverse approach of using the same dial-up procedure, physical signaling, and display over the human-machine interface to control different ISDN services can also be accommodated. It requires only a change in the local adaption process between the applications process and the layer at which it interfaces with the TE functional group.

Although the required level of intelligence to operate a functional protocol is likely to be present in such network equipment as a PBX or local exchange, for certain types of user devices it may not be justifiable. One important example is an individual ISDN telephone. For practical reasons the function of such an instrument must be restricted to generating and recognizing a small number of tones on the part of its connection control process (CCP). Thus it is unlikely to contain any capability above layer 3. In addition, the protocol between the layer 3 entities in the user and network functional groups must be limited in its procedural complexity and in the number and logical complexity of the protocol messages that are exchanged between them.

For this type of user terminal the so-called *stimulus protocol* suggests itself. In this approach the major responsibility for controlling the relationship between user and network rests with the network. A layer 3 entity in the TE functional group interacts with its applications process solely for the purpose of conveying signals that occur at its human-machine interface directly to the network, without interpreting these signals or mapping them into corresponding protocol messages and procedures. Thus it only performs a simple relay function for the signals generated and received by the end-user. The layer 3 entity in the network functional group in turn interprets these signals or stimuli in accordance with the requirements of the protocol between itself and the applications process. It also responds with appropriate signals that are conveyed by the layer 3 entity in the TE functional group to the applications process across the human-machine interface. These are directly interpretable by the applications process. The signals themselves are carried between the user entities and network entities by means of a small number of information elements and protocol messages whose logical complexity is low enough that they can be generated and interpreted by the limited capability of the layer 3 entity in the TE.

Aside from the lower level of end-user equipment complexity, the advantage of the stimulus protocol lies in the fact that changes and enhancements in the protocol can be entirely implemented in the network and do not require any modifications on the part of the end-user equipment. Furthermore, specific procedures implemented in the applications process on the user side can be adapted to multiple purposes by changes in how the network interprets and responds to the received stimuli. But these advantages entail a trade-off. They occur at the expense of greater information storage and processing requirements in the network equipment, due to the need to accommodate many different types of user equipment, their associated signaling characteristics, and service-specific procedures.

Clearly, the essential difference between the functional and stimulus protocols lies in the migration of the intelligence from the user equipment to the network in the latter case. The choice between one or the other is therefore one of centralized versus distributed intelligence.

6.2 Protocol Messages

Let us now specify the structural and functional properties of the protocol messages by means of which the layer 3 control information flows, user-to-user signaling information flows, and user information

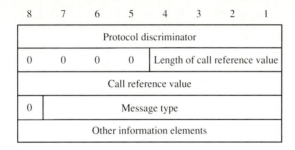

Figure 6.2 *General structure of D-channel protocol messages*
© Reprinted from CCITT Blue Book, vol. VI.11, 1988.

flows are conveyed across the S or T reference point. As we mentioned earlier, these messages are carried in the information field of a LAPD data link layer I frame or UI frame. They are exchanged over the UNI between layer 3 entities in the TE and NT2, TE and ET, or NT2 and ET functional groups over the D channel on either end of the connection.

6.2.1 General Message Structure

All messages exchanged between the peer layer 3 entities communicating over the D channel conform to the format shown in Figure 6.2. Generally, a message consists of an ordered set of three or more so-called *information elements (IE)*, of which the first three are contained in all messages. All IEs consist of an integral number of octets, which follow in increasing order the control field of the data link layer frame.

The first IE is a one-octet protocol discriminator, whose purpose is to identify the specific protocol in which the messages are interpreted. In the present case of a D-channel protocol used for connection control and user-to-user signaling, the protocol discriminator is set to 0 0 0 0 1 0 0 0.

The second IE, whose format is shown in Figure 6.3, specifies the length and value of a call reference that identifies the particular layer 3 signaling connection to which the message pertains. This IE therefore allows various signaling activities for the control of multiple circuit switched and packet switched connections and supplementary services to be carried out simultaneously over the same UNI. A call reference identifies the connection at the local UNI only, but has no end-to-end significance. A connection is therefore identified by two independent call references valid at the near-end and far-end UNIs.

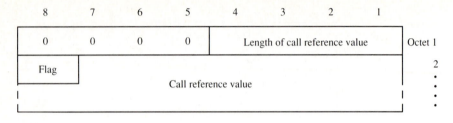

Figure 6.3 *Structure of call reference information element*
© Reprinted from CCITT Blue Book, vol. VI.11, 1988.

For a given UNI they are assigned by the side originating the message exchange at the time a signaling connection is initiated and remain valid until the connection is released. In addition, the call reference for a given connection must be unique within a particular D-channel logical link layer connection that is simultaneously supporting protocol message transfer for more than one layer 3 connection or activity.

Digits 1 through 4 of the first octet specify in binary coded decimal form the number of octets used for the call reference value. The latter may occupy any number of octets up to 15, with a minimum value of 1 for basic access and 2 for primary access. It may also be absent, in which case the first four digits of the first octet are set to 0. The flag contained in the first octet of the call reference value is set to zero by the originating side and to 1 by the destination side of the signaling connection.

The global call reference consists of two octets, the length octet 0 0 0 0 0 0 0 1 and the value octet 0 0 0 0 0 0 0 0. Messages containing this value pertain to all layer 3 signaling connections associated with the given logical link layer connection.

The message type IE identifies the particular function carried out by the message. It consists of a single octet in which digit 8 is set to 0 and reserved for possible future use as a code extension digit.

The set of messages defined for the layer 3 D-channel protocol is divided into four groups of messages for call establishment, call clearing, messages used during the information phase of the connection, and a set of miscellaneous messages. Table 6.1 lists all currently identified messages and their message type code. All messages must contain the protocol discriminator, call reference, and message-type IEs, and so they are at least three octets long.

Of the remaining information elements contained in a message, some are mandatory and some are optional, depending on the specific

TABLE 6.1   Message types for the D-channel protocol

MESSAGE TYPE	BINARY CODE							
	8	7	6	5	4	3	2	1
Call Establishment Messages								
ALERTING	0	0	0	0	0	0	0	1
CALL PROCEEDING	0	0	0	0	0	0	1	0
PROGRESS	0	0	0	0	0	0	1	1
SETUP	0	0	0	0	0	1	0	1
CONNECT	0	0	0	0	0	1	1	1
SETUP ACKNOWLEDGE	0	0	0	0	1	1	0	1
CONNECT ACKNOWLEDGE	0	0	0	0	1	1	1	1
Call Information Phase Messages								
USER INFORMATION	0	0	1	0	0	0	0	0
SUSPEND REJECT	0	0	1	0	0	0	0	1
RESUME REJECT	0	0	1	0	0	0	1	0
HOLD	0	0	1	0	0	1	0	0
SUSPEND	0	0	1	0	0	1	0	1
RESUME	0	0	1	0	0	1	1	0
HOLD ACKNOWLEDGE	0	0	1	0	1	0	0	0
SUSPEND ACKNOWLEDGE	0	0	1	0	1	1	0	1
RESUME ACKNOWLEDGE	0	0	1	0	1	1	1	0
HOLD REJECT	0	0	1	1	0	0	0	0
RETRIEVE	0	0	1	1	0	0	0	1
RETRIEVE ACKNOWLEDGE	0	0	1	1	0	0	1	1
RETRIEVE REJECT	0	0	1	1	0	1	1	1
Call Clearing Messages								
DISCONNECT	0	1	0	0	0	1	0	1
RESTART	0	1	0	0	0	1	1	0
RELEASE	0	1	0	0	1	1	0	1
RESTART ACKNOWLEDGE	0	1	0	0	1	1	1	0
RELEASE COMPLETE	0	1	0	1	1	0	1	0
Miscellaneous Messages								
SEGMENT	0	1	1	0	0	0	0	0
FACILITY	0	1	1	0	0	0	1	0
REGISTER	0	1	1	0	0	1	0	0
NOTIFY	0	1	1	0	1	1	1	0
STATUS ENQUIRY	0	1	1	1	0	1	0	1
CONGESTION CONTROL	0	1	1	1	1	0	0	1
INFORMATION	0	1	1	1	1	0	1	1
STATUS	0	1	1	1	1	1	0	1

message and its use. Their general characteristics and applications are discussed next.

6.2.2 Additional Information Elements

Two categories of additional IEs, the single-octet IE and the variable-length IE, are defined. Two types of single-octet IEs are also defined. Their formats are shown in Figure 6.4. Each IE contains an identifier that distinguishes it from all others. These identifiers, and the names of the corresponding IEs, are given in Table 6.2(a) and (b) for all currently defined single-octet and variable-length IEs, respectively.

A message may contain multiple IEs, but only specific IEs may be present in a particular message. Single-octet IEs may appear anywhere in a message after the message-type IE. The variable-length IEs on the other hand must appear in the ascending numerical order de-

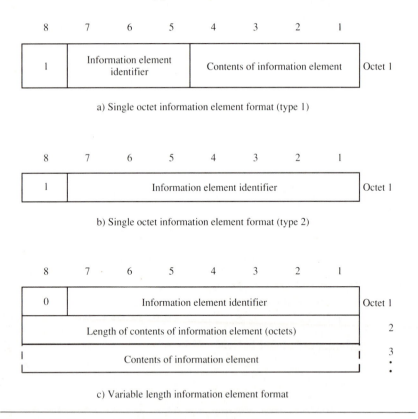

a) Single octet information element format (type 1)

b) Single octet information element format (type 2)

c) Variable length information element format

Figure 6.4 *Formats of additional information elements*
© Reprinted from CCITT Blue Book, vol. VI.11, 1988.

fined by their identifiers when the latter are interpreted as the binary coded decimal representation of an integer. This convention permits a receiving entity to determine the presence or absence of a particular IE without the need to search the entire message.

To delimit one IE in a message from the next, the variable-length IEs contain an octet that determines in binary coded decimal the number of octets used to represent the contents of the element. The remaining octets of an IE specify its contents, which consists largely of information relating to the characteristics of a connection.

The following discussion is limited to an outline of the major aspects of the contents field, since a complete treatment is somewhat beyond the scope of this text. For a precise specification of the formats and codes of all IEs listed in Table 6.2, see Recommendation I.451 of the CCITT. The subset of IEs relevant to the primary-access interface specification of AT&T is given in AT&T Publication 41449.

The *Shift IE* provides the capability of specifying one of eight codesets in which the IEs contained in a message are to be interpreted. It is therefore possible to extend the number of available IEs beyond the limit imposed by the number of digits assigned to the identifier field to meet future requirements. At the beginning of every message, the active codeset is always codeset 0. A new active codeset may be specified by including either the locking or the nonlocking version of the Shift IE. In the first case the new codeset applies until it is changed by another Shift IE or until the end of the message. In the second case it is valid for the next IE only, after which codeset 0 again becomes the active codeset. Digit 4 in the Shift IE is set to 0 for the Locking Shift IE and to 1 for the Nonlocking Shift IE.

TABLE 6.2a Single-octet information elements

INFORMATION ELEMENT	BINARY CODE							
	8	7	6	5	4	3	2	1
SHIFT	1	0	0	1	–	–	–	–
MORE DATA	1	0	1	0	0	0	0	0
SENDING COMPLETE	1	0	1	0	0	0	0	1
CONGESTION LEVEL	1	0	1	1	–	–	–	–
REPEAT INDICATOR	1	1	0	1	–	–	–	–

TABLE 6.2b   Variable-length information elements

INFORMATION ELEMENT	BINARY CODE							
	8	7	6	5	4	3	2	1
SEGMENTED MESSAGE	0	0	0	0	0	0	0	0
BEARER CAPABILITY	0	0	0	0	0	1	0	0
CAUSE	0	0	0	0	1	0	0	0
CALL IDENTITY	0	0	0	1	0	0	0	0
CALL STATE	0	0	0	1	0	1	0	0
CHANNEL IDENTIFICATION	0	0	0	1	1	0	0	0
FACILITY	0	0	0	1	1	1	0	0
PROGRESS INDICATOR	0	0	0	1	1	1	1	0
NETWORK SPECIFIC FACILITIES	0	0	1	0	0	0	0	0
NOTIFICATION INDICATOR	0	0	1	0	0	1	1	1
DISPLAY	0	0	1	0	1	0	0	0
DATE/TIME	0	0	1	0	1	0	0	1
KEYPAD FACILITY	0	0	1	0	1	1	0	0
INFORMATION REQUEST	0	0	1	1	0	0	1	0
SIGNAL	0	0	1	1	0	1	0	0
SWITCHHOOK	0	0	1	1	0	1	1	0
FEATURE ACTIVATION	0	0	1	1	1	0	0	0
FEATURE INDICATION	0	0	1	1	1	0	0	1
SERVICE PROFILE IDENTIFICATION	0	0	1	1	1	0	1	0
ENDPOINT IDENTIFIER	0	0	1	1	1	0	1	1
INFORMATION RATE	0	1	0	0	0	0	0	0
END-TO-END TRANSIT DELAY	0	1	0	0	0	0	1	0
TRANSIT DELAY SELECTION AND INDICATION	0	1	0	0	0	0	1	1
PACKET LAYER BINARY PARAMETERS	0	1	0	0	0	1	0	0
PACKET LAYER WINDOW SIZE	0	1	0	0	0	1	0	1
PACKET SIZE	0	1	0	0	0	1	1	0
MINIMUM THROUGHPUT CLASS	0	1	0	0	0	1	1	1
CALLING PARTY NUMBER	0	1	1	0	1	1	0	0
CALLING PARTY SUBADDRESS	0	1	1	0	1	1	0	1
CALLED PARTY NUMBER	0	1	1	1	0	0	0	0

TABLE 6.2b (*Cont.*)

	BINARY CODE							
INFORMATION ELEMENT	8	7	6	5	4	3	2	1
CALLED PARTY SUBADDRESS	0	1	1	1	0	0	0	1
REDIRECTING NUMBER	0	1	1	1	0	1	0	0
TRANSIT NETWORK SELECTION	0	1	1	1	1	0	0	0
RESTART INDICATOR	0	1	1	1	1	0	0	0
LOW-LAYER COMPATIBILITY	0	1	1	1	1	1	0	0
HIGH-LAYER COMPATIBILITY	0	1	1	1	1	1	0	1
USER-USER	0	1	1	1	1	1	1	0
ESCAPE FOR EXTENSION	0	1	1	1	1	1	1	1

The *More Data IE* notifies the end-user on the other side of a connection that additional messages containing end-user information are to be transmitted. It is therefore an IE that has end-to-end significance.

The *Sending Complete IE* is used in certain situations to indicate that the transfer of the called party identification is complete. The *Congestion-Level IE* is used to describe the degree of congestion experienced on a connection. The 4 digits provided allow the specification of one of 16 levels of congestion, two of which are the receiver ready condition and the receiver not ready condition.

The *Repeat Indicator IE* defines how IEs that are repeated within a message are to be interpreted, which of these IEs is to be considered, or the order in which they are to be considered.

The variable-length IEs, shown in Table 6.2(b), are divided into several specific categories.

Three elements are provided for the purpose of specifying the nature of the user connection and the network over which it is to be established. The *Bearer Capability IE* is used to indicate to the network side the major service characteristics of a desired connection for the transfer of user information flows between TEs. It includes information on whether the connection is permanent or established on demand, circuit switched or packet switched, point-to-point or multipoint, and unidirectional or bidirectional. It also defines the information transfer rate over the connection, the type, structure, and rate of the information conveyed over the connection, and the user information transfer protocols at layers 1, 2, and 3. This IE may be repeated in a message to identify more than one service characteristic over multiple connections or networks. Facilities that are available on a specific network may be invoked by the *Network Specific Facilities IE*. The latter includes information identifying the type of network, the network itself, and the selected facility. The *Transit Network Selection IE* allows the user to request a specific transit network over which the connection is to be established. Sequences of transit networks may be specified by repeated use of this IE in the same message.

Two variable-length IEs provide for the identification of a connection and the interface configuration over which the call exists. The *Call Identity IE* allows a user to identify a suspended call. Its value is assigned at the beginning of the call suspension and consists of a single octet whose composition is arbitrary. It could, for example, represent the call by a name coded in the *International Alphabet No. 5 (IA5)*. The call identity numbers of suspended calls are maintained by the network as unique values and are referenced by the user to request the resumption of a suspended call. The *Channel Identification IE* is used to specify the type of interface that exists between the user and network and the particular B, D, or H channel within that interface that is controlled by the signaling protocol. It includes fields for indicating a basic-access, primary-access, or broadband-access interface and for selecting a specific channel on a preferred or exclusive basis.

Two variable-length information elements are used to signal the status of a call. The *Cause IE* makes it possible to convey diagnostic information about procedural problems that may arise in the operation of the layer 3 protocol, the inability to provide requested services, and the location of the network originating the IE. Cause IEs are divided into eight classes, denoted Normal Event (Class 0), Normal Event (Class 1), Resource Unavailable (Class 2), Service or Option Not Available (Class 3), Service or Option Not Implemented (Class 4), Invalid Message (Class 5), Protocol Error (Class 6), and Interworking (Class 7). These correspond to the general nature of the event generating the IE. Within each class a number of specific cause values have been defined which, together with additional diagnostic information, describe the detailed nature of the event. Table 6.3 contains the current list of these values, divided into the eight classes just defined. The Cause IE may be repeated in a message to report multiple errors associated with a given connection. The *Call State IE* describes the current state of a connection on the network and user sides. Its value is contained in a single octet. As shown in Table 6.4, on the user side the connection may be in any one of 16 states labeled U0 to U25, whereas from the network's point of view there are 17 states labeled N0 to N25.

Seven IEs are provided for specifying the parameters of a packet switched connection operated in virtual circuit mode. The parameters themselves, as well as the set of their values, are derived from the packet level part of CCITT Recommendation X.25. The *Information Rate IE* is used to define the throughput rate of a virtual circuit and allows the specification of average and minimum rates, independently in the two directions of transmission. The *End-to-End Transit Delay IE* provides the facility to request a specific value of the end-to-end delay incurred over a virtual circuit, as well as to specify its maximum permissible value. The nominal and maximum permissible transit delay over a virtual circuit may be requested and indicated by means of the *Transit Delay Selection and Indication IE*. The *Packet Layer Binary Parameters IE* is used to request a set of optional features on the virtual circuit. Among these are the Fast Select, Expedited Data, Delivery Confirmation, and Modulo 8 or 128 Sequence Numbering options provided by the X.25 packet-level protocol. The *Packet Layer Window Size IE* is used to request a particular value of the flow control window that will be in effect on the virtual circuit. Values in the forward and reverse direction may be selected independently. In similar manner the *Packet Size IE* conveys the requested size of the packet in octets. The *Minimum Throughput Class IE* specifies a lower bound on the packet-level throughput class required on a virtual circuit, independently in the two directions.

Three variable-length IEs provide indications of certain events related to a call. The *Notification Indicator IE* is used to convey information regarding the suspension or resumption of a call by the user and a change of bearer service. The *Progress Indicator IE* describes an event that occurred during the life of a call. It includes information describing the location where the event occurred and the nature of the event. The *Restart Indicator IE* is used to indicate the facility involved in a restart of a call and identifies the specific component channel or channel structure.

Five variable-length IEs convey addressing information between the user and network sides. Their formats are shown in Figures 6.5 to 6.7. The *Calling Party Number* and *Called Party Number IEs* identify the origination endpoint and intended destination endpoint of a

TABLE 6.3 Cause values for cause information element

CAUSE	CLASS			VALUE			
	7	6	5	4	3	2	1
Unallocated (unassigned) number	0	0	0	0	0	0	1
No route to specified transit network	0	0	0	0	0	1	0
No route to destination	0	0	0	0	0	1	1
Channel unacceptable	0	0	0	0	1	1	0
Call awarded and being delivered in an established channel	0	0	0	0	1	1	1
Normal call clearing	0	0	1	0	0	0	0
User busy	0	0	1	0	0	0	1
No user responding	0	0	1	0	0	1	0
No answer from user (user alerted)	0	0	1	0	0	1	1
Call rejected	0	0	1	0	1	0	1
Number changed	0	0	1	0	1	1	0
Nonselected user clearing	0	0	1	1	0	1	0
Destination out of order	0	0	1	1	0	1	1
Invalid number format	0	0	1	1	1	0	0
Facility rejected	0	0	1	1	1	0	1
Response to STATUS ENQUIRY	0	0	1	1	1	1	0
Normal, unspecified	0	0	1	1	1	1	1
No circuit/channel available	0	1	0	0	0	1	0
Network out of order	0	1	0	0	1	1	0
Temporary failure	0	1	0	1	0	0	1
Switching equipment congestion	0	1	0	1	0	1	0
Access information discarded	0	1	0	1	0	1	1
Requested circuit/channel not available	0	1	0	1	1	0	0
Resources unavailable, unspecified	0	1	0	1	1	1	1
Quality of service unavailable	0	1	1	0	0	0	1
Requested facility not subscribed	0	1	1	0	0	1	0
Bearer capability not authorized	0	1	1	1	0	0	1
Bearer capability not presently available	0	1	1	1	0	1	0
Service or option not available, unspecified	0	1	1	1	1	1	1

TABLE 6.3 (*Cont.*)

CAUSE	BINARY CODE						
	CLASS			VALUE			
	7	6	5	4	3	2	1
Bearer capability not implemented	1	0	0	0	0	0	1
Channel type not implemented	1	0	0	0	0	1	0
Requested facility not implemented	1	0	0	0	1	0	1
Only restricted digital information bearer capability is available	1	0	0	0	1	1	0
Service or option not implemented, unspecified	1	0	0	1	1	1	1
Invalid call reference value	1	0	1	0	0	0	1
Identified channel does not exist	1	0	1	0	0	1	0
A suspended call exists, but this call identity does not	1	0	1	0	0	1	1
Call identity in use	1	0	1	0	1	0	0
No call suspended	1	0	1	0	1	0	1
Call having the requested call identity has been cleared	1	0	1	0	1	1	0
Incompatible destination	1	0	1	1	0	0	0
Invalid transit network selection	1	0	1	1	0	1	1
Invalid message, unspecified	1	0	1	1	1	1	1
Mandatory information element is missing	1	1	0	0	0	0	0
Message type nonexistent or not implemented	1	1	0	0	0	0	1
Message not compatible with call state or message type nonexistent or not implemented	1	1	0	0	0	1	0
Information element nonexistent or not implemented	1	1	0	0	0	1	1
Invalid information element contents	1	1	0	0	1	0	0
Message not compatible with call state	1	1	0	0	1	0	1
Recovery on timer expiry	1	1	0	0	1	1	0
Protocol error, unspecified	1	1	0	1	1	1	1
Interworking, unspecified	1	1	1	1	1	1	1

TABLE 6.4   User-side and network-side call states

USER STATE	NETWORK STATE	BINARY CODE					
		6	5	4	3	2	1
U0—Null	N0—Null	0	0	0	0	0	0
U1—Call Initiated	N1—Call Initiated	0	0	0	0	0	1
U2—Overlap Sending	N2—Overlap Sending	0	0	0	0	1	0
U3—Outgoing Call Proceeding	N3—Outgoing Call Proceeding	0	0	0	0	1	1
U4—Call Delivered	N4—Call Delivered	0	0	0	1	0	0
U6—Call Present	N6—Call Present	0	0	0	1	1	0
U7—Call Received	N7—Call Received	0	0	0	1	1	1
U8—Connect Request	N8—Connect Request	0	0	1	0	0	0
U9—Incoming Call Proceeding	N9—Incoming Call Proceeding	0	0	1	0	0	1
U10—Active	N10—Active	0	0	1	0	1	0
U11—Disconnect Request	N11—Disconnect Request	0	0	1	0	1	1
U12—Disconnect Indication	N12—Disconnect Indication	0	0	1	1	0	0
U15—Suspend Request	N15—Suspend Request	0	0	1	1	1	1
U17—Resume Request	N17—Resume Request	0	1	0	0	0	1
U19—Release Request	N19—Release Request	0	1	0	0	1	1
———	N22—Call Abort	0	1	0	1	1	0
U25—Overlap Receiving	N25—Overlap Receiving	0	1	1	0	0	1

© Reprinted from CCITT Blue Book, vol. VI.11, 1988.

connection. The Called Party Number IE may be repeated in a message to indicate multiple destination endpoints in multipoint connections. The *Calling Party* and *Called Party Subaddress IEs* identify a subaddress in the originating and destination endpoints such as a *network-service-access point (NSAP). The Redirecting Number IE* contains the destination address from which a call redirection or transfer took place. It may be repeated in a message to identify multiple redirecting endpoints. All five address IEs contain fields to distinguish between national and international numbers, local numbers, subaddresses, and abbreviated addresses. They also contain the numbering plan used to specify the number, the actual address digits (represented by the integers from 0 to 9), and several special addressing symbols. The digits and symbols are coded in the International Alphabet No. 5.

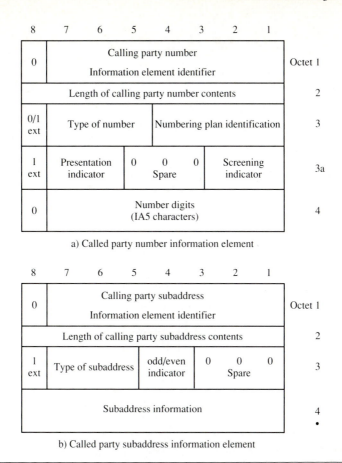

a) Called party number information element

b) Called party subaddress information element

Figure 6.5 *Calling party address formats*
© Reprinted from CCITT Blue Book, vol. VI.11, 1988.

Both the Calling Number IE and the Redirecting IE include a presentation indicator allowing the originator or redirector to control the presentation of his or her number to the receiving party. The Redirecting Number IE also contains diagnostic information on the reason for the redirection.

Three IEs convey information between end-users as part of a user-to-user signaling connection. They are passed transparently by the network. The *Low-Layer Compatibility IE* and *High-Layer Compatibility IE* provide the remote user with the ability to check its compatibility with the sender of the IE. They contain data describing the nature of the connection being established in terms of the transmission

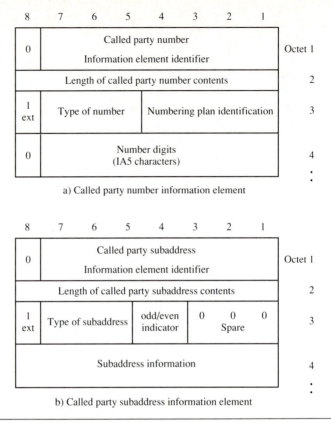

a) Called party number information element

b) Called party subaddress information element

Figure 6.6 *Called party address formats*
© Reprinted from CCITT Blue Book, vol. VI.11, 1988.

parameters, the protocol structure at layers 1 to 3, and the characteristics of the teleservices at layers 4 to 7. Any other information intended for the end-user is carried in the *User-User IE*. Its content is not restricted in any way.

Four variable-length IEs are provided for the exchange of end-user related information between the user and the network in connection with various stimulus protocols. The purpose of the *Display IE* is to provide a means for the network to convey information to the user that is to be visually displayed by the end-user device. This information is normally coded in the International Alphabet No. 5. Information from the keypad of an end-user device may be transferred across the UNI via the *Keypad Facility IE*. The information is again coded

8	7	6	5	4	3	2	1	
0	Redirecting number Information element identifier							Octet 1
Length of redirecting number contents								2
0/1 ext	Type of number		Numbering plan identification					3
0/1 ext	Presentation indicator		0	0 Spare	0	Screening indicator		3a*
1 ext	0	0 Spare	0	Reason for redirection				3b*
0 spare	Number digits (IA5 characters)							4 • •

Figure 6.7 *Redirecting address format*
© Reprinted from CCITT Blue Book, vol. VI.11, 1988.

in IA5 characters. The *Signal IE* is sent by the network to a user to cause the end-user device to generate certain tones and alerting signals related to an incoming call or the status of a call. Table 6.5 contains a list of such signals and their binary representation. Among other uses, the different alerting tone patterns serve to differentiate between on-premises or off-premises calls. The *Switchhook IE* is employed by the user side to indicate the on-hook or off-hook status of the end-user device to the network.

Six IEs have been defined specifically for use in the control of supplementary services. The *Facility IE* serves to indicate and invoke a particular supplementary service. The *Information Request IE* is used by the network to request additional information required to carry out certain actions, to indicate the type of information requested, and to notify the user that the requested information has been received. The *Feature Activation IE* allows the user to invoke a particular supplementary service by reference to a feature identifier number. On the network side the *Feature Indication IE* is used to indicate to the user the status of the supplementary service specified by the feature identifier number. The *Service Profile Identification IE* allows a user to request the assignment of two identifiers labeled user service ID and terminal ID. These identifiers are necessary in situations

TABLE 6.5   Tones and alerting signals

SIGNALS	BINARY CODE							
	8	7	6	5	4	3	2	1
Dial tone on	0	0	0	0	0	0	0	0
Ring back tone on	0	0	0	0	0	0	0	1
Intercept tone on	0	0	0	0	0	0	1	0
Network congestion tone on	0	0	0	0	0	0	1	1
Busy tone on	0	0	0	0	0	1	0	0
Confirm tone on	0	0	0	0	0	1	0	1
Answer tone on	0	0	0	0	0	1	1	0
Call waiting tone on	0	0	0	0	0	1	1	1
Off-hook warning tone on	0	0	0	0	1	0	0	0
Tones off	0	0	1	1	1	1	1	1
Alerting on—pattern 0	0	1	0	0	0	0	0	0
Alerting on—pattern 1	0	1	0	0	0	0	0	1
Alerting on—pattern 2	0	1	0	0	0	0	1	0
Alerting on—pattern 3	0	1	0	0	0	0	1	1
Alerting on—pattern 4	0	1	0	0	0	1	0	0
Alerting on—pattern 5	0	1	0	0	0	1	0	1
Alerting on—pattern 6	0	1	0	0	0	1	1	0
Alerting on—pattern 7	0	1	0	0	0	1	1	1
Alerting off	0	1	0	0	1	1	1	1

© Reprinted from CCITT Blue Book, vol. VI.11, 1988.

where the user and network support multiple service profiles and multipoint connections. Two or more users conforming to the same service profile may then be distinguished by the terminal ID, whereas the service profile itself is specified by the user service ID. The assignment of the two identifiers is carried out by the network by transferring to the user the *Endpoint Identifier IE*.

Several miscellaneous IEs have also been defined. The *Segmented Message IE* indicates that the protocol message in which it appears is part of a sequence of such messages that are segments of a longer message. The *Date/Time IE* allows the network to indicate to the user the date and time the network generated the message containing it. The *Escape for Extension IE* is intended for the definition of additional information elements for future use.

6.2.3 Message Functional Definitions

As shown in Table 6.1, the protocol messages that are exchanged between peer layer 3 entities over the layer 3 D-channel protocol are divided into four groups.

- Messages for the establishment of layer 3 circuit switched or packet switched connections between users
- Messages exchanged during the information transfer phase of a connection to convey user information flows or user-to-user signaling information flows, to suspend a connection or resume its use, and to provide supplementary services
- Messages for the clearing of layer 3 circuit switched or packet switched connections between users
- Miscellaneous messages used to indicate the status of a connection, to effect flow control, to invoke or cancel the use of supplementary services, and to convey additional information between the users and the network

A given message is not necessarily involved in all types of interactions across the UNI. Table 6.6 indicates the applicability of each message in circuit or packet switched connection control, the transfer of user-to-user signaling information flows, and the provision of supplementary services. The messages used for the transfer of user information flows have not been specified.

As we noted earlier, across the UNI the messages are exchanged between functional groups on the user and network sides of the S or T reference points on both the calling and called sides of the connection. Depending on the specific message and the information elements contained in it, they may be sent by the user side, the network side, or both.

The following paragraphs provide a summary description of the function of each message in Table 6.1. Again, a complete discussion is beyond the scope of this text; the reader should consult the appropriate documents of the CCITT and AT&T. The actual use of the messages in specific situations is discussed in later sections of this chapter.

Let us first consider the messages used for call establishment. A

TABLE 6.6   Correspondence of message types and D-channel protocol functions

D-CHANNEL PROTOCOL MESSAGES	CIRCUIT SWITCHED	PACKET SWITCHED	USER-USER CONNEC-TIONS	SUPPLE-MENTARY SERVICES
ALERTING	X	X	X	X
CALL PROCEEDING	X	X	X	X
PROGRESS	X	X		
SETUP	X	X	X	X
CONNECT	X	X	X	X
SETUP ACK	X		X	X
CONNECT ACK	X	X	X	
USER INFO	X		X	
SUSPEND REJECT	X			
RESUME REJECT	X			
HOLD				X
SUSPEND	X			
RESUME	X			
HOLD ACK				X
SUSPEND ACK	X			
RESUME ACK	X			
HOLD REJECT				X
RETRIEVE				X
RETRIEVE ACK				X
RETRIEVE REJECT				X
DISCONNECT	X	X		X
RESTART	X			
RELEASE	X	X	X	X
RESTART ACK	X			
RELEASE COMPLETE	X	X	X	X
SEGMENT				
FACILITY				X
REGISTER				X
NOTIFY	X			
STATUS ENQUIRY	X	X	X	
CONGESTION CONTROL	X		X	
INFORMATION	X		X	X
STATUS	X	X	X	

user initiates the establishment of a connection by sending the SETUP message. This message always contains a call reference number as an identifier for the connection and usually includes additional information elements specifying the network on which the connection is to be established, the calling and called party network addresses, and details on the type of connection desired.

The SETUP message is also sent by the network on the destination side to indicate an incoming call and includes all information elements provided by the originator.

In the case where the SETUP message transmitted by the originating user does not contain all the information required to establish the call, the network on the originating side and the user on the destination side respond with a SETUP ACKNOWLEDGE message requesting additional detail relating to the characteristics of the call. This information is supplied by the originating user side in one or more INFORMATION messages from the category of miscellaneous messages to its network side, which in turn may relay these messages to the destination user as INFORMATION messages.

When all required call establishment information has been received, the network on the originating side sends a CALL PROCEEDING message ending the dial-up phase of connection establishment. A similar message may be sent by the destination user to its network side.

The ALERTING message is sent by the destination user to indicate its general ability to accept the call and is relayed by the network to the originating user side. If several users are prepared to accept the call, each of them transmits the ALERTING message.

The actual call acceptance by the destination user is signaled by sending the CONNECT message, which is also relayed to the calling user. The latter may confirm the connection to the network by transmitting a CONNECT ACKNOWLEDGE message. A similar message is sent by the network on the called side to the destination user to complete the call establishment procedure. At any time during the call establishment phase the user or the network may transmit the PROGRESS message to report on certain events relevant to the connection.

The clearing of an established call may be initiated by either of the two users or the network by sending the DISCONNECT message. The normal response from the side receiving this message is the RELEASE message, which in turn prompts the sending of the RELEASE COMPLETE message.

In certain situations the user or network may return a connection to a predefined state in response to the occurrence of a fault. In such a case a RESTART message is sent, to which the receiver responds with a RESTART ACKNOWLEDGE message.

In the category of call information phase messages, six messages provide the capability to temporarily suspend a connection and resume its use at a later time. The suspend procedure is initiated by the user side by sending a SUSPEND message containing the call reference and optionally a number identifying the suspended call to its network side. The latter responds with either the SUSPEND ACKNOWLEDGE message, or a SUSPEND REJECT message if the information supplied in the SUSPEND message is insufficient for a subsequent call reestablishment.

The call may be reestablished by the user side by sending the RESUME message containing the call identification number supplied with the SUSPEND message. When it receives this message the network side will either reestablish the suspended call and send a RESUME ACKNOWLEDGE message to the user or it will indicate its inability to reestablish the call by sending the RESUME REJECT message.

User-to-user signaling information flows are transferred between a pair of users by sending the USER INFORMATION message between the user and network sides.

The remaining six call information phase messages are used in the provision of supplementary services. The HOLD message may be sent by the user or the network to request that an existing call be put in a temporary hold condition. Information regarding the call identity, as well as certain resources assigned to the call, are maintained by the network while the call is in this state. The response to this message is either the HOLD ACKNOWLEDGE message if the request can be carried out, or the HOLD REJECT message if the request for a hold is denied. In the latter case the message contains a Cause IE indicating the reason for the rejection.

A call previously placed in the hold state may be retrieved by sending the RETRIEVE message. A successful retrieve request is acknowledged by the RETRIEVE ACKNOWLEDGE message, whereas the RETRIEVE REJECT message with an appropriate Cause IE indicates the inability to retrieve the call.

In the group of miscellaneous messages, the CONGESTION CONTROL message may be sent by the user or network to indicate the initiation or termination of flow control procedures governing the transmission of USER INFORMATION messages on the connection.

The INFORMATION message conveys additional information regarding the state of the connection between user and network.

The NOTIFY message is sent by the user or network side to convey information pertinent to a call. One example of its use is in the notification of a user that a call has been suspended by the other user.

The STATUS message allows the user and network to report the condition of the connection or to respond to an unexpected message. To solicit a status message both the user and network may transmit a STATUS ENQUIRY message, to which the receiver must respond with a STATUS message.

The FACILITY message is used to request or acknowledge a supplementary service that is related to an existing call. It contains IEs specifying the particular service and its parameters and allows the invocation of supplementary services independently from the normal call control procedures.

Supplementary services not associated with an existing call are invoked and acknowledged by sending the REGISTER message.

The purpose of the SEGMENT message is to carry information that has been segmented across the UNI.

6.3 Functional Protocol Procedures for Circuit Switched Connections

With the definition of the protocol messages and information elements given in the previous section, we are now ready to specify the procedural aspects of the layer 3 D-channel protocol. We begin by discussing the functional protocol for the establishment, operation, and termination of circuit switched connections involving a B channel or H channel. Again, we restrict ourselves to a survey of the most important aspects of the subject. The reader should consult the CCITT Recommendations I.450 and I.451 for a more precise and complete exposition.

6.3.1 Protocol Messages and Protocol States

To carry out its functions of call establishment, call clearing, and call operation, the functional protocol for circuit switched connections utilizes the specific subset of the protocol messages shown in Table 6.6. The RESUME and SUSPEND messages flow only in the direction of the network, whereas the RESUME ACKNOWLEDGE and

TABLE 6.7 Call establishment messages for circuit switched connections

IE	SETUP	SETUP ACK	CALL PROC	ALERTING	CONNECT	CONNECT ACK	PROGRESS
MESSAGE → TYPE AND DIRECTION							
SENDING COMPLETE	O,B						
BEARER CAPABILITY	M,B						
CAUSE							O,B
CHANNEL ID	M,B	O,B	O,B	O,B	O,B	O,U	
FACILITY				O,B	O,B		
PROGRESS INDICATOR			O,B	O,B	O,B		M,B
NETWORK SPECIFIC FACILITIES	O,B						
DISPLAY	O,U	O,U	O,U	O,U	O,U	O,U	O,U
KEYPAD FACILITY	O,N						
SIGNAL				O,U	O,U	O,U	
CALLING PARTY NUMBER	O,B						
CALLING PARTY SUBADDRESS	O,B						
CALLED PARTY NUMBER	O,B						
CALLED PARTY SUBADDRESS	O,B						
TRANSIT NETWORK SELECTION	O,N						
LOW-LAYER COMPATIBILITY	O,B				O,B		
HIGH-LAYER COMPATIBILITY	O,B						
USER-USER	O,B				O,B	O,B	O,U

RESUME REJECT messages and the SUSPEND ACKNOWLEDGE and SUSPEND REJECT messages are only sent by the network to the user. All other messages may be transmitted in both directions across the UNI. The composition of these messages depends on the application and is shown in Tables 6.7 to 6.10, which list the manda-

TABLE 6.8   Call clearing messages for circuit switched connections

MESSAGE	DISCONNECT	RELEASE	RELEASE COM	RESTART	RESTART ACK
IE	TYPE AND DIRECTION				
CAUSE	M,B	O,B	O,B		
CALL STATE					
CHANNEL ID				O,B	O,B
FACILITY	O,B	O,B	O,B		
PROGRESS INDICATOR	O,B				
DISPLAY	O,U	O,U	O,U	O,U	O,U
SIGNAL	O,U	O,U	O,U		
RESTART INDICATOR				M,B	M,B
USER-USER	O,B	O,B	O,B		

tory (M) and optional (O) IEs that may be contained in a message and whether an IE may be contained in a message transmitted in the direction of the network (N), the user (U), or in both directions (B).

During the operation of the protocol the circuit switched connection is considered to undergo a series of state changes. These states, which are independently perceived by the user and network sides, are listed in Table 6.4. In each state the user and network sides may receive certain protocol messages and in turn may be required to carry out certain internal actions and transmit to the other side certain protocol messages. Many of these activities are under the control of timers that determine the maximum amount of time allowed for a response to a received message. Generally, the reception and/or transmission of a protocol message by one of the sides results in a change of state at that side.

TABLE 6.9 Call information phase messages for circuit switched connections

MESSAGE	R E S U M E	R E S U M E A C K	R E S U M E R E J	S U S P E N D	S U S P E N D A C K	S U S P E N D R E J	U S E R I N F O
IE				**TYPE AND DIRECTION**			
MORE DATA							O,B
CAUSE			M,U			M,U	
CALL IDENTITY	O,N			O,N			
CHANNEL ID		M,U					
DISPLAY		O,U	O,U		O,U	O,U	
USER-USER							M,B

Tables 6.11(a) and 6.11(b) contain the list of primitives that are exchanged between the layer 3 and 4 connection control entities on the user and network sides.

6.3.2 Call Establishment Procedures

Let us assume now that the user and network sides initially perceive the connection to be in the Null state U0 and N0.

The CCE-3 on the user side, in response to a SETUP Request primitive from its CCE-4, initiates call establishment by transferring across the UNI to its peer CCE-3 on the network side one or more protocol messages containing the information elements required by the network to process the call. This information may be transmitted by one of two methods, known as en-bloc and overlap signaling.

In *en-bloc signaling,* all information is contained in a single SETUP message and this fact is indicated by the presence of the Sending Complete IE. After transferring this message the connection on the user side enters the Call Initiated state U1. The network-side CCE-3, on receiving the SETUP message, provides a SETUP Indi-

TABLE 6.10   Miscellaneous messages for circuit switched connections

IE	CONGEST CON	INFORMATION	NOTIFY	STATUS	STATUS ENQ
	MESSAGE				
	TYPE AND DIRECTION				
SENDING COMPLETE		O,B			
CONGESTION LEVEL	M,B				
BEARER CAPABILITY			O,U		
CAUSE	O,B	O,U		M,B	
CALL STATE				M,B	
NOTIFICATION INDICATOR			M,B		
DISPLAY	O,U	O,U	O,U	O,U	O,U
KEYPAD FACILITY		O,N			
SIGNAL		O,U			
SWITCHHOOK		O,N			
CALLED PARTY NUMBER		O,B			

cation primitive to its CCE-4 and also places the connection into the Call Initiated state N1. If the CCE-4 judges the information to be complete and compatible with its capabilities, it issues a PROCEEDING Request primitive, which causes the CCE-3 to acknowledge the SETUP message to the user side with the CALL PROCEEDING message. This indicates that the call is being processed and that no further call establishment information will be accepted. This message also includes the identity of the component channel allocated to the call. At this point the connection on the network side enters the Outgoing Call Proceeding state N3. On the user side the receipt of the CALL PROCEEDING message results in the transfer of a PROCEEDING Indication primitive to the CCE-4 and a transition to the Outgoing Call Proceeding state U3.

TABLE 6.11a Layer 3 primitives (user side)

PRIMITIVE NAME	USER-SIDE PRIMITIVE TYPE			
	REQUEST	INDICA-TION	RESPONSE	CONFIRM
SETUP	X	X	X	X
SETUP COMPLETE		X		
MORE INFORMATION	X	X		
INFORMATION	X	X		
PROCEEDING	X	X		
ALERTING	X	X		
REJECT	X	X		
SUSPEND	X			X
SUSPEND REJECT				
RESUME	X			X
RESUME REJECT				
DISCONNECT	X	X		
RELEASE	X	X		X
RESTART	X			X
PROGRESS	X	X		
NOTIFY	X	X		
STATUS		X		
ERROR		X		
DATA LINK FAILURE		X		
MANAGEMENT RESTART	X			

The SDL diagrams of these en-bloc procedures are shown in Figures 6.8(a) and 6.9(a) for the user side and network side, respectively.

In *overlap signaling,* only partial call establishment information is transferred by the user side in the initial SETUP message. In this case the CCE-4 on the network side returns the MORE INFORMATION Request primitive, instructing the CCE-3 to obtain additional data regarding the call. The network-side CCE-3 then sends to the user side the SETUP ACKNOWLEDGE message containing the identity of the allocated component channel and enters the Overlap Sending state N2. On the user side the CCE-3, on receiving the SETUP AC-KNOWLEDGE message, indicates the requirement for additional in-

TABLE 6.11b   Layer 3 primitives (network side)

	NETWORK-SIDE PRIMITIVE TYPE			
PRIMITIVE NAME	REQUEST	INDICA-TION	RESPONSE	CONFIRM
SETUP	X	X	X	X
SETUP COMPLETE	X			
MORE INFORMATION	X	X		
INFORMATION	X	X		
PROCEEDING	X	X		
ALERTING	X	X		
REJECT	X	X		
SUSPEND		X	X	
SUSPEND REJECT	X			
RESUME		X	X	
RESUME REJECT	X			
DISCONNECT	X	X		
RELEASE	X	X		X
RESTART	X			X
PROGRESS	X	X		
NOTIFY	X	X		
STATUS		X		
ERROR		X		
DATA LINK FAILURE		X		
MANAGEMENT RESTART				

formation to its CCE-4 by means of the MORE INFORMATION Indication primitive and also enters the Overlap Sending state U2. When the CCE-4 provides additional information to its CCE-3 as part of an INFORMATION Request primitive, the latter transfers it in an INFORMATION message. On the network side this message causes an INFORMATION Indication primitive to be sent to the CCE-4. This procedure may be invoked several times if necessary to convey all the required call setup detail.

Once the network-side CCE-4 determines that it has obtained sufficient information to process the call, or it receives an indication from the user that sending is complete by means of the Sending Complete

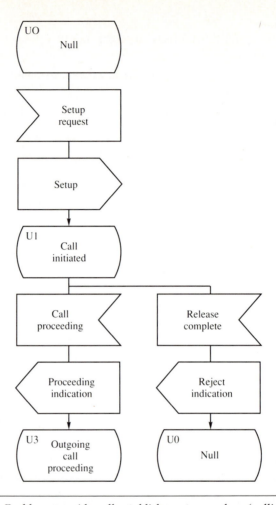

Figure 6.8a   *En-bloc user-side call establishment procedure (calling side)*
© Adapted from CCITT Blue Book, vol. VI.11, 1988.

IE contained in an INFORMATION message, the procedure reverts to the one followed in the en-bloc signaling case.

Figures 6.8(b) and 6.9(b) show the SDL diagram corresponding to the overlap procedures.

Several exception conditions may arise during the operation of this protocol. First, a specific component channel or facility requested by the user side may not be available for the call. Second, the call establishment information provided in en-bloc or overlap signaling may be insufficient. Third, the network timer that governs the maxi-

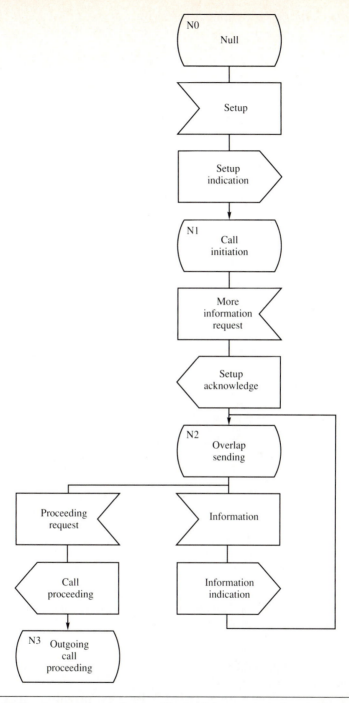

Figure 6.9b *Overlap network-side call establishment procedure (calling side)*
© Adapted from CCITT Blue Book, vol. VI.11, 1988.

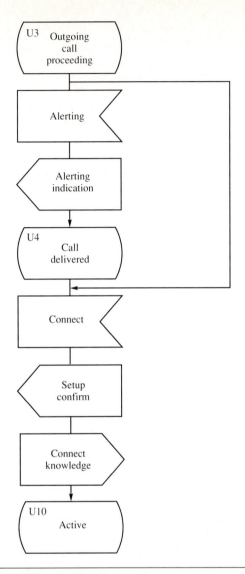

Figure 6.8c *User-side call establishment procedure (calling side)*
© Adapted from CCITT Blue Book, vol. VI.11, 1988.

mum time allowed for a response from the user side may expire. In all such cases the CCE-4 on the network side responds to the initial SETUP message with a REJECT Request primitive. Its CCE-3 then sends the RELEASE COMPLETE message containing a Cause IE that specifies the nature of the problem. The state of the connection

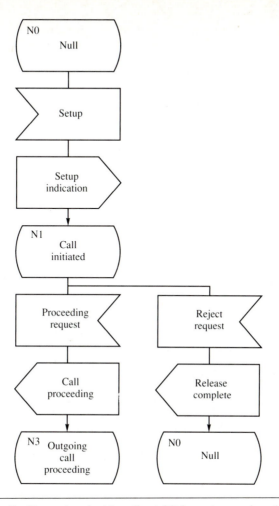

Figure 6.9a *En-bloc network-side call establishment procedure (calling side)*
© Adapted from CCITT Blue Book, vol. VI.11, 1988.

then reverts to the Null state N0. On the user side the receipt of the RELEASE COMPLETE message results in the transmission of a REJECT Indication primitive to the CCE-4 and a change to the Null state U0.

These interactions are also shown in Figures 6.8(a) and 6.9(a).

Following the transmission of the CALL PROCEEDING message, the network initiates appropriate interexchange signaling to transfer the call establishment information to the destination side. There the network-side CCE-3, on receiving a SETUP Request

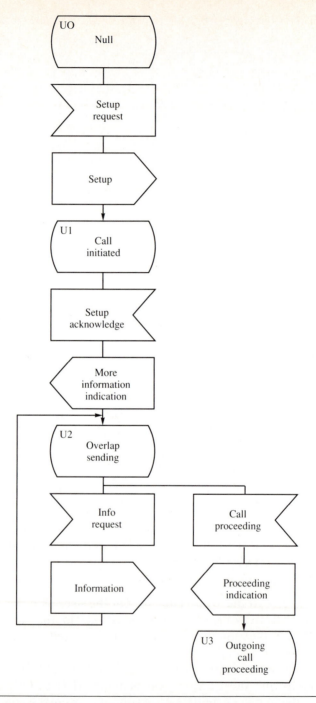

Figure 6.8b *Overlap user-side call establishment procedure (calling side)*
© Adapted from CCITT Blue Book, vol. VI.11, 1988.

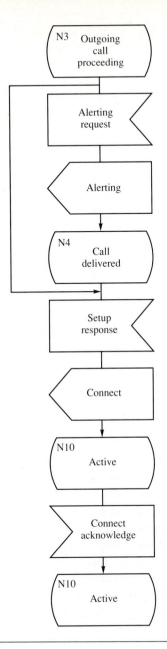

Figure 6.9c *Network-side call establishment procedure (calling side)*
© Adapted from CCITT Blue Book, vol. VI.11, 1988.

primitive from its CCE-4, indicates the arrival of a call by transmitting a SETUP message to the called user side and enters the Call Present state N6. If the existing data link layer connection is point-to-point, the message is sent in Multiple Frame Acknowledged mode. Otherwise it is broadcast to all the attached users inside a layer 2 UI frame. The CCE-3 on the called user side then issues a SETUP Indication primitive to its CCE-4 and also enters the Call Present state U6. Again, the procedures of en-bloc or overlap signaling, as outlined earlier, may be employed to convey any additional call establishment detail not contained in the SETUP message.

Assuming now that the called user CCE-4 is willing and able to accept the characteristics of the call defined in the received SETUP and INFORMATION messages, including the specified component channel, and that the specification of the call is complete, it issues a PROCEEDING Request primitive to its CCE-3. This causes the latter to transmit the CALL PROCEEDING message to indicate that the requested call establishment has been initiated and to verify the selected component channel. After this message has been transmitted and has been received at the network side, the connection enters the Incoming Call Proceeding state U9 and N9.

Once the proper conditions exist in the called user-side equipment, its CCE-4 issues to the CCE-3 an ALERTING Request primitive, which causes the transmission of an ALERTING message and a change to the Call Received state U7. The receipt of this message at the network side prompts an ALERTING Indication primitive and a similar change to state N7. Next, the user-side CCE-4 issues the SETUP Response primitive, giving rise to the transmission and reception of the CONNECT message and a change to U8 and N8.

Two alternatives that bypass the transmission of one or both of the CALL PROCEEDING and ALERTING messages are also possible. The choice between these three modes is essentially dependent on internal operational modes of the user equipment.

Figures 6.10(a) and 6.11(a) contain the SDL diagrams for the en-bloc version of these procedures.

Again, a number of anomalies must be considered. A called user could be in a busy condition, could be incompatible with the characteristics of the requested call, or could refuse the call for other reasons. In all such cases the CCE-4 on the called user side issues a REJECT Request primitive, causing its CCE-3 to transmit a RELEASE COMPLETE message to the network side. The latter includes appropriate Cause IEs indicating the reason for the refusal of

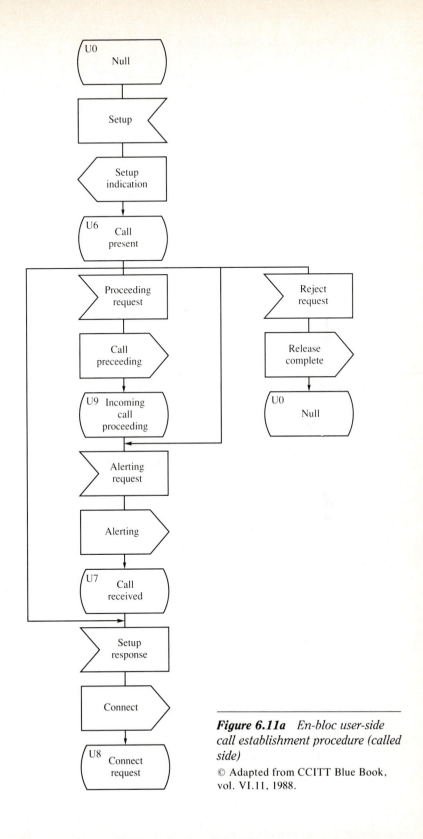

Figure 6.11a *En-bloc user-side call establishment procedure (called side)*

© Adapted from CCITT Blue Book, vol. VI.11, 1988.

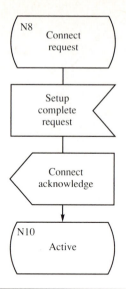

Figure 6.10b *Network-side call establishment procedure (called side)*
© Adapted from CCITT Blue Book, vol. VI.11, 1988.

the call. The connection then reverts to the Null state U0. In response, the network-side CCE-3 conveys the REJECT Indication primitive to its CCE-4, which in turn initiates appropriate clearing procedures. The state of the connection then likewise reverts to N0.

Figures 6.10(a) and 6.11(a) also show the SDL diagrams for these procedures.

In the normal operating mode, the network, on receiving the ALERTING message on the called side, causes its CCE-3 on the calling side to transmit a corresponding ALERTING message to the user on the calling side. The connection then enters the Call Delivered state N4. The subsequent reception of the CONNECT message by the network on the called side prompts the transmission of the CONNECT message on the calling side and a change of the connection to the Active state N10. If the alerting procedure is not used on the called side, the corresponding ALERTING message on the called side is also absent.

On receiving the ALERTING message, the user on the calling side provides the ALERTING Indication primitive to its CCE-4 and enters the Call Delivered state U4. The subsequent reception of the CON-NECT message prompts the SETUP Confirm primitive, the optional

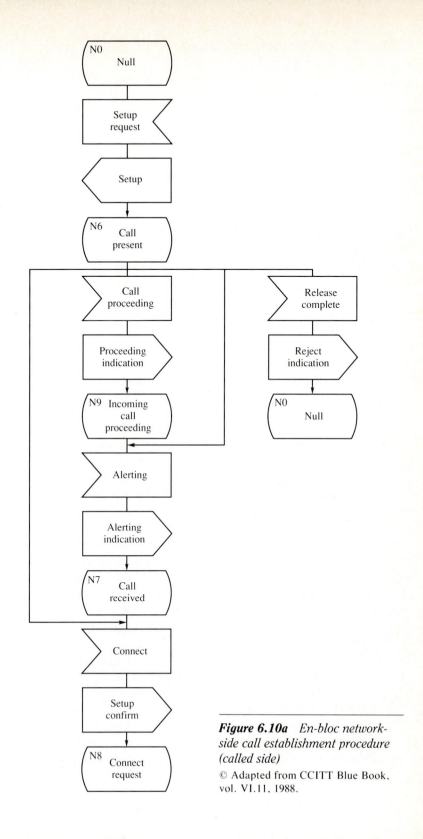

Figure 6.10a *En-bloc network-side call establishment procedure (called side)*

© Adapted from CCITT Blue Book, vol. VI.11, 1988.

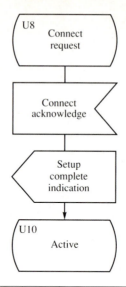

Figure 6.11b   *User-side call establishment procedure (called side)*
© Adapted from CCITT Blue Book, vol. VI.11, 1988.

transmission of the CONNECT ACKNOWLEDGE message, and a change to the Active state U10. This message is a purely local indication that the call is in the active state. The user and network on the calling side now consider the connection to be established.

Figures 6.8(c) and 6.9(c) contain the SDL diagrams of this part of the procedure.

As the final step in the call establishment procedure, the network on the called side transfers to the user from which it received the first CONNECT message a CONNECT ACKNOWLEDGE message to indicate the completion of a circuit switched connection. At this point it considers the connection to that user to be in the active state. On receiving the CONNECT ACKNOWLEDGE message, the user issues a SETUP COMPLETE primitive to its CCE-4 and also considers the connection to be in the active state U10.

These final procedures are shown in Figures 6.10(b) and 6.11(b).

To all other users that had responded to the SETUP message with an ALERT or CONNECT message, the network transmits the RELEASE message to indicate that the call is no longer available. All such users must respond with the RELEASE COMPLETE message.

The exchange of the protocol messages for the successful establishment of a circuit switched call is diagrammed in Figure 6.12.

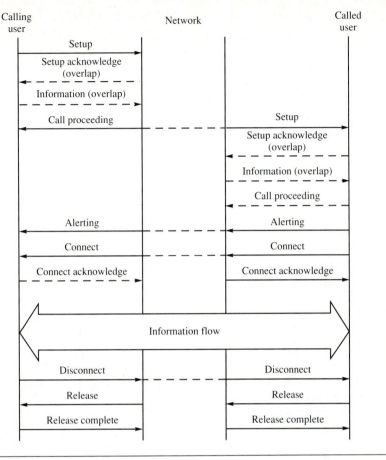

Figure 6.12 *Message exchange for call establishment and clearing*

6.3.3 Call Clearing Procedures

The structure of the protocol messages involved in the clearing of a circuit switched connection is shown in Table 6.8. An established circuit switched connection can be cleared by either the calling user, the called user, or the network, using an essentially similar procedure. In the following example we assume clearing by the user side.

Call clearing is initiated by the CCE-4 through the issuing of a DISCONNECT Request primitive to its CCE-3, which in turn transmits a DISCONNECT message to its peer CCE-3 across the UNI. The user side then enters the Disconnect Request state U11. On receipt of this message the network side disconnects the component channel used in the call and issues the DISCONNECT Indication primitive to its CCE-4. It then considers the connection to also be in the Disconnect Request state N11. Once the CCE-4 on the network side accepts the clearing of the call, it issues the RELEASE Request primitive, which causes its CCE-3 to transmit a RELEASE message and produces a change of the connection to the Release Request state N19. On the user side, receiving the RELEASE message causes the transmission of the RELEASE Indication primitive to the CCE-4 and the RELEASE COMPLETE message to the peer CCE-3. The connection then enters the Null state U0. On the network side, receiving the RELEASE COMPLETE message causes the release of the component channel and call reference, the transmission of the RELEASE Confirm primitive to the CCE-4, and a change of the connection to the Null state N0.

The clearing of the call by the network on the other side of the connection as part of the clearing by one of the users is accomplished in essentially the same manner, with the roles of user and network interchanged.

SDL diagrams of these procedures are given in Figures 6.13 and 6.14, and the messages exchanged between the peer CCE-3s during the clearing procedure are shown in Figure 6.12.

In certain situations, such as when the peer entity does not respond to call control messages, the user or network may require that the component channel be returned to an idle condition. This is accomplished by transmitting the RESTART message, which contains the Channel Identification IE specifying the channel in question. The recipient of this message returns the specified channel to the idle condition, resets the Call Reference IE to the null value, and responds with the RESTART ACKNOWLEDGE message to complete the procedure. As a result the connection is considered to be in the Null state on both sides.

6.3.4   Call Suspension and Reestablishment

A connection in the Active state may be suspended by a user for a period of time and resumed at a later time, thereby releasing certain resources for other uses. Such a suspension is a purely local matter and does not affect the state of the connection at the other end.

The procedure is initiated by the user-side CCE-4 conveying the SUSPEND Request primitive to its CCE-3. The latter then transmits a SUSPEND message, which contains the call reference IE and a Call Identity IE by which the suspended call will be known. The connec-

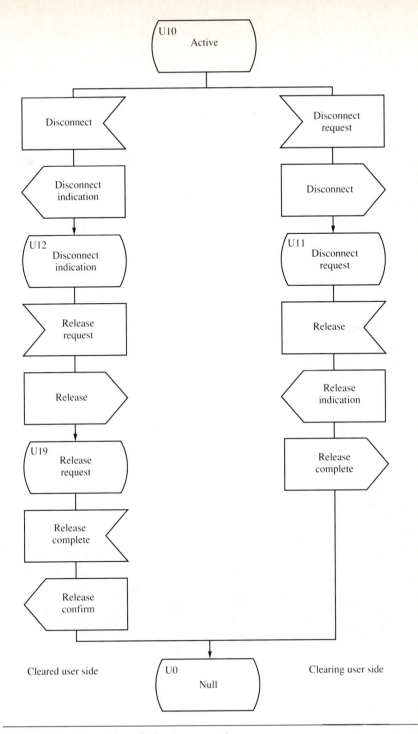

Figure 6.13 *User-side call clearing procedure*
© Adapted from CCITT Blue Book, vol. VI.11, 1988.

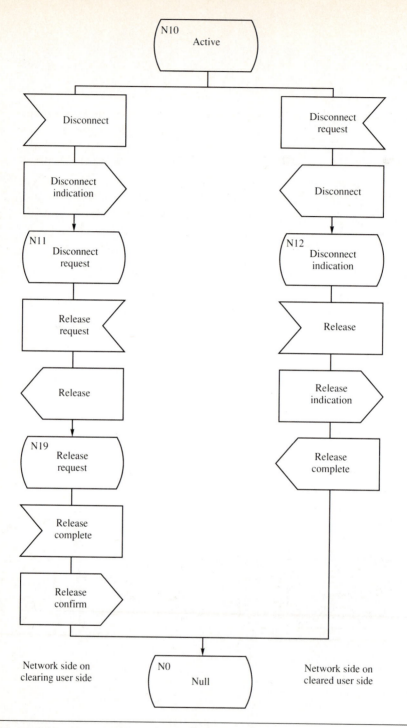

Figure 6.14 *Network-side call clearing procedure*
© Adapted from CCITT Blue Book, vol. VI.11, 1988.

tion then enters the Suspend Request state U15. On receiving this message the network-side CCE-3 conveys a SUSPEND Indication primitive to its CCE-4 and the connection enters the Suspend Request state N15. The CCE-4 in turn validates and stores the received Call Identity IE and releases the call reference. It also reserves the component channel involved in the connection for eventual reuse and issues a SUSPEND Response primitive to its CCE-3. The latter then transmits a SUSPEND ACKNOWLEDGE message to the suspending user and a SUSPEND Confirm primitive to its CCE-4. It also causes the network side on the other end of the connection to send a NOTIFY message to the other user to indicate that the call has been suspended. The connection then enters the Null state N0.

When the CCE-3 in the originating user receives the SUSPEND ACKNOWLEDGE message it conveys a SUSPEND Confirm primitive to its CCE-4, which in turn releases the component channel and the call reference. It may also disconnect the underlying data link connection. The connection is now considered in the Null state U0.

In some circumstances the original SUSPEND message may not contain a Call Identity IE or the provided call identity may already be in use. In either case the network side would be unable to resume the use of the connection at a later time. In response to this problem, the CCE-4 on the network side will reject the attempt to suspend the call by issuing the SUSPEND REJECT Request primitive, causing its CCE-3 to transmit to the suspending user the SUSPEND REJECT message. The latter contains the Cause IE indicating the reason for the rejection. The connection then returns to the active state N10. On the user side the reception of the SUSPEND REJECT message prompts the issuing of a SUSPEND REJECT Indication primitive and a similar reversion of the connection to the Active state U10.

These procedures are given in SDL form in Figures 6.15 and 6.16 for the user and network sides, respectively.

The reestablishment of the call is accomplished by the user sending the RESUME message containing the call identity submitted in the original SUSPEND message. The network then validates this call identity and sends the RESUME ACKNOWLEDGE message containing the identity of the reserved component channel. It also notifies the other user by means of the NOTIFY message that the call has been resumed and releases the call identity for further use. On receipt of the RESUME ACKNOWLEDGE message the connection enters the Active state.

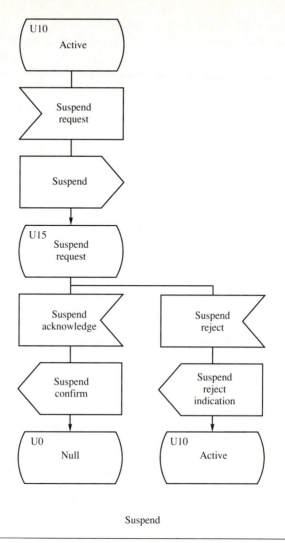

Suspend

Figure 6.15 *User-side suspend and resume procedures*
© Adapted from CCITT Blue Book, vol. VI.11, 1988.

Various exception conditions can occur during the attempt to resume a suspended call. For example, the call identity may not exist in the network or the suspended call may have been inadvertently cleared. In such cases the network returns the RESUME REJECT message to the user. Both sides then release

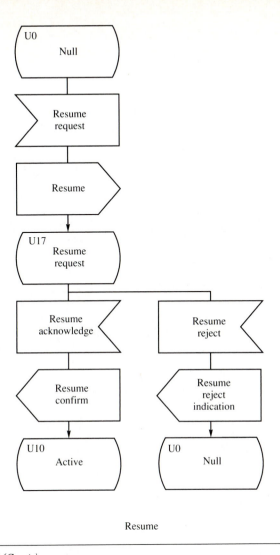

Resume

Figure 6.15 *(Cont.)*
© Adapted from CCITT Blue Book, vol. VI.11, 1988.

the call reference and return the connection to the Null state. Figures 6.15 and 6.16 give SDL diagrams of the suspend and resume procedures.

The protocol message exchange for a successful suspend and resume is shown in Figure 6.17.

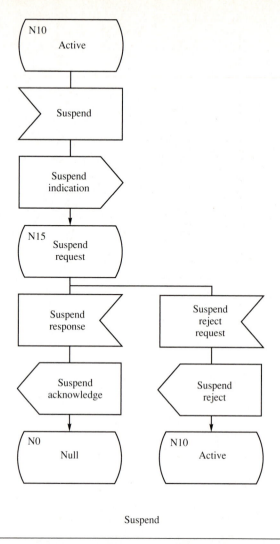

Suspend

Figure 6.16 *Network-side suspend and resume procedures*
© Adapted from CCITT Blue Book, vol. VI.11, 1988.

6.4 Stimulus Protocol Procedures for Circuit Switched Connections

Having discussed the basic procedures by which a functional terminal may control circuit switched connections, we now turn to the types of user terminals operating in stimulus mode.

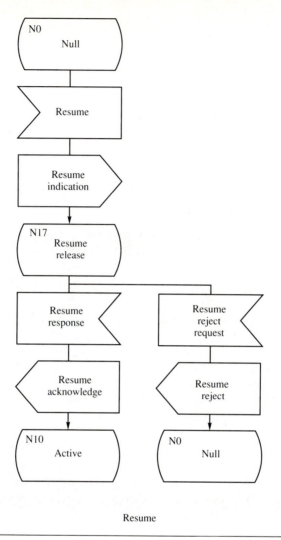

Resume

Figure 6.16 *(Cont.)*
© Adapted from CCITT Blue Book, vol. VI.11, 1988.

The design of the stimulus mode protocol is based on the use of a relatively small number of protocol messages that are exchanged between the layer 3 connection control entities on the user and network sides of the UNI. In keeping with the goal of low logical complexity, the messages contain only a small number of information elements,

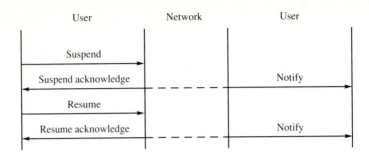

Figure 6.17 *Call suspend and reestablishment procedure*

including the Keypad Facility and Switchhook in the direction user-to-network and Display and Signal in the direction network-to-user. On the user side these IEs are generated by the CCE-3 as a direct response to an action at the human-machine interface and describe in simple form the nature of the action. On the network side they are also generated by the CCE-3 and contain simple instructions of direct significance to the end user. The IEs received by the user side are interpreted by the CCE-3 and mapped into signals that can be executed by the end-user device. These signals are then conveyed across the human-machine interface.

To the extent that the user side is able to process them, the messages may contain additional IEs that do not directly affect the end-user.

In the following sections we discuss the stimulus mode procedures for the establishment and clearing of a simple circuit switched connection over a B channel or H channel. Not all details of these procedures are firmly defined. Thus we limit ourselves to a consideration of the major concepts.

6.4.1 Stimulus Call Establishment Procedure

The establishment of a call on the user side is normally initiated by the end-user placing the switchhook of the end-user device in the off-hook state. As a result, the CCE-3 on the originating user side generates a SETUP message that includes the Switchhook IE with its value set to "off-hook." As a minimum, the message must also include the Bearer Capability IE—by which the network is informed of the type of connection being established—and the Call Reference IE, whose value identifies the connection. The latter may be set to a dummy value when the underlying data link connection supports only one layer 3 signaling connection. It is most likely that this information is permanently contained in the logic of the CCE-3, rather than being generated by the end-user device and conveyed across the human-machine interface.

If en-bloc signaling is employed the SETUP message must also include any other information such as the address of the called party required by the network to establish the connection. This information is contained in a Keypad Facility IE generated by the user-side CCE-3 in response to signals received from its end-user device and is coded as characters from the International Alphabet No. 5. Thus, for example, the signals representing the called party address that are generated at the keypad of the end-user device are converted by the CCE-3 into IA5 characters and transferred as a Keypad Facility IE to the network.

After receiving an en-bloc SETUP message the network-side CCE-3 interprets the Switchhook and Keypad Facility IEs and returns a CALL PROCEEDING message. This message includes the Channel Identification IE specifying the assigned B channel or H channel, the Call Reference IE, and a Display IE. The latter contains connection related information that is intended to be displayed by the end-user device. The IA5 characters of the Display IE are again mapped by the user-side CCE-3 into signals that can be executed directly by the end-user device.

In overlap signaling the network side responds to the initial SETUP message with the SETUP ACKNOWLEDGE message. The latter contains the Signal IE, whose purpose is to relay to the end-user certain prompts for additional information. Its various values are listed in Table 6.5. As an example of its use, the value "dial tone on" instructs the end-user device to generate a dial tone indicating that the transfer of called party address information may be initiated. The appropriate digits are then sent by the end-user device across the human-machine interface and conveyed to the network side as Keypad Facility IEs within one or more INFORMATION messages. The network may respond with INFORMATION messages of its own for conveying other Signal IEs. For example, after receiving the INFORMATION message containing the first digit of the called party address, it may send the Signal IE with value "tones off" to stop the generation of the dial tone by the end-user device. When all call establishment information has been received by the network side it sends the CALL PROCEEDING message, as in the en-bloc case.

On the destination side of the connection the SETUP message conveyed by the network side to the user side contains the Bearer Capability IE, the Call Reference IE, and the Channel Identification IE, the latter specifying the particular component channel over which the connection is to be established. It may also include a Display IE for detailed call-related information to be displayed on the screen of the end-user device and a Signal IE that is set to one of the "alerting on" values shown in Table 6.5. The latter IE instructs the end-user device to generate a ringing signal to indicate an incoming call. Eight such ringing signals, corresponding to different terminal requirements, have been defined.

On receiving the SETUP message the called user performs a compatibility check on the received Bearer Capability IE. Assuming a positive result, its CCE-3 responds by sending the ALERTING message, which contains the Call Reference IE with the value selected by the network. When the end-user device goes off-hook in response to the ringing signal, its CCE-3 generates the CONNECT message containing the Switchhook IE with its value set to "off-hook" and sends it to its network side.

At the originating UNI, when the network side receives an indication that user alerting on the destination side has been initiated, it transmits the ALERTING message to its user side. This message includes the Signal IE with value "ring back tone on." The subsequent indication that the destination end-user has sent the CONNECT message then causes the transfer of the CONNECT message with the Signal IE value set to "tones off." This message may also include a Display IE containing information such as the rate at which the call is charged and the address of the connected terminal.

The final step in the connection establishment procedure requires the network side at the destination UNI to transfer the CONNECT ACKNOWLEDGE message to its user side, with the Signal IE value set to "alerting off." This causes the receiving end-user device to stop the generation of the ringing tone.

Figure 6.18 shows these procedures for the case of overlap sending.

6.4.2 Stimulus Call Clearing Procedure

The clearing of a call in stimulus mode follows essentially the procedure shown in Figure 6.12.

A user may initiate the clearing of a call by placing the switchhook

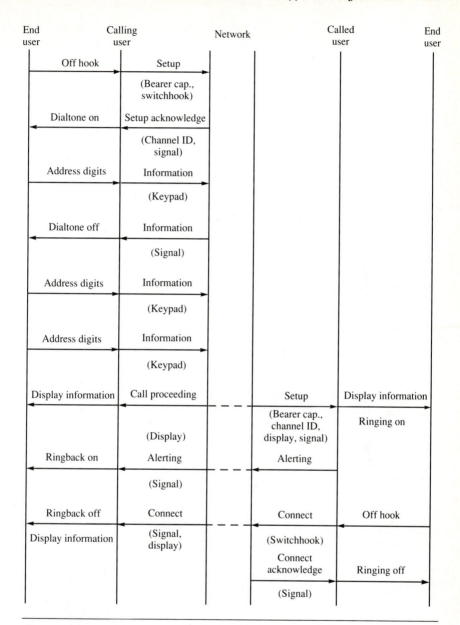

Figure 6.18 *Stimulus mode call establishment procedure*

in the "on-hook" position, which causes the generation and transmission of a DISCONNECT message containing the Switchhook IE set to the value "on-hook." On receiving this message the network conveys a DISCONNECT message to the remote user, possibly containing a Display IE to indicate that the call is being cleared. When the remote user replaces the switchhook a RELEASE message is generated and transmitted with the Switchhook IE also set to the value "on-hook." Once the clearing user receives the RELEASE message it detaches from the component channel and returns a RELEASE COMPLETE message which, when delivered to the remote user, completes the clearing procedure.

6.5 Protocol Procedures for Supplementary Services

Let us now consider the layer 3 protocol required for the control of the types of services considered to be supplementary to a basic telecommunications service. As mentioned earlier, this protocol involves the exchange of I.451 messages over the D channel between peer CCE-3s on either side of the UNI.

Supplementary services can exist either in association with a circuit switched or packet switched call or independently of any such call. In any case, the layer 3 protocol must have the capability for the user to invoke or cancel a service and for the network to allow or reject the invocation or cancellation. Call associated services may be invoked and canceled during the establishment phase, the active phase, or the clearing phase of the associated call and are always identified with the call reference of the associated call. On the other hand, supplementary services that can exist independently of a call may be invoked or canceled anytime, as long as a layer 2 connection between peer CCE-2s exists.

Although the detailed procedures for the control of a specific supplementary service are still to be defined and may in some instances be network dependent, the CCITT in Recommendation Q.932 has specified three generic types of protocols, two of which are based on the stimulus mode and the third requiring the capabilities of a functional terminal on the user side. In this section we summarize their major features.

6.5.1 The Keypad Protocol

The *Keypad Protocol* is a stimulus mode procedure that allows the invocation and cancellation of a supplementary service associated with a call for which at least a call reference has been established. The service may be invoked and canceled at any time during the establishment, operation, and clearing phases of the call.

The principal mechanism of the protocol is the transfer of the Keypad Facility IE in the direction user-to-network and the Display, Signal, and Information Request IEs in the direction network-to-user. These IEs are contained in SETUP and INFORMATION messages, which also contain the call reference of the associated call.

A human end-user at the human-machine interface invokes a supplementary service by dialing at the keyboard certain integers and symbols that identify the desired service. This information is then transferred to the network as a Keypad Facility IE. The service identifier is coded in IA5 characters, but the semantics and syntax of specifying the service are not standardized and may be different from one network to another. They must therefore be agreed on at subscription time.

All supplementary service information may be sent in either en-bloc or overlap mode. If the service is invoked during the call establishment phase, the information is conveyed via a Keypad Facility IE in the SETUP message for en-bloc signaling and additional Keypad Facility IEs in INFORMATION messages, for overlap sending. During the other phases of the call the information is transmitted to the network via one or more Keypad Facility IEs in INFORMATION messages.

During overlap sending or at other times the network may repeatedly prompt the user for additional information by transmitting INFORMATION messages containing either the Display IE, the Signal IE, or the Information Request IE. As with the Keypad Facility IE, the contents of the Display IE are coded in IA5 characters, but the semantics and syntax are network dependent. The contents are intended to be displayed on the user device and interpreted by the human end-user. The Signal IE contains a binary code for a number of network-specific tones that are converted by the user into audible prompts. These are interpreted by the human end-user as requests for specific types of information. The requested information may also be identified explicitly by the Information Request IE.

Once the network has obtained sufficient information concerning the supplementary service being invoked, it responds with an INFORMATION message containing the Display IE that indicates whether the invocation was successful or not. In the latter case—which may occur when the user has not subscribed to the service or when the information received by the network is invalid—the network may prompt the user to retransmit the required information, ignore the invocation, or clear the call.

Over the remote UNI the network normally provides an indication to the user that a supplementary service is being invoked. This information is conveyed by means of a Display or Signal IE contained in an INFORMATION message. No reaction from the user to such an indication is required.

6.5.2   *The Feature Key Management Protocol*

The second protocol for the control of supplementary services, known as the *Feature Key Management Protocol,* is also of the stimulus type, but allows the invocation and cancellation of a supplementary service either in association with a call or independently. It relies on the use of the Feature Activation IE and Feature Indication IE to request a supplementary service and to communicate the network's response to that request. These IEs contain a feature identifier number that specifies the particular service by reference to a user service profile maintained by the network. The association of this number to a service may in general differ from one user to another and from one network to another, and the user is not necessarily aware of the detailed nature of the service. The Feature Indication IE also contains a status field that allows the network to indicate the disposition of the service invocation or cancellation.

A user normally invokes a supplementary service by transferring across the UNI, in response to the depression of a feature key at the human-machine interface, the Feature Activation IE containing the appropriate feature identifier number. This IE may be sent in either a SETUP message if the service is invoked during the establishment phase of an associated call or at any time in an INFORMATION message. For a call associated service the messages also contain the appropriate call reference. Otherwise a dummy call reference is included. If additional information is required, the network may solicit it by sending an INFORMATION message containing the Information Request IE. The user then follows normal overlap procedures, providing the information via Keypad IEs contained in INFORMATION messages.

Once the network has determined that sufficient information exists to identify the supplementary service being invoked, it returns to the user a Feature Indication IE with a status field indicating whether the service is deactivated, activated, or pending. Alternatively, the network may send the Signal, Cause, or Display IEs to describe the disposition of the service. These IEs may be conveyed in the INFORMATION message or in one of the call establishment and clearing messages indicated in Table 6.6. An error condition arises if the user attempts to invoke a supplementary service to which he or she has not subscribed or if the feature identifier number is not understood by the network. In such cases the network may respond by either prompting the user for additional information, return a Cause, Signal, or Display IE indicating the nature of the problem, or ignore the request.

The cancellation of a supplementary service can be implemented in two ways. In the first method, cancellation is accomplished in the manner of a toggle switch by the transmission of a second Feature Activation IE following the one used for service invocation. In the second method, a special feature identifier number transmitted by the user in a Feature Activation IE is interpreted by the network as a request for the cancellation of the supplementary service.

6.5.3 The Functional Protocol

For user devices with the ability to generate and analyze complex protocol messages the CCITT in Recommendation Q.932 has defined the outlines of a functional protocol that allows the operation of supplementary services in a highly automated fashion. The protocol is based on the use of a separate and dedicated set of messages and information elements to effect the invocation and cancellation of particular services. By appropriate structuring of the IEs, the procedure allows the specification of services with multiple options and service parameters and the invocation of several supplementary services within a single message. It also permits the introduction of new services by the simple expedient of defining new elements of the data structure of the IEs.

Two categories of procedures have been defined. In the first, known as the *common information element procedure,* all supplementary service information is conveyed via the Facility IE. For call-independent services this IE is contained in a FACILITY or

REGISTER message, whereas for call associated services it may also be transmitted in any of the basic call control messages. The IE consists of four types of components, known as Invoke, Return Result, Return Error, and Reject. Each of these contains information specifying the relevant supplementary service and the disposition of the service. A number of diagnostic indications relating to certain problems that may be encountered in the execution of a service are also included.

The second category of procedures, known as the *separate message procedure,* differs from the first in that it utilizes messages that are exclusively identified with a particular service, rather than defining the service by means of the Facility IE. To date only the six messages HOLD, HOLD ACKNOWLEDGE, HOLD REJECT, RETRIEVE, RETRIEVE ACKNOWLEDGE, and RETRIEVE REJECT have been defined. These are used to place an existing call in the hold state and retrieve it at a later time. The hold and retrieve capability is available to both the user and the network and can be used, for example, to reconfigure the customer-premises installation without disconnecting existing calls.

The transmission of the HOLD message causes the receiver to place the call identified by the call reference into the hold state, while retaining the component channel and call reference for future retrieval of the call. The successful execution of the hold function is acknowledged by the HOLD ACKNOWLEDGE message. The hold function may also be rejected by transmitting the HOLD REJECT message, which contains a Cause IE indicating the reason for the rejection.

Call retrieval is accomplished through the transmission of the RETRIEVE message and acknowledged by the RETRIEVE ACKNOWLEDGE message. These messages may contain the Channel Identification IE, specifying a particular or preferred component channel over which the call is to be reestablished. Failure to retrieve the call is indicated by the RETRIEVE REJECT message, which also contains a Cause IE specifying the reason for the failure.

6.6   Functional Protocol Procedures for User-to-User Signaling Connections

As we mentioned earlier in this chapter, the D channel, in conjunction with a packet switched connection over the CCSN, can support the transparent transfer of user-to-user signaling information flows between user-to-user signaling entities in the end-user equipment. This exchange can be accomplished either in association with a circuit switched or packet switched connection over a B channel or H channel or independently of any such connection. In the first case, the service is considered to be supplementary to the associated connection and is governed by the supplementary services protocols described in Section 6.5. In the second case, the user-to-user signaling information flows are transferred over a temporary signaling connection.

In this section we specify the protocol used in the establishment, operation, and clearing of such a connection and the transfer of the information flow over it.

The messages used in the operation of the user-to-user signaling protocol are listed in Table 6.6, and the composition of the messages is given in Tables 6.12 to 6.15.

The procedures followed in the establishment and clearing of the signaling connection over the D channel are essentially simplified versions of those employed for circuit switched connections over a B channel or H channel, as discussed in Section 6.3. Of course, the peer-to-peer interactions are between the USE-3s on the two sides of the UNI and the adjacent layer interactions are between USE-3 and USE-4.

Connection establishment follows the procedures shown in Figure 6.12. The initial SETUP message issued by the calling USE-3 includes the Bearer Capability IE and Channel Identification IE. The first specifies the transfer of unrestricted digital information in packet switched mode and the second identifies the D channel as the component channel over which the connection is to be established.

The information transfer phase begins on the calling side on receipt of the CONNECT message and on the called side when the CONNECT ACKNOWLEDGE message has been received. The user-to-user signaling information flows are conveyed between the USE-3s on the calling and called sides by means of the USER INFORMATION message, with the information contained in the User-User IE. This IE is passed by the network to the receiving user USE-3 without modification. The message may also contain the More Data IE to indicate that another USER INFORMATION message is to follow.

Both the user and the network may control the transmission of USER INFORMATION messages from the other side across the UNI by means of a flow control procedure. A receiver willing to accept a predefined number W of USER INFORMATION messages sends the CONGESTION CONTROL message, with the Congestion Level IE

TABLE 6.12 Establishment messages for signaling connections

IE \ MESSAGE	SETUP	SETUP ACK	CALL PROC	ALERTING	CONNECT	CONNECT ACK
	TYPE AND DIRECTION					
SENDING COMPLETE	O,B					
BEARER CAPABILITY	M,B					
CHANNEL ID	M,B	O,B	O,B	O,N	O,N	
NETWORK SPECIFIC FACILITIES	O,B					
DISPLAY	O,U	O,U	O,U	O,U	O,U	O,U
KEYPAD FACILITY	O,N					
CALLING PARTY NUMBER	O,B					
CALLING PARTY SUBADDRESS	O,B					
CALLED PARTY NUMBER	O,B					
CALLED PARTY SUBADDRESS	O,B					
TRANSIT NETWORK SELECTION	O,N					
LOW-LAYER COMPATIBILITY	O,B					
HIGH-LAYER COMPATIBILITY	O,B					
USER-USER	O,B			O,B	O,B	

set to the value "receiver ready." The other side may then transfer up to W such messages. Any further transfer must await the receipt of another "receiver ready" indication.

If, on the other hand, the receiver wants to temporarily interrupt the flow of USER INFORMATION messages from the other side, it transmits a CONGESTION CONTROL message with the Congestion Level IE set to "receive not ready." While in this flow control state

TABLE 6.13   Information phase message for signaling connections

MESSAGE	USER INFO
IE	**TYPE AND DIRECTION**
MORE DATA	O,B
USER-USER	M,B

TABLE 6.14   Miscellaneous messages for signaling connections

MESSAGE	CONGEST CON	INFORMATION	STATUS	STATUS ENQ
IE		**TYPE AND DIRECTION**		
SENDING COMPLETE		O,B		
CONGESTION LEVEL	M,B			
CAUSE	M,B	O,U	M,B	
CALL STATE			M,B	
DISPLAY	O,U	O,U	O,U	O,U
KEYPAD FACILITY		O,N		
CALLED PARTY NUMBER		O,B		

TABLE 6.15   Clearing messages for signaling connections

MESSAGE	R E L E A S E	R E L E A S E C O M
IE	TYPE AND	DIRECTION
CAUSE	O,B	O,B
DISPLAY	O,U	O,U
USER-USER	O,B	O,B

the receiver will discard a received USER INFORMATION message and respond with a CONGESTION CONTROL message in which the Congestion Level IE is set to "receiver not ready" and the Cause IE indicates the discard of the message. Clearing of the signaling connection is initiated by the user through the transmission of the RELEASE message, which is conveyed by the network to the remote user. The latter then responds with a RELEASE COMPLETE message, which is relayed by the network to the clearing user.

As Tables 6.12 and 6.15 show, the SETUP, ALERTING, CONNECT, RELEASE, and RELEASE COMPLETE messages may contain the User-User IE. Since all of these messages are conveyed between the end-users, user-to-user signaling information may therefore also be transferred during the establishment and clearing phases of the signaling connection.

6.7   Summary and Recommended Reading

Chapter 6 examined the layer 3 services and protocols of the C plane and U plane for the control of connections, for information transfer, and for the control of supplementary services. We defined functional and stimulus connection control protocols and specified the formats of the corresponding protocol messages. We also described the procedures for the establishment, suspension, reestablishment, and clearing of circuit switched connections over the ISDN. Three types of protocols for the control of supplementary services—the Keypad Protocol, the Feature Key Management Protocol, and the Functional Protocol—were defined. The Functional Protocol was used in the control of a user-to-user signaling connection.

A good tutorial summary of the layer 3 protocol for connection control and supplementary service control can be found in [HARM89]. See also [KANO86].

CHAPTER 7

The Terminal Adapter

In the previous three chapters we have concentrated on the physical and logical protocols that govern the relationship between the user and the network across the S and T reference points of the ISDN. As we have noted, these protocols are in many ways unique to the ISDN and thus require the development of new types of data terminals and network equipment as part of the ISDN implementation.

It is clear that this equipment will be largely incompatible with today's telecommunications devices. Since the ISDN is expected to evolve from the existing telecommunications networks, during the transitional period solutions to the problem of interworking between ISDN and non-ISDN equipment need to be developed.

From a technical point of view there are two major compatibility issues that must be addressed. The first relates to the interworking between the interexchange facilities of an ISDN and those of an existing non-ISDN such as the public switched telephone network. Such interworking will likely be required for an interim period, either to provide connections between pairs of TE1s attached to disjointed ISDNs or between a TE1 attached to an ISDN and a conventional terminal attached to an existing network. The second issue, and the one of interest to us in the present chapter, concerns the adaption of existing non-ISDN telecommunications terminals to the user-to-network interface of an ISDN, so as to allow their continued use during a period of transition to the ISDN.

In recent years considerable effort has gone into the development of specifications for the conversion of the most important types of non-ISDN data terminal equipment (DTE) in use today—namely, those whose communications characteristics have previously been standardized by the CCITT. The current status of this work is summarized in six CCITT recommendations. I.461 (X.30) applies to the adaption of the synchronous and asynchronous DTEs based on Recommendations X.21, X.21bis, and X.20bis for use over circuit switched data networks. I.462 (X.31) covers synchronous DTEs operating in the packet mode according to Recommendation X.25. The terminals with V-series type interfaces, which utilize a modem for operation over the public switched telephone network, are considered in I.463 (V.110) and I.465 (V.120). The two remaining recommendations—I.460 and I.464—concern themselves with various aspects of the terminal adaption problem common to all terminal types.

In the following sections we discuss the terminal adaption for the interfaces specified in these recommendations. We assume a basic familiarity with the major features of the relationship between the data terminal equipment (DTE) and the data-circuit terminating equipment (DCE), as specified in CCITT Recommendations X.20bis, X.21bis, X.21, X.25, and the recommendations of the V-series.

Many aspects of adapting the CCITT terminal standards to the ISDN requirements have not yet been specified, so that our treatment is somewhat tentative. We also point out that adaption is not restricted to equipment standardized by the CCITT but is equally important for terminals conforming to proprietary protocols. In view of the numerous existing terminal types, a complete treatment of the adaption problem would involve a great amount of detail and is beyond the scope of this book.

7.1 The Terminal Adaption Problem

We may formulate the terminal adaption problem in terms of the abstract subscriber-access reference configuration discussed in Chapter 2, a part of which is reproduced in Figure 7.1. The terminal equipment is represented by the functional group TE2, which interfaces with the terminal adapter functional group TA via the R reference point. On the network side the TA conforms to the standard ISDN specifications, so that the combination of TE2 and TA is equivalent to the functional group TE1 and presents an S or T type interface to the network side.

From a less abstract point of view, this reference configuration can be expanded into the model shown in Figure 7.2. Here the TE2 functional group is contained in a DTE, which interacts with a non-ISDN network termination functional group contained in a DCE within the

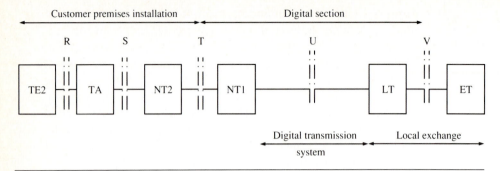

Figure 7.1 *Reference configuration for terminal adaption*

TA. The interactions between DTE and DCE are governed by one of the native protocols mentioned earlier. A mapping function in the TA converts these interactions into equivalent interactions between the S/T controller and an NT2, NT1, or ET across the S or T reference points.

To assure complete compatibility, the mapping function must provide a conversion of all pertinent physical and logical interactions that are carried out between DTE and DCE into equivalent interactions over the S or T reference point. For several reasons this may not always be feasible. First, as we have seen in earlier chapters, the interactions across S and T are structured into layers and planes. Across R, however, for the types of DTEs and DCEs considered here the concept of a plane does not exist; nor is the capability of the DTE and DCE necessarily divided into well-defined layers.

Second, the functions of a DTE, in total or in a given layer, may exceed or fall short of the total or layer functions of a TE1, so that a

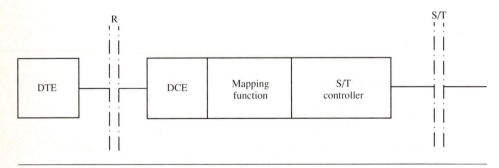

Figure 7.2 *Terminal adapter components*

particular interaction over one reference point may have no equivalent at another reference point.

Given these inconsistencies, it is usually not possible to provide a one-to-one mapping of the complete set of interactions at R to and from the interactions at S or T. As a result, only a reduced subset of functions may be available to the DTE, which may prevent it from accessing the full capability of the ISDN.

As currently conceived, the design of the TA is limited to layers 1, 2, and 3 of the protocol architecture.

At layer 1 all physical aspects of the relationship between DTE and DCE are converted by the mapping function of the TA into the layer 1 basic-access or primary-access structures discussed in Chapter 4. This includes, among other things, the change from one cabling system to another, the adaption of data rates, and the conversion of electrical signal levels, line codes, pulse shapes, and power feeding arrangements. Both user data and control information exchanged between DTE and DCE are mapped into a common layer 1 frame according to CCITT Recommendation I.430 or I.431, with user data mapped into either B-channel or D-channel flows and control data mapped into flows over the D channel.

At layer 2 the conversion applies to the normal data link layer control functions such as error control, flow control, frame synchronization, and logical link initialization and termination. These control interactions are carried out over the D channel and are mapped from the DTE-to-DCE protocol to the LAPD protocol discussed in Chapter 5. For user data transported over a B channel, this mapping remains to be defined, due mainly to the fact that no layer 2 B-channel protocol has been specified.

At layer 3 the call control functions carried out between DTE and DCE are converted to the I.451 D-channel protocol described in Chapter 6. Included here are all the establishment, operation, and clearing functions for calls over the circuit switched and packet switched facilities of the ISDN. Again, no mapping of the layer 3 procedures for user data is provided.

7.2 X.21 Terminal Adaption

We focus now on the adaption of a DTE conforming to the specifications of CCITT Recommendation X.21 to the requirements of the S or T reference point. As noted previously, this conversion encompasses the lower three layers of the protocol hierarchy within both the control plane and user plane. Except for the rate adaption problem, we will not discuss the physical layer, since it involves considerable detail on the electrical aspects of signals and circuits that is beyond our scope. At the link layer, X.21 provides only a rudimentary synchronization capability, so that no major conversion issues arise. Consequently, we will focus on the three remaining aspects of this problem. These include the adaption of the X.1 user data rates to the 64-kbit/s B-channel rate, the mapping of the X.21 call control procedure to the I.451 D-channel protocol, and the synchronization of the data transfer phase at the two ends of a connection.

We illustrate the essential aspects of the call control conversion by discussing in some detail the adaption procedure for the successful establishment and clearing of a circuit switched connection. For a complete understanding of this subject it is, of course, necessary to also consider the various anomalies that may arise and the corresponding recovery procedures. For a discussion of these and a number of other important issues, see CCITT Recommendation I.461 (X.30).

7.2.1 Rate Adaption

Over the R reference point the user data flows between DTE and DCE are transmitted synchronously at rates corresponding to user classes of service 3 (600 BPS), 4 (2400 BPS), 5 (4800 BPS), 6 (9600 BPS), 7 (48 kbit/s), and 19 (64 kbit/s), as specified in CCITT Recommendation X.1. Since these flows are conveyed over the B channel, the TA must convert the rates for classes 3 to 7 to the 64-kbit/s rate required over the B channel. The precise method to accomplish this depends on the specific class.

For classes 3 to 6 the adaption is carried out in two stages. Stage 1 produces an intermediate rate of 8 kbit/s for classes 3 to 5 and 16 kbit/s for class 6 by constructing a 40-bit frame organized into a two-frame multiframe according to the format of Figure 7.3.

The digits in octet 0 of all odd frames, together with the first digits of the remaining 9 octets of the multiframe, form the 17-digit frame synchronization sequence.

Digits E1 to E3 are used to indicate the user data rate, while digits E4 to E7 are reserved for future use.

The status digits SP, SQ, and SR carry the control signals that are exchanged across the R reference point from one DTE to another, and digit X is available for optional end-to-end flow control. Since these digits are transmitted within the capacity of the B channel, they evi-

		Bit number							
		1	2	3	4	5	6	7	8
Octet 0	Odd frames -	0	0	0	0	0	0	0	0
	Even frames -	1	E1	E2	E3	E4	E5	E6	E7
Octet 1		1	P1	P2	P3	P4	P5	P6	SQ
Octet 2		1	P7	P8	Q1	Q2	Q3	Q4	X
Octet 3		1	Q5	Q6	Q7	Q8	R1	R2	SR
Octet 4		1	R3	R4	R5	R6	R7	R8	SP

Figure 7.3 *Rate adaption frame structure (user classes 3–5)*
© Reprinted from CCITT Blue Book, vol. VIII.2, 1988.

dently constitute inband control. Their precise use is discussed in Section 7.2.4.

The remaining digit groups P1 to P8, Q1 to Q8, and R1 to R8 constitute the user data. To achieve a rate of 8 kbit/s, a given user data digit is present eight times in succession for user class 3 and twice in succession for user class 4. For classes 5 and 6, however, each of the P, Q, and R digits is unique. As an example, the multiframe for the class 4 rate appears as in Figure 7.4.

In the second step of the rate adaption process the 40-digit frame is transmitted over the B channel by placing its digits in position 1 of consecutive B-channel octets for the 8-kbit/s intermediate rate and in positions 1 and 2 for the 16-kbit/s intermediate rate. The remaining digits in the B-channel octets are set to binary 1.

0	0	0	0	0	0	0	0
1	P1	P1	P2	P2	P3	P3	SP
1	P4	P4	P5	P5	P6	P6	X
1	P7	P7	P8	P8	Q1	Q1	SQ
1	Q2	Q2	Q3	Q3	Q4	Q4	SQ
1	1	1	0	E4	E5	E6	E7
1	Q5	Q5	Q6	Q6	Q7	Q7	SR
1	Q8	Q8	R1	R1	R2	R2	X
1	R3	R3	R4	R4	R5	R5	SR
1	R6	R6	R7	R7	R8	R8	SP

Figure 7.4 *Intermediate rate adaption frame (user class 4)*
© Reprinted from CCITT Blue Book, vol. VIII.2, 1988.

A somewhat similar approach to the rate adaption problem is used for user class-of-service 7. Here the information is organized in a four-octet frame, shown in Figure 7.5. The first digit of each octet forms the synchronization sequence. Also included are the three status digits SP, SQ, and SR and 24 digits of user data. The entire 32 digits are transmitted in four consecutive B-channel octets, so that three out of every four B-channel octets consist of user data, yielding a data rate of 48 kbit/s.

7.2.2 X.21 Interface Specifications

To understand the principles involved in the conversion of the X.21 procedure for the control of a circuit switched connection to the I.451 D-channel protocol, it is necessary to consider briefly the relationship between DTE and DCE across the R reference point according to the X.21 specifications.

As shown in Figure 7.6, physically the interface between DTE and DCE consists of four major circuits, labeled Transmit (T) and Control (C) in the direction DTE to DCE and Receive (R) and Indication (I) in the direction DCE to DTE. In addition, two timing circuits in the direction DCE to DTE are provided, one for Signal Element Timing (S) and the other for Byte Timing (B). Electrically these six circuits are balanced and conform to the specifications of CCITT Recommendation X.27. Together with a signal ground G and a DTE common return Ga, they are terminated in a 15-pin interface connector as specified in ISO 4903.

The signals exchanged across C and I are referred to as ON or OFF and consist of continuous sequences of binary 0 or binary 1, respectively. On the T and R circuits various characters from the

	Bit number							
	1	2	3	4	5	6	7	8
Octet 1	1	P1	P2	P3	P4	P5	P6	SQ
Octet 2	0	P7	P8	Q1	Q2	Q3	Q4	X
Octet 3	1	Q5	Q6	Q7	Q8	R1	R2	SR
Octet 4	1	R3	R4	R5	R6	R7	R8	SP

Figure 7.5 *Rate adaption frame structure (user class 6)*
© Reprinted from CCITT Blue Book, vol. VIII.2, 1988.

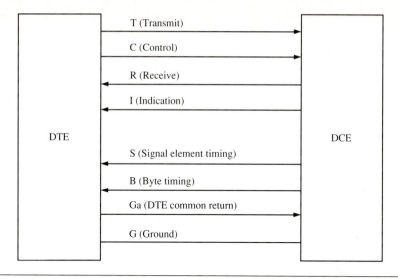

Figure 7.6 *X.21 interface circuits*

IA5—which are always preceded by one or two SYN characters from IA5—as well as the three continuous sequences of binary 0, binary 1, and alternating 0 1 are transmitted. These convey, in combination with the signals on C and I, a particular condition or control. The end-user data from one DTE to another is also transmitted over T and R. All of these transmissions are synchronous and are timed by the DCE over S or B, with the user data transfer restricted to user-classes-of service 1 to 7 and 19, as indicated earlier.

Logically, the interface may exist in one of four distinct phases, known as *quiescent, call control, data transfer,* and *clearing.* Within each phase the interface at a particular time is in one of several states, with the specific state being determined by the combination of signals conveyed over the T, C, R, and I circuits.

During the quiescent phase the two sides signal their ability or inability to enter the call control or data transfer phase. The DTE indicates its readiness to enter one of these phases by signaling on its T circuit a continuous sequence of binary 1 and on its C circuit the condition OFF. If the DCE is sending similar signals on its R and I circuits, the interface is said to be in the Ready state. On the other hand, either DTE or DCE may signal its inability to enter an operational phase by transmitting a continuous sequence of 0s on T or R and the condition OFF on C or I, respectively. Finally, both DTE and DCE may signal a temporary inability to enter an operational phase by signaling the controlled not ready condition. The latter is conveyed by the transmission of an alternating sequence of 0 and 1 on T or R and the OFF condition on C or I.

Let us now describe the X.21 procedure for the successful establishment of a simple circuit switched call to a remote DTE. An event diagram is shown in Figure 7.7 for the calling side and in Figure 7.8 for the called side.

Assuming that the interface at the calling DTE is in the Ready state, the DTE may initiate the call request by transmitting T = 0 and C = ON. As a response the DCE issues on R the Proceed to Select signal, represented by the continuous transmission of the + character from IA5, and sets I to OFF. The appropriate selection signals are then transmitted by the DTE as a sequence of IA5 characters ending with the + character on T, with C remaining in the ON condition. Then the DTE conveys the signal T = 1 and C = ON, and the interface enters the DTE Waiting state. In response, the DCE returns a sequence of two or more SYN characters on R as well as the OFF condition on I and enters the DCE Waiting state. While in this state it may transmit various call progress signals or other DCE-provided information as sequences of IA5 characters on R, with C remaining in the OFF condition. It may also signal the connection-in-progress condition represented by R = 1 and I = OFF.

Once all call selection information has been relayed across the network to the called side, and assuming the called side interface is also in the Ready state, the called DCE initiates alerting of the called DTE by transmitting the incoming call signal. The latter is represented by the continuous transmission of the BEL character from IA5 on R and the OFF condition on I. The called DTE then responds with the call accepted signal by switching the condition on C from OFF to ON. In a manner similar to the calling DCE, the called DCE may provide various types of information and the connection-in-progress signal.

The final step in the call establishment procedure is the transfer of the ready for data signal R = 1, I = ON by the DCEs on the calling and called sides to their respective DTEs. The interface on both sides of the call then enters the Data Transfer state.

In this state end-user data from DTE to DCE is transferred over the T circuit, while in the opposite direction it flows over the R circuit. C and I remain in the ON condition. All such data flow transparently between the two DTEs.

Figures 7.7 and 7.8 also show the events during the clearing phase of the call. The calling DTE submits a DTE clear request by switching

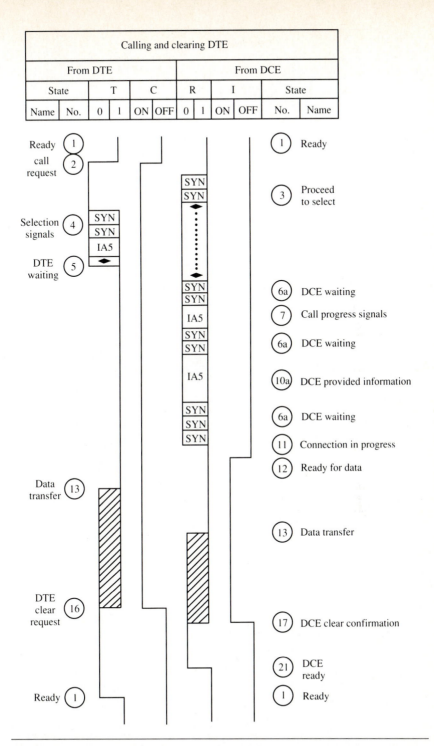

Figure 7.7 *Sequence of events for establishment and clearing of connection (calling and clearing DTE)*

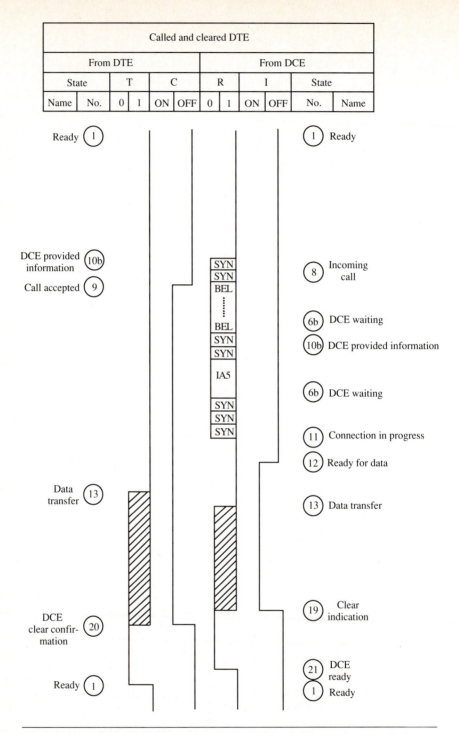

Figure 7.8 *Sequence of events for establishment and clearing of connection (called and cleared DTE)* © Reprinted from CCITT Blue Book, vol. VIII.2, 1988.

the C circuit to OFF and setting $T = 0$. On completion of its own data transfer, the calling DCE responds with the DCE clear confirmation signal by also sending $R = 0$ and $I = $ OFF. Then the interface is returned to the Ready state by the transmission of the DCE ready signal and the DTE ready signal, as indicated earlier. On the called side the DCE clear indication signal $R = 0$ and $I = $ OFF is transmitted by the DCE. After the cleared DTE has responded with its DTE clear confirmation signal $T = 0$, $C = $ OFF the interface is likewise placed in the Ready state by the earlier procedure.

7.2.3   Adaption of the X.21 Call Establishment Procedure

We turn now to a consideration of the mapping of the X.21 procedure for setting up a circuit switched connection between two DTEs to the I.451 D-channel protocol. A diagram of the conversion is shown in Figure 7.9. We assume that initially the X.21 interface on both the calling and called sides is in the Ready state.

When it receives the end-of-selection signal from the calling DTE, the S/T controller of the TA generates a SETUP message that includes the Called Number IE and the Bearer Capability IE. The first IE contains en bloc the complete selection information provided by the DTE in the selection signals. In the second IE the transfer mode is set to "circuit" and the information transfer rate is set to 64 kbit/s. This message is then transferred across the S or T reference point to the ET over the D channel in accordance with the I.430/431 procedures at the physical layer and the LAPD protocol at the data link layer. The network side normally responds to the receipt of the SETUP message with the CALL PROCEEDING message, causing the S/T controller to allocate a B channel and the DCE to signal to its DTE the DCE waiting condition.

The network relays the SETUP message to the ET on the called side, which in turn sends it to the S/T controller of the TA, again in accordance with the I.430/431 and LAPD procedures. As a response the S/T controller generates an ALERTING message, which is relayed over the network to the TA on the calling side. On the calling side it prompts the transmission of the call progress signal by the calling DCE to the calling DTE. On the called side the DCE transmits the X.21 incoming call signal to its DTE. When the latter accepts the call by sending the X.21 call accepted signal, the S/T controller sends the CONNECT message to its ET, which in turn relays it to the calling side S/T controller via the calling side ET. The called side ET also acknowledges the CONNECT message to its S/T controller with a

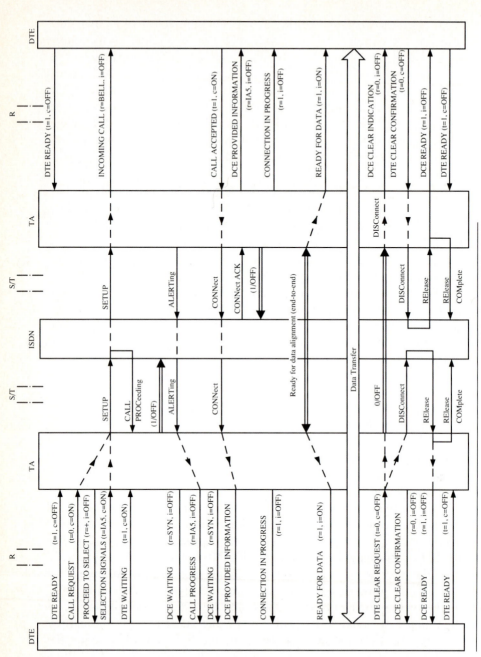

Figure 7.9 *Conversion of X.21 call control to I.451*

CONNECT ACKNOWLEDGE message, allocating a particular B channel to the connection. The DCE in the called TA then sends any DCE-provided information and the connection-in-progress signal to its DTE. On the calling side the TA, on receiving the CONNECT message, proceeds in the same way by instructing its DCE to transmit to its DTE any DCE-provided information followed by the connection-in-progress signal. At this point both R reference points are in the Connection in Progress state.

Before the interface can enter into the Ready for Data state it is necessary to align the B channels on both sides of the connection. The procedure for accomplishing this task is discussed next.

7.2.4   Ready for Data Alignment

At the point in the call establishment procedure where a B channel has been allocated, the S/T controller initiates the transfer of rate adaption frames over that channel. These frames contain the synchronization pattern and the status digits SP, SQ, and SR set to the connection-in-progress signal R = 1 and I = OFF. No end-user data is allowed.

The transmission of frames is maintained until the R interface is in the Connection in Progress state. At this point the S/T controller scans the B channel for the synchronization pattern of a rate adaption frame received from the other side. When synchronization has been achieved the B channel is connected to the DTE and the S/T controller begins to relay the T = 1, C = ON condition from the DTE to the remote S/T controller in the SP, SQ, and SR status digits. There the DCE relays it to its DTE as the ready-for-data signal R = 1, I = ON. Data transfer over the B channel from the remote DTE may then begin and may continue as long as the DTE receives this signal.

It is clear that in the data transfer phase the B channel must accommodate both the end-user data and the continuous transmission of the ready-for-data signal. Since this inband signaling reduces the capacity of the B channel for carrying user information, it is not permitted for user class-of-service 19, where the entire B-channel capacity is required for the end-user data. In this case the following procedure is employed. On receiving the CONNECT ACKNOWLEDGE message the called S/T controller transmits a continuous sequence of 1s to the calling S/T controller over the B channel. When the calling S/T controller recognizes at least 24 of these digits in sequence, it sends a similar pattern to the called S/T controller and prompts its DCE to send the ready-for-data signal to its DTE. Once the called S/T controller has recognized 24 of these digits, it likewise causes its DCE to issue the ready-for-data signal to its DTE, completing the procedure.

7.2.5 *Adaption of the X.21 Call Clearing Procedure*

The mapping of the procedure for clearing a circuit switched connection is shown in Figure 7.9.

The DTE initiating the clearing generates the DTE clear request signal T = 0, C = OFF and transfers it over the R reference point to the DCE. From there it is conveyed over the B channel between the two S/T controllers in the status digits of the rate adaption frame and from cleared DCE to cleared DTE as the DTE clear indication signal R = 0, I = OFF. This inhibits any further transfer of data from the remote DTE.

On the clearing side the DCE responds by sending to its DTE the DCE clear confirmation signal R = 0, I = OFF. A DISCONNECT message is also conveyed between the clearing S/T controller and its ET over the D channel. The ET then returns the RELEASE message to its S/T controller, which prompts the clearing DCE to indicate the DCE ready condition R = 1, I = OFF to its DTE. When the latter responds with the DTE ready signal T = 1, C = OFF, the S/T controller transfers a RELEASE COMPLETE message to its ET to complete the procedure at the clearing side.

On the cleared side the DTE responds to the receipt of the DCE clear indication signal with the DTE clear confirmation signal, causing the S/T controller on the cleared side to transmit the DISCONNECT message to its ET. The latter then returns the RELEASE message, which is mapped into the DCE ready signal transmitted by the cleared DCE. When the cleared DTE responds with the DTE ready signal the S/T controller sends the RELEASE COMPLETE message to its ET as the final step in the procedure.

7.3 X.20bis, X.21bis, and V-Series Terminal Adaption

We consider next the adaption problem for the type of terminal that normally interfaces with a signal conversion device such as a modem for the purpose of transmitting data over public data networks or over the public switched telephone network. Such terminals operate over a wide range of synchronous and asynchronous data rates and utilize several different DTE-to-DCE interface configurations.

The current state of development of this terminal adaption is summarized in CCITT Recommendations I.461 (X.30) and I.463 (V.110). To date only the data rate conversion technique has been completely specified, whereas many details of the mapping of the call control procedure remain to be considered.

7.3.1 Rate Adaption

The synchronous and asynchronous data rates that must be adapted to the 64-kbit/s B-channel rate are shown in Table 7.1. As in the case of the X.21 interface, the adaption process is carried out in multiple stages, using an intermediate frame structure into which the user data is organized. Since the details of adaption depend somewhat on the specific rate, we consider several cases.

For the synchronous data rates up to 19.2 kbit/s the adaption is accomplished in two steps, with an intermediate rate as given in Table 7.1. The conversion uses the 80-bit frame shown in Figure 7.10, whose structure is similar to the multiframe employed in the X.21 rate adaption. Frame synchronization is carried out with the aid of the synchronization sequence located in octet 0 and the first digit of octets 1 to 9. Digits E1 to E3 define the synchronous data rate, E4 to E6 carry network-independent clock signals, and E7 provides a multiple frame synchronization indication. The status digits S1, S3, S4, S6, S8, S9, and X are used to convey information that controls entry to and exit from the data transfer phase, with the X digit optionally available for flow control between the two TAs. The data digits are located in positions D1 to D48.

The adaption of the synchronous data rates of the DTE to the appropriate intermediate rate specified in Table 7.1 is accomplished by either the repetition of a given DTE data digit a certain number of times in the frame or the insertion of filler digits. For rates of 0.6 kbit/s, 1.2 kbit/s, and 2.4 kbit/s each data digit occurs 8 times, 4 times, or twice in succession, respectively. A given 80-digit frame therefore contains exactly 6, 12, or 24 distinct data digits, and the frame digit rate must be the multiple of 80/6, 80/12, or 80/24 of the data rate, respectively. No repetition of the data digits is required for rates of 4.8 kbit/s, 9.6 kbit/s, and 19.2 kbit/s. For rates of 7.2 kbit/s and 14.4 kbit/s, the adaption to 16 kbit/s and 32 kbit/s, respectively, is achieved by inserting 12 filler digits in positions D11, D12, D15, D16, D19, D20,

TABLE 7.1 Conversion rates for synchronous and asynchronous data rates

SYNCHRONOUS RATE (kbit/s)	INTER-MEDIATE RATE (kbit/s)	ASYNCHRONOUS RATE (kbit/s)	SYNCHRONOUS CONVERSION (kbit/s)	INTER-MEDIATE RATE (kbit/s)
0.6	8	0.050	0.6	8
1.2	8	0.075	0.6	8
2.4	8	0.110	0.6	8
4.8	8	0.150	0.6	8
7.2	16	0.200	0.6	8
9.6	16	0.300	0.6	8
12	32	0.600	0.6	8
14.4	32	1.2	1.2	8
19.2	32	2.4	2.4	8
48	—	3.6	4.8	8
56	—	4.8	4.8	8
		7.2	9.6	16
		9.6	9.6	16
		12	19.2	32
		14.4	19.2	32
		19.2	19.2	32

D35, D36, D39, D40, D43, and D44. Each frame therefore contains 36 distinct data digits, yielding the appropriate frame rate of (80/36)7200 = 16 kbit/s or (80/36)14.4 = 32 kbit/s. Finally, the rate of 12 kbit/s requires an additional 6 filler digits in positions D22, D23, D24, D46, D47, and D48.

The adaption of these intermediate rates to the B-channel rate of 64 kbit/s is accomplished in a manner similar to the X.21 interface. Thus, for the intermediate rates of 8 kbit/s, 16 kbit/s, and 32 kbit/s the frame digits are placed in position 1, positions 1 and 2, and positions 1, 2, 3, and 4, respectively, of successive B-channel octets. The remaining bit positions of the octets are set to binary 1.

The adaption of the two synchronous rates of 48 kbit/s and 56

Octet number	Bit number							
	1	2	3	4	5	6	7	8
0	0	0	0	0	0	0	0	0
1	1	D1	D2	D3	D4	D5	D6	S1
2	1	D7	D8	D9	D10	D11	D12	X
3	1	D13	D14	D15	D16	D17	D18	S3
4	1	D19	D20	D21	D22	D23	D24	S4
5	1	E1	E2	E3	E4	E5	E6	E7
6	1	D25	D26	D27	D28	D29	D30	S6
7	1	D31	D32	D33	D34	D35	D36	X
8	1	D37	D38	D39	D40	D41	D42	S8
9	1	D43	D44	D45	D46	D47	D48	S9

Figure 7.10 *Rate adaption frame structure*
© Reprinted from CCITT Blue Book, vol. VIII.2, 1988.

kbit/s is accomplished in one step. For the first, a frame consisting of four octets and containing 24 data digits is used. The rate of 56 kbit/s employs an eight-octet frame containing 56 data digits. The digits of these frames occupy the entire B channel.

Rate adaption of the asynchronous data rates listed in Table 7.1 is preceded by initially converting the rates to their next higher synchronous rate. This is accomplished by the insertion of an appropriate number of stop bits following each character. The resultant synchronous data stream is then applied to the rate adaption mechanism for synchronous data rates discussed previously.

7.3.2 Interface Specifications

Generally the connection between the DTE and DCE across an X.20bis, X.21bis, or V-series interface is provided by a set of circuits whose nomenclature and functional characteristics are specified in CCITT Recommendation V.24. Depending on the particular DTE and DCE, different subsets of the V.24 circuits may be present in different interfaces.

As far as the adaption of the interface to the S/T reference point is concerned, the most pertinent circuits are listed in Table 7.2. Of these, circuits 103, 105, 108/1, and 108/2 are used in the direction DTE to DCE, while the remaining circuits function in the opposite direction. The circuits are distinguished as data circuits (103 and 104), control circuits (105 to 109 and 125), and timing circuits (114 and 115).

For data rates less than or equal to 19.2 kbit/s, the electrical properties of the preceding circuits conform to the specifications of CCITT Recommendation V.28. They are terminated in connectors specified in ISO 2110. For data rates in excess of 19.2 kbit/s, the generators and receivers of all data and timing circuits are as specified in CCITT Recommendation V.11. Control circuits, on the other hand, may conform to either V.11 or V.10. The connector in this case is as specified in ISO 4902.

Let us now briefly discuss the function of each circuit. Data circuits are said to be in binary state 1 or 0, whereas all other circuits are either in the ON or OFF state. The electrical signal that defines a particular state depends, of course, on the electrical specifications to which the circuits conform.

TABLE 7.2   V.24 interface circuits

INTERCHANGE CIRCUIT	
No.	*Description*
103	Transmitted data
104	Received data
105	Request to send
106	Ready for sending
107	Data set ready
108/1	Connect data set to line
108/2	Data terminal ready
109	Data channel received line signal detector
114	Transmitter signal element timing (DCE source)
115	Receiver signal element timing (DCE source)
125	Calling indicator

Circuit 103 carries the end-user data from DTE to DCE, and circuit 104 is used for a similar purpose in the direction DCE to DTE. For synchronous transmission the timing of both of these data streams is the responsibility of the DCE, which sends appropriate clock signals on circuits 114 and 115 to the DTE.

The control circuits 105 to 109 and 125 are set to ON or OFF to indicate certain actions to the other side. In the ON condition circuit 105 conveys to the DCE a request from the DTE to transmit data. The DCE in turn signals the ON condition on circuit 106 to indicate to the DTE that it is prepared to accept such data. Circuit 107, when set to ON, notifies the DTE that the DCE is ready to exchange control signals for the purpose of initiating data transfer. The ON condition on circuit 108/1 instructs the DCE to connect its signal conversion device to the network, and circuit 108/2 is set to ON whenever the DTE is ready to transmit or receive data. Circuit 109 is set to ON by the DCE to signal to the DTE that the data signal received on circuit 103 is within required quality limits. Finally, circuit 125 is set to ON to indicate an incoming call to the DTE.

As a simple example of the interactions between DTE and DCE, we consider the automatic establishment of a connection over the public switched telephone network between two DTEs. Although the sequence of events is subject to several options, we follow one of the procedures specified in CCITT Recommendation V.25bis and shown in Figure 7.11.

Let us assume that the interface on both sides of an eventual connection is initially in the DTE Not Ready state, shown as state 1 in Figure 7.11 and defined by the transmission of the OFF condition on the four circuits 108/2, 107, 106, and 125, as also indicated in Figure 7.11. When the DTE wants to communicate with its DCE, it signals the ON condition on its circuit 108/2, to which the DCE responds with the ON condition on circuit 106. The interface is then in the Dialogue state, during which the DTE can transfer so-called commands to its DCE and the latter can respond with so-called indications. These messages are coded as IA5 characters and may be accompanied by one or more parameters. They are conveyed over circuits 103 and 104, respectively.

While in the Dialogue state, a DTE may request the establishment of a call by transmitting the call request message, with the called number as a parameter, to its DCE, at which time the interface enters the Call Establishment state. On the network side the DCE now seizes

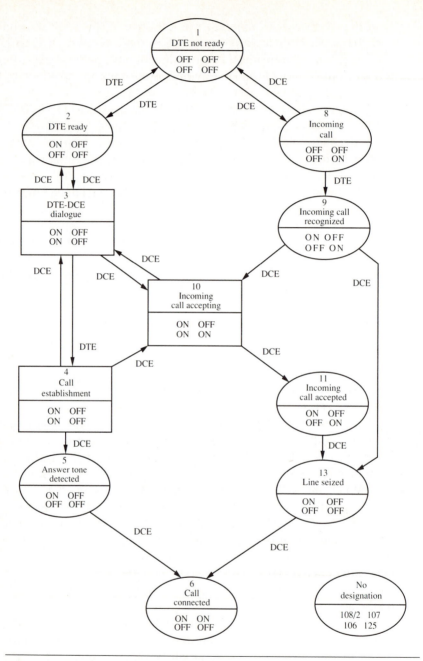

Figure 7.11 V.25bis call control procedure

the line by going off hook, and when it receives the dial tone, it conveys the called DTE number to the network.

As a result of these actions, the called DCE receives the ringing signal from the network, which causes it to indicate the call to its DTE by placing circuit 125 in the ON condition. In response the called DTE places circuit 108/2 in the ON condition, at which time the interface enters the Incoming Call Recognized state. The DCE now indicates the ON condition on circuit 106, which places the interface in the Incoming Call Accepting state.

In certain situations an exchange of messages between called DTE and DCE may be required, so that the two sides must first enter the Dialogue state according to the procedure discussed earlier. The transition to the Incoming Call Accepting state at the end of the dialogue can then be effected by the DCE placing circuit 125 in the ON condition.

If the interface remains in the Incoming Call Accepting state for a predetermined period of time the DCE effects the transition to the Incoming Call Accepting state by turning circuit 106 OFF. It then goes off hook toward the network and conveys the OFF condition on circuit 125 toward the DTE, placing the interface into the Line Seized state. In the final step at the called side, the DCE indicates ON over circuit 107 and enters the Call Connected state.

On the calling side the DCE, on receiving the answer tone from the called DCE, turns circuit 106 to OFF and enters the Answer Tone Detected state. It then completes the call establishment procedure by turning circuit 107 ON and entering the Call Connected state.

7.3.3 Protocol Adaption

Since the relationship between DTE and DCE discussed in the previous section includes only a rudimentary data link control, its mapping onto the S or T interface involves mainly layers 1 and 3.

At layer 3 the conversion to I.451 messages of the commands, indications, and circuit states used by the DTE and DCE to effect call control has not been completely specified. As an example, Figure 7.12 indicates the call establishment procedure when the R reference point conforms to the X.21bis interface.

At layer 1, the entry to and exit from the data transfer state involves the connection of the B channel to circuits 103 and 104 and the alignment of the rate adaption frame structure with the layer 1 B-channel frame. The procedure for accomplishing these tasks is described in CCITT Recommendation I.463 and summarized next.

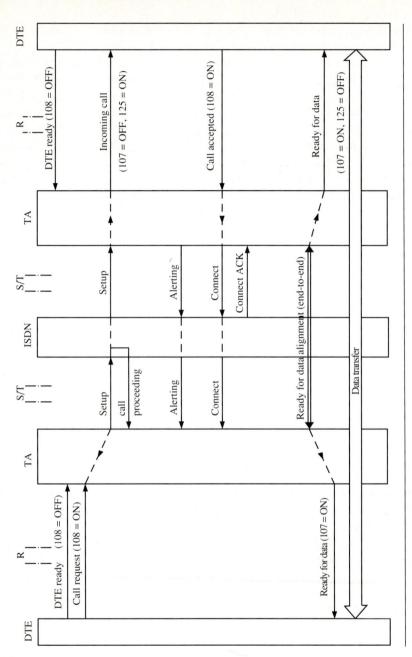

Figure 7.12 *Conversion of X.21bis call establishment procedure*

We assume that the interface has entered the data transfer state—that is, that a connection between the communicating DTEs across a network has been established. Prior to transmitting any real data the DTE conveys a continuous sequence of binary 1s on circuit 103 and the ON condition on circuit 108/2. In the opposite direction the DCE likewise transmits a sequence of binary 1s on circuit 104 and the OFF condition on circuit 106. The S/T controller conveys these circuit states across the S or T interface by transmitting a continuous sequence of binary 1s at the appropriate rate over both the B channel and D channel, in effect setting all digits in the rate adaption frame to binary 1. To condition the interface for data transmission over the B channel, the S/T controller transmits over the B channel the rate adaption frame containing the frame synchronization pattern, with all data digits set to binary 1 and with the S and X status digits set to OFF (binary 1). At the same time it monitors the received B-channel digit stream, and on recognizing the synchronization pattern of the rate adaption frame turns the S and X status digits in the transmitted frame to ON (binary 0). When this condition is sensed by the S/T controller on the other side, it conveys the ON condition on circuit 106 and connects the DTE and DCE data streams on circuits 103 and 104 to the rate adaption frame.

At the completion of data transfer the DTE places circuit 108/2 in the OFF condition, to indicate a disconnect request. This action prompts the local S/T controller to set the S status digits to OFF and all data digits in the rate adaption frame to binary 0. It also conveys the OFF condition on circuit 106 to its DTE. When the remote TA receives this frame it recognizes it as a disconnect signal and turns circuit 107 to OFF. Its DTE then responds by turning circuit 108/2 to OFF and terminating the transmission of data. This action causes the S/T controller to transfer a rate adaption frame with S set to OFF and all data digits set to binary 0. When this frame is received by the TA originating the disconnect, it interprets the status digit as a disconnect confirm, completing the procedure.

7.4 X.25 Terminal Adaption

As currently envisioned by the CCITT, the provision of packet switched data communication services for X.25 terminals attached to an ISDN may be accomplished in two different ways. In the first method, shown in Figure 7.13, the ISDN provides only a physical circuit switched connection over a B channel between the TA and an *access unit (AU)* of an existing packet switched data network. This connection may either be permanent or may be established by means of the I.451 circuit switching call control procedure carried out over the D channel, in response to a request by a DTE to its DCE across the R reference point. Thus a mapping of the R interface protocol for the control of a circuit switched connection to the I.451 procedure is required.

Once the connection exists, the B channel can be used to convey X.25 layer 2 and 3 protocol information between DTE and AU for the purpose of establishing, controlling, and terminating a virtual circuit to another X.25 DTE and transferring data between the DTEs. These procedures are entirely transparent to the ISDN and no terminal adaption is required. At the physical layer the TA-to-AU communication must, of course, conform to the I.430/431 requirements for the B channel, necessitating the conversion of the electrical parameters of the R interface to the S or T interface, the adaption of the DTE data rate to the 64-kbit/s B-channel rate, and the provision of data alignment.

In this scenario the packet mode terminal and the access unit are

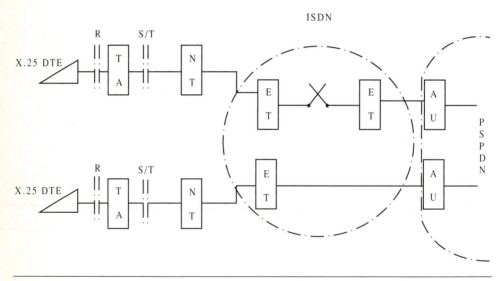

Figure 7.13 *B-channel connection of X.25 DTE to PSPDN access unit*
© Adapted from CCITT Blue Book, vol. VIII.2, 1988.

logically part of the packet switched data network. The only support the ISDN offers is a circuit switched connection over the B channel between the TA and the AU, across which the DTE may exchange X.25 data link–level and packet-level information with the AU in a manner transparent to the ISDN. As a consequence it is necessary for the DTE to provide to the ISDN the address of the AU for B-channel connection, and to the AU the packet switched network address of the remote DTE for X.25 virtual circuit service. It is also evident that the service characteristics of the virtual circuits and the facilities made available to a packet mode DTE are those of the packet switched network.

In the second method, depicted in Figure 7.14, the ISDN provides a complete X.25 virtual circuit service between X.25 DTEs by incorporating a so-called *packet handler (PH)* with which a TA can communicate at layers 2 and 3 of the X.25 protocol.

The connection between a TA and the PH can utilize either the B channel or the D channel and can be permanent or established on demand. The procedure for establishing the B channel and the operation over it are similar to the first method. Once the connection exists, the I.430/431 formats must again be used at the physical layer between TA

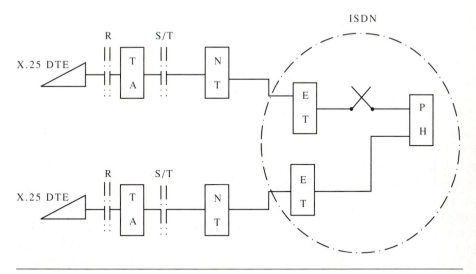

Figure 7.14 *B-channel or D-channel connection of X.25 DTE to ISDN packet handler*

© Adapted from CCITT Blue Book, vol. VIII.2, 1988.

and PH. At the data link layer and packet layer the DTE and PH can exchange information according to the X.25 layer 2 and 3 procedures in a manner transparent to the TA.

If the communication between TA and PH is carried by the D channel, the TA and PH must establish a logical link between them. This requires the mapping of the LAPB logical link control procedures followed over the R reference point into the equivalent LAPD procedures over the S or T reference point. The layer 3 X.25 information may then be transferred between DTE and PH in a manner transparent to the TA by sharing the D-channel capacity with signaling information in a multiplex arrangement. Unlike in the first method, the PH—being an integral part of the ISDN—does not have to be individually addressed by the DTE. Likewise, the DTE is considered a part of the ISDN in both the physical and logical sense and is identified by an ISDN address. Finally, since the virtual circuit services and other network facilities are entirely provided by the ISDN, their characteristics are those of the ISDN rather than an independent packet switched network.

In the following section we again offer a summary discussion of the major issues in X.25 terminal adaption, including the rate adaption technique and the control of the B channel and D channel.

7.4.1 X.25 Rate Adaption

For access to the PH or AU via the B channel, the rates at which an X.25 packet mode DTE may communicate across the R reference point are restricted to categories of access T1/Y1 (2.4 kbit/s), T2/Y2 (4.8 kbit/s), T3/Y3 (9.6 kbit/s), T4/Y4 (48 kbit/s), and T5/Y5 (64 kbit/s), as specified in CCITT Recommendation X.10. The same rates, corresponding to categories of access U1 to U5, may be used for D-channel access. Category U5, however, is not permitted if the S/T interface conforms to basic access, since the D channel in this case operates at 16 kbit/s. All transmissions are synchronous.

For data rates less than 64 kbit/s two methods of rate adaption have been specified. In the case of B-channel access to an AU the conversion of the rates normally follows the procedure described for X.21 terminals. For B-channel or D-channel access to the PH the conversion is achieved through the insertion in the data stream of an appropriate number of HDLC flags between successive HDLC frames. Note that this requires the ability on the part of the TA to recognize the beginning and end of an HDLC frame, even in the case of B-channel access.

7.4.2 Protocol Adaption for B-Channel Connection

Let us now consider the protocol adaption problem for the case when a B channel is used to provide the connection between a TA and the PH or AU. At the physical layer the relationship between an X.25 DTE and its DCE across the R reference point normally conforms to the specifications of CCITT Recommendation X.21, X.21bis, or one of the V-series recommendations. Therefore many of the details of the B-channel connection are similar to those covered in the previous sections of this chapter.

To initiate connection establishment, the DTE can follow one of two procedures. If the address of the AU is available in the TA, the DTE may simply signal call request by setting circuit C or circuit 108 to the ON condition, depending on the type of DTE-to-DCE interface present. The TA then interacts with the PH or AU according to the I.451 circuit switching procedure and notifies the DTE that the B channel is connected by setting circuit I or circuit 107 to the ON condition. If, on the other hand, the AU address is provided by the DTE, the full circuit switching selection procedure and its mapping into the I.451 protocol—as described in the previous sections of this chapter—apply.

Disconnection of the B channel is normally prompted by the detection of a clearing of the X.25 layer 3 virtual circuit and layer 2 data link connection between DTE and PH or AU. The DTE may then initiate the disconnection by transmitting the OFF condition on circuit C or 108. In response the TA follows the normal I.451 procedures for the clearing of a circuit switched connection over the B channel between it and the PH or AU.

7.4.3 Protocol Adaption for D-Channel Connection

The ability of an X.25 DTE to establish, maintain, and terminate a virtual circuit to another DTE over a D channel requires the existence of a logical link to the PH over the same D channel. To establish, maintain, and terminate such logical links the TA acts to convert the LAPB protocol governing the layer 2 relationship between DTE and DCE to the LAPD protocol between S/T controller and PH.

Certain aspects of these relationships are purely local and do not have to be mapped from one protocol to the other. For example, the frame check sequence present in a LAPB frame is used strictly for the control of errors across R, while a completely independent FCS is applied to LAPD frames for error control across the S or T reference

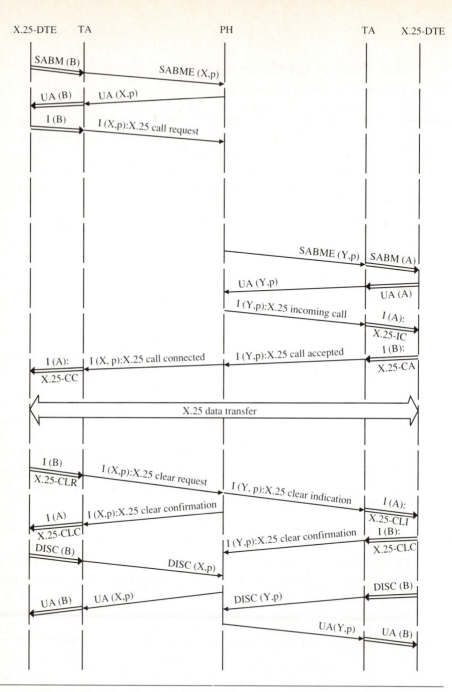

Figure 7.15 *Procedure for D-channel access*

point. Likewise, the exchange of S frames across one interface to acknowledge or request the retransmission of I frames has no effect on the other interface. As far as the mapping of the frame structure is concerned, we note the difference in format of the address and sequence number fields of LAPB and LAPD frames.

We now describe the various interactions across R and S/T to establish a logical link between DTE and PH over the D channel. A diagram of the message exchange is shown in Figure 7.15. Here (A) and (B) are the LAPB addresses of the DTE and PH, respectively, and (X,p) and (Y,p) denote the TEI and SAPI of the two TAs.

The procedure is initiated by the DTE through the transmission of the LAPB SABM frame to its DCE. As a result the S/T controller transmits the equivalent LAPD SABME frame with a SAPI of p = 16 to the PH. The latter then responds with the LAPD UA frame, causing the DCE to complete the setup of the logical link by transferring the LAPB UA frame to its DTE.

Thereafter the calling DTE and PH may exchange layer 3 X.25 packets for the purpose of establishing, maintaining, and clearing virtual circuits across the ISDN to another DTE and transferring user data between them. These packets are transported between DTE and DCE in the information field of LAPB I frames and between S/T controller and PH in the information field of LAPD I frames. They are completely transparent to the TA. Of course, the transfer of a layer 3 X.25 packet between the TA and DTE on the called side also requires the existence of a logical link. This is established at the initiative of the PH, but in a similar manner. Figure 7.15 illustrates the sequence of interactions on the two sides of a network connection leading to the establishment of a virtual circuit between two X.25 DTEs.

The DTEs may clear the virtual circuit between them through the exchange of clearing packets that are again carried transparently in I frames over the logical links between DTE and PH. This procedure, and the subsequent disconnection of the logical links, are also shown in Figure 7.15.

7.5 Summary and Recommended Reading

Chapter 7 covered the problem of converting non-ISDN terminal equipment to the formats and protocols specified in the previous chapters. In general the adaption of a terminal involves the conversion to the ISDN specifications of the data rates, the physical interface, and the logical interactions that the terminal carries out. We discussed the adaption of three types of terminals whose native protocols have been standardized by the CCITT. These are the X.21 terminals for synchronous operation over circuit switched data networks, terminals conforming to the interfaces of the V-series, X.20bis, and X.21bis recommendations, and the X.25 terminals for operation over packet switched networks.

For a discussion of the concepts of minimum and maximum integration and the conversion of X.21, X.21bis, and X.25 terminals see [RUMS86].

CHAPTER 8

The Digital Section

The preceding four chapters focused on the physical and logical aspects of the ISDN, insofar as they pertain to the user-to-network interface points S, T, and R. Thus, our concern was with the part of the ISDN subscriber-access network that is normally located on the customer premises and that is under the direct control of the end-user. It is important to note that from the end-user's perspective, an ISDN manifests itself largely through the physical interconnections and logical interactions between the various functional groups across these reference points. Consequently, the end-user's relationship with the network is embodied in the standardized interface structures studied in Chapters 4 to 7.

We turn our attention now to the second major part of the subscriber-access network: the so-called digital section. Its primary purpose is to provide the physical connectivity, the electrical signaling, and the control structure required to carry the various information flows across the U reference point between the customer premises and the transit network.

As shown in Figure 8.1, the digital section extends from the T reference point on the customer premises to the V reference point that separates the physical and logical terminations of the subscriber-access network at the local exchange. It therefore consists of the NT1 and LT functional groups and the physical medium between them. The latter is known as the *digital transmission system* and may be a metallic pair of wires, a coaxial cable, an optical fiber cable, or a radio transmission system. Together these components provide the physical transmission function of the subscriber-access network and permit the logical interaction between a TE or NT2 and an ET.

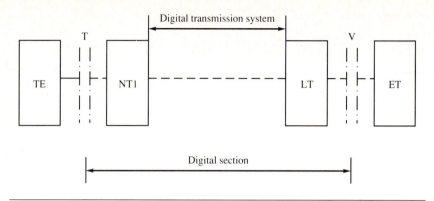

Figure 8.1 *The digital section*

Several different configurations of the local exchange termination are possible. They are shown in Figure 8.2. Normally, the digital section provides direct access to the ET in the local exchange via the V1 reference point for basic access and the V3 reference point for primary access. In those serving areas of the network where the density of subscribers is low, or during a period of transition where the expense of converting the local exchange to ISDN capability cannot be justified economically, it may be desirable to provide the physical termination of the subscriber-access network at a site remote from the local exchange. In such cases the digital section terminates at either a remote concentrator or a static multiplexer. These combine traffic from several subscriber-access networks and transmit the resulting data flows to the ET between pairs of V2 or V4 reference points and separate digital sections. Depending on the level of activity, a concentrator may combine up to several hundred basic-access digital sections in a statistical multiplex arrangement. In the current specification of the static multiplexer, on the other hand, 12 basic-access digital sections are combined in a synchronous TDM arrangement.

According to the standard and internationally accepted definition of the ISDN, the T reference point marks the boundary between the subscriber and the network, so that the digital section is entirely under the control of the network. As a result, its characteristics are masked from the end-user. They may be specified by the network according to its own requirements, as long as the requirements of the S and T reference points—insofar as they are relevant to the digital section—are met. Given the substantial differences in the subscriber-access net-

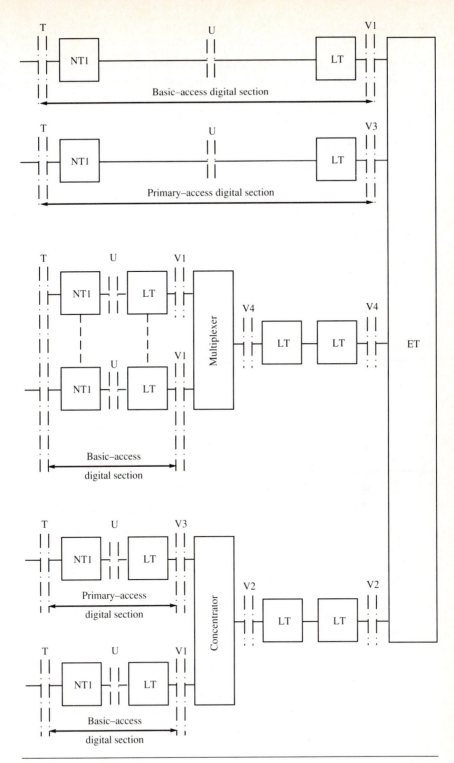

Figure 8.2 *Digital section terminations*

work infrastructure of the world's telecommunications networks, it is not surprising that several different and inherently incompatible versions of the digital section have been proposed and implemented. To date no international standard has been issued by the CCITT, although a preliminary version is currently under consideration.

By contrast, in the North American definition of the ISDN the network terminates at the U reference point. Therefore, to assure the independence between the customer premises and the network, it becomes necessary to standardize at least those aspects of the digital section that are relevant to the end-user. In recognition of this fact the T1 committee of the Exchange Carriers Standards Association has developed a particular implementation of the digital section as a standard for use in the North American ISDN. This work currently applies only to basic-access interface structures.

Our objective in this chapter is to offer a summary of the technical issues involved in the specification of the digital section. Although many details remain to be resolved, a consensus has been reached on most of the major aspects. We refer the reader to CCITT Recommendations G.960, G.961, and the recommendations of the Q.500 and G.700 series of the 1988 *Blue Book* for the most recent version of the emerging international standard and to ANSI document T1.601–1988 for the North American standard.

8.1 The Digital Section for Basic Access

The primary task of the digital section for the basic-access interface is the bit-sequence independent full duplex transmission across the U reference point of the user information flows, control information flows, and user-to-user signaling flows. These flows are contained in the 2B+D channel structure implemented across the S or T reference point. In support of this task the digital section carries out certain additional control functions and a maintenance function to assure an appropriate level of performance and reliability.

The functional aspects of the digital section can be divided into four major parts, as shown in Figure 8.3.

The transmission function is responsible for the full duplex transmission of the 2B+D channel structure and certain additional control information. The total data rate that must be conveyed in full duplex

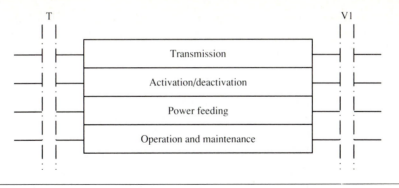

Figure 8.3 *Functionality of the digital section for basic access*

manner between the T and V1 reference points depends somewhat on the specific transmission technique chosen, but it is typically on the order of 160 kbit/s. To characterize the transmission function requires the specification of the digital transmission system, including the physical and electromagnetic properties of the medium, the structure of the information flows transmitted across it, the line code employed, the method used to achieve full duplex transmission, and the procedures for timing and synchronization.

The activation procedure places the NT1 and LT functional groups, as well as the digital transmission system, into their normal operating mode in preparation for data transmission. It also supports the activation of the interface across the S or T reference point, as described in Chapter 4. Activation is usually carried out at the initiative of the ET but may also be initiated by the TE.

The deactivation function is necessary in order to place the digital section and the interface across T into a mode of low power consumption. It is usually initiated by the ET.

The power feeding function allows the supply of power from the network to the NT1 and TE customer-premises equipment and therefore supports the power feeding options discussed in Chapter 4.

The procedures for operation and maintenance are intended to assure reliable operation of the digital section and provide the required level of performance across the entire user-to-network interface. In support of this goal they are designed to detect loss of frame alignment, to provide supervision of the power feeding function, and to monitor the transmission performance parameters.

Several different techniques for accomplishing the objectives of the digital section have been developed and implemented. These are discussed in the following sections.

8.1.1 The Transmission Medium for Basic Access

The most important transmission medium between the NT1 and LT for basic access is the standard metallic two-wire twisted pair commonly used as the subscriber loop in the telephone networks. This choice is mandated primarily by its widespread availability, which makes possible the large-scale introduction of the ISDN without the major investment in subscriber-access lines otherwise required. Other media such as coaxial cables, optical fibers, and radio links have been proposed and are occasionally implemented. Their role, however, is restricted to special situations where the metallic pair is unsuitable or unavailable.

As shown in Figure 8.4, a metallic pair cable typically consists of multiple sections of pairs of high-purity copper wires covered with either a polyethylene or wood pulp insulation. The wires are twisted into loops of different twist length to reduce electromagnetic coupling to other pairs located nearby in a bulk cable, which contains from several hundred to several thousand pairs. The diameter of the wires typically varies section by section over the range of 0.4 to 0.8 mm or #19, #22, #24, and #26 American Wire Gauge (AWG).

For the transmission of information in digital format, only non-loaded cables are suitable. Existing loading coils must therefore be removed. In many networks the cables also contain one or more so-called *bridge taps (BT)*, which are open-circuit metallic pairs that are

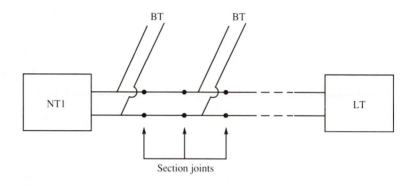

Figure 8.4 *General composition of metallic twisted pair cable*

attached in parallel to the main cable. Since their removal is not feasible for practical reasons, their effects on the transmission system must be compensated.

The statistical distribution of cable length varies substantially from one telephone network to another. Representative values taken from the 1982 GTE Outside Plant Survey [MODE86] for nonloaded loops are given in Figure 8.5. For this network the maximum cable length is on the order of 5.5 km (18 kft), with an average length of approximately 2.7 km (9 kft). Approximately 90 percent of the cables are shorter than 4.6 km (15 kft).

By contrast, Figure 8.6, taken from [ASAT82], shows the cumulative distribution of line length for the Japanese telephone network. Note that the maximum and average lengths here are on the order of 8 km (26 kft) and 1.9 km (6 kft), respectively, and that 90 percent of the loops are shorter than 4 km (13 kft).

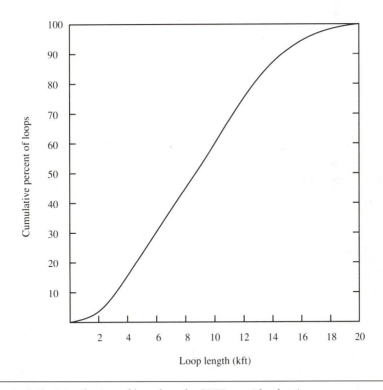

Figure 8.5 *Distribution of loop lengths (GTE outside plant)*
© Adapted from [MODE86].

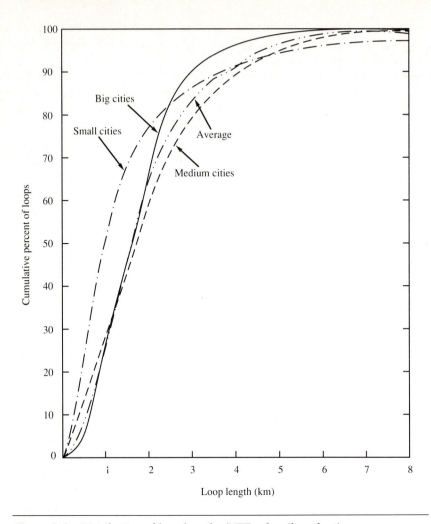

Figure 8.6 *Distribution of loop lengths (NTT subscriber plant)*
© Adapted from [ASAT82].

A typical distribution of the number of BTs on the cables, again taken from the GTE survey [MODE86], is shown in Figure 8.7. More than 20 percent of the loops contain no BTs and 80 percent contain two or fewer BTs. The maximum length of a BT is usually restricted to a value of 1.8 km (5.9 kft), and its average length tends to be around 0.4 km (1.3 kft).

The distance of transmission, data rate, and transmission quality at which digital information can be conveyed over metallic pairs are

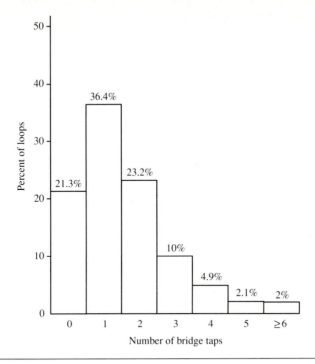

Figure 8.7 *Distribution of bridge taps (GTE outside plant)*
© Adapted from [MODE86].

limited by several factors, among the most important of which is the
so-called insertion loss of the cable, defined as follows. For a given
frequency, let P_1 be the power transferred by a source on one side of
the cable into a load on the other side and let P_2 be the power transferred directly into the same load, but without the intervening cable.
The insertion loss, expressed in dB, is given by

$$\text{Insertion loss} = 10 \log_{10} (P_2/P_1)$$

Although the insertion loss of a twisted pair depends on many factors,
including its manufacture, age, and physical environment, it is primarily a function of its length and diameter, and the number of section
joints, gauge changes, and bridge taps. Figure 8.8, taken from
[SUZU82], shows a typical case involving a line of length 2 km, with
up to four bridge taps of length 0.5 km.

Considering first the line without bridge taps, we note that the
insertion loss is generally a nonlinear function of frequency. At the

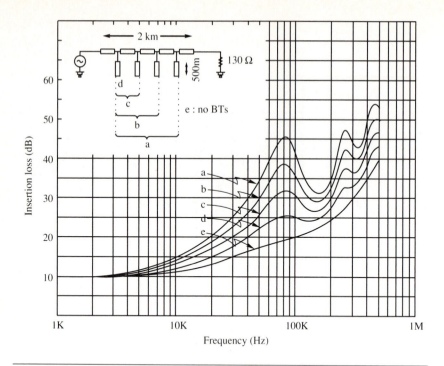

Figure 8.8 *Insertion loss versus frequency*
© Adapted from [SUZU82].

higher frequencies, where skin effects are the primary cause, the insertion loss varies approximately as the square root of frequency.

The time domain response of such a line due to a single isolated square pulse of 1 V amplitude transmitted at a rate of 160 kilobaud is shown in Figure 8.9 for various cable lengths [MESS86]. Clearly, the nonlinear insertion loss causes a dispersion of the waveshape in time, leading to intersymbol interference of successive pulses. This effect generally becomes more severe with increasing cable length and increasing transmission rate.

Now let us consider the effect of the bridge taps. Since the end of a BT is normally open, a pulse traveling along it is reflected from its end back to the transmitting side, causing a reduction in the amount of energy at the receiver. In Figure 8.8 these echoes manifest themselves as large values of insertion loss at certain resonance points in the frequency domain related to the length of the tap. A fraction of the energy reflected by the BTs is also echoed in a forward direction,

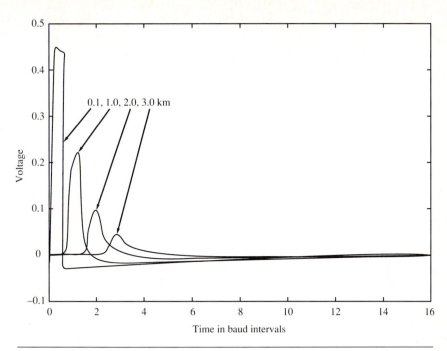

Figure 8.9 *Time domain response of twisted pair without BTs*
© Adapted from [MESS86].

causing the superposition at the receiver of a pulse and its delayed and attenuated version. Finally, reflections of the echo from the transmitter side to the receiver side produce additional delayed and attenuated copies of the pulse. As an example of these effects, Figure 8.10 shows the time domain distortion for a square pulse transmitted at 160 kilobaud over the same line as in Figure 8.9, for a line of length 3 km and a single BT of length 0.5 km [MESS86].

Using various echo cancellation and equalization techniques, it is possible to remove much of the time domain pulse distortion caused by the nonlinear nature of the insertion loss and the bridged taps and thus to restore a received pulse to its original shape. Since the insertion loss on the cable increases with the length of the cable, the distance of transmission that can reliably be achieved depends on the amount of tolerable system gain. The latter is for the most part limited by two factors, the level of crosstalk and the amount of impulse noise present on the line.

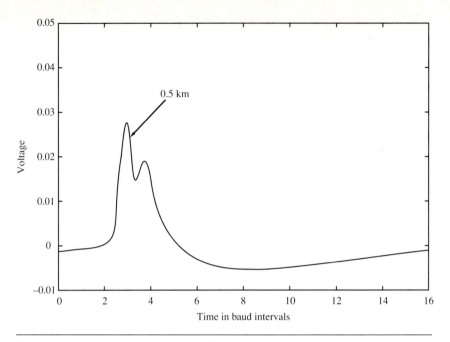

Figure 8.10 *Time domain response for twisted pair with one BT*
© Adapted from [MESS86].

Crosstalk is the coupling of a portion of the electromagnetic energy flowing from one pair onto a neighboring pair. As depicted in Figure 8.11, we distinguish between two types. *Near-end crosstalk (NEXT)* represents the coupling of energy from a transmitter into a receiver located in close proximity to the transmitter. *Far-end crosstalk (FEXT),* on the other hand, is the coupling of transmitted energy into a remote receiver. Since FEXT is subject to the attenuation of the line, NEXT is usually the dominating factor.

Impulse noise is characterized by very large amplitude noise voltages that occur in relatively infrequent bursts. These arise from a variety of sources, including natural phenomena such as lightning, and transients caused by switching and dial pulsing in the central office.

Crosstalk and impulse noise, relative to the amount of insertion loss, determine the signal-to-noise ratio at the receiver and consequently the performance of the transmission system. Since insertion loss is a function of transmission distance, it is clear that a specified level of performance can be reached only over limited distances.

For acceptable performance, the design of the line is typically

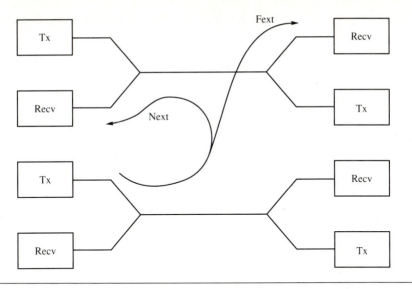

Figure 8.11 *Illustration of NEXT and FEXT*

based on a maximum insertion loss of 40 to 45 dB over the range of frequencies of interest. Measurements have shown that for a #26 AWG cable without bridge taps or section joints, this amounts to a maximum cable length of 15 kft. The length extends to 30 kft for #22 AWG cables. The additional losses due to mixed gauges and the presence of bridge taps may reduce the maximum line length considerably.

8.1.2 Line Codes

Whether the requirements just summarized can be met by a digital transmission system based on a single metallic pair strongly depends on the design of the line code for the information quantities that must be conveyed across the U reference point. By this we mean the pattern of pulse polarities and the waveshapes of the pulses that represent the logical digits 0 and 1, individually and as a sequence.

For the metallic pair the choice of a line code is constrained by several important considerations.

- The code's power spectral density, which is a function of the number of different pulse amplitudes, their shape, the correlation among pulses in a sequence, and the rate at which the pulses are transmitted, must be compatible with the frequency response of the cable and sufficiently compact to fit within its bandwidth. To avoid DC wander, the code should also have little or no DC power in the transmitted spectrum.

- Any arbitrary sequence of line code pulses should have a sufficient number of polarity changes to allow for synchronization and timing of the code at the receiver. Thus, long sequences of line code pulses of the same polarity should be avoided. Most important, the line code should be transparent in the sense that the transmission system's performance should be independent of the particular sequence of binary digits being transmitted, including the sequence of all 0's and the sequence of all 1's.

- The sequence of code symbols should contain a certain amount of redundancy to allow for the detection and possible correction of errors that may occur during transmission.

- The complexity of the circuits at the sending and receiving sides that implement the generation and detection of the line code must be limited.

During the last decade, several different line codes have been investigated as to their suitability for achieving the reliable transmission of data at a rate of 160 kbit/s over a metallic pair and over distances commensurate with the existing infrastructure of subscriber lines [LECH89]. In the most important class of these codes, the rate of the line code pulses is less than the rate of the corresponding binary digits, so that more than one binary digit is represented by a particular pulse. These codes are generally known as *baud rate reduction codes*. Their major advantage lies in the reduced crosstalk generated by the corresponding line signal and the narrower power spectral density, compared to codes based on binary pulses.

One particularly prominent class among the baud rate reduction codes are the so-called mBnL codes, which represent sequences of m binary digits by sequences of n pulses whose amplitudes are chosen from an L-level alphabet, where $n < m$ and $L > 2$. Here the number of L-level pulses per binary digit is n/m, which is clearly less than 1.

In addition to the baud rate reduction, certain mBnL codes also contain redundancy, which may be exploited for error control. Since the number of different binary sequences that must be represented by an mBnL line code equals 2^m and the number of available line code sequences is L^n, the amount of information contained in each pulse equals

$$(m/n) \text{ bits per pulse}$$

assuming that the binary digits occur with equal probability. On the other hand, each pulse is able to carry a maximum of $\log_2 L$ bits of information. The code's redundancy is therefore given by

$$\log_2 L - (m/n) \text{ bits per pulse}$$

Two particular mBnL line codes have been considered for use on the basic-access digital transmission system.

The first of these, known as the *Modified Monitoring State 4B3T* code and denoted *MMS 43*, has been selected by the CCITT for inclusion in the emerging international standard for the basic-access digital section. It maps groups of four consecutive binary digits into three consecutive ternary symbols, denoted $+$, $-$, 0. The rate at which ternary symbols are transmitted is therefore 75 percent of the binary digit rate and the baud rate reduction is 25 percent. The code also contains redundancy since it maps the set of 16 possible binary sequences of four digits into a set of 16 sequences selected from the set of 27 possible sequences of three ternary pulses. The amount of redundant information in each ternary symbol is given by

$$\log_2 3 - 4/3 = 0.23 \text{ bits per pulse}$$

The coding table for the MMS 43 code, which determines the particular choice of the 16 code sequences and consequently the code's power spectral density, is shown in Table 8.1.

Each sequence of four binary digits is represented by a sequence of three symbols chosen from the ternary alphabet $+$, $-$, 0 according to one of the four possible code tables S1, S2, S3, and S4. By convention, both the binary digits and the corresponding ternary digits are read from left to right. Next to the code sequence for a given binary sequence is listed the number of the code table to be used for the immediately following binary sequence.

As an example, consider the binary sequence

1 0 1 1 1 0 0 1 0 0 1 0 0 0 1 1 0 1 0 1 0 0 0 1 1 1 1 0

Assuming arbitrarily that the first four binary digits are encoded according to table S1, we obtain

$$+ 0 - + - + + - 0 0 0 + - 0 0 0 - + 0 + -$$

for the corresponding ternary sequence.

If we associate the $+$ and $-$ symbols with pulses of positive and negative polarity, respectively, and the 0 symbol with the absence of

TABLE 8.1   Coding table for the MMS 43 line code

	S1		S2		S3		S4	
0001	0 − +	1	0 − +	2	0 − +	3	0 − +	4
0111	− 0 +	1	− 0 +	2	− 0 +	3	− 0 +	4
0100	− + 0	1	− + 0	2	− + 0	3	− + 0	4
0010	+ − 0	1	+ − 0	2	+ − 0	3	+ − 0	4
1011	+ 0 −	1	+ 0 −	2	+ 0 −	3	+ 0 −	4
1110	0 + −	1	0 + −	2	0 + −	3	0 + −	4
1001	+ − +	2	+ − +	3	+ − +	4	− − −	1
0011	00 +	2	00 +	3	00 +	4	− − 0	2
1101	0 + 0	2	0 + 0	3	0 + 0	4	− 0 −	2
1000	+ 00	2	+ 00	3	+ 00	4	0 − −	2
0110	− + +	2	− + +	3	− − +	2	− − +	3
1010	+ + −	2	+ + −	3	+ − −	2	+ − −	3
1111	+ + 0	3	00 −	1	00 −	2	00 −	3
0000	+ 0 +	3	0 − 0	1	0 − 0	2	0 − 0	3
0101	0 + +	4	− 00	1	− 00	2	− 00	3
1100	+ + +	4	− + −	1	− + −	2	− + −	3

A received 3T block 000 is decoded into the 4B block 0000.

a pulse, then the normalized power spectrum density of the MMS 43 code for a random sequence of binary 0's and 1's is as shown in Figure 8.12. Note that the signal power is mostly contained in the part of the spectrum extending from DC to approximately the symbol rate of the code and that the spectrum density is relatively large at low frequencies.

The second important line code, known as *2B1Q*, is used as the standard code in the North American version of basic access. It associates pairs of binary digits with a single pulse chosen from a four-pulse alphabet. The pulses are known as *quats* and are symbolically represented by the alphabet +3, +1, −1, −3. According to the encoding rule the first digit in each binary pair determines the sign of the quat and the second digit determines its amplitude. Note that this line

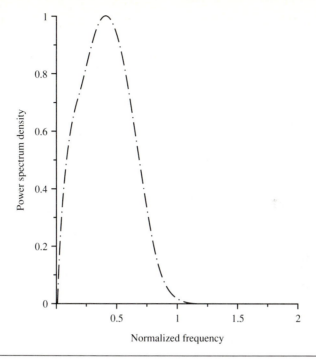

Figure 8.12   *Normalized power spectrum density (MMS 43 code)*

code does not contain any redundancy, but reduces the baud rate by 50 percent.

Figure 8.13 depicts the encoded pulse pattern for a typical binary sequence, using square pulses to represent the various symbol levels.

8.1.3   Scrambling

An examination of the line codes discussed in the previous section reveals the possible occurrence of periodicities in a sequence of pulses for certain common binary sequences. For example, a binary string of 0s encoded in the MMS 43 code will result in the recurring line code + 0 + 0 − 0 0 − 0 of periodicity 9.

These patterns are undesirable for several reasons. First, they increase the probability of loss of synchronization and false lock. Second, they give rise to large discrete components at low frequencies in the line code's power spectral density. Finally, they produce large amounts of crosstalk and cochannel interference.

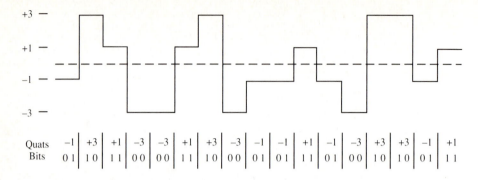

Figure 8.13 *Example of 2B1Q pulse sequence*
© Reprinted from ANSI T1.601, 1988.

For these reasons, the binary data stream containing the information in the two B channels and the D channel is usually subjected to a scrambling procedure prior to line encoding and is descrambled after line decoding at the receiving side. The scrambling polynomials used are the same for both the CCITT and ANSI versions of the digital section specification. At the LT transmitter the polynomial is given by

$$s(x) = 1 + x^{-5} + x^{-23}$$

whereas in the network direction the NT1 uses the polynomial

$$s(x) = 1 + x^{-18} + x^{-23}$$

Here the symbol $+$ denotes the binary exclusive-or operation. The same polynomial as used at the transmitter is applied to descramble the data stream at the receiver.

Figure 8.14 shows the 23-stage linear feedback shift register implementations corresponding to these polynomials. The scrambled data D_s is obtained by summing the original unscrambled data D_i and the output of the feedback shift register. The latter is itself the sum of the contents of the last stage and the contents of stage 5 or 18. D_s is also the input to the shift register. Descrambling is accomplished by combining the scrambled data D_s with the output of the register, again in an exclusive-or gate, to produce the descrambled data D_o.

8.1.4 Frame Structures

The totality of the information that must be transmitted across the U reference point is normally organized into constant-size frames whose structure depends to some extent on the particular line code em-

Scrambler: NT to LT

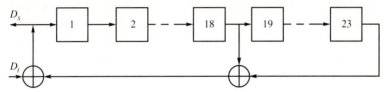

Scrambler: LT to NT

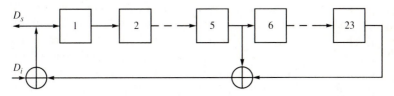

Descrambler: NT to LT

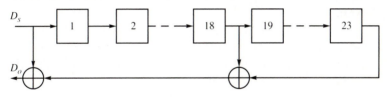

Descrambler: LT to NT

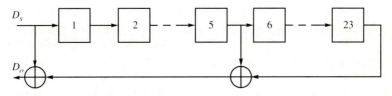

Figure 8.14 *Scrambler and descrambler circuits*
© Adapted from ANSI T1.601, 1988.

ployed. Although many schemes have been proposed and investigated, for basic access only two different frame structures—corresponding to the use of either the MMS 43 line code or the 2B1Q line code—have been utilized.

In the case of the MMS 43 line code, the data are arranged in constant-length frames containing 120 ternary symbols each. These are transmitted in 1 ms, for a symbol rate of 120 kilobaud or an equivalent bit rate of 160 kbit/s. The overall structure of the frame is shown in Figure 8.15 [SZEC86].

Each frame contains four groups of 27 ternary symbols, labeled T1 to T4 for LT-to-NT frames and T5 to T8 for NT-to-LT frames. These carry the information contained in the two B channels and the D channel of the basic-access channel structure. The assignment of one group of 27 ternary symbols to the corresponding 36 binary B-channel and D-channel digits is shown in Figure 8.16. Sixteen binary digits are allocated to each of the two B channels, and the remaining four correspond to the D channel. At the rate of 1000 frames per second the four groups per frame yield the appropriate basic-access channel rates of 64 kbit/s for each B channel and 16 kbit/s for the D channel.

The ternary symbols in positions 110 to 120 for LT-to-NT frames and positions 50 to 60 for NT-to-LT frames form the frame synchronization words SW1 and SW2, respectively. The patterns are 11-symbol Barker codes given by

$$SW1 = - + - - + - - - + + +$$

$$SW2 = + + + - - - + - - + -$$

The remaining ternary symbols M1 and M2 in position 85 of LT-to-NT frames and position 25 of NT-to-LT frames form a 1-kilobaud service channel known as the *M channel*. Its purpose is to control the use of test loops on the subscriber and network sides of the U reference point.

We note that the positions of the synchronization words and the M1 and M2 symbols in the LT-to-NT and NT-to-LT frames are offset by 60 symbols, corresponding to 50 ms of transmission time. This eliminates any cross correlation between the frames flowing in the two directions.

For the 2B1Q code the information is formatted as shown in Figure 8.17. Each frame consists of 120 quats—corresponding to 240 bits—that are transmitted in 1.5 ms. Thus, the baud rate is 80 kilobaud

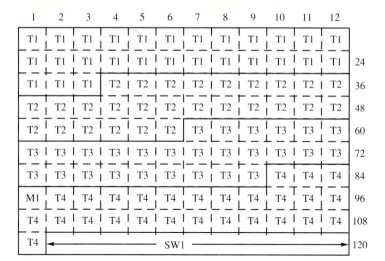

LT–to–NT1 frames

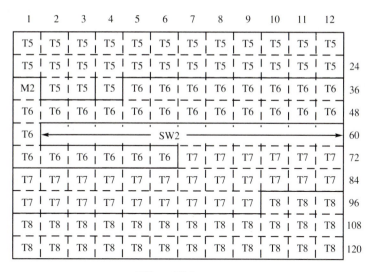

NT1–to–LT frames

Figure 8.15 *MMS 43 frame structures*
© Reprinted from [SZEC86].

1	2	3	4	5	6	7	8	9	10	11	12	13	14	15	16	17	18	19	20	21	22	23	24	25	26	27
Ti	Ti	Ti	Ti	Ti	Ti	Ti	Ti	Ti	Ti	Ti	Ti	Ti	Ti	Ti	Ti	Ti	Ti	Ti	Ti	Ti	Ti	Ti	Ti	Ti	Ti	Ti

1	2	3	4	5	6	7	8	9	10	11	12	13	14	15	16	17	18	19	20	21	22	23	24	25	26	27	28	29	30	31	32	33	34	35	36
B_1	B_1	B_1	B_1	B_1	B_1	B_1	B_1	B_2	B_2	B_2	B_2	B_2	B_2	B_2	B_2	D	D	B_1	B_1	B_1	B_1	B_1	B_1	B_1	B_1	B_2	B_2	B_2	B_2	B_2	B_2	B_2	B_2	D	D

i=1...8

Figure 8.16 *B channel and D channel assignment to MMS 43 frame*

and the equivalent bit rate is 160 kbit/s, as in the MMS 43 case. Eight of these basic frames are organized into a superframe whose composition depends on the direction of transmission. The two formats are shown in Figures 8.18 and 8.19. The first 9 quats in each of the basic frames 2 through 8 of any superframe form a *synchronization word (SW)*, which is used to register the beginning of the basic frame. Its line code is given by

$$SW = +3 +3 -3 -3 -3 +3 -3 +3 +3$$

The first 9 quats in the first basic frame in every superframe are the complement of the preceding line code and serve to synchronize the superframe. They are known as the *inverted synchronization word (ISW)*, whose line code is given by

$$ISW = -3 -3 +3 +3 +3 -3 +3 -3 -3$$

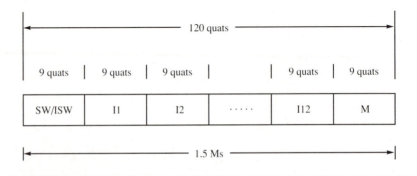

Figure 8.17 *Frame structure for 2B1Q line code*

Basic Frame #	Framing	2B+D	Overhead bits (M₁-M₆)					
Quat positions	1-9	10-117	118		119		120	
Bit positions	1-18	19-234	235	236	237	238	239	240
Sync word / 2B+D	Sync word	2B+D	M_1	M_2	M_3	M_4	M_5	M_6
1	ISW	2B+D	eoc $_{a1}$	eoc $_{a2}$	eoc $_{a3}$	act	1	1
2	SW	2B+D	eoc $_{dm}$	eoc $_{i1}$	eoc $_{i2}$	dea	1	febe
3	SW	2B+D	eoc $_{i3}$	eoc $_{i4}$	eoc $_{i5}$	1	crc $_1$	crc $_2$
4	SW	2B+D	eoc $_{i6}$	eoc $_{i7}$	eoc $_{i8}$	1	crc $_3$	crc $_4$
5	SW	2B+D	eoc $_{a1}$	eoc $_{a2}$	eoc $_{a3}$	1	crc $_5$	crc $_6$
6	SW	2B+D	eoc $_{dm}$	eoc $_{i1}$	eoc $_{i2}$	1	crc $_7$	crc $_8$
7	SW	2B+D	eoc $_{i3}$	eoc $_{i4}$	eoc $_{i5}$	1	crc $_9$	crc $_{10}$
8	SW	2B+D	eoc $_{i6}$	eoc $_{i7}$	eoc $_{i8}$	1	crc $_{11}$	crc $_{12}$

Figure 8.18 *Superframe format for 2B1Q line code (LT-to-NT1)*
© Adapted from ANSI T1.601, 1988.

Basic frame #	Framing	2B+D	Overhead Bits (M₁-M₆)					
Quat positions	1-9	10-117	118		119		120	
Bit positions	1-18	19-234	235	236	237	238	239	240
Sync word / 2B+D	Sync word	2B+D	M_1	M_2	M_3	M_4	M_5	M_6
1	ISW	2B+D	eoc $_{a1}$	eoc $_{a2}$	eoc $_{a3}$	act	1	1
2	SW	2B+D	eoc $_{dm}$	eoc $_{i1}$	eoc $_{i2}$	ps $_1$	1	febe
3	SW	2B+D	eoc $_{i3}$	eoc $_{i4}$	eoc $_{i5}$	ps $_2$	crc $_1$	crc $_2$
4	SW	2B+D	eoc $_{i6}$	eoc $_{i7}$	eoc $_{i8}$	ntm	crc $_3$	crc $_4$
5	SW	2B+D	eoc $_{a1}$	eoc $_{a2}$	eoc $_{a3}$	1	crc $_5$	crc $_6$
6	SW	2B+D	eoc $_{dm}$	eoc $_{i1}$	eoc $_{i2}$	1	crc $_7$	crc $_8$
7	SW	2B+D	eoc $_{i3}$	eoc $_{i4}$	eoc $_{i5}$	1	crc $_9$	crc $_{10}$
8	SW	2B+D	eoc $_{i6}$	eoc $_{i7}$	eoc $_{i8}$	1	crc $_{11}$	crc $_{12}$

Figure 8.19 *Superframe format for 2B1Q line code (NT1-to-LT)*
© Adapted from ANSI T1.601, 1988.

Except for the synchronization words, all binary digits in a basic frame are scrambled according to the procedure discussed earlier.

The 12 successive fields I1 to I12 of 9 quats each in a basic frame carry the information contained in the basic-access channel structure. Their common format is shown in Figure 8.20. Each field contains 4 quats or 8 bits for each of the two B channels and 1 quat or 2 bits for the D channel. Thus, the 12-field frame yields the appropriate rates of 64 kbit/s for each B channel and 16 kbit/s for the D channel.

The remaining 3 quats in each basic frame, considered over the entire superframe, form the M channel. The corresponding six binary digits are labeled M_1 to M_6. Collectively, the 24 M_1, M_2, and M_3 bits of a superframe define a 2-kbit/s *embedded operations channel (EOC)*, which is used by the network to convey to the NT certain instructions regarding the performance of diagnostic functions. The 24 bits are divided into two identical frames of 12 bits. Each of these contains a 3-bit address eoc_a of the NT, a data/message indicator bit eoc_{dm}, and an 8-bit information field eoc_i. The latter carries instructions from network to NT and acknowledgments from NT to the network.

Bits M_5 and M_6 in frames 3 to 8 of a superframe form a 12-bit *cyclic redundancy check code (CRC-12)*, with generator polynomial

$$g(x) = x^{12} + x^{11} + x^3 + x^2 + x + 1$$

This code is applied to all the binary B-channel digits, D-channel digits, and M_4 bits in the superframe.

The remaining M-channel bits are dedicated to a number of operations and maintenance functions.

The *far-end block error (febe)* bit M_6 in frame 2 is set to 0 or 1 to indicate the presence or absence of errors, respectively, in a received superframe. It is transmitted in the next available outgoing superframe to the other side.

Data	B_1				B_2				D
Bit pairs	$b_{11}b_{12}$	$b_{13}b_{14}$	$b_{15}b_{16}$	$b_{17}b_{18}$	$b_{21}b_{22}$	$b_{23}b_{24}$	$b_{25}b_{26}$	$b_{27}b_{28}$	$d_1\ d_2$
Quat #	1	2	3	4	5	6	7	8	9

$\longleftarrow$ IJ (J=1,2,$\cdots$12) $\longrightarrow$

Figure 8.20 *Encoding of 2B + D information flow*
© Adapted from ANSI T1.601, 1988.

The act bit M_4 in the first frame of every superframe and the dea bit M_4 in the second frame of an NT-to-LT superframe are used as part of the activation procedure. Their precise function is discussed later.

The ps_1 and ps_2 bits M_4 in NT-to-LT superframes indicate the status of the primary and secondary power supplies of the NT functional group.

The ntm bit M_4 in NT-to-LT superframes is set to 1 to indicate that the NT is in normal operation and to 0 to signal that the NT is in a customer-initiated test mode. The latter condition is entered if the D channel or any of the B channels are involved in a maintenance procedure.

All remaining M_4, M_5, and M_6 bits are currently reserved and set to 1.

8.1.5 Transmission Systems

As we noted in our discussion of frame structures in the previous section, the total amount of information contained in a basic-access frame equals 160 kbit/s. This bit rate must be carried in full duplex mode between the NT1 and LT across a single metallic pair of the type found in the local loop plant of the world's telephone networks. Thus the transmission scheme must be designed to perform the conversion from the four-wire arrangements existing across the T or V1 reference points to the two-wire structure across the U reference point and provide satisfactory performance in the presence of the signal impairments caused by insertion loss, gauge changes, bridge taps, impulse noise, and crosstalk. Ideally, it should be able to accommodate all currently deployed subscriber lines regardless of their length, to achieve complete coverage.

There are essentially two technologies that lend themselves to these tasks. In the first, commonly known as *time compression multiplexing (TCM), burst mode transmission,* or *ping-ponging,* the transmission of frames between NT1 and LT alternates in the two directions. Taking into account the propagation delay between sender and receiver and a necessary quiescent period between transmission reversals, during which no data can be transmitted, it is clear that the actual one-way transmission rate must be somewhat in excess of twice the full duplex data rate.

The second method, known as *hybrid echo cancellation (HEC),* allows transmission in both directions simultaneously, so that the data rate and transmission rate are equal. Signal separation at the transceiver is provided by a hybrid circuit, and echoes of the transmitted signal that are superimposed on the received signal are removed by an echo canceller.

Let us first consider the TCM system, a block diagram of which is shown in Figure 8.21 [BOSI82]. The input data at either the NT1 or LT, which occurs at a rate of 160 kbit/s, is applied to a buffer, where it is stored until the next transmission opportunity. When that opportunity arises, a rate changer adapts its rate to the transmission rate on the subscriber line and subsequently applies it to the transmitter and the line through a transmit/receive switch.

Received data is passed to a regenerator, a rate changer, and a buffer, from which it is delivered to the receiver at the appropriate data rate.

The general organization of the frames on the line is shown in Figure 8.22.

Each side transmits one frame at a time in an alternating fashion. They are labeled A1, A2, . . . in the direction LT-to-NT1 and B1, B2, . . . in the opposite direction. The transmission time for each frame is assumed to be the same and is denoted by T_t. If the frame contains the equivalent of F binary digits that are transmitted at the equivalent rate of R bits per second on the line, we have

$$T_t = FR$$

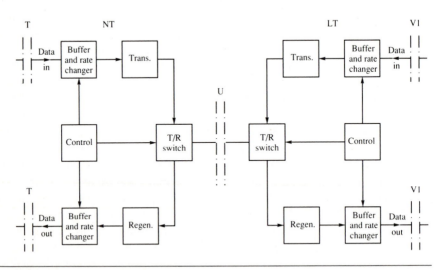

Figure 8.21 *TCM block diagram*
© Adapted from [BOSI82].

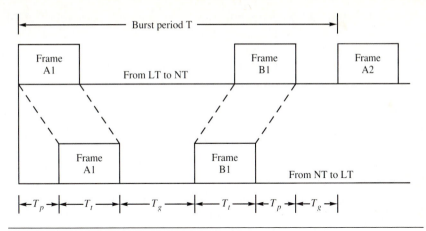

Figure 8.22 *TCM frame transmission parameters*

The line propagation delay is T_p and typically equals 5 to 7 μs per kilometer of line length, depending on cable diameter. To accommodate a transmission distance on the order of 6 to 8 km (20 to 26 kft) therefore requires a value of T_p on the order of 40 μs.

The guard time between receiving a frame and the transmission of the next frame is T_g. Its value must be large enough to allow the decay of the last received frame before initiating the transmission of the next frame. Studies have shown that a decay of 65 dB or more is required and that such a decay commonly occurs during a time interval of approximately 60 μs.

The total time required for the transmission of one frame from each side—which must not exceed the time between frames generated by the NT1 or LT—is the burst period and is given by

$$T = 2 \left(F/R + T_p + T_g \right)$$

The amount of data that is actually transmitted during that time interval depends, of course, on the size of the frame. For the MMS 43 line code, each frame contains the equivalent of 160 binary digits of information. Since one such frame must be conveyed between NT1 and LT every 1 ms, the required line transmission rate R under the preceding assumptions on T_p and T_g is lower bounded by 400 kbit/s, or equivalently 300 kilobaud. This represents an increase by a factor of 2.5 over the actual full duplex transmission rate.

For the 2B1Q case each frame contains the equivalent of 240 binary digits that are transmitted in 1.5 ms. Thus the transmission rate must be at least 370 kbit/s or 185 kilobaud, which represents an increase by a factor of 2.3 over the full duplex rate.

From the preceding discussion it is clear that an increase in the range of transmission also implies an increase in the rate of transmission, all other factors being equal. This higher rate presents certain problems, mainly the expansion of the power spectral density of the line signal and the increased level of near-end crosstalk. As a practical matter the use of TCM appears to be limited to lines shorter than 4 km.

Let us discuss next the hybrid echo cancellation (HEC) system, a block diagram of which is shown in Figure 8.23 [AGAZ82a].

The HEC consists of two major components, a hybrid circuit, whose function is to separate the transmitted and received signals, and the echo canceller, which removes echoes of the transmitted signal from the received signal.

Figure 8.24 illustrates in somewhat simplified form the principle of operation of the hybrid [BELL71]. Let Z_4 be the impedance of the two-wire circuit at the U side of the hybrid and let Z_3 be an impedance equal to Z_4 and acting as a balance to Z_4. Similarly, let Z_1 and Z_2 be the impedances of the two circuits on the T side or the V1 side of the hybrid and assume $Z_1 = Z_2$. With the proper choice of turns ratios for the two transformers T1 and T2, the power delivered to port 1 will be equally split and delivered to Z_3 and Z_4, with a negligible amount being

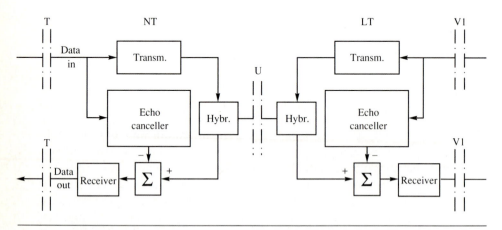

Figure 8.23 *Hybrid echo cancellation system*
© Adapted from [AGAZ82].

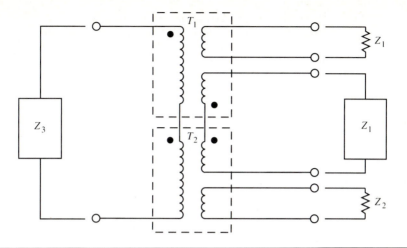

Figure 8.24 *Hybrid circuit*
© Adapted from [BELL71].

passed to Z_2. Likewise, the power entering port 3 is directed almost completely to port 2.

Ideally, the signal obtained by the receiver of the NT1 or LT from its hybrid circuit should be an exact copy of the signal transmitted from the far end. In practice, it also contains attenuated and delayed copies or echoes of the signal transmitted by the near side, in addition to the distortion introduced by crosstalk, impulse noise, and insertion loss.

The echo canceller, whose function it is to remove these echoes, must accommodate three distinct types. First, the separation of the transmitted and received signals by the hybrid circuit is imperfect, because the balancing network of the hybrid does not perfectly match the impedance of the two-wire line. Thus, a certain amount of the energy from the transmitter leaks through into the local receiver, producing a near-end echo. Second, the gauge changes and bridge taps on the line between NT1 and LT represent impedance discontinuities that cause reflections of the transmitted signal back to the transmitter. Third, a portion of the transmitted signal is reflected from the hybrid circuit at the far side and manifests itself in the receiver as a far-end echo.

In typical applications the level of the echoes present in the local receiver is 10 to 20 DB below the transmitted signal and is usually dominated by the hybrid leakthrough. If the subscriber line contains bridge taps close to the transmitter, the reflections from these taps may also make a significant contribution. Far-end echoes, on the other hand, are generally negligible unless the transmission distance is very short.

For distances of about 5 km between transmitter and receiver the signal will experience a line attenuation of 40 to 50 DB, over the frequency range of interest. If we require a minimum receiver signal-to-echo ratio of 20 DB for signal detection at an acceptable error rate, the echo canceller must provide echo suppression of as much as 60 DB.

Figure 8.25 illustrates in block diagram form a typical echo canceller.

The central component of the device, which is shown in Figure 8.26, is an adaptive digital transversal filter or tapped delay line. The input to the filter is the transmitted signal $a(t)$, which is sampled at T-second intervals by the N taps on the delay line. The N sample values $a(k), a(k-1), \ldots, a(k-N+1)$ corresponding to the kth sampling instant are then applied to a set of N multipliers whose values at the kth sampling instant are $c_0(k), c_1(k), \ldots, c_{n-1}(k)$. The products are subsequently summed, to form the echo replica $\hat{e}(k)$.

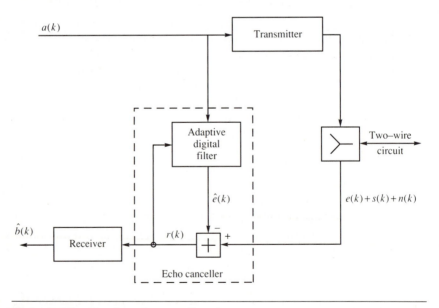

Figure 8.25 *Adaptive echo canceller*
© Adapted from [VERH79].

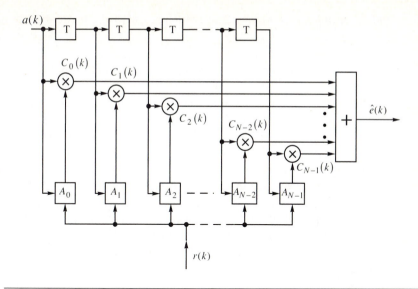

Figure 8.26 *Adaptive transversal filter*
© Adapted from [VERH79].

The signal received from the transmission line at the kth sampling instant is the sum of the far-end signal $b(k)$ as it appears at the near end, which we denote by $s(k)$, the noise signal $n(k)$, and the echo signal $e(k)$. Subtracting $\hat{e}(k)$ from this sum yields an error signal

$$r(k) = s(k) + n(k) + e(k) - \hat{e}(k)$$

which serves as an estimate $\hat{b}(k)$ of the desired signal $b(k)$. The error signal $r(k)$ is also combined with the transmitted signal $a(k-i)$ in an adaption unit A_i to determine the value of $c_i(k)$. Various combining schemes that minimize the error between the actual echo and its replica have been investigated. The interested reader is referred to the relevant literature for additional details [VERH79].

The size of the transversal filter—that is, the number of delay stages and multipliers—is normally matched to the longest time delay of the echo, measured in sampling intervals, and thus depends on the line length, the configuration of bridge taps, and the sampling rate. As an example, for a 5-km line, a transmitted pulse will return as a far-end echo in approximately 50 μs. At a transmission rate of 80 kilobaud and 2 samples per pulse, this translates into eight stages of delay. Typical echo cancellers may contain from 20 to 50 taps, depending on the application.

Of the two transmission systems discussed in this section, the implementation of TCM is generally somewhat simpler than that of a hybrid system, due to the complexity of the echo cancellation requirement in the latter. For TCM it is usually possible to essentially eliminate near-end crosstalk by coordinating the transmission intervals in all systems affected by crosstalk. On the other hand, because of its wider bandwidth requirements and the increased levels of noise, far-end crosstalk, and insertion loss at the high frequencies, TCM suffers from a somewhat shorter transmission range. If we take into consideration the possible need for repeaters and concentrators to offset this limitation, the implementation advantage of TCM may be eliminated. In addition, the high signaling rate causes increased levels of interference to other transmission systems.

As a result, both the ANSI standard and the emerging CCITT specifications include hybrid echo cancellation as the transmission method for the basic-access digital section.

8.1.6 *Activation and Deactivation of the Digital Section*

Mainly for economical operation, the equipment on both sides of the U reference point is normally maintained in a state of low power consumption during idle periods. While in this state the NT1 and LT are unable to perform certain functions such as frame synchronization. Thus they are prevented from exchanging any B-channel and D-channel flows over the digital section. It therefore becomes necessary to activate the transceivers in this equipment prior to the transfer of any operational data and to place them into the deactivated state at the conclusion of the information transfer phase. In this section we present a somewhat simplified description of the procedures for accomplishing these tasks. We restrict ourselves to the ANSI version of the digital section and refer the reader to Recommendations G.960 and G.961 for the CCITT procedures.

Activation of the digital section may in general be initiated by either the network side or the customer side, whereas only the former may deactivate. Let us consider first activation by the network.

The layer 2 logic in the local exchange issues a PH-ACTIVATE Request primitive to its layer 1, which prompts the transmission of a wake-up tone from LT to NT1. This tone is represented by an unscrambled and unframed alternating pattern of four positive and four negative quats of amplitude 3, transmitted at the synchronous rate of 80 kiloquats per second in accordance with the network clock. When it receives it, the NT1 extracts the clock signal and responds with a similar tone. After a predetermined interval of time it then transmits a series of basic frames containing the synchronization word SW and logical 1s in the B-channel, D-channel, and M-digit locations. Except for SW, all digits are scrambled prior to encoding into quats. Once the NT1 has achieved full power status and is able to receive frames from the LT, it stops the transmission of its frames and thereby signals its new status to the LT. The latter then responds with the transmission of similar basic frames while it establishes its own operational status, following which it conveys a series of properly synchronized superframes in which the B channel and D channel contain logical 0s and the dea digit is set to 1 to request the activation of the interface. When the NT1 has acquired superframe synchronization and has interpreted the dea digit, it notifies the TE of the activation request in accordance with the procedures discussed in Chapter 4 and resumes the earlier transmission of basic frames until the TE has positively responded to the activation request. It then inserts the superframe synchronization pattern in its transmissions, sets the act digit to 1, and includes normal operational data in the B-channel, D-channel, and M-digit locations. In the final step of the procedure, when the LT recognizes the superframe pattern in the received frames, it also reaches fully operational status and indicates this fact by the transmission of similar superframes, also with act set to 1.

Activation from the customer side is initiated by the transmission of the Info 1 signal from the TE to the NT1 in accordance with the S/T activation protocol discussed in Chapter 4. This causes the transmission of the wake-up tone from NT1 to LT, after which the same procedure as in the previous case is followed.

Deactivation of the digital section is under the control of the network and is initiated by the LT in response to a PH-DEACTIVATE Request primitive from the layer 2 logic in the local exchange. This request is conveyed by the LT to the NT1 by setting the dea digit in the current LT-to-NT1 superframe to 0. Subsequently the LT enters the deactivated state by ceasing all transmissions at the end of the next superframe. Deactivation of the NT1 then occurs as a consequence of the loss of signal from the LT.

8.2 The Digital Section for Primary Access

The digital section for primary access differs from the one for basic access in two respects.

First, because of the much higher data rates it is generally not possible to transmit the information flows contained in the B, H, and D channels over a single pair of wires. As a result, the usual implementation involves two symmetrical metallic pairs, one for each direction of transmission. For distances in excess of 1 km repeaters may also be necessary. Virtually all aspects of the transmission scheme on these pairs conform to the primary-access specifications at the S or T reference points, as presented in Chapter 4.

Second, in the usual installation the digital section is permanently in the activated state, so that no activation or deactivation procedures are required.

8.3 Summary and Recommended Reading

This chapter has treated the engineering of the digital section that provides the physical connection between the customer premises and the network. We discussed the electrical characteristics of the metallic pair as a subscriber loop and considered the line coding and framing aspects of a digital transmission scheme over the metallic pair. We also discussed the technical features and relative merits of two transmission systems, time compression multiplexing and hybrid echo cancellation. Finally, we described the activation and deactivation procedures that allow the digital section to be maintained in a state of low power consumption during periods of inactivity.

There is a large and varied technical literature on the digital section. The September 1982 special issue on subscriber loops of the *IEEE Transactions on Communications* and the November 1986 issue of the *IEEE Journal on Selected Areas in Communications* contain many papers describing the engineering of the digital section. The most important of these are listed in the references section. An excellent tutorial on echo cancellation is [VERH79]. [LECH89] discusses the issues in the selection of a line code and [BOSI84] describes TCM.

CHAPTER 9

Common Channel Signaling

The establishment, operation, and termination of user connections over the interexchange network, the management of the network resources, and the provision of intelligent network services require the exchange of control signals among the local and transit exchanges of the interexchange network and between the repositories of the network intelligence. In most telecommunications networks this signaling is conveyed over the same circuits that carry the user information. The necessary channel capacity is obtained either by permanently allocating a portion of the total capacity of the circuit to signaling or by assigning the total circuit capacity to signaling for a period of time.

Although this so-called *in-channel signaling* has many desirable properties and served its purpose for many years, recently its limitations have become a matter of concern, especially in connection with the introduction of the ISDN and its associated stored program controlled switches and intelligent network features. If the entire available channel capacity associated with a connection is allocated to signaling, the latter is clearly restricted to periods of user inactivity. On the other hand, the permanent allocation of a portion of the capacity to signaling implies a reduction of throughput for the user data. In either case the capacity of the user connection places limits on the rate of signaling that can be carried out. In many situations this has a serious effect on the speed with which user connections can be established and terminated. The requirement to conform to the physical characteristics of the user connection, which may be matched to the characteristics of the user information flows, also tends to limit the number and variety of control signals and affects the level of sophistication of the signaling system. Finally, we note that in-channel signaling is normally confined to the exchanges across which a user data connection is established, so that separate signaling facilities for communication among other network facilities must be provided.

To alleviate these difficulties the telecommunications networks in recent years initiated the conversion from the traditional signaling arrangements to so-called *common channel signaling* in which the direct association between user information transfer and signaling over the same circuit is eliminated [DONO86]. Here all signaling is carried out over a separate network that is designed to interconnect all relevant network facilities and provide sufficient capacity for whatever signaling requirements may exist. Furthermore, the protocols governing the exchange of signaling information are optimized for this task and are not constrained by the characteristics of the user information or the user connection.

During the past decade the CCITT has developed the specifications for a common channel signaling network, together with a signaling system that governs the transfer of signaling information. The most recent version of these specifications is contained in the Q.700 series recommendations of the 1988 *Blue Book*. The parallel activities of the American National Standards Institute are documented in ANSI Documents T1.110 to T1.114. We devote the present chapter to a discussion of the most important aspects of this work.

9.1   The Common Channel Signaling Network

Common channel signaling is carried out over a *common channel signaling network (CCSN)* that is logically independent of the interexchange network. The CCSN is a distributed network whose nodes are intelligent processors that are associated with either the exchanges of the IEN or the network databases for maintenance, call accounting, and other network services and operations. The signaling messages that must be conveyed among these resources are structured as packets and are transferred in packet switched mode over digital circuits under the control of a protocol known as a *signaling system*.

There are a number of important advantages of this arrangement over in-channel signaling.

- The IEN and the CCSN may evolve independently of each other in terms of their connectivity, channel capacity, and logical complexity.

- Call setup and clearing times can be decreased through the use of high-speed digital signaling links and a high level of connectivity of the signaling network.

- The transmission, switching, and storage facilities of the CCSN can be designed to support sophisticated connection control protocols, using an essentially unlimited set of signals that incorporate the potential for future enhancements to support new services.

- User data connections and signaling connections may exist simultaneously in time. This feature offers the capability of conveying user information during the establishment and clearing phases of a connection and allows changes in the characteristics of a connection without interruption of user data transfer.

- In addition to connection control, the CCSN may also be employed for the transfer of other internal network information flows. Thus all data communications activities relating to network maintenance, performance monitoring, management, and call accounting can be centralized and carried out over the CCSN, resulting in a high utilization of its resources.

- The facilities of the CCSN may be used for the transfer of user-to-user signaling information flows in packet switched mode, as discussed in Chapters 3 and 6.

There are also several disadvantages. Since a given transmission circuit of the CCSN typically carries the call control messages for many connections, the network must be highly secure against line failures, transmission errors, and the possibility of message loss and must have a high degree of availability. This requires a substantial amount of redundancy in the network nodes and circuits and a sophisticated control structure for data transmission and network resource management.

The transfer of connection control signals and user information over separate connections also implies the need to assure each of the connections individually, since the existence of one does not guarantee the existence of the other.

Finally, since the signaling messages for different connections are interleaved on common channels, each message must carry an explicit identification of its corresponding user connection.

Topologically a CCSN consists of two types of nodes called *signaling points (SP)* and *signaling transfer points (STP)*, that are connected into a distributed network by data transmission circuits known as *signaling links*. Nodes that are directly connected are said to be adjacent to each other; otherwise they are nonadjacent. Typically, several signaling links in parallel are used between a pair of adjacent nodes. Collectively these links are known as *link sets*. Within a link set signaling links with identical transmission characteristics are combined into link groups. Figure 9.1 shows an example of the interconnection of a SP and a STP by means of a link set consisting of five signaling links combined into two link groups.

SPs are nodes in which signaling messages originate and terminate or in which applications-level processing of the messages takes place. Several types of SPs can be distinguished. The most important of these are the *switch SPs,* which are resident in the local and transit exchanges of the interexchange network with common channel signaling capabilities. Their main function is to support the call control signaling for the establishment, operation, and termination of circuit switched and packet switched connections over the IEN. Examples of exchanges with SP capabilities are the 4ESS and 5ESS exchanges of AT&T, the Northern Telecom DMS 100 and DMS 250, and the Siemens EWSD exchange.

Two other types of SPs, the *service switching points (SSP)* and the *service control points (SCP),* support various intelligent network functions. The purpose of the SSP is to provide end-user access to the internal network databases containing the network intelligence or to feature nodes that are external to the ISDN. The SCP, on the other hand, is the repository of the network databases. It includes information such as subscriber records, directories, billing data, and conversion tables between real and virtual addresses.

STPs are packet switches with high throughput and low delay that provide little more than message routing between adjacent SPs or STPs. They determine the next node to which a message is to be

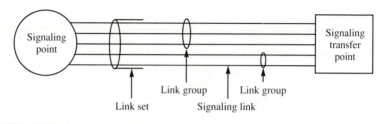

Figure 9.1 *Common channel signaling network components*

routed, select appropriate signaling links, and assure the delivery of the messages in the proper sequence.

In general a given node of the signaling network may function as either a SP or a STP, depending on the particular signaling relation in which it participates. Certain nodes, however, may be dedicated entirely to the STP function.

The signaling links used to connect adjacent nodes are usually digital circuits with a capacity of 64 kbit/s, although bit rates of 56 kbit/s and analog circuits operating at 2.4 kbit/s or 4.8 kbit/s are also sometimes employed [DONO86]. In some implementations they consist of the transmission capacity of one octet in a primary PCM multiplex frame being transported between two exchanges of the IEN, with the remaining octets reserved for user data. In other networks separate physical circuits are provided.

For purposes of reliability the STPs in a common channel signaling network are deployed as identical mated pairs, each with its own complete signaling capability. This pair is connected by a set of signaling links known as *cross links (C links)*. Two mated pairs are joined into a *quad* of four STPs in a fully connected mesh, using four sets of *bridge links (B links)*. To avoid service interruption due to the failure of one STP of a mated pair, each SP is connected to both STPs of the pair, using sets of signaling links called *access links (A links)*. Multiple routing capability and a degree of immunity to line and node failures are achieved by including in a link set two or more circuits that are deployed over geographically diverse routes. Figure 9.2 shows the

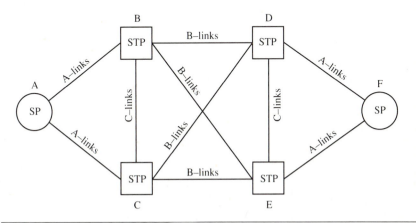

Figure 9.2 *Common channel signaling network quad configuration*

interconnection of two mated pairs (B,C) and (D,E), each pair with one attached SP.

It is sometimes useful to create two levels of hierarchy within the CCSN, a primary level for handling general signaling traffic and a secondary level dedicated to traffic that is confined to a local area of the network. Figure 9.3 shows an example. Here the STPs of the primary network again occur in mated pairs that are connected by C links, with two mated pairs connected via B links into a quad. The mated pair of secondary STPs is also connected to a mated pair of primary STPs in the form of a quad via so-called *diagonal links (D links)*. Local traffic confined to the secondary part of the network can then be routed only among the secondary STPs, whereas more general traffic can be exchanged between the primary and secondary STPs.

In networks that must accommodate high levels of traffic a SP is sometimes joined to a second mated pair of STPs and to another SP via so-called *E links* and *F links*, respectively. Examples of these configurations are also shown in Figure 9.3 [HEIS87].

Over a common channel signaling network of the type discussed earlier, signaling can be carried out in two ways. In one arrangement the signaling messages are routed between SPs via one or more intermediate STPs and are therefore carried over circuits that are physically separated from the user data circuits. This mode of operation is

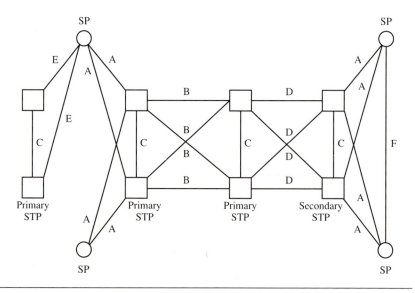

Figure 9.3 *Common channel signaling network topology*

known as *nonassociated mode*. As an alternative, the SPs along the route of a user connection can be directly connected by F links, in which case signaling and user data transfer are said to be *associated*.

The topological design of the CCSN is the result of stringent performance specifications that require among other things a maximum unavailability of a route set between a pair of SPs of not more than 10 minutes per year. This requirement is satisfied through the replication of critical links and signaling transfer points and the quad configuration of the STPs. Collectively these offer the possibility of routing messages over sets of multiple routes between the SPs, using different combinations of intermediate STPs and signaling links chosen from the available link sets. Let us illustrate these capabilities by means of the quad configuration shown in Figure 9.2.

Under normal operating conditions the C links between the mated pairs (B,C) and (D,E) are not used. Thus, A and F are connected via the four routes ABDF, ABEF, ACEF, and ACDF, each of them involving two intermediate STPs. Of course, any one of these routes may be served by multiple circuits constructed from the different links of the link sets connecting the SPs and STPs.

In the presence of link failures one or both of the C links may be activated to carry the traffic diverted from any failed links. This creates the possibility of eight additional routes involving only one C link and three intermediate STPs, and four additional routes with four intermediate STPs if both C links are used. Thus there exists a total of 16 routes between signaling points A and F. Of course, because of link and node failures and the restriction on the use of the C links mentioned earlier, not all of these are available at all times.

In general, it is desirable to restrict the number of intermediate STPs along any route in order to limit the maximum transfer delay from an originating SP to a destination SP. As an objective in the design of the CCSN topology and routing plan the CCITT recommends the inclusion of no more than two STPs under normal conditions and no more than four STPs in the presence of link or node failures.

9.2 Common Channel Signaling

Having discussed the topological aspects of the CCSN in the previous section, we now turn to an examination of the type of signaling information that must be exchanged between the nodes of the network.

In the context of the ISDN the network internal signaling functions can be divided into two major categories. First, to establish, maintain, and terminate user connections over the IEN, the signaling system must convey supervisory and status information to the exchanges involved in the connections. This requires the transfer of certain signaling messages over the CCSN between the set of signaling points associated with the local exchange terminations and any intermediate network switches. Second, the signaling system must allow communication between the various intelligent network nodes that function as repositories of network information. In this category we include access to specialized databases for call accounting, network diagnostics, and maintenance and the multitude of intelligent network features offered by an ISDN.

The accomplishment of these tasks requires the availability of a signaling system which governs the transfer of signaling messages between the SPs and STPs of the CCSN.

Over the past decade several different general-purpose signaling systems have been developed by the CCITT and other standards organizations. The most important of these, and the one of major relevance to the ISDN, is the set of procedures known as *Signaling System #7,* as described in CCITT Recommendations Q.700 to Q.795 of the 1988 *Blue Book.* To date the specification of SS#7 is nearly complete, although a number of relatively minor details remain to be resolved and are the subject of active investigation during the 1988–1992 study period.

In the United States the American National Standards Institute has developed a variant of SS#7 that accommodates the peculiarities of the U.S. telecommunications environment. This version is currently being deployed by the public carriers.

The remainder of this chapter is devoted to those parts of SS#7 that apply to the ISDN. Since a complete and rigorous treatment of all its features is beyond the scope of our work, we restrict ourselves to an exposition of its most important functions.

9.3 Protocol Architecture of SS#7

Logically, SS#7 is structured as a layered architecture, with its functionality divided into four levels, as shown in Figure 9.4. The first three levels contain the so-called *message transfer part (MTP),* which provides a reliable relaying and distribution service for signaling mes-

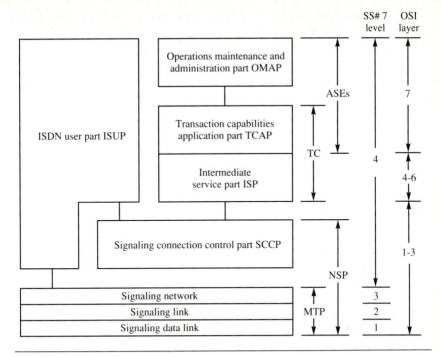

Figure 9.4   *Protocol architecture of Signaling System #7*

sages between a pair of SPs over an interconnecting set of signaling links and STPs. They correspond approximately to layers 1, 2, and 3 of the OSI protocol reference model, but do not offer the full capability of these layers.

Level 1, called the *signaling data link,* specifies the physical and electrical characteristics of the signaling links interconnecting the SPs and STPs of the CCSN.

Level 2, referred to as the *signaling link,* provides for the reliable transfer of signaling messages between adjacent SPs or STPs that are connected by a signaling link conforming to the signaling data link specifications. It performs detection and recovery from transmission errors and assures the proper sequencing of the signaling messages.

Level 3, the so-called *signaling network,* has the responsibility of relaying the signaling messages along an appropriate set of STPs from one SP to the next, distinguishing messages that have arrived at their destination SP from messages that must be forwarded and distributing arrived messages to the appropriate part of level 4. Level 3 also plays a major role in the management of the resources of the CCSN.

The lower part of level 4 contains the *signaling connection control part (SCCP)*, which provides additional networking features on an optional basis. Among other facilities, it offers a connection-oriented transmission service for signaling messages with flow control and sequence control on top of the relaying service provided by the MTP, and an enhanced addressing capability.

Collectively, the MTP and SCCP are known as the *network service part (NSP)*. Functionally they are equivalent to the full capability of the lower three layers of the OSI architecture.

The remaining parts of level 4 of the SS#7 architecture perform much the same functions as layers 4 to 7 in OSI.

The *ISDN user part (ISUP)* supplies the basic ISDN call control functions for the establishment, operation, and clearing of connections over the IEN. In addition, it offers support for the control of a variety of optional and supplementary services such as call forwarding, calling line identification, and the exchange of user-to-user signaling information flows over the CCSN. The ISUP may interact with either the SCCP or the MTP, depending on the level of service required for the transport of its signaling messages.

The *transaction capabilities (TC)* part provides services in support of various applications such as access to network databases and other specialized facilities. It is itself divided into two parts. The *intermediate service part (ISP),* whose precise functionality is at present undefined, is intended to offer the equivalent of the OSI transport, session, and presentation layers. The *transactions capabilities application part (TCAP),* which functions as an *application service element (ASE),* provides applications-layer services to its user application processes. Its functionality corresponds to layer 7 in the context of OSI.

Level 4 of the SS#7 architecture also contains various other ASEs that utilize the services of the TCAP and offer support for network operations, administration, management, testing, validation, and provisioning. To date only the *operations maintenance and administration part (OMAP)*—which supports the system management application process—has been defined.

9.4 The Message Transfer Part

We now consider the message transfer part of the SS#7 architecture, which, as we mentioned earlier, provides a relaying and distribution service for signaling messages between level 4 parts resident in a pair

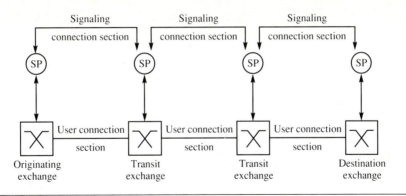

Figure 9.5 *User and signaling connections and connection sections*

of communicating SPs. These SPs are either connected via one or more intermediate STPs as shown in Figure 9.2, or are attached via a direct signaling link set, as indicated by the F link in Figure 9.3. A pair of communicating SPs, together with their intermediate STPs and signaling links, are known as a *connection section*. Typically, several connection sections in tandem are required to interconnect the SPs associated with the IEN exchanges involved in a connection between a pair of end-users. Figure 9.5 illustrates the example of a user connection between originating and destination local exchanges via two intermediate transit exchanges. Here the SPs in each connection section are directly connected, without any intermediate STPs.

Figure 9.6 depicts the relationships between the SPs from the point

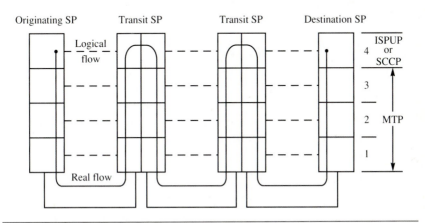

Figure 9.6 *Signaling connection information flow*

of view of the SS#7 protocol layering, for the example of Figure 9.5. Note that each SP is involved in the handling of the level 4 information flow.

Let us now examine the functions performed by the three levels of the MTP in carrying a signaling message from one SP to another across a single connection section.

9.4.1 The Signaling Data Link Level

The purpose of the signaling data link is to provide a digital communications capability for the transfer of signaling information over a signaling link between adjacent SPs or STPs. In the usual implementation of the common channel signaling network, the transmission capacity of the signaling links is derived from the trunk circuits of the interexchange network by allocating portions of their channel capacity to signaling. The physical and electrical specifications of the signaling links are therefore those of the IEN circuits. For trunks operating at 2048 kbit/s, signaling is confined to slot 16, whereas for 8448-kbit/s trunks one of the slots 67 to 70 may be used in descending order of priority. In either case, the signaling rate is 64 kbit/s.

Other transmission rates and the use of analog transmission channels are also permissible for certain applications. For example, CCITT Recommendation Q.702 specifies a full duplex rate of 4.8 kbit/s over separate metallic pairs, with the modems conforming to CCITT Recommendation V.27 or V.27bis and electrical specifications according to Recommendations V.10/V.11 or V.24/V.28.

In North America the signaling links are based on the T1 carrier specifications and normally operate at 56 kbit/s.

9.4.2 The Signaling Link Level

Given the transmission service offered by level 1, the level 2 protocol of SS#7 is responsible for the reliable exchange of frames of information called *signaling units (SU)* between adjacent SPs or STPs of the CCSN—that is, between a pair of nodes that are directly connected by a signaling link. In support of this task it offers six major functions.

- With the aid of level 1, it provides the capability to generate, transmit, and receive properly delimited and synchronized SUs.

- It establishes a logical relationship between sender and receiver for the exchange of SUs.

- It performs detection and correction of bit errors and sequence errors that may occur during the transmission of an SU over the signaling link.

- The receiving node controls the flow of SUs from the sending node in order to prevent congestion.

- The nodes may notify each other of a problem in their level 3 or 4 entities that precludes the use of the signaling link.

- The receiver monitors the quality of the signaling link by measuring the frequency of rejected SUs.

These functions are carried out by means of a set of procedures that are in many respects conceptually similar to the LAPD protocol used over the D channel, as described in Chapter 5.

Three types of SUs are defined. They are known as *message signal unit (MSU)*, *link status signal unit (LSSU)*, and *fill-in signal unit (FISU)*. Their structural properties are depicted in Figure 9.7.

The beginning and end of each SU are marked with the standard LAPD synchronization pattern 0 1 1 1 1 1 1 0. As usual, for proper operation all information between opening and closing flags must be

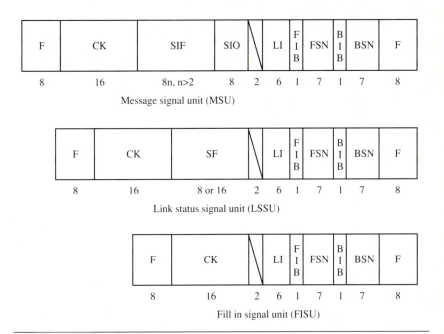

Message signal unit (MSU)

Link status signal unit (LSSU)

Fill in signal unit (FISU)

Figure 9.7 *Signal unit formats*

© Adapted from CCITT Blue Book, vol VI.7, 1988

bit stuffed to avoid the occurrence of the pattern anywhere else in the SU. Any SU that does not have an integral number of octets between flags or that has fewer than 5 octets or more than 278 octets between flags is discarded by the receiver.

The *forward* and *backward sequence numbers (FSN* and *BSN)*, together with the *forward* and *backward indicator bits (FIB* and *BIB)*, are used in an acknowledgment and retransmission scheme to control transmission errors, sequence errors, and the occurrence of duplicates in a sequence of MSUs. They are contained in all SUs but refer only to MSUs.

The six digits of the *length indicator (LI)* are a count of the number of octets between the LI and the *check bits (CK)*. For MSUs the LI varies over the range 3 to 63, for LSSUs it is either 1 or 2, and for FISUs it equals 0. Thus the value of LI also distinguishes between the three types of SU.

The CK field contains the 16 digits of a frame check sequence obtained from the standard CCITT generator polynomial

$$P(x) = x^{16} + x^{12} + x^5 + 1$$

The procedure for calculating these digits is identical to the one discussed in Section 5.2.4.

The *service information octet (SIO)* and *signaling information field (SIF)* in a MSU carry information obtained from level 3 and the various level 4 entities of the protocol architecture. Their functions are described in subsequent sections. Here we note that the size of the SIF is limited to 272 octets and that the LI is set to value 63 if the SIF exceeds 61 octets.

The *status field (SF)* of a LSSU contains information regarding the alignment status of the link, the level of congestion, and the condition of the level 3 or 4 entities that are using the level 2 service, as perceived by the sender of the LSSU.

Let us now examine the detailed procedures for performing the functions just outlined. Prior to the transmission of MSUs the level 2 logical relationship between two communicating adjacent nodes must be established. In somewhat simplified terms this alignment of the signaling link is accomplished through the exchange of a series of LSSUs that contain in their status field the status indications out-of-alignment (O), normal alignment (N), emergency alignment (E), and out-of-service (OS). Four states of the signaling link can be distinguished. In the idle state the alignment procedure is suspended but the signaling link is in a condition where alignment may be initiated. Transmitting the status indication O causes a transition to the not aligned state in which the signaling link is still unaligned but alignment has been initiated. On receiving this LSSU the remote node returns a similar signal, after which the two sides exchange the status indication N. The signaling link then enters a proving state in which the quality of the link is tested. During testing each node continuously transmits LSSUs with the status field set to N until a total of 2^{16} octets have been sent. The link is considered acceptable and enters the aligned ready state if no more than four of these LSSUs are received in error. Otherwise the proving period is aborted as soon as a count of 5 is reached and the link reverts to the idle state. The entire procedure may be repeated up to four more times, after which the link is declared out of service by transmitting a LSSU with the status indication OS.

Under certain emergency conditions where a lower level of link performance is acceptable the less stringent quality requirement of one faulty LSSU in 2^{12} octets can be imposed. This is indicated by replacing the N status indication with the E status indication in the transition to the proving state and during the proving period.

Once the signaling link has been properly aligned, higher-level information may be transferred inside message signal units. This process is controlled by the sequence numbers FSN and BSN, the indication bits FIB and BIB, and an acknowledgment and retransmission protocol for the correction of channel bit errors, sequence errors, and message signal unit duplication.

The FSN in a MSU uniquely identifies that MSU within the limitations of the modulo-128 counting scheme and is associated with it until it is accepted by the receiver. The *forward indicator bit (FIB)* marks this MSU as either new or, if different from its value in the previous MSU, as a retransmission. The ESN refers to the most recent MSU received from the other side. If the *backward indicator bit (BIB)* is inverted from its value in the previous MSU, the MSU identified by the BSN is rejected. Otherwise it marks this MSU as accepted and also implies the acceptance of all previously received MSUs that may not yet have been explicitly acknowledged.

LSSUs and FISUs carry the FSN of the last transmitted MSU and the BSN of the last correctly received MSU.

An example of the use of the sequence numbers and indicator bits for the case of error-free transmission is shown in Figure 9.8. Here nodes A and B exchange five MSUs that are interspersed with FISUs

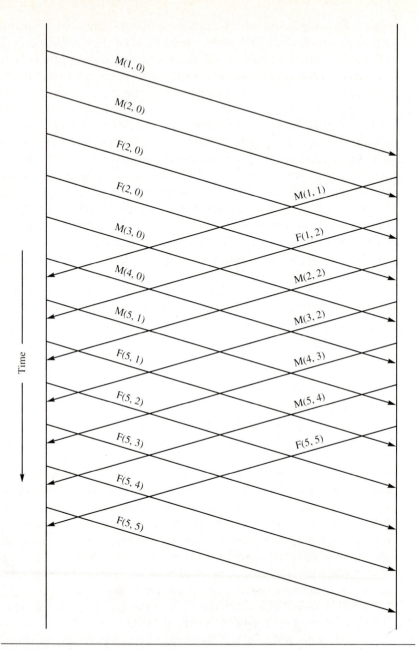

Figure 9.8 Exchange of signal units without transmission errors

during periods where they have no data to send. Since there are no retransmissions or negative acknowledgments, all FIB and BIB have the same value.

Next we consider the case when errors occur on the transmission of MSUs across the signaling link. All received MSUs detected to be in error by the error checking procedure are discarded by the receiver. An error-free MSU received with a FSN not equal to one higher than the FSN of the last accepted MSU is likewise discarded. Otherwise it is accepted, provided its FIB has the same value as the last sent BIB.

Two different protocols have been defined for the recovery of discarded MSUs. They are applicable to different traffic conditions and transmission distances.

The first method, known as *basic error correction*, is normally used on short delay circuits. It relies on the retransmission of a faulty MSU upon explicit request from the receiver. All transmitted but not yet acknowledged MSUs are retained in a buffer for possible retransmission until they have been positively acknowledged. The transmission of new MSUs is interrupted during periods of retransmission. When the last received BIB is not equal to the last sent FIB, all MSUs with FSN greater than the received BSN are transmitted in their proper sequence. Figure 9.9 shows the same example as in Figure 9.8, but with an error occurring on the transmission of MSU number 4.

The second method of error control, known as *preventive cyclic retransmission,* is intended for signaling links with large propagation delays such as satellite circuits, where the first method would result in unacceptable reductions of throughput and large storage requirements. In this scheme a sequence of MSUs that have already been transmitted once but have not yet been positively acknowledged by the receiver is cyclically retransmitted during periods when no new MSUs are presented for transmission. This process continues until the receiver positively acknowledges one of the MSUs, at which time that MSU and all previous MSUs are dropped from the sequence. Retransmissions are always interrupted whenever new MSUs or LSSUs must be sent. If, however, the rate of arrival of such new SUs or their lengths are too large the loading of the retransmission buffer will increase to an unacceptable level. Consequently, if either the number of MSUs or the total number of data octets in the retransmission buffer exceeds certain thresholds, the transmission of new SUs is interrupted and retransmission of all MSUs in the retransmission buffer resumes until both the number of MSUs and the number of data octets fall below their respective thresholds.

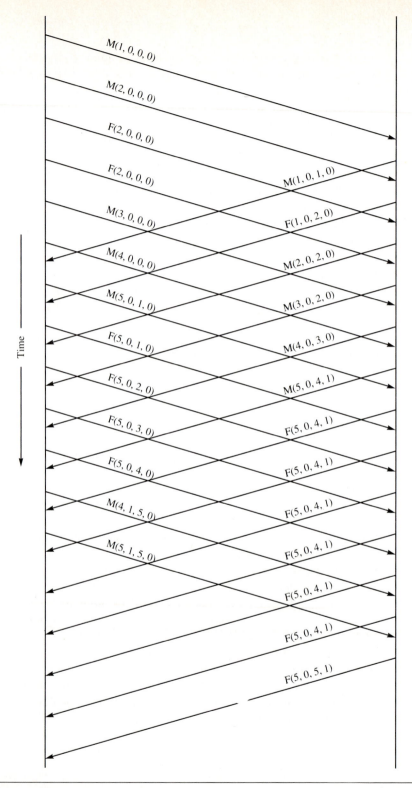

Figure 9.9 *Exchange of signal units with transmission errors*

To manage congestion on the signaling link, a flow control procedure is implemented that allows a receiver to control the rate at which MSUs are transmitted to it. As soon as the receiver senses the onset of congestion it conveys to the sender a LSSU with the status field marked busy and periodically repeats this transmission every 80 to 120 ms as long as the condition persists. While in this state, the receiver withholds all positive and negative acknowledgments of any received MSUs, but continues its own transmissions, unless congestion has also been signaled by the other side. Congestion abatement is indicated to the sender by suspending the transmission of the busy LSSU and resuming normal operation. To avoid adverse effects on the higher levels of the architecture, the maximum duration of the busy condition is limited to a range of 3 to 6 seconds, after which the sender conveys a link failure indication to its level 3 entity.

Under certain conditions such as the failure of a central processor the level 3 or 4 entities in a node may be unable to accept messages from their signaling link level. Whenever the latter obtains an indication of such an event it discards any received MSUs that have not yet been forwarded to level 3 and notifies the remote node of the condition by sending a LSSU with the status indication set to *processor outage (PO)*. The remote node then notifies its level 3 entity, stops the transmission of MSUs, and initiates the continuous transmission of FISUs. When the outage condition is cleared the local node resumes the transmission of MSUs or FISUs to the remote node which, on receiving any of these messages, also returns to normal operation.

To maintain the quality of an operational signaling link an error rate monitor is implemented in the receiver that declares the link to be out of service whenever it registers an excessive rate of rejected SUs. A counter C is incremented by 1 for every received SU that is rejected and decremented by 1 (but not below 0) for every sequence of 256 received SUs, whether rejected or not. The link is considered unreliable whenever C reaches the threshold value T. The latter is set to 64 for 64-kbit/s links and 32 for lower transmission rates.

9.4.3 The Signaling Network Level

We turn now to a description of level 3 of the *message transfer part,* the signaling network level. As depicted in Figure 9.10, its functions can be divided into two categories, referred to as *signaling message handling* and *signaling network management*. We begin with a consideration of signaling message handling.

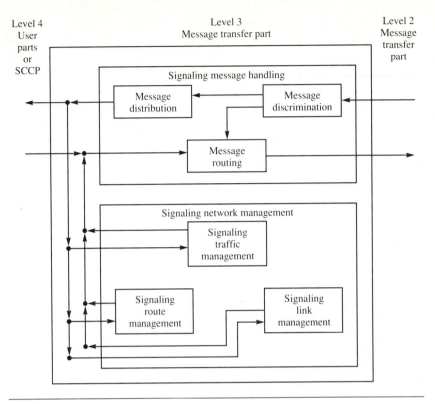

Figure 9.10 *SS#7 layer 3 functions*
© Adapted from CCITT Blue Book, vol VI.7, 1988

Signaling message handling concerns itself with the proper relaying and delivery of signaling messages across a signaling connection section. The signaling messages consist of information derived from the various level 4 entities of the protocol architecture, as well as certain level 3 network management data. They are transported in the signaling information field of level 2 MSUs.

Signaling message handling serves three specific purposes, as indicated in Figure 9.10. The *message routing function* determines the signaling link on which a signaling message obtained from level 3 or 4 that has not yet reached its destination SP is to be forwarded. The *message discrimination function,* on the other hand, determines whether a signaling message received from level 2 has arrived at its destination SP or must be forwarded by the routing function. The *message distribution function* is responsible for the delivery to the appropriate level 3 or 4 entity of signaling messages that have reached their destination SP.

These functions are carried out by means of signaling message handling messages whose structural details are shown in Figure 9.11. Each message consists of two fields, the *service information octet (SIO)* and a *routing label*.

The SIO is divided into two parts, the *service indicator* and the *sub–service field*. The first identifies the particular level 3 or 4 entity associated with the signaling message and the second is used to differentiate between national or international signaling messages.

The routing label is used by level 3 to route the signaling message across the connection section from one SP to another. It contains three subfields.

The *originating point code (OPC)* and *destination point code (DPC)* are the addresses of the SPs in the connection section where the signaling message originated and to which it must be delivered. The 14 digits assigned to these codes permit the globally unique identification of up to 12288 signaling points. The structure of international point codes has been standardized by the CCITT and is composed of three subfields of 3 bits, 8 bits, and 3 bits, respectively. The first subfield identifies one of 8 SPs in the context of a national network, the second identifies one of 256 national networks within a world geographic zone, and the third defines one of 6 world geographic zones in which the national network exists. All network and zone codes are assigned by the CCITT and are listed in CCITT Recommendation Q.708. Local SP identifiers, however, are assigned by the national network authority.

The *signaling link selection code (SLS)* defines one of up to 16 virtual routes between the pair of SPs in the connection section. It is used to assign the signaling messages belonging to different transactions to separate routes for the purpose of load sharing and routing around failures.

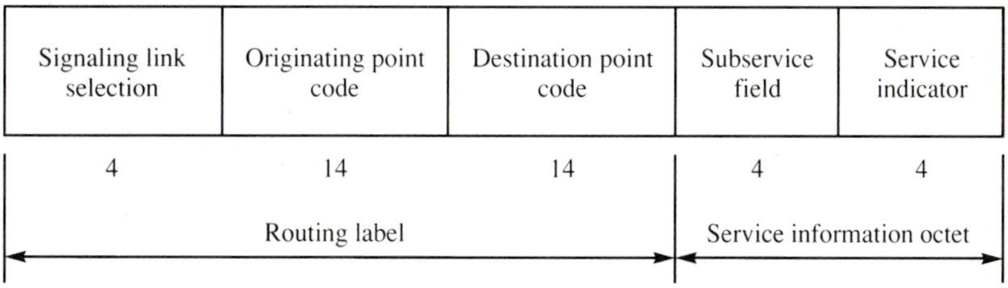

Signaling link selection	Originating point code	Destination point code	Subservice field	Service indicator
4	14	14	4	4
Routing label			Service information octet	

Figure 9.11   *Format of signaling message handling message*

As shown in Figure 9.12, the SIO and routing label are carried within a level 2 MSU, together with any signaling messages obtained from the level 3 network management entity and the level 4 user parts.

The message routing function relies on the routing label to relay a signaling message from the originating SP to the destination SP in a connection section. Each SP and intermediate STP contains information in the form of a routing table that allows it to determine on the basis of the DPC and SLS the signaling link on which to forward the message to the next SP or STP. This link is chosen by the SP or STP independently of the preceding portion of the route. Note, however, that in order to ensure proper sequencing, all signaling messages belonging to a given transaction are normally transferred over the same signaling link to the next node and consequently over the same route between originating and destination SPs in a connection section. Load sharing is achieved by assigning different links for different transactions involving the same pair of SPs.

The decision at a node of which link to use to the next node for a given destination SP and transaction is based on the level of traffic currently experienced by the signaling links leaving that node. It is also possible to establish priorities based on other factors such as link quality, transmission rate, and cost.

At each SP or STP the message discrimination function examines the DPC in the routing label of a received message. If it does not correspond to the local address, the message is directed to the message routing function. Otherwise it is forwarded to the message distribution function, which in turn directs it to the proper level 3 or 4 entity on the basis of the service indicator of the SIO. These interactions are shown in Figure 9.10.

Let us now consider the second major category of level 3 functions, namely signaling network management. Its purpose is to control the topology, routing plan, and traffic flow of the CCSN in response to link and node failures and the occurrence of congestion. Thus it

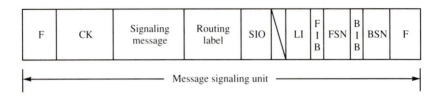

Figure 9.12 *MSU structure*

plays a critical role in meeting the extreme requirements of reliability placed on the CCSN.

Before discussing the specific tasks of the signaling network management and the manner in which they are carried out, it is necessary to define the various states in which the signaling links and signaling routes may exist within the CCSN.

A signaling link is considered to be either available or unavailable to carry traffic from one node to another. An unavailable link is said to be either failed, deactivated, or blocked and becomes available when it is restored, activated, or unblocked. Typically, a signaling link failure is declared by level 2 when the error rate monitor indicates an excessive number of rejected MSUs or when the link alignment procedure fails. The link is restored when both sides have carried out a successful realignment procedure. Link deactivation occurs as a result of a request from the signaling network management function or an external management entity and activation is again the result of a successful alignment. A link is blocked when an outage occurs in the message handling processor within a node and is unblocked when the processor reenters service.

Signaling routes are said to be available, restricted, or unavailable. The latter conditions are recognized when one of the STPs along the route indicates a degree of difficulty or its complete inability to transfer messages to their destination along the route in question.

Signaling links are either uncongested or congested. The latter condition is recognized by level 2 when the number of MSUs queuing for transmission or retransmission across the link exceeds a threshold. This threshold may be specified as either a percentage of the available buffer space or a certain number of MSUs. The link is declared uncongested when the buffer occupancy falls below the threshold by a predetermined amount.

Signaling routes between origin and destination SPs are likewise considered to be uncongested or congested. The latter condition pertains if any signaling link along the route is congested.

To manage the signaling links and routes of the CCSN in a way that assures the appropriate level of performance under conditions of link failure, node failure, and congestion the signaling network management provides three specific functions, referred to as *signaling traffic management, signaling link management,* and *signaling route management.* These are shown in Figure 9.10. Traffic management concerns itself with the diversion of traffic from points of congestion or failure or a temporary reduction of the volume of traffic over certain routes. The link management function offers the capability of restoring failed links, of activating idle links to replace failed links, and of deactivating operational links when they are no longer needed. It also supervises the links to determine their operational status. Route management is responsible for the distribution to the network nodes of messages that indicate the availability or unavailability of specific signaling routes.

These various tasks of signaling network management are accomplished through the exchange among the SPs and STPs of level 3 signaling network management messages. Their format is shown in Figure 9.13, and a list of all currently defined messages is contained in Table 9.1.

Two 4-bit headers, labeled H0 and H1, identify the groups of messages and specific messages within a group, respectively, as shown in Table 9.1. Some of the messages also include an additional field of up to three octets that specify various *signals and indications (SI)* relating to the specific function being carried out.

For transmission across the CCSN a signaling network management message is attached to a signaling message handling message and the entire structure is carried in a level 2 MSU, as shown in Figure 9.14. The service indicator in the SIO is set to 0 0 0 0 to identify the message as a signaling network management message. The actual routing, discrimination, and delivery is performed by the signaling message handling part of level 3, as described earlier and indicated in Figure 9.10.

We now proceed to illustrate with the aid of several examples the essential aspects of the procedures by which the signaling network management carries out its tasks. For a complete and rigorous treatment of this topic, see CCITT Recommendation Q.704.

Our first example involves the use of the signaling traffic management functions known as *changeover* and *changeback,* which redirect traffic from a signaling link that has become unavailable to an alternative link and reverse this diversion when the original link becomes available again.

Signals and indications SI	Heading code H1	Heading code H0
0,8,16 or 24	4	4

Figure 9.13 *Format of signaling network management message*

TABLE 9.1   Signaling network management messages

Changeover and Changeback Messages	
COO	Changeover Order
COA	Changeover Acknowledgment
CBD	Changeback Declaration
CBA	Changeback Acknowledgment
Emergency Changeover Messages	
ECO	Emergency Changeover Order
ECA	Emergency Changeover Acknowledgment
Transfer Control Messages	
TFP	Transfer Prohibited
TFA	Transfer Allowed
TFR	Transfer Restricted
Signaling Traffic Flow Control Messages	
RCT	Signaling Route Set Congestion Test
TFC	Transfer Controlled
Signaling Route Set Test Messages	
RST	Signaling Route Set Test
Management Inhibit Messages	
LIN	Link Inhibit
LUN	Link Uninhibit
LIA	Link Inhibit Acknowledgment
LUA	Link Uninhibited Acknowledgment
LID	Link Inhibit Denied
LFU	Link Force Uninhibit
LLT	Link Local Inhibit Test
LRT	Link Remote Inhibit Test
Signaling Data Link Connection Order Messages	
DLC	Signaling Data Link Connection Order
CSS	Connection Successful
CNS	Connection Not Successful
CNP	Connection Not Possible
Traffic Restart Allowed Messages	
TRA	Traffic Restart Allowed
User Part Flow Control Messages	
UPU	User Part Unavailable

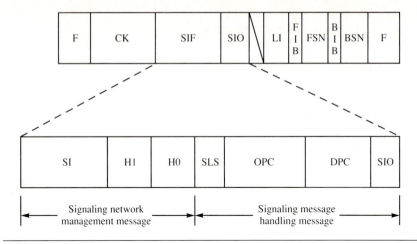

Figure 9.14 *MTP frame structure*

A node recognizing the unavailability of a link terminates the transmission and acceptance of MSUs relative to that link and sends the Changeover Order message COO to the node on the other side of the unavailable link. This message may be transmitted either over another link in the link set connecting the two nodes, or if no such alternative is available, over a route involving one or more relay nodes. In the SI field, the message contains the forward sequence number of the last MSU accepted from the unavailable signaling link. The remote node, on receiving the COO, responds by likewise suspending its transmission and acceptance of MSUs relative to the unavailable signaling link and sending the Changeover Acknowledgment message COA containing the forward sequence number of its last accepted MSU in the SI field. Through the exchange of these numbers the two sides are able to resume the transmission of MSUs over an alternative set of signaling links in the proper sequence and without duplication or loss. The route containing these links is identified by the appropriate signaling link selection code in the routing label of the signaling message handling message part of the MSUs.

Figure 9.15 illustrates this procedure for the case of a link failure between signaling point A and signaling transfer point B that causes an interruption of the route between A and D. Here the changeover messages between A and B are exchanged via signal transfer point C over links AC and BC. Subsequent to the changeover, the flow of MSUs is then diverted from link AB to links AC and BC, respectively.

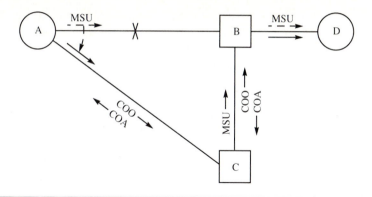

Figure 9.15 *Illustration of the changeover procedure*

When the original signaling link becomes available again, the changeback procedure can be used to effect the reversal of the traffic previously diverted to the alternative link. Changeback is initiated by terminating the transmission of the relevant MSUs on the alternative link and sending instead the Changeback Declaration message CBD to the remote node. This message, which is conveyed over the alternative signaling link, indicates that no more MSUs associated with the traffic being diverted will be sent on the alternative link. It contains the identity of the newly available link in the routing label and a changeback code in the SI field. The latter allows discrimination of the changeback declaration from other changeback operations that may currently be in progress. When the remote node receives the changeback declaration, it responds with a Changeback Acknowledgment message CBA containing the same changeback code. This signal, which can be routed via any available signaling link, acknowledges receipt of all MSUs sent on the alternative signaling link. The originating node then resumes transmission of MSUs over the newly available link.

As a second example of a signaling traffic management function, we consider signaling traffic flow control. Its purpose is to limit the amount of signaling traffic generated by a source when the set of routes to the desired destination is congested and unable to handle all submitted messages. Such a condition can be the result of route unavailability, congestion, or failure of signaling links and congestion or failure of SPs and STPs.

Generally, any message received by level 3 of a SP or STP when the route set to the destination is congested is nonetheless handed over as a MSU to level 2 for transmission. The originating SP effects flow control by conveying to its appropriate level 4 entity from which it received the message a congestion indication primitive containing the address of the relevant destination as a parameter. This primitive is sent when the first signaling message from level 4 is received and after every set of eight such messages, until congestion abates. By contrast, a STP receiving a MSU for a congested route returns to the originating SP the Transfer Controlled message TFC after the first received MSU and after every set of eight MSUs, as long as the congestion condition persists. On receiving the TFC message, which identifies in its SI field the destination involved in the congested route, the originating SP informs its appropriate level 4 entity as above.

As an example of a signaling route management function we consider the case where the route through a node of the CCSN becomes unavailable for the transfer of messages to a particular destination.

A node receiving a signaling message while in such a state returns to the node from which it received the message the Transfer Prohibited message TFP, containing an indication of the unreachable destination in the SI field. On the other hand, if no messages are being received at the time the node recognizes the unavailability of a route to a given destination, it broadcasts the TFP message to all its adjacent nodes.

As a result of receiving the TFP message a node performs a rerouting function and periodically tests the status of the original route by sending in 30- to 60-second intervals the Signaling Route Set Test message RST to the node from which it received the TFP message.

When the original route becomes available again, the relevant node transmits in broadcast fashion to all adjacent nodes the Transfer Allowed message TFA. The receiving nodes then perform another rerouting to the original route and cease the transmission of the RST message.

9.4.4 *Performance of the Message Transfer Part*

Collectively the three levels of the message transfer part of the SS#7 are designed to carry signaling messages generated by the level 3 or 4 entities in one SP to a corresponding entity in another SP across a connection section without loss or duplication, in the proper sequence, and error free. Of course, given the unavoidable occurrence of transmission errors on the signaling links and the potential for line and node failures, perfect performance cannot be guaranteed. The CCITT has therefore developed a set of performance measures and has specified minimum levels of performance to meet the require-ments of the respective users of the message transfer part.

Currently the performance specifications require an undetected bit error rate of 10^{-10}, a lost message rate of 10^{-7}, an out-of-sequence message rate of 10^{-10}, and a duplicated message rate of 10^{-10}.

The CCITT has also given recommended values regarding the availability of any particular route set between a pair of SPs, the avail-ability of routes in signaling connections, the maximum number of in-termediate SPs and STPs to be used in an end-to-end signaling relation, and the maximum link-to-link and end-to-end signaling de-lays. For details concerning these specifications, see CCITT Recom-mendations Q.706 and Q.709.

9.5 The Signaling Connection Control Part

From our discussion in the previous section it is evident that the three levels of the message transfer part of the SS#7 protocol architecture provide the ability to exchange messages in a sequenced and connec-tionless manner over a connection section between a pair of SPs that may be connected directly or via one or more intermediate STPs. By invoking this SP-to-SP signaling capability over appropriate succes-sive connection sections, it is possible to transfer setup and control information among the SPs associated with the set of exchanges in the IEN through which a user connection is established.

We consider now the signaling connection control part which, to-gether with the message transfer part, forms the network service part (NSP) of the SS#7 protocol architecture, as shown in Figure 9.4. Its purpose is to add a routing capability on top of the MTP service that allows the NSP to offer to the transaction capability and ISDN user part an end-to-end transmission service between the endpoint SPs of a signaling relation. Together, the MTP and SCCP are equivalent to the functions of layers 1, 2, and 3 of the OSI architecture.

The end-to-end service provided by the NSP can be associated with a user connection over the IEN, but is normally used for the transfer of signaling information of relevance only to the endpoint SPs. The exchange of supplementary service information between the orig-inating and destination local exchanges of an existing user connection over the IEN provides an example of this type of signaling. Since the

SPs associated with the transit exchanges of the user connection are not affected by this information, they do not need to process it in any way. An end-to-end signaling relation may also be entirely independent of any IEN user connections. Examples of this mode of operation are the exchange of information between a service switching point and a service control point for the support of an intelligent network service and the transfer of user-to-user signaling information flows between a pair of ISDN end-users.

In general, an end-to-end signaling connection between a pair of SPs involves one or more connection sections between the end SPs and intermediate SPs, as shown in Figure 9.16. A connection section may provide a direct connection between attached SPs or may involve one or more intermediate STPs. In any case, the transfer of messages across a connection section is performed by the MTP. As far as the service users are concerned, the intermediate SPs involved in a signaling relation act purely as STPs and do not participate in the processing of the service user messages. The end-to-end signaling relation therefore simplifies the treatment of such end-to-end messages at intermediate nodes, resulting in a reduction of workload, complexity, and end-to-end delay. Figure 9.17 shows the associated real and logical information flows across a connection section and end-to-end.

9.5.1 SCCP Services and Service Primitives

We begin our study of the SCCP with the specification of its service capabilities. Figure 9.18 depicts the interactions of the SCCP with the users of its services, known as *subsystems,* and the underlying MTP. The subsystems in question are, of course, the ISDN user part and the transaction capabilities.

Functionally the SCCP can be divided into four major blocks, as shown in Figure 9.19. Two of these, the *SCCP connection-oriented*

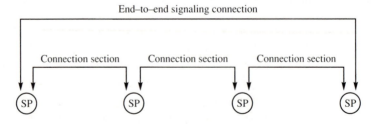

Figure 9.16 *Signaling connections*

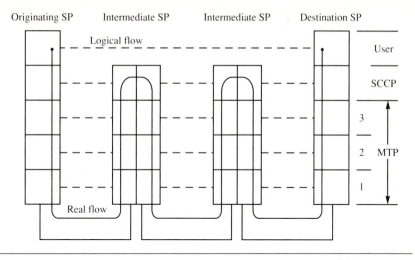

Figure 9.17   *Node-to-node and end-to-end information flows*

control (SCOC) and the *SCCP Connectionless Control (SCLC),* offer the user subsystems engaged in a signaling relation the capability to transfer messages called *network service data units (NSDU).* The SCOC provides these services in a connection-oriented manner through the establishment of signaling connections between the end subsystems, whereas the SCLC offers only a connectionless transfer capability. These control blocks rely on the *SCCP routing control (SCRC),* which performs the distribution of messages that have arrived at their destination to either the SCOC or SCLC and directs messages that must be forwarded to the MTP for relaying across a connection section. The SCCP, through its *SCCP management control block (SCMG),* also provides facilities for maintaining network performance in the presence of congestion and failure of subsystems and signaling points. The SCMG, using the services provided by the SCLC and SCRC blocks, distributes information regarding the availability of its subsystems and signaling point to other SCMGs and relays such information received from other SCMGs to its own subsystems. Collectively, the four blocks of the SCCP provide services to the ISDN user part and the transaction capabilities and rely on the services of the MTP.

As usual, the interactions between service user and service provider involve the exchange of primitives across an appropriate service-access point.

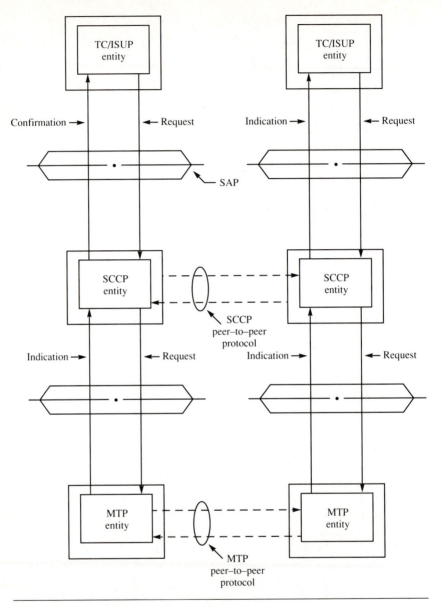

Figure 9.18 *SCCP service relationships*

SCCP Users   SCCP   MTP

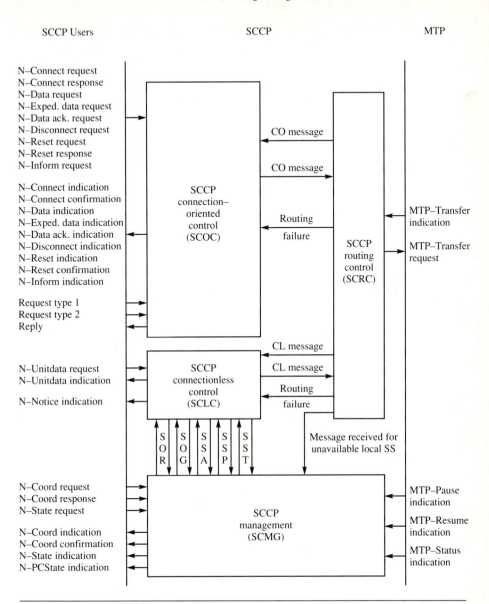

Figure 9.19 *Functionality of the SCCP*
© Reprinted from CCITT Blue Book, vol VI.7, 1988

The MTP message relaying services are invoked and obtained by the SCRC through the MTP-TRANSFER Request primitive and the MTP-TRANSFER Indication primitive. These primitives, together with their parameters, are listed in Table 9.2.

The end-to-end message transfer services of the SCCP can be configured in either a connection-oriented or a connectionless mode. Within each category, two classes of service are defined.

Class 0, the so-called *basic connectionless class,* provides a simple connectionless service with no control over the sequence in which the NSDUs are delivered to the destination. Each message is considered as an independent entity without regard to its relationship with previous or subsequent messages. Class 1, the *sequenced connectionless class,* builds on the capabilities of class 0 by utilizing the sequence control function of the underlying MTP across a connection section to assure a high probability of correct sequencing at the receiver.

These two classes of service are provided by the SCLC and utilize the N-UNITDATA and N-NOTICE primitives listed in Table 9.3 in their interactions with the subsystem. The first is used to transfer messages between the SCCP and a subsystem and the second allows the return of undeliverable messages to the sending subsystem.

Class 2 service, known as the *basic connection-oriented class,* offers the capability to establish and terminate temporary logical signaling connections and to transfer the NSDUs over such temporary or

TABLE 9.2   MTP service primitives

PRIMITIVES		
Generic Name	*Specific Name*	**PARAMETERS**
MTP-TRANSFER	Request	OPC
	Indication	DPC
		SLS
		SIO
		User Data
MTP-PAUSE	Indication	Affected DPC
MTP-RESUME	Indication	Affected DPC
MTP-STATUS	Indication	Affected DPC
		Cause

© Adapted from CCITT Blue Book, vol VI. 7, 1988

TABLE 9.3   SCCP connectionless service primitives

PRIMITIVES		PARAMETERS
Generic Name	*Specific Name*	
N-UNITDATA	Request	Called address
	Indication	Calling address
		Sequence control
		Return option
		User data
N-NOTICE	Indication	Called address
		Calling address
		Reason for return
		User data

© Reprinted from CCITT Blue Book, vol VI. 7, 1988

permanent connections. As in class 1 service, the control over the sequence in which the NSDUs are received is delegated to the MTP. Class 3, the *flow control connection-oriented class,* adds a flow control function and its own capability for the detection of out-of-sequence NSDUs. It also includes the ability to detect lost NSDUs. These connection-oriented services are provided by the SCOC and utilize the primitives shown in Table 9.4. The services are divided into connection establishment and clearing services that use the N-CONNECT and N-DISCONNECT primitives, normal and expedited data transfer services using the N-DATA, N-EXPEDITED, DATA and N-DATA ACKNOWLEDGE primitives, and a reset service employing the N-RESET primitives. The latter may be invoked during the data transfer phase in order to reinitialize the sequencing control. Also included is a diagnostic service implemented by means of the N-INFORM primitive.

   The services of the SCMG can be activated by either the MTP or a subsystem. In the first case the MTP provides service status information by means of three primitives. The MTP-PAUSE Indication and MTP-STATUS Indication are used to notify the SCCP of the total or partial interruption of the MTP service, and the MTP-RESUME Indication is used to indicate service resumption. These primitives are shown in Table 9.2. In the second case the subsystem and the SCCP interact through use of the management primitives shown in Table 9.5.

TABLE 9.4   SCCP connection-oriented service primitives

PRIMITIVES		PARAMETERS
Generic Name	*Specific Name*	
N-CONNECT	Request Indication Response Confirmation	Called address Calling address Responding address Receipt confirmation selection Expedited data selection Quality of service parameter set User data Connection identification
N-DATA	Request Indication	Confirmation request User data Connection identification
N-EXPEDITED DATA	Request Indication	User data Connection identification
N-DATA ACKNOWLEDGE	Request Indication	Connection identification
N-DISCONNECT	Request Indication	Originator Reason User data Responding address Connection identification
N-RESET	Request Indication Response Confirmation	Originator Reason Connection identification
N-INFORM	Request Indication	Reason Connection identification QOS parameter set

© Adapted from CCITT Blue Book, vol VI. 7, 1988

The four N-COORD primitives are utilized by SPs or SCCP users that exist in multiple copies to remove themselves as active participants or users of the SCCP services. The two N-STATE primitives allow a subsystem and the SCCP to exchange status information with each other. Finally, the N-PCSTATE primitive serves the purpose of providing SP status information to a subsystem.

TABLE 9.5   SCCP management primitives

PRIMITIVES		
Generic Name	*Specific Name*	**PARAMETERS**
R-COORD	Request Indication Response Confirmation	Affected subsystem Subsystem multiplicity indicator
N-STATE	Request Indication	Affected subsystem User status Subsystem multiplicity indicator
N-PCSTATE	Indication	Affected DPC Signaling Point Status

© Reprinted from CCITT Blue Book, vol VI. 7, 1988

9.5.2   SCCP Message Structure

To perform their service of end-to-end message transfer between peer subsystems, the SCCPs involved in an end-to-end signaling relation exchange *SCCP messages* across one or more connection sections, as shown in Figure 9.17. These messages are generated and received in the SCOC or SCLC blocks of an SP and are transferred across a connection section via the SCRC and MTP. The structural details of the SCCP messages are shown in Figure 9.20. For transmission purposes each SCCP message is carried in the signaling information field of a level 2 MSU.

All messages consist of a routing label, a message type code, and a number of parameters.

The three-octet routing label is generated in the SCRC and has the structure shown in Figure 9.11. As we discussed in Section 9.4.3, it is passed to the MTP and used by the latter to relay the message across a connection section.

The one-octet message type code is used to identify a particular message. Table 9.6 is a list of all currently specified messages, together with their message type code and an indication of the appropriate protocol class.

The message parameters are either fixed or variable in length and may be mandatory or optional. The mandatory fixed-length parameters occur only in specific messages and their names, order

TABLE 9.6   List of SCCP messages

MESSAGE TYPE	CLASSES				CODE
	0	1	2	3	
CR Connection Request			X	X	0000 0001
CC Connection Confirm			X	X	0000 0010
CREF Connection Refused			X	X	0000 0011
RLSD Released			X	X	0000 0100
RLC Release Complete			X	X	0000 0101
DT1 Data Form 1			X		0000 0110
DT2 Data Form 2				X	0000 0111
AK Data Acknowledgment				X	0000 1000
UDT Unitdata	X	X			0000 1001
UDTS Unitdata Service	X	X			0000 1010
ED Expedited Data				X	0000 1011
EA Expedited Data Acknowledgment				X	0000 1100
RSR Reset Request				X	0000 1101
RSC Reset Confirm				X	0000 1110
ERR Protocol Data Unit Error			X	X	0000 1111
IT Inactivity Test			X	X	0001 0000

© Reprinted from CCITT Blue Book, vol VI. 7, 1988

of appearance, and length are uniquely identified by the corresponding message-type code. Consequently only their value must be specified. The mandatory variable-length parameters are also associated with specific messages and occur in a specific order determined by the message. Therefore only their length and value must be specified. The location of the one-octet length indicator of each such parameter in a message is identified by a one-octet pointer that indicates the number of octets between it and the length indicator of the parameter. The pointers for all such parameters are arranged in the order in which the parameters appear and precede the mandatory variable-length parameters in the message. Optional parameters may be of both fixed or variable length and may be included in a message in any order. They are specified by a one-octet length field, a one-octet length indicator, and a variable number of octets containing the parameter value. The start of the optional parameter field is also identified by a pointer, and the octet of all zeros marks its end.

Table 9.7 is a list of all currently defined parameters and the messages with which they are associated. Here the letters F, V, and O identify the corresponding parameter as either mandatory and of fixed length (F), mandatory and of variable length (V), or optional and of fixed or variable length (O).

In the following paragraphs we briefly describe the functions of these parameters. For their detailed binary coding, see CCITT Recommendation Q.713.

Four of the parameters in Table 9.7 are used for addressing purposes. The *Destination Local Reference* is fixed and three octets in length. It contains a reference number that identifies a connection between the two peer SCCP entities in a connection section and is specified by the entity receiving the message in which it is contained. The *Source Local Reference* has a similar structure, but identifies the connection at the sending entity. The *Called Party Address* and *Calling Party Address* are variable in length and contain information identifying the users of the SCCP services and their location.

The one-octet *Protocol Class* specifies the class of the protocol to be used in the relationship between the two subsystems. For classes 0 and 1 it also indicates whether an undeliverable message is to be returned to the sending subsystem.

Three of the parameters are used in controlling message segmentation and proper message sequencing. The *Segmenting/Reassembling* parameter consists of one octet containing the more data indication. The latter specifies whether the message is an intermediate or final segment of a longer message that was segmented for transmission purposes. The one-octet *Receive Sequence Number* contains the sequence number of the next expected message, modulo 128. Two octets are allocated to the *Sequencing/Segmenting* parameter, which combines the modulo-128 send and receive sequence numbers with a more data indication.

Control over the rate at which messages may be sent is accomplished by the one-octet *Credit* parameter, which indicates the size of the flow control window.

Five one-octet parameters are used for various diagnostic purposes. The *Release Cause* and *Reset Cause* contain the reason for the release or resetting of an existing connection, respectively. The *Return Cause* denotes the reason for the return of a message to the sender, and the *Error Cause* specifies the type of error in the event of

TABLE 9.7 List of parameters contained in SCCP messages

PARAMETER	MESSAGE															
	CR	CC	CREF	RLSD	RLC	DT1	DT2	AK	UDT	UDTS	ED	EA	RSR	RSC	ERR	IT
End of optional parameters	O	O	O	O												
Destination local reference		F	F	F	F	F	F	F			F	F	F	F	F	F
Source local reference	F	F		F	F								F	F		F
Called party address	V		O						V	V						
Calling party address	O								V	V						

TABLE 9.7 (Cont.)

	MESSAGE															
PARAMETER	CR	CC	CREF	RLSD	RLC	DT1	DT2	AK	UDT	UDTS	ED	EA	RSR	RSC	ERR	IT
Protocol class	F	F							F							F
Segmenting/ reassembling						F										
Receive sequence number								F								
Sequencing/ segmenting							F									F
Credit	O	O						F								F
Release cause				F												
Return cause										F						
Reset cause													F			
Error cause															F	
Refusal cause			F													
Data	O	O	O			V	V		V	V	V	V				

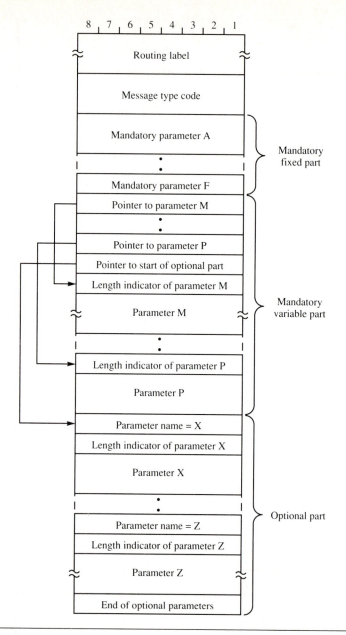

Figure 9.20 *Frame structure of SCCP messages*
© Reprinted from CCITT Blue Book, vol VI.7, 1988

a protocol mismatch. The *Refusal Cause* denotes the reason why a connection is being refused.

The *Data* parameter is variable in length and contains the information to be transferred between communicating SCCP users. In addition to the messages and their associated parameters defined earlier, a number of SCCP management messages that are exchanged between SCCP management entities have been specified. Such a message is usually carried as a Data parameter in a *Unitdata message,* with the latter being transferred in connectionless mode according to protocol class 0. The Calling Party Address and Called Party Address of the Unitdata message are set to the respective subsystem numbers of SCCP management.

The structure of the Data parameter when it contains a SCCP management message also conforms to Figure 9.20. Five messages have been defined. Their names and message type code, as well as the three mandatory and fixed parameters associated with each message, are shown in Table 9.8.

The *Affected SSN* is a one-octet subsystem number that identifies a particular SCCP management user or subsystem that has failed or withdrawn from service, is congested, or is allowed. The *Affected PC* consists of two octets and specifies the signaling point code of a signaling point that has failed or withdrawn, is congested, or is allowed.

TABLE 9.8   SCCP management messages and parameters

MESSAGE TYPE	CODE
SSA Subsystem-Allowed	00000001
SSP Subsystem-Prohibited	00000010
SST Subsystem-Status-Test	00000011
SOR Subsystem-Out-of-Service-Request	00000100
SOG Subsystem-Out-of-Service-Grant	00000101
PARAMETER	**TYPE**
SCMG format identifier	F
Affected SSN	F
Affected PC	F
Subsystem multiplicity indicator	F

© Adapted from CCITT Blue Book, vol VI. 7, 1988

The one-octet *Subsystem Multiplicity Indicator* specifies whether the subsystem in question is duplicated or not, or whether its multiplicity is unknown.

9.5.3 SCCP Protocol Procedures

The services of the SCCP are implemented with the aid of a protocol that governs the interactions between peer SCCPs in a connection section. In analogy with the classification of services, four classes of protocols have been defined. They utilize the messages shown in Table 9.6.

Classes 0 and 1 offer the capability of exchanging Unitdata and Unitdata Service messages in connectionless mode. The first provides no sequence control for successive messages, whereas the second relies on the MTP for this function.

Class 2 provides procedures for the establishment of logical signaling connections through the exchange of the Connection Request and Connection Confirm messages and the termination of such connections by means of the Released and Release Complete messages. It also performs unacknowledged data transfer by means of the Data Form 1 message, but does not provide sequence or flow control. The performance of the protocol in terms of lost or out-of-sequence messages is therefore determined by the MTP.

Class 3 adds to the capabilities of class 2 by allowing the acknowledged, flow controlled transfer of data in normal mode through use of the Data Form 2 and Data Acknowledgment messages or in expedited mode, using the Expedited Data and Expedited Data Acknowledgment messages. It also includes a sequence numbering capability for the detection of lost or out-of-sequence data messages and a reset function implemented by the exchange of the Reset Request and Reset Confirmation messages to recover from these types of errors.

To illustrate the main aspects of these protocols we offer three examples. For a complete description of the procedures, see CCITT Recommendation Q.714.

We start with the transfer of a NSDU in connectionless mode between a pair of SCCP service users.

A NSDU generated by one of the subsystems is delivered to the SCLC of its SCCP by means of the N-UNITDATA Request primitive that contains as parameters the calling and called addresses of the relevant users and the data to be transferred. If a series of NSDUs are to be transferred and sequencing is required by the user, the sequence control parameter is also included.

In general, the addresses may be specified as any combination of a subsystem number (SSN) identifying a particular subsystem such as the ISUP or TC, the point code of the SP containing the subsystem, and a global title. The latter can take various forms but is usually a subscriber number represented according to some numbering plan. It may contain the signaling point code and/or the subsystem number, but not necessarily explicitly. Consequently a translation function may be required in order to extract the signaling point code and SSN needed for routing, if they are not part of the address.

When it receives this primitive, the SCLC generates a Unitdata message that contains the four parameters Data, Protocol Class, Calling Party Address, and Called Party Address. The first parameter carries the user data part of the NSDU that must be transferred transparently to the remote SCCP user. The second parameter specifies the use of either the class 0 or class 1 service, with the latter being requested by the presence of the sequence control parameter in the N-UNITDATA Request primitive. The address parameters define the origin and destination of the NSDU and are derived from the addresses obtained in the N-UNITDATA Request primitive.

The Unitdata message is then passed to the SCRC for transmission. If the Called Party Address parameter contains the DPC in explicit form, the SCRC selects an initial connection section on which to transfer the message and generates a routing label containing the OPC and DPC of the corresponding SPs. Otherwise the DPC of the message must first be derived from the global title by a translation function. The SCRC also determines a route across the connection section and identifies it by a signaling link selection code. For protocol class 0 the SLS may vary from one message to the next, whereas for class 1 the same SLS must be used to assure the in-sequence delivery of successive messages. The entire routing label is then attached to the Unitdata message, and the complete message is conveyed by the SCRC as part of a MTP-TRANSFER Request primitive to the MTP. The latter relays it along a series of STPs and signaling links identified by the SLS to the MTP in the destination SP of the connection section. From there it is sent via a MTP-TRANSFER Indication primitive to the SCRC. The discrimination function in the SCRC now determines, based on the Called Party Address and a possible translation of the global title, whether the message has arrived at its ultimate destination. If so, it passes the message to the SCLC, which in turn transfers it in an N-UNITDATA Indication primitive to the subsystem identified by the Called Party Address parameter. Otherwise the SCRC selects another connection section and proceeds as described earlier. The calling and called users are unaware of the identity or the number of connection sections involved in the transfer of the message.

As a second example we describe the procedures for the establishment and termination of a signaling connection between two SCCP users and the transfer of data over it.

Connection establishment is initiated through the conveyance of the N-CONNECT Request primitive by the calling subsystem to its SCOC. This primitive contains the addresses of the calling and called users and a set of quality-of-service parameters. In response the SCOC generates a Connection Request message in which the selected QOS is reflected in the appropriate value of the Protocol Class parameter. The message also includes the Source Local Reference parameter that identifies to the SCOC the connection that is being established and allows the SCOC to distinguish it from other existing connections between the same users. Its value is significant only over the connection section to which the calling SP is attached. It must be included in all subsequent messages conveyed in the opposite direction toward the calling SCCP user over this connection section. For class 3 service the Connection Request message also contains the Credit parameter, which indicates the requested size of the flow control window to be used on the signaling connection. Its value is selected to satisfy the quality of service requested by the user. The Connection Request message is then transferred to the SCRC, which performs any necessary global address conversion, constructs and appends a routing label for the connection section, and delivers the complete message as part of a MTP-TRANSFER Request primitive to its MTP for transmission.

At the receiving SP of the connection section the message is transferred to the SCRC by means of a MTP-TRANSFER Indication primitive. As in the previous example, the SCRC now determines whether the message has reached the SP associated with the called subsystem and if so transfers it to the SCOC. From there it is conveyed to the appropriate called subsystem as part of an N-CONNECT Indication primitive. Otherwise the SCRC assigns new values of the Source Local Reference parameter, Credit parameter, and routing label for the next connection section and transfers the message to the MTP for relaying across that connection section. This process continues until the message has arrived at its called subsystem.

Assuming that the called subsystem is willing to accept a signaling connection to the calling subsystem, it responds by transferring the N-CONNECT Response primitive to its SCOC. The process outlined earlier is then repeated in transferring a Connection Confirm message

from the called SCOC to the calling SCOC across one or more connection sections. This message contains the previously established
value of the Source Local Reference parameter pertinent for the particular connection section, the selected Protocol Class, and—for class
3 service—a flow control credit allocation as a value of the Credit
parameter. Also included is the Destination Local Reference parameter whose value identifies the connection from the destination's point
of view. Again this number is only valid for a particular connection
section. Thus it varies as the message is transferred across the different connection sections of the signaling connection. Once the message
has arrived at the calling subsystem, the signaling connection is considered established.

In the data transfer phase the SCCP users employ the N-DATA
Request and N-DATA Indication primitives in their interactions with
the calling and called SCOCs. The latter exchange Data Form 1 or
Data Form 2 messages—depending on whether class 2 or 3 service is
used—to exchange user information. These data messages always
contain the local reference of the receiving SCCP on the particular
connection section. They do not require any other addressing information. For class 3 service with flow control the Data Form 2 messages also include send and receive sequence numbers that indicate
the number of the current message and the number of the next message expected from the other side. These numbers are governed by
the usual window flow control procedure and are valid only for individual connection sections. In addition, flow control may be provided
through the use of the Data Acknowledgment message, which also
contains the send and receive sequence numbers and a credit window.
By setting the Credit parameter to zero, a SCCP experiencing congestion can thereby stop any further transfer of data messages from the
remote SCCP on its connection section. The subsequent transmission
of a Data Acknowledgment message with a positive credit value allows the resumption of such transmissions, starting with the indicated
receive sequence number.

Release of the signaling connection is initiated by a SCCP user by
conveying to its SCOC the N-DISCONNECT Request primitive containing as a parameter the reason for the disconnection. In response
the SCOC transfers on its connection section a Released message containing the Source Local Reference and Destination Local Reference
parameters and the Release Cause parameter derived from the corresponding parameter of the primitive. The receiving SCOC on the
connection section then confirms the release by returning to the

originating SCOC a Release Complete message containing the Source Local Reference and Destination Local Reference parameters as well and releases the resources associated with the connection section. If it is an intermediate SCOC, it also transfers a Released message to a peer SCOC on the next connection section toward the end-user. Otherwise it issues the N-DISCONNECT Indication primitive with the Reason parameter to its subsystem to complete the procedure.

As our final example, we consider the transfer of a SCCP management message generated in the SCMG to a peer entity. We assume that a SCCP user in a signaling point has gone out-of-service, in which case it transfers to its SCMG an N-STATE Request primitive in which one of its two parameters identifies the affected subsystem and the other is set to out-of-service. In response the SCMG generates a Subsystem Prohibited message (SSP) and hands it over to the SCLC for transmission to all concerned signaling points. The SCLC then generates for each destination node a Unitdata message with the Data parameter containing the SSP message and forwards them to the SCRC for transfer across the signaling network. This message is transferred in connectionless mode across one or more connection sections according to the procedures outlined earlier. At the destination node the message is routed to the SCLC and from there to the SCMG. In the final step the N-STATE Indication primitive is used by the SCMG to inform the SCCP user of the out-of-service condition.

9.6 The ISDN User Part

We now consider the *ISDN user part (ISUP)*, which provides its end-users with the capability to establish, supervise, and terminate basic bearer services over an integrated services digital network, to invoke supplementary services in support of a basic service, and to provide for the end-to-end transfer of signaling information that is either independent of or related to an existing user connection.

As currently defined, the ISUP is restricted to the control of 64-kbit/s circuit switched connections between the local exchanges of a pair of ISDN subscribers and allows the invocation of five supplementary services. These include calling line identification, call forwarding, closed user group, direct dialing in, and user-to-user signaling. For a precise definition of these services, see Sections 10.2.1 to 10.2.4 and 10.4.

In addition to these services, three modes of end-to-end signaling that rely on either the MTP or the SCCP for information transfer are also specified.

The message structures and functional procedures for carrying out the ISUP tasks have been given by the CCITT in Recommendations Q.730, Q.761 to Q.764, and Q.766. In the following sections we offer a summary of these documents.

9.6.1 ISUP Services and Service Primitives

In carrying out their functions of basic call control, supplementary services control, and end-to-end information transfer, the ISUPs in the SPs of the common channel signaling network create signaling relations between themselves. These can be of two types. SP-to-SP relations are used to convey signaling information in an incremental manner from one SP to another along a given path. They are intended for the establishment, supervision, and termination of user connections between a pair of local exchanges over the interexchange network. The set of SPs and corresponding ISUPs involved in the relation are associated with the local and transit exchanges over which the user connection is established and each ISUP participates in the processing of the ISUP call control messages. In this type of signaling relation an ISUP utilizes the services of the message transfer part to exchange messages with a peer ISUP.

In contrast, end-to-end signaling relations, which are used to convey supplementary services control information flows or user-to-user information flows, involve only the ISUPs in the end SPs to which the originating user and destination user are attached. The ISUPs in any intermediate SPs are transparent to the messages at the ISUP level. Two types of such end-to-end relations are defined. In the so-called *pass-along signaling relation,* ISUP messages flow along the same signaling path that was used to establish an existing user connection. They are conveyed from one SP to another by the MTP. In the *SCCP signaling relation,* on the other hand, the ISUP messages are transferred over a path that is independent of any user connection between the endpoints, even if one exists. Here the ISUP messages are conveyed in connectionless or connection-oriented mode by the SCCP.

Figure 9.4 shows the interactions between the ISUP, the MTP, and the SCCP. For the SP-to-SP and pass-along signaling relations the ISUP interacts directly with the MTP through the exchange of the MTP service primitives listed in Table 9.2. In the SCCP signaling relation the services of the SCCP are accessed through the exchange of the appropriate connectionless or connection-oriented service primitives listed in Tables 9.3 and 9.4.

9.6.2 ISUP Messages and Message Structures

To carry out its services an ISUP generates, interprets, and exchanges with a peer ISUP so-called *ISUP messages*. Table 9.9 contains the currently defined list of messages, their acronyms, and the corresponding message type code. The structural details and the handling of an ISUP message depend to some extent on its application.

SP-to-SP and pass-along end-to-end ISUP messages, which are of course conveyed directly by the MTP, have the structure given in Figure 9.21. They are carried in the routing label and signaling message field of a message signal unit, as shown in Figure 9.12.

The service indicator of the SIO is set to 0 1 0 1 to indicate the presence of an ISUP message, and the routing label has the usual interpretation. The two-octet circuit identification code is used to specify the physical circuit connecting a pair of adjacent exchanges involved in the end-user connection with which the signaling relation is associated. For example, if a pair of exchanges along the path of the user connection is connected by several digital time division multiplex trunk circuits, the circuit identification code specifies which particular trunk circuit and time slot are being used to transfer the user information between these exchanges.

End-to-end ISUP messages that are conveyed via the SCCP have their routing label applied by the SCCP. Furthermore, since they are not associated with a user connection, the circuit identification code is absent. These messages are carried in the Data parameter of a SCCP message.

The set of ISUP messages is divided into eight groups for forward call setup, backward call setup, general setup, call supervision, circuit supervision, circuit group supervision, in-call modification, and end-to-end signaling.

The eight messages in the three setup groups are used for the establishment of a bidirectional connection between a calling and called ISDN user. The forward setup group includes the *Initial Address* message *(IAM)* and *Subsequent Address* message *(SAM)*. The first is sent by the calling ISUP toward the called ISUP to convey addressing and other information relating to the routing of the user connection. If the information contained in the IAM is insufficient, any additional addressing information required to establish the connection is then

TABLE 9.9   ISDN user part messages

ACRONYM	MESSAGE TYPE	CODE
ACM	Address complete	00000110
ANM	Answer	00001001
BLO	Blocking	00010011
BLA	Blocking acknowledgment	00010101
CMC	Call modification completed	00011101
CMR	Call modification request	00011100
CMRJ	Call modification reject	00011110
CFG	Call progress	00101100
CGB	Circuit group blocking	00011000
CGBA	Circuit group blocking ac'nowledgment	00011010
CQM	Circuit group query	00101010
CQR	Circuit group query response	00101011
GRS	Circuit group reset	00010111
GRA	Circuit group reset acknowledgment	00101001
CGU	Circuit group unblocking	00011001
CGUA	Circuit group unblocking acknowledgment	00011011
CFN	Confusion	00101111
CON	Connect	00000111
COT	Continuity	00000101
CCR	Continuity check request	00010001
FCA	Facility accepted	00100000
FRJ	Facility reject	00100001
FAR	Facility request	00011111
FOT	Forward transfer	00001000
INF	Information	00000100
INR	Information request	00000011
IAM	Initial address	00000001
PAM	Pass-along	00101000
REL	Release	00001100
RLC	Release complete	00010000
RSC	Reset circuit	00010010
RES	Resume	00001110
SAM	Subsequent address	00000010
SUS	Suspend	00001101
UBL	Unblocking	00010100
UBA	Unblocking acknowledgment	00010110
USR	User-to-user information	00101101

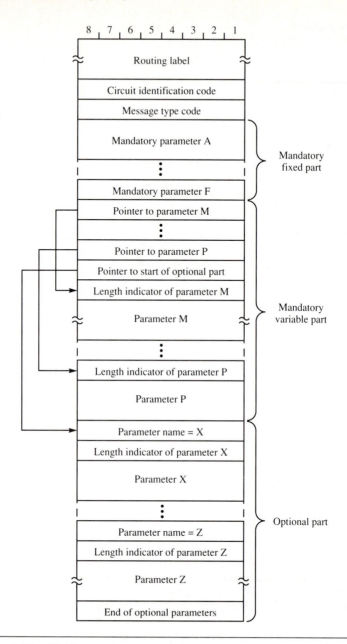

Figure 9.21 *ISDN user part message structure*
© Adapted from CCITT Blue Book, vol VI.8, 1988

conveyed by one or more SAMs. Setup in the backward direction is accomplished by means of three messages. The *Address Complete* message *(ACM)* is sent by the called ISUP in the backward direction to indicate that all information required to route the call has been received. Certain events occurring during the establishment of the connection are reported by the called ISUP to the calling ISUP by means of one or more *Call Progress* messages *(CPG)*. The *Connect* message *(CON)* serves to indicate to the calling ISUP that all information regarding the call has been received and that the call has been answered by the remote user. The group of general setup messages contains three messages. Additional information regarding a call may be requested by an ISUP through the transfer of the *Information Request* message *(INR)* and is provided to the requesting ISUP by means of the *Information* message *(INF)*. The *Continuity* message *(COT)* allows an ISUP to inform its peer ISUP whether or not the incoming and outgoing circuits of a user connection through its associated exchange are continuous.

Call supervision is accomplished through the exchange of three messages. An indication to the calling ISUP that the call has been answered is given by means of the *Answer* message *(ANM)* and release of a user connection is initiated by sending the *Release* message *(REL)*. Operator communications to solicit assistance in the setup of a call are carried out through the exchange of the *Forward Transfer* message *(FOT)*.

Circuit supervision is carried out by means of the ten messages in the circuit supervision group. The *Release Complete* message *(RLC)* is sent in response to the reception of a REL message to indicate that the circuit in question has been placed in an idle condition. To request a check on the continuity of a circuit through an exchange a *Continuity Check Request* message *(CCR)* is sent. The reset of a circuit is accomplished by sending the *Reset Circuit* message *(RSC)*. The *Blocking* message *(BLO)* is sent to an exchange to cause the blocking of the specified circuit for calls outgoing from the exchange receiving the message. This action can be reversed by sending the *Unblocking* message *(UBL)*. Acknowledgments of the BLO and UBL messages are provided by the *Blocking Acknowledgment* message *(BLA)* and *Unblocking Acknowledgment* message *(UBA)*, respectively. The temporary disconnection of a party is indicated to the other party by sending the *Suspend* message *(SUS)*, and its subsequent reconnection is indicated by the *Resume* message *(RES)*. The inability to recognize all or

TABLE 9.10   ISDN user part message parameters

PARAMETER NAME	CODE
Access transport	00000011
Automatic congestion level	00100111
Backward call indicators	00010001
Call modification indicators	00010111
Call reference	00000001
Called party number	00000100
Calling party number	00001010
Calling party's category	00001001
Cause indicators	00010010
Circuit group supervision message-type indicator	00010101
Circuit state indicator	00100110
Closed user group interlock code	00011010
Connected number	00100001
Connection request	00001101
Continuity indicators	00010000
End of optional parameters	00000000
Event information	00100100
Facility indicator	00011000
Forward call indicators	00000111

© Adapted from CCITT Blue Book, vol VI. 7, 1988

part of a received message is indicated to the sender by the *Confusion* message *(CFN)*.

Eight messages in the circuit group supervision category are dedicated to the supervision of groups of circuits. The *Circuit Group Blocking* message *(CGB)* is sent from one exchange to another in order to inhibit the use of a specific group of circuits in subsequent user connections outgoing from the remote exchange. The cancellation of this action is effected by the *Circuit Group Unblocking* message *(CGU)*. Acknowledgment of these two messages is given by the *Circuit Group Blocking Acknowledgment* message *(CGBA)* and the *Circuit Group Unblocking Acknowledgment* message *(CGUA)*, respectively. To ascertain the status of a specified group of circuits at a remote exchange and the reporting of that status involves the ex-

TABLE 9.10 *(Cont.)*

PARAMETER NAME	CODE
Information indicators	00001111
Information request indicators	00001110
Nature of connection indicators	00000110
Optional backward call indicators	00101001
Optional forward call indicators	00001000
Original called number	00101000
Range and status	00010110
Redirecting number	00001011
Redirection information	00010011
Redirection number	00001100
Signalling point code	00011110
Subsequent number	00000101
Suspend/Resume indicators	00100010
Transit network selection	00100011
Transmission medium requirement	00000010
User service information	00011101
User-to-user indicators	00101010
User-to-user information	00100000

change of the *Circuit Group Query* message *(CGQ)* and the *Circuit Group Query Response* message *(CQR)*. Release of a specified group of circuits is accomplished through the exchange of the *Circuit Group Reset* message *(GRS)* and the *Circuit Group Reset Acknowledgment* message *(GRA)*.

Changes in the characteristics of an existing user connection are controlled by means of the six messages in the *In-call Modification* group. The *Call Modification Request* message *(CMR)* indicates the request to modify an existing call, and the *Call Modification Reject (CMRJ)* and *Call Modification Completed (CMC)* messages represent the negative or positive response to that request. The activation of a specific facility can be requested by the *Facility Request* message *(FAR)*. The negative and positive responses to that request are given by the *Facility Reject* message *(FRJ)* and the *Facility Accepted* message *(FAA)*.

End-to-end information may be conveyed in either the *Pass-along* message *(PAM)* or the *User-to-User Information* message *(USR)*.

The details of the ISUP messages just described are contained in a number of mandatory and optional parameters of fixed or variable size. Their representation is the same for all ISUP messages and is similar to that of the parameters in a SCCP message, as discussed in Section 9.5.2. A list of currently defined parameters is given in Table 9.10.

9.6.3 SP-to-SP Procedures

As an illustration of the use of the messages and parameters described earlier, let us now discuss in somewhat simplified terms the essential aspects of the SP-to-SP procedures to set up and terminate a basic circuit switched user connection over the IEN between a pair of ISDN terminals. We assume in our example that the user connection involves three user connection sections via two transit exchanges. The signaling information flows between the SPs associated with the exchanges are conveyed over the corresponding signaling connection sections. The entire procedure is diagrammed in Figure 9.22.

The ISDN user originating the call transfers to its local exchange a SETUP message containing as IEs sufficient information to allow the routing of the call to the destination local exchange. The format of this message and the transfer procedure conform, of course, to the principles described in Chapter 6. After analyzing the IEs, and with reference to a network database containing routing information, the local exchange selects an appropriate initial transit exchange and an interconnecting circuit, the latter being specified by its circuit identification code. It also derives from the IEs the transmission medium requirement and various other characteristics of the desired connection. The ISUP in its associated SP then generates an IAM that contains as parameters the IEs supplied by the calling user in the SETUP message, including the Calling Party Number and Called Party Number, as well as the Transmission Medium Requirement and all other information necessary to route the call to the destination local exchange. In addition, the Calling and Called Party Number parameters contain an indication of whether or not the numbers may be presented to the other party. If present in the SETUP message, the Bearer Capability IE is mapped into the User Service Information parameter, and any User-User IE is represented by the User-to-User Information

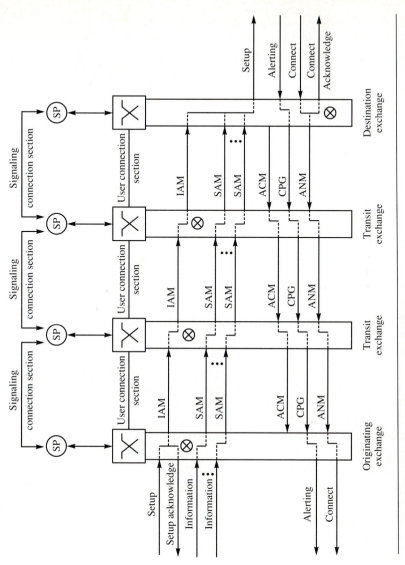

Figure 9.22 User connection establishment procedure

parameter. All IEs that must be transferred transparently between originating and destination exchanges are carried in the Access Transport parameter. The latter is therefore transparent to the SPs associated with the transit exchanges of a user connection. The formats of the parameters are identical to those of the corresponding IEs, as described in Section 6.2.

The ISUP also appends the selected circuit identification code and a routing label containing its point code and the point code of the SP associated with the initial transit exchange, together with the signaling link selection code. It then conveys the IAM to the MTP as part of a MTP-TRANSFER Request primitive for transmission to the peer ISUP in the initial transit exchange, where it is delivered as part of a MTP-TRANSFER Indication primitive.

Immediately after transmission of the IAM the local exchange completes the user transmission path between it and the transit exchange and establishes the first signaling connection section. On receiving the IAM at the SP of the transit exchange, the Called Party Number, the Transmission Medium Requirement, and other parameters are analyzed to determine the next transit exchange and an appropriate interconnecting circuit. The IAM, with a new routing label and circuit identification code, is then relayed via the services of the MTP to the ISUP in the next transit exchange, the user transmission path is connected through the transit exchange, and the second signaling connection section is established.

This procedure is repeated at all subsequent transit exchanges until the IAM arrives at the SP associated with the destination local exchange.

If overlap signaling is used over the UNI on the originating side, the originating local exchange returns a SETUP ACKNOWLEDGMENT message in response to the SETUP message and receives additional detail regarding the call in one or more INFORMATION messages. This detail is then conveyed to the ISUPs in the SPs of the previously selected transit exchanges and the destination local exchange as a Subsequent Number parameter in one or more SAM messages.

When all call control detail has been received at the destination local exchange the Called Party Number, the Bearer Capability IE, and other call control details obtained in the IAM and SAM messages are analyzed to determine whether a connection can be established to the called ISDN terminal. Assuming that no incompatibilities exist, a SETUP message is then transferred over the remote UNI. At the same time an ACM message is conveyed in the reverse direction over the established path to the originating local exchange to indicate that complete addressing information is now available at the destination local exchange. When the called terminal responds to the SETUP message with an ALERTING message, the destination local exchange causes the relaying of a CPG message via the SPs of the transit exchanges to the SP of the originating local exchange. The latter then sends an ALERTING message to the calling terminal. The subsequent receipt of the CONNECT message from the called terminal results in the return of a CONNECT ACKNOWLEDGE message to the called terminal, the through-connection of the circuit in the direction of the originating local exchange, and the relaying of an ANM message to the originating local exchange. There a CONNECT message is conveyed to the calling terminal as the final step in the establishment procedure.

Figure 9.23 diagrams the procedure for clearing a user connection when the clearing terminal is the called terminal. An essentially symmetric procedure applies to clearing by the calling terminal. Release of the connection is initiated by sending the DISCONNECT message across the UNI to the local exchange where it causes the release of the circuit to the transit exchange, the transfer of a RELEASE message to the clearing terminal, and the relaying of the REL message toward the remote local exchange. The clearing terminal normally acknowledges the RELEASE message by a RELEASE COMPLETE message.

At each transit exchange the reception of the REL message causes the release of the through-connection, the return of a RLC message to the preceding exchange, and the relaying of the REL message to the next exchange. At the remote local exchange the reception of the REL message also causes the transfer of the DISCONNECT message to the cleared terminal, which responds with the RELEASE message. The transfer of the RELEASE COMPLETE message to the cleared terminal then completes the procedure.

9.6.4 Pass-Along End-to-End Procedures

From our discussion in the previous section it is evident that the establishment of a user connection between a pair of end-users is accompanied by the creation of a signaling relation between the SPs associated with the local and transit exchanges. This relation, which may consist of a number of signaling connection sections as shown in

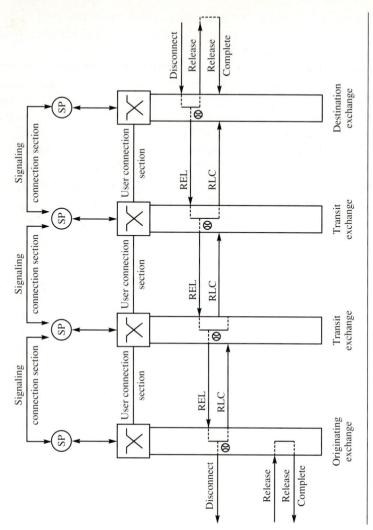

Figure 9.23 *User connection release procedure*

Figure 9.22, is used in the pass-along method to relay signaling information that is associated with the user connection but relevant only at the originating and destination local exchanges.

The procedure makes use of the PAM message that contains the same routing label and circuit identification code as other ISUP messages associated with the existing signaling relation, but carries a single end-to-end ISUP message as a parameter. The PAM message itself is transferred over the signaling connection in the same manner as any other ISUP message, but its included ISUP message is only examined at the endpoint ISUPs of the signaling connection.

9.6.5 *End-to-End Procedures Using Connectionless SCCP*

We now consider the end-to-end transfer of an ISUP message when an underlying connectionless SCCP service is available. Two scenarios can be distinguished, based on whether the ISUP message is independent of or associated with a user connection.

In the first case the information is contained as a User-to-User Information parameter in a User-to-User Information message (USR). The latter is passed as part of an N-UNITDATA Request primitive to the SCLC of the SCCP and is transferred end-to-end by the connectionless procedure described in Section 9.5.3.

In the second case it becomes necessary to establish a relationship between an end-to-end ISUP message and its associated user connection, prior to the transfer of the message. This is accomplished by exchanging across the signaling connection sections associated with the user connection certain ISUP call control messages containing the Call Reference parameter. The latter consists of a three-octet call identity, together with the point code of the SP where the call identity is established. It is specified independently for each connection section and in each direction, with an appropriate coupling where the connection sections are joined.

The actual call control messages used to convey the Call Reference parameter depend on the operational phase of the signaling connection at the time that the call reference is created. During the establishment phase of the signaling connection, the parameter is included in the IAM in the forward direction and its presence implies the request to create an end-to-end signaling relation. If the request can be satisfied, the parameter is also included in the first ISUP message sent in the backward direction in response to the IAM. The corresponding ISUP messages during other phases of the signaling connection are the Information Request message (INR) and the Information message (INF).

Once the Call Reference parameter has been established, it is included in all ISUP messages that must be transferred end-to-end. Its value changes from one connection section to the next, but always corresponds to that specified by the destination SP of the section.

As in the first case above, end-to-end ISUP messages are conveyed by the ISUP to its SCLC in the User Data parameter of an N-UNITDATA Request primitive and transferred in connectionless mode in the User Data parameter of a Unitdata message.

9.6.6   End-to-End Procedures Using Connection-Oriented SCCP

As we discussed in Section 9.5.3, an ISUP may use the services of its SCCP to establish an end-to-end connection-oriented signaling relation with a peer ISUP and to transfer end-to-end signaling information through the exchange of Data Form 1 or Data Form 2 SCCP messages. This method is entirely independent of whether a user connection exists or not. As an alternative the CCITT has defined the so-called embedded method in which an end-to-end connection-oriented signaling relation is created by transporting the Connection Request and Connection Confirm SCCP messages in certain ISUP messages. The latter may be exchanged as part of the procedure to establish a user connection or during its operation. Figure 9.24 diagrams the interactions.

The embedded method makes use of three interface elements that are exchanged between an ISUP and the SCOC of its SCCP. These are indicated in Figure 9.19. When an ISUP wants to establish an end-to-end signaling connection, it notifies its SCOC by means of the Request Type 1 interface element. This element contains an indication of the type of connection desired and requests the SCOC to provide a source local reference and other information necessary for the establishment of the connection. The SCOC then generates a Connection Request message containing this information and transfers it to its ISUP as a Reply interface element. The ISUP embeds the message as a parameter in either an IAM, a FAR, or an INF message and transfers it to the ISUP in the remote SP of the first connection section, using normal transfer procedures. At the receiving SP a Request Type 2 interface element is conveyed by the ISUP to its SCOC, in response to which the latter generates another Connection Request message with a new local reference and point code and relays it to the ISUP as part of a Reply interface element. There the message is again embedded in

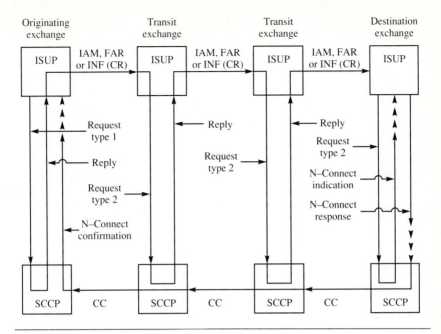

Figure 9.24 *Embedded end-to-end signaling connection establishment*

an appropriate ISUP message and transferred to the next relay point. This process continues until the Connection Request message has been received by the SCOC in the destination local exchange, at which time the latter informs its ISUP by an N-CONNECT Indication primitive that a signaling connection is to be established. The remaining parts of the procedure now follow the normal arrangement. When the ISUP responds with an N-CONNECT Response primitive to its SCOC, the latter transfers the Connection Confirm message via the relay SPs to the SCOC in the SCCP associated with the originating local exchange. In the final step of the procedure the SCOC conveys a N-CONNECT Confirmation primitive to its ISUP to confirm the establishment of the connection.

9.7 Summary and Recommended Reading

This chapter focused on the subject of common channel signaling. We began with a consideration of the structure of a common channel signaling network and characterized its nodes and interconnecting circuits. We then turned to an examination of the CCITT Signaling System #7, whose protocols control the interactions between the signaling entities in the common channel signaling network. We investigated the architectural aspects of SS#7, described the structure of the messages used at the various levels, and illustrated the operation of the signaling system at each level by means of specific examples.

A general introduction to SS#7 can be found in [PHEL86] and [SCHL86]. A good summary of the user part of SS#7 is contained in [APPE86]. [BENA85], [CRAW85], and [DONO86] describe the introduction and evolution of common channel signaling in the AT&T network. [VEA 84] gives an early assessment of SS#7. Other papers of interest in connection with SS#7 are [WALK86] and [PUNS87].

CHAPTER 10

ISDN Telecommunications Services

In previous chapters we have concentrated on the technological developments embodied in the design of the ISDN as they affect the subscriber-access network. From that point of view an ISDN is fully defined to the end-user by the technical specifications of the user-to-network interface, as they manifest themselves at the R, S, T, and U reference points.

A detailed understanding of these interface specifications is necessary for the design and implementation of the user equipment. Ultimately, however, the user's main interest lies in the telecommunications services available from the network. By this we mean specifically the user's ability to establish and control connections, to exchange information with another user, to control the processing and storage of this information by the network, and to allow access to sources of information offered by the network itself or by independent service suppliers. It is in fact the provision of new, innovative, easy-to-use, and cost-effective telecommunications services—together with the enhancement of the traditional services offered by today's networks—that constitute the primary reason for the implementation of the ISDN and the major potential for its economic viability.

As we have pointed out, the development of such services is made possible by two features of the ISDN. First, the existence of high-quality transparent digital end-to-end connections of various bit rates makes it feasible to transfer all types of information at levels of performance and cost generally not obtainable over existing networks. Second, the availability to the end-user of multiple information transfer channels and a separate signaling channel, together with the ISDN's stored program controlled switches and common channel signaling network, provide the user with the ability to engage in more than one connection at the same time, while simultaneously exercising sophisticated control over these connections and the information transferred across them. The same features also offer the possibility of network-provided storage and processing of user information.

This chapter covers the most important telecommunications services currently being considered for implementation in the ISDN. In describing these services and defining their salient characteristics, we follow, at least in part, the formal service description framework developed by the CCITT, as contained in Recommendations I.121, I.130, I.140, and the recommendations of the I.200 series.

10.1 Characterization of Telecommunications Services

As currently specified by the CCITT, the telecommunications services supported by an ISDN are divided into two categories, known as *bearer services* and *teleservices*. They are further divided into *basic services* that provide the essential aspects of the service and *supplementary services,* which modify or augment a basic service and are offered only in conjunction with a basic service. Table 10.1 summarizes this terminology.

With reference to Figure 10.1, Bearer Services are made available by the network to the user at reference points S and T—that is, at access points 1 and 2. They provide the capability for information transfer between the communications functions of the terminals, as well as signaling between those functions and the network. Generally, these functions for both information transfer and signaling extend only

TABLE 10.1   Classification of telecommunications services

TELECOMMUNICATIONS SERVICE			
Bearer Service		*Teleservice*	
Basic bearer service	Basic bearer service + supplementary services	Basic teleservice	Basic teleservice + supplementary services

© Reprinted from CCITT Blue Book, vol III.7, 1988.

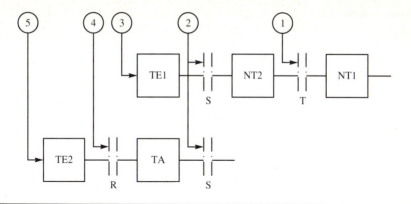

Figure 10.1 *ISDN telecommunications service-access points*
© Reprinted from CCITT Blue Book, vol III.7, 1988

to layers 1, 2, and 3 of the OSI reference model. Any interactions at layers 4 to 7 are end-to-end according to user-defined procedures and are transparent to the service.

In contrast, teleservices build on and extend the functions of bearer services by also including capabilities at layers 4 to 7. They are accessed at the user-to-terminal interface points 3 and 5 in Figure 10.1 and thus include the user-oriented noncommunication functions of the terminals.

Non-ISDN services corresponding to the X-series and V-series recommendations are obtained at access point 4.

The capabilities of a telecommunications service are described in terms of a set of salient features known as *service attributes,* each of which may assume one or more values. A particular service is then characterized by specifying the values of all its pertinent attributes.

The set of service attributes, shown in Table 10.2, is divided into *low-layer attributes,* corresponding to layers 1 to 3 of the OSI reference model, *high-layer attributes,* corresponding to layers 4 to 7, and *general attributes,* referring to the service in general. Low-layer attributes are further divided into *information transfer attributes* and *access attributes.* Bearer services include only low-layer attributes and general attributes, whereas teleservices contain all three classes.

The class of information transfer attributes characterizes the ability of the telecommunications service to transfer information from one S or T reference point to one or more other S or T reference points. It currently includes seven distinct components. The *Information Transfer Mode* describes the transmission and switching techniques

TABLE 10.2   Telecommunications service attributes

Low-layer attributes

Information transfer attributes

1. Information transfer mode
2. Information transfer rate
3. Information transfer capability
4. Structure
5. Establishment of communication
6. Symmetry
7. Communication configuration

Access attributes

8. Access channel and rate
9.1 Signaling access protocol Layer 1
9.2 Signaling access protocol Layer 2
9.3 Signaling access protocol Layer 3
9.4 Information access protocol Layer 1
9.5 Information access protocol Layer 2
9.6 Information access protocol Layer 3

High-layer attributes

10. Type of user information
11. Layer 4 protocol functions
12. Layer 5 protocol functions
13. Layer 6 protocol functions
14. Layer 7 protocol functions

General attributes

15. Supplementary services provided
16. Quality of service
17. Interworking possibilities
18. Operational and commercial

© Adapted from CCITT Blue Book, vol. III.7, 1988

employed by the service in the transfer of user information. The *Information Transfer Rate* refers to the rate at which digital information is conveyed between a pair of S or T reference points. *Information Transfer Capability* defines the service's ability to transfer different types of information through the ISDN. The *Structure* attribute refers to the service's ability to maintain the structural characteristics of the information streams conveyed by the service. The *Establishment-of-*

Communication attribute describes the method used to establish the service's communication link. The remaining two attributes—*Symmetry* and *Communication Configuration*—characterize the type of communication link over which the service is provided.

The class of access attributes describes the layer 1, 2, and 3 capabilities required to gain access to the service. The *Access Channel and Rate* attribute specifies the particular B, D, or H channel provided by the service and its bit rate. The *Signaling and Information Access Protocol* attribute defines the signaling and information transfer protocols at layers 1, 2, and 3 across the user-to-network interface that govern the access to the service.

The high-layer attributes describe the message-oriented characteristics of a service and relate to the capabilities of OSI layers 4 to 7. The *Type of User Information* attribute characterizes the restrictions placed on the data streams and formats that are conveyed by the service. The attribute *Layer 4 Protocol Functions* defines the transport-level protocols that may be employed by the service to effect the efficient and reliable transport of the user information. The *Layer 5 Protocol Functions* attribute refers to the protocols managing the two-way dialogue. The *Layer 6 Protocol Functions* attribute concerns itself with the presentation details of the user information being exchanged, including such issues as the code, resolution, and graphic mode in which the user information is represented. The attribute *Layer 7 Protocol Functions* refers to the characteristics of the information that are meaningful in the context of the service.

The class of general attributes deals with qualifications and additional aspects of the service not included in the other categories.

The *Supplementary Services* attribute refers to the modifications and additional services that may be associated with a particular basic bearer service or teleservice. The *Quality-of-Service* attribute characterizes various performance aspects of the service such as delay, throughput, and error rate. The attribute *Interworking Possibilities* concerns the types of services available to a user attached to a particular ISDN in communicating with users attached to another ISDN or a non-ISDN network and the procedures by which these services are obtained. Finally, the *Operation and Management* attribute relates to tarif and subscription issues.

Table 10.3 lists the range of values of the low-layer attributes, as currently defined. Subject to further study, other values may be added in the future.

Information transfer may be accomplished in either circuit switched or packet switched mode, with the rates of information

TABLE 10.3 Low-layer attribute values

ATTRIBUTES	POSSIBLE VALUES OF ATTRIBUTES						
Information transfer attributes							
1. Information transfer mode	Circuit					Packet	
2. Information transfer rate	Bit rate kbit/s					Throughput	
	64	2 × 64	384	1536	1920		
3. Information transfer capability	Unrestricted digital information	Speech	3.1 kHz audio	7 kHz audio	15 kHz audio	Video	Options for further study
4. Structure	8 kHz integrity	Service data unit integrity		Unstructured		TSSI	RDTD
5. Establishment of communication	Demand	Reserved		Permanent			

	Unidirectional		Bidirectional symmetric			Bidirectional asymmetric		
6. Symmetry								
7. Communication configuration	Point-to-point		Multipoint			Broadcast		
Access attributes								
8. Access channel and rate	D(16)	D(64)	B	H0	H11	H12		
9.1 Signaling access protocol Layer 1	I.430/I.431	I.461	I.462	I.463	(V.120) I.465			
9.2 Signaling access protocol Layer 2	I.440/I.441		I.462	X.25				
9.3 Signaling access protocol Layer 3	I.450/I.451		I.461	I.462	X.25	I.463		
9.4 Information access protocol Layer 1	I.430/I.431	I.460	I.461	I.462	I.462	(V.120) I.465	I.463	
9.5 Information access protocol Layer 2	HDLC LAP B	X.25			I.462		G.711	G.722
9.6 Information access protocol Layer 3	T.70-3	X.25			I.462			

transfer conforming to the channel structures for basic access and primary access. The information transfer capabilities include the transfer of digital information streams with totally unrestricted contents, A-law or Mu-law coded digital speech, digitally encoded 3.1 kHz, 7 kHz, and 15 kHz audio, and various forms of digitally encoded video. The structure attribute value "8 kHz integrity" refers to information streams such as 64-kbit/s digital speech samples, that are implicitly or explicitly demarcated at 125-μs intervals. Other attribute values relate to information flows that are structured into service data units or sequences of time slots (time slot sequence integrity—TSSI). Depending on the attribute value selected, the service will maintain the integrity of the corresponding boundaries and structure of the information flows. The attribute value *Restricted Differential Time Delay (RDTD)* refers to the delivery of the information submitted to the service in a given time slot within a limited delay. A telecommunications service with the structure attribute *Unstructured*, on the other hand, does not preserve the boundaries or the structural integrity of the information flows.

Communications may be established in three ways. In the *demand* mode a connection is created through a dial-up procedure and is available from the end of that procedure until a disconnect is issued. In *reserved* communication the time of connection establishment and the connection duration are predetermined and the connection is made available and disconnected by the service at the predetermined time without any explicit connection or disconnection request being issued by the user. *Permanent* communications exist during the entire time interval of a subscription to the service and are available at any time between fixed endpoints specified by the subscriber.

The Symmetry attribute can assume three specific values. *Unidirectional* communication restricts the flow of information between a pair of access points to one direction. In *bidirectional* communication, in contrast, information flows in both directions are possible. The characteristics of these flows are the same or different in the two directions, depending on whether the service is *symmetric* or *asymmetric*.

The Communication Configuration attribute may also assume three values. *Point-to-point communication* exists between a single pair of access points, whereas *multipoint* and *broadcast* communication involve more than two access points. In the last case the information is conveyed between a unique source access point and all other destination access points in only one direction.

The access channel and rate attribute allows as values all the component B, D, and H channels of the basic and primary rate access structures and their associated rates.

The choice of access protocols for information transfer and signaling includes the layer 1, 2, and 3 procedures of the ISDN Recommendations I.430/I.431, I.441, and I.451 for basic and primary access, the terminal adapter recommendations I.460, I.461, I.462, I.463, and I.465, as well as a number of non-ISDN protocols such as Recommendations X.25 and T.70.

The currently specified values of the high-layer attributes are listed in Table 10.4. The values of the type-of-user-information attribute range over most commonly encountered forms, including speech, sound, text, facsimile, and mixed-mode text, as well as graphics, videotex, and other image-based information.

The Layer 4, 5, and 6 Protocol attributes take as values a number of standard CCITT protocols.

At layers 4 and 5 the currently specified range includes the general transport layer protocol defined in Recommendation X.224 and the session layer protocol of Recommendation X.225. The subset of X.224 defined in Recommendation T.70 and the subset of X.225 defined in Recommendation T.62, both applicable to teletex and Group 4 facsimile terminals, are also permissible.

The Layer 6 Protocol attribute currently specifies the use of the T.400-series recommendations, in addition to the procedures defined in T.6 and T.61. The latter two apply to Group 4 facsimile machines and teletex terminals, respectively. The representation of analog voice in digital mode according to Recommendation G.711 is also a possible value of the Layer 6 Protocol attribute. For facsimile the attribute "resolution" can vary over the range 200, 240, 300, and 400 picture elements per inch (ppi), whereas "graphic mode" allows most of the standard methods of representing graphic information, including alphamosaic, geometric, and photographic coding.

The Layer 7 Protocol attribute again takes on a number of standard CCITT protocols, including Recommendation T.60 for teletex and the recommendations of the T.500 series.

Based on the list of attributes and their values presented earlier, it is possible to define a large number of individual telecommunications services by setting the service attributes to specific values. Not all of these are necessarily useful or desirable. In fact, one of the major issues in the design and implementation of the ISDN involves the development of a limited set of standard services that can accommodate

TABLE 10.4 High-layer attribute values

ATTRIBUTES	POSSIBLE VALUES OF ATTRIBUTES							
10. Type of user information	Speech (Tele-phony)	Sound	Text (Tele-tex)	Facsimile (Tele-fax 4)	Text-facsimile (Mixed mode)	Videotex	Video	Text inter-active (Telex)
11. Layer 4 protocol	X.224		T.70					
12. Layer 5 protocol	X.225		T.62					
13. Layer 6 protocol	T.400-Series	G.711	T.61		T.6			
Resolution	200 ppi	240 ppi	300 ppi	400 ppi				
Graphic mode	Alphamosaic		Geometric		Photographic			
14. Layer 7 protocol	T.60		T.500-Series					

© Adapted from CCITT Blue Book. vol VIII.7, 1988

the user's current needs in a cost-effective manner, that offer the potential for the development of new applications, and that are economically viable from the network's point of view. Within these constraints, the CCITT has specified several categories of bearer services and teleservices. Their characteristics are summarized in the next two sections.

10.2 Definition of Bearer Services

It is convenient to distinguish between bearer services based on circuit switched connections and bearer services using the packet mode of information transfer.

Circuit mode bearer services conform entirely to the ISDN protocol reference model described in Chapter 3. Thus, the user information is transferred over one or more B or H channels of the basic access or primary access and is under the control of the U-plane protocols. Layer 1 of the U plane conforms to the procedures defined in CCITT Recommendations I.430 for basic access and I.431 for primary access, as described in Chapter 4. The protocols at layers 2 and 3, however, are end-user defined and the bearer services are completely transparent to them.

Signaling information for connection control is conveyed over the 16-kbit/s D channel of basic access or the 64-kbit/s D channel of primary access, under control of the C-plane protocols. At layer 1 the transfer is again governed by I.430 or I.431, respectively. At layers 2 and 3 the I.441 and I.451 procedures, as described in Chapters 5 and 6, apply.

Since the U-plane and C-plane procedures are carried out independently over separate component channels of the interface, user information transfer and connection control may operate concurrently.

In defining packet mode bearer services, the CCITT has been guided by two considerations. First, the need to accommodate, at least for an interim period, the existing X.25-based packet switching networks and terminals led to the development of a hybrid service in which the packet switching functions are carried out according to the X.25 protocols, but access to the resources of the packet switching network, whether they are a part of the ISDN or separate from it, is provided by the ISDN circuit switched connection control procedures.

More recently, the CCITT has considered packet mode bearer services in which these differences are eliminated and in which there is a clear separation of the procedures for user information transfer and connection control, in accordance with the ISDN protocol reference model.

Two types of hybrid packet mode bearer services provided by an ISDN, referred to as *minimum integration* and *maximum integration*, have been defined.

The first is mainly intended for a period of time during which a full-scale implementation of a packet switching capability in the ISDN does not exist. It allows packet mode DTEs attached to an ISDN, but conforming to CCITT Recommendation X.25, to communicate with each other via an independent X.25 packet switched network, using their native protocols. The ISDN, in this case, acts only as a circuit switched physical transmission medium from the DTE to an inter-working port (IP) between the ISDN and the packet switched network. This physical connection is provided over a B channel. If it is a permanent connection, only the physical transmission aspects of the packet mode DTE must conform to the ISDN specifications. This may require among other things the conversion of frame formats and data rates through a terminal adapter to the I.430/431 specifications. If, on the other hand, the connection between DTE and IP is established and terminated on demand, the terminals must also be able to carry out the normal layer 2 logical link control procedure of I.441 and the layer 3 circuit switching call control procedures of I.451 over the D channel, possibly also via a terminal adapter. In any case, the procedures for establishing, as well as terminating the B channel are contained in the C plane.

Once the B channel is in place, communication between the DTEs, including the establishment and termination of virtual circuits and the transfer of user information, follows their native X.25 layer 2 and 3 procedures and is conducted entirely over the B channel. These procedures and the information conveyed are totally transparent to the ISDN and any terminal adapter. At level 1, however, the normal I.430/431 specifications apply. Since in X.25, connection control and information transfer are integrated within one and the same protocol, the separation of the B-channel communication between the DTEs into U-plane and C-plane components is not possible. This service therefore does not conform to the ISDN protocol reference model.

In the second type of hybrid packet mode bearer service, the ISDN acts as a complete packet switched network and thus provides a packet handling (PH) function to which the packet mode terminal can be attached and which supports the packet switching protocols. This function may be located in a remote exchange within the ISDN, in the local exchange, or in the NT2. Two modes of operation are possible. In the first, a circuit switched connection to the PH is set up over a B channel, using the standard ISDN C-plane protocols I.430/431, I.441, and I.451 over the D channel. If the terminal itself is unable to support these procedures, an appropriate terminal adapter is required to present the standard S interface toward the network. Once the connection to the PH is established, the level 2 and 3 packet switching protocols apply to the establishment and termination of the virtual circuit and the transfer of information between the terminals over the B channel. This mode is therefore similar to the one discussed previously, except that the ISDN also provides the packet handling functions.

In the second mode, the level 3 procedures for virtual circuit establishment and termination, as well as the user information, are conveyed across the D channel. Since the latter provides a semipermanent connection between terminal and PH, only a logical link must be established between them. This is accomplished through the LAPD procedure of I.441. All level 3 virtual circuits are then multiplexed into a single logical link under LAPD control and transmitted according to I.430/431 at level 1. This may again require the existence of a terminal adapter that can present levels 1 and 2 of the S interface toward the network, but is transparent to level 3.

In both of these modes, no separation of the packet switched communication between the terminals into C plane and U plane is possible.

In contrast to the two types of packet mode bearer services discussed previously, the so-called *additional packet mode bearer services* that have recently been considered by the CCITT integrate the protocols for control of the access channel and the virtual circuits. Furthermore, they separate the connection control functions from the user information transfer functions into C-plane and U-plane procedures, according to the ISDN protocol reference model.

Four bearer services of this type are currently under consideration. Their characteristics, as far as they have been specified, are summarized in CCITT Recommendation I.122. Many aspects, however, including the specification of their attribute values, are still the subject of active study by the CCITT and no formal definition of actual services has been given.

All of the additional packet mode bearer services provide for the bidirectional transfer of user information, structured into service data units, in virtual circuit mode over any of the D, B, or H channels implemented on the interface. The quality of the service is expressed in terms of parameters whose values can be selected during call establishment. Among these are throughput, transit delay, information integrity, residual error rate, delivered errored frames, delivered duplicated frames, delivered out-of-sequence frames, lost frames, and *misdelivered frames*.

In all cases layer 1 of the U plane specifies the use of I.430 for basic access and I.431 for primary access. The higher-layer U-plane protocols, however, depend on the particular service. In the first two of these, known as *frame relaying 1* and *frame relaying 2,* the user service data units are LAPD frames and are transferred in unacknowledged mode between S or T reference points. The transfer across the network is implemented in such a way that the frames are delivered in the order in which they are submitted. The services also detect transmission, format, and operational errors, using the so-called *core functions* of LAPD for frame delimiting, transparency, multiplexing, and error detection. Except for the Frame Check Sequence and Address fields, which are involved in these operations, the frames are conveyed transparently through the virtual circuit. In addition to these functions that are common to both services, the first service may implement in the U plane above the LAPD core functions any end-to-end procedures for acknowledgments, error control, and flow control. The network is unaware of the actual protocol used. The second service, on the other hand, must use the relevant parts of LAPD for these purposes and the network may take advantage of these functions to facilitate its own operations, without actually participating in the control procedures [CHEN89].

The third additional packet mode bearer service is known as *frame switching*. As in the previous cases, it also provides for the sequenced bidirectional transfer of LAPD frames and detects transmission, format, and operational errors. In addition, the U plane includes capabilities for flow control and the detection and recovery from lost or duplicated frames. All these functions are carried out by means of the LAPD protocol I.441.

The last additional packet mode bearer service is referred to as *X.25-based additional packet mode*. At layer 2 in the U plane it again uses LAPD. The user service data units in this case are X.25 packets, which are transferred under control of the data transfer part of layer

3 of X.25. The latter includes all X.25 layer 3 functions except call establishment and call termination.

The procedures for the establishment and release of the virtual circuits are carried out in the C plane over the D channel, using the layer 1, 2, and 3 specifications of I.430/431, I.441, and I.451, respectively. These procedures are common to all four additional packet mode bearer services.

Let us now consider the specifications of the actual services defined by CCITT to date. Currently, eight circuit mode bearer services and one hybrid packet mode bearer service have been identified. These correspond to the most important applications of the ISDN, as presently envisioned. In the following sections we discuss their information transfer attribute values. For additional details regarding these services, see CCITT Recommendations I.230, I.231, and I.232.

10.2.1   Circuit Mode 64-kbit/s Unrestricted 8-kHz Structured Bearer Service

As potentially the most important of the narrowband ISDN services, this bearer service provides for the transfer of unrestricted information between two users in a point-to-point mode or between more than two users in a multipoint mode, while maintaining any 8-kHz structural boundaries that may be present in the data. It is primarily intended to support applications involving the transfer of speech, 3.1-kHz audio, and multiple subrate information flows that are multiplexed and rate adapted by the user into a 64-kbit/s stream. The service may also be used to provide transparent access to services offered by other networks, such as an X.25 packet switched network. The connection may be unidirectional or bidirectional symmetric and can be established on a demand, reserved, or permanent basis.

Of the general attributes, only the supplementary services have been specified to date. These are discussed in Section 10.4.

10.2.2   Circuit Mode 64-kbit/s 8-kHz Structured Bearer Service for Speech

This bearer service is mainly intended to support the unidirectional or bidirectional symmetric transfer of digital speech that conforms to the A-law or Mu-law encoding rules. The original analog speech signal does not necessarily have to correspond to normal analog telephone voice. The service delivers the information over point-to-point connections, maintaining the basic 8-kHz sampling rate of digital speech.

It does not, however, guarantee the integrity of the binary information.

The applicable supplementary services and their characteristics are discussed in Section 10.4. All other general attributes are for further study.

10.2.3   Circuit Mode 64-kbit/s 8-kHz Structured Bearer Service for 3.1-kHz Audio

This bearer service is similar to the one in the previous section in that it also permits the transfer of A-law or Mu-law coded digitized speech in point-to-point or multipoint mode over unidirectional or bidirectional symmetric connections. In this case, however, the original analog voice signal is confined to a 3.1-kHz bandwidth and thus corresponds to the one normally transmitted over the public switched telephone network. Alternately, the service allows the transmission of data that have been derived from the A/D conversion of the output of modems whose carrier signals have been modulated either by arbitrary data streams or by the signals derived from Group 1, 2, and 3 facsimile machines, as defined in CCITT Recommendations T.2, T.3, and T.4. Here the analog modem output signal prior to digitization must also be confined to a bandwidth of 3.1 kHz, which implies a limit on the modulating data rate that is a function of the modulation technique employed. In addition, the digitization must also satisfy the A-law or Mu-law coding rules.

10.2.4   Circuit Mode 64-kbit/s Bearer Service for Alternate Speech or Unrestricted Data

This bearer service provides for the alternate transfer over the same connection of either digital speech encoded according to the A-law or Mu-law or unrestricted digital information at 64 kbit/s. It is primarily intended for the support of end-user devices with multiple capabilities, but may also be used by simple voice or data terminals. The changeover from one mode to another can be indicated without interrupting the connection. However, it requires an agreement on the part of the communicating partners and is subject to the availability of the appropriate network resources at the time the change is indicated. The protocol by which a changeover is effected is currently not defined.

Since the two alternative services conform individually to the services described in Sections 10.2.1 and 10.2.2, they are characterized by the combined attributes and attribute values of the latter.

10.2.5   *Circuit Mode 2 × 64-kbit/s Unrestricted 8-kHz Structured Bearer Service*

This bearer service provides point-to-point or multipoint connections capable of simultaneously transferring two 64-kbit/s unrestricted digital information flows between the same set of end-users. Its primary application is in situations where the data rate requirements of the users exceed the capabilities of the 64-kbit/s services defined earlier. Thus, for example, a 128-kbit/s information stream can be split into two 64-kbit/s streams at the sending side and reassembled into the original form at the receiver.

The user information flows are transmitted over two component B channels of either basic access or primary access. The layer 1 control procedures over each of the B channels are as specified in I.430/I.431, with layer 2 and 3 functions defined by the end-users and transparent to the service. Connection control for the combined B channels is carried out over the corresponding D channel, using the ISDN standard layer 1, 2, and 3 procedures given in I.430/431, I.441, and I.451.

The service maintains the integrity of the binary data, ensures any 8-kHz structure of the information, and guarantees the delivery of each data unit within a limited time after its submission. The connection may be unidirectional, bidirectional symmetric, or bidirectional asymmetric and can be established on either the demand, reserved, or permanent basis.

None of the general attributes are at present specified.

10.2.6   *Circuit Mode 384/1536/1920-kbit/s Unrestricted 8-kHz Structured Bearer Services*

Three wideband bearer services, differing only in their information carrying capacity, have been defined. They provide for the transfer of unrestricted information at either 384 kbit/s, 1536 kbit/s, or 1920 kbit/s over primary access. These data rates are selected mainly to conform to the requirements of high-quality audio programs and various forms of compressed video.

The user information is conveyed over an H0 channel at 384 kbit/s, an H11 channel at 1536 kbit/s, and an H12 channel at 1920 kbit/s, whereas signaling is carried out over either a 16-kbit/s or 64-kbit/s D channel. The connections may be point-to-point or multipoint, unidirectional, bidirectional symmetric, or bidirectional asymmetric and are established on a demand, reserved, or permanent basis. The service maintains any 8-kHz structure contained in the information stream but does not guarantee data integrity.

None of the general attribute values have as yet been defined.

10.2.7 *Packet Mode Virtual Call and Permanent Virtual Circuit Bearer Service*

This bearer service is designed to allow terminals operating in the packet mode according to CCITT Recommendation X.25 to communicate with each other via the ISDN. As such it provides for the transfer of unrestricted user information in a packet switched mode over a point-to-point bidirectional symmetric virtual circuit within a B channel or a D channel over basic or primary access. The service offers both the virtual call established on demand and the permanently established virtual circuit. Throughput rates on the virtual circuit are limited by the maximum bit rate of the B or D channel on the one hand, and the throughput class of the virtual circuit on the other. The integrity of the data service unit or packet is guaranteed.

The establishment of the B-channel connection to the packet handling function is carried out over either a 16-kbit/s D channel or a 64-kbit/s D channel and follows the procedures in I.430/431, I.441, and I.451. Since the D channel is permanently connected to the PH, only a logical link needs to be established. This is accomplished via the I.430/431 and I.441 procedures.

The layer 1 protocol for virtual circuit call control and user information transfer over the B or D channel conforms to I.430/I.431 and layer 3 is governed by the packet level procedures of CCITT Recommendation X.25. Layer 2 uses either LAPB of X.25 or the LAPD procedures of I.441 for virtual circuits over the B channel and D channel, respectively.

10.3 Definition of Teleservices

We turn now to a consideration of the second type of telecommunications service provided by an ISDN: the teleservices. As we mentioned earlier, these build on bearer services by providing additional functions that correspond to the higher layers of the OSI reference model. Their low-layer attributes are in general identical to those of the bearer services.

Normally teleservices support applications that involve an interaction at the transport, session, presentation, and application layers between the end-user terminals and the network, as well as between the terminals themselves. They therefore incorporate the non-communication-oriented aspects of the terminals and are accessed at user-to-terminal interface points 3 and 5, as shown in Figure 10.1. Typically, the devices supported by teleservices include digital telephones for voice communication, telex and teletex terminals for text communication, videotex terminals and facsimile machines for image-based information, and so-called mixed-mode devices that combine aspects of teletex and facsimile. The higher-layer protocols offer these devices the means to exchange information in a reliable and efficient manner, independently of the characteristics of the underlying bearer service over which the information is transferred. They also provide the ability to establish, maintain, and terminate sessions between devices, organize data into information units, and control the nature of the dialogue between them. Finally, they create a level of compatibility between terminals through conversion functions for voice coding laws, character sets, document layout, and image representations.

Although not yet formalized, teleservices are also envisioned to include the short- or long-term storage of end-user information and its processing while the information is in transit or in storage within the network. This would make possible the implementation of a variety of store and forward message handling services such as electronic text, voice, and image mail. In addition, teleservices could be defined that provide access to word processing systems and other applications software found in specialized processors, network, or end-user-supplied databases such as directories, data management systems, and a host of other intelligent features.

To date, the CCITT has defined six specific teleservices, which are described in detail in Recommendations I.240 and I.241. In the following sections we restrict ourselves to a summary of their major features.

10.3.1 Telephony

This teleservice is intended for the transmission of ordinary analog telephone speech that conforms to a 3.1-kHz bandwidth limitation. It is in many respects similar to the bearer service discussed in Section 10.2.3 and in a given ISDN implementation may be offered as either a bearer service or a teleservice.

Owing to the undesirable fluctuation of end-to-end delay inherent in packet mode bearer services, only circuit mode bearer services may be used as the transmission function. The only relevant high-layer attributes are the type-of-user-information attribute, which is set to the value "speech", and the Layer 6 Protocol Functions attribute, which requires the A-law or Mu-law encoding of the digital signal as specified in CCITT Recommendation G.711. No general attribute values are currently defined.

10.3.2 *Teletex*

This teleservice provides for the exchange of office correspondence between subscribers that is text based and represented by means of standardized character sets. The information is organized into pages and documents, with the page being the smallest unit of text treated as an entity.

Both circuit mode and packet mode bearer services may be used for information transmission. The values of the higher-layer attributes correspond to the various CCITT T-series recommendations for teletex. At the transport layer the service specifies the use of the network-independent transport layer protocol defined in CCITT Recommendation T.70. The latter is equivalent to the class 0 subset of the CCITT standard X.224. The session layer protocol conforms to CCITT Recommendation T.62 and allows both one-way and two-way alternate communication. It also provides for the detection and correction of errors produced by the transport mechanism. All commands and responses are a subset of CCITT Recommendation X.225 and are fully compatible with it. The layer 6 attribute characterizes the graphic character sets in which the information is represented and the control functions that govern the presentation of the information. They are both derived from an extension of the International Alphabet No. 5 and are specified in CCITT Recommendation T.61. Finally, the value of the layer 7 attribute conforms to CCITT Recommendation T.60, which characterizes teletex terminals in terms of their functions and information display formats.

10.3.3 *Telefax 4*

The Telefax 4 service offers subscribers the capability to exchange office documents coded according to the CCITT Group 4 facsimile standards between compatible devices. The general characteristics of these devices are given in Recommendations T.5 and T.6. The first of these recommendations specifies the basic facsimile scanning parameters in terms of the number of scan lines per document and the number of picture elements per scan line. Four levels of resolution at 200 × 200, 240 × 240, 300 × 300, and 400 × 400 picture elements per square inch are permitted. Recommendation T.6 defines a two-dimensional data compression scheme for the binary digit strings produced by a black-and-white image.

As in the Teletex case, layers 4 and 5 conform to Recommendations T.70 and T.62, respectively. At layer 6, the protocol of Recommendation T.400 applies, and layer 7 conforms to Recommendations T.503, T.521, and T.563.

The bearer service may be either circuit switched or packet switched, although the former is generally preferred.

10.3.4   Mixed Mode

This service combines the capabilities of teletex and telefax to provide subscribers with the ability to exchange documents containing both textual and image-based information. The high-layer attributes are therefore similar to those of the Teletex and Telefax 4 services. No general attribute values have been specified.

10.3.5   Videotex

Generally, videotex services allow the communication of textual and pictorial information of the type commonly represented on television screens. They also possess a repertoire of functions by means of which the display attributes of the information can be controlled. The information may be represented in one of four different ways by means of mosaic or dynamically redefinable character sets, geometric primitives, and photographic picture elements.

The ISDN videotex service involves communications between subscriber and videotex center, as well as between different videotex centers. In the first case a point-to-point circuit switched bidirectional bearer service for 64-kbit/s unrestricted data transfer is employed. The bearer service in the second case can be either circuit switched or packet switched. The precise characteristics are, however, as yet undefined.

Most aspects of the higher-layer attributes for videotex have also not been specified and need further study.

10.3.6 Telex

This teleservice is intended for interactive text communication between subscribers. It may be based on either a circuit mode or packet mode bearer service, although the latter possibility has not been formally approved. The bearer service must be bidirectionally symmetric and may be point-to-point or multipoint. Signaling and user information transfer at layers 2 and 3 conform to Recommendation U.202 for telex service. No higher-layer or general attribute values have been specified.

10.4 Supplementary Services

So far in this chapter we have concerned ourselves with the basic ISDN telecommunications services that provide the minimum functionality for efficient and reliable information transmission. We have characterized the bearer services and teleservices in terms of a set of attributes and their possible values and have defined the characteristics of a number of specific services of major importance to the user.

We consider next the supplementary services, whose purpose, we recall, is to augment the functionality of a basic telecommunications service. The primary objective in specifying these services is to provide a higher level of convenience and user friendliness, especially with respect to a user's ability to manage connections. In addition, they are intended to improve a service's security through certain user identification functions and to provide users with the information required to control costs.

In line with these goals, the CCITT has defined a number of supplementary services that the service provider may make available to the service user on a subscription basis in association with a particular basic telecommunications service. They are divided into seven distinct categories of services that correspond to various aspects of call control, call charging, and information transfer. Table 10.5 contains a list of all currently defined services, and Table 10.6 shows the association of each supplementary service with the basic circuit switched bearer services and teleservices.

Many of the services in Table 10.5 are intended for use in connection with voice calls and correspond to services that are presently offered on the public switched telephone network. Various aspects of their implementation within an ISDN have not been completely

TABLE 10.5   List of supplementary services

Number Identification Supplementary Services
    Direct Dialing In (DDI)
    Multiple Subscriber Number (MSN)
    Calling Line Identification Presentation (CLIP)
    Calling Line Identification Restriction (CLIR)
    Connected Line Identification Presentation (COLP)
    Connected Line Identification Restriction (COLR)
    Malicious Call Identification (MCI)
    Subaddressing (SUB)

Call Offering Supplementary Services
    Call Transfer (CT)
    Call Forwarding Busy (CFB)
    Call Forwarding No Reply (CFNR)
    Call Forwarding Unconditional (CFU)
    Call Deflection (CD)
    Line Hunting (LH)

Call Completion Supplementary Services
    Call Waiting (CW)
    Call Hold (HOLD)
    Completion of Calls to Busy Subscribers (CCBS)

Multiparty Supplementary Services
    Conference Calling (CONF)
    Three-Party Service (3PTY)

Community of Interest Supplementary Services
    Closed User Group (CUG)
    Private Numbering Plan (PNP)

Charging Supplementary Services
    Credit Card Calling (CRED)
    Advice of Charge (AOC)
    Reverse Charging (REV)

Additional Information Transfer Supplementary Service
    User-to-User Signaling (UUS)

© Adapted from CCITT Blue Book, vol VIII.7, 1988

defined and are the subject of further study. We therefore restrict ourselves in our discussion to a summary description of each service's major features. The reader requiring a complete treatment of the subject is referred to CCITT Recommendations I.250 to I.257.

TABLE 10.6   Association of supplementary and basic services

SUPPLEMENTARY SERVICES	CIRCUIT MODE BEARER SERVICES						TELESERVICES				
	64 kbit/s Unrestricted Demand	64 kbit/s Speech Demand	64 kbit/s 3.1 kHz Audio Demand	64 kbit/s Unrestricted Permanent	64 kbit/s 3.1 kHZ Audio Permanent	1920 kbit/s Unrestricted Permanent	Telephony	Teletex	Telefax 4	Videotex	Mixed Mode
Direct Dialing In	X	X	X				X	X	X	X	X
Multiple Subscriber Number	X	X	X				X	X	X	X	X
Calling Line Identification Presentation	X	X	X				X	X	X	X	X
Calling Line Identification Restriction	X	X	X				X	X	X	X	X
Connected Line Identification Presentation	X	X	X				X	X	X	X	X
Connected Line Identification Restriction	X	X	X				X	X	X	X	X
Malicious Call Identification											
Subaddressing											
Call Transfer	X	X	X				X				
Call Forwarding Busy	X	X	X				X				
Call Forwarding No Reply	X	X	X				X			X	

© Adapted from CCITT Blue Book, vol VIII.7, 1988

In the United States, the supplementary services that will be offered in connection with an ISDN are in the process of definition by Bellcore and several 800-series Technical References detailing their characteristics have been issued. A number of differences between the

TABLE 10.6 *(Cont.)*

SUPPLEMENTARY SERVICES	CIRCUIT MODE BEARER SERVICES						TELESERVICES				
	64 kbit/s Unrestricted Demand	64 kbit/s Speech Demand	64 kbit/s 3.1 kHz Audio Demand	64 kbit/s Unrestricted Permanent	64 kbit/s 3.1 kHZ Audio Permanent	1920 kbit/s Unrestricted Permanent	Telephony	Teletex	Telefax 4	Videotex	Mixed Mode
Call Forwarding Unconditional	X	X	X				X			X	
Call Deflection											
Line Hunting	X	X	X				X				
Call Waiting	X	X	X				X				
Call Hold	X	X	X				X				
Completion of Calls to Busy Subscribers											
Conference Calling	X	X	X				X				
Three-Party Service	X	X	X				X				
Closed User Group	X	X	X				X	X	X	X	X
Private Numbering Plan											
Credit Card Calling											
Advice of Charge	X	X	X				X	X	X	X	X
Reverse Charging											
User-to-User Signaling	X	X	X				X	X	X		X

CCITT and Bellcore specifications may be noted. These are principally due to the RBOC's desire to maintain the currently available features associated with Centrex service and the perceived preferences and needs of the U.S business community.

10.4.1 Number Identification Services

The services in this category concern themselves with the identification of the particular subscribers involved in a connection. Such identification may be provided to the calling subscriber, the called subscriber, and the service provider—that is, the network.

The first of these services, known as *Direct Dialing In*, enables users to directly call a specific subscriber among a number of subscribers attached to a private system such as a private branch exchange, without attendant intervention. The mechanism by which this is accomplished is the forwarding by the network of that part of the called subscriber's number that distinguishes the multiple subscribers on the private system.

The service *Multiple Subscriber Number* is somewhat similar in that it allows the assignment of more than one identifying number to a single user-to-network interface, so as to be able to distinguish between multiple terminals operating across that interface. Thus, incoming calls to a user subscribing to this service may be routed to a specific terminal on the interface and outgoing calls from that user may be ascribed to a specific originating terminal for the purpose of charging or identifying the calling user to a called user.

The service *Calling Line Identification Presentation* offers a subscribing user the identity of the calling party during the call setup phase on all incoming calls. This information may originate within the network or may be relayed by the network from the calling party to the called party.

A user may also subscribe to the service *Calling Line Identification Restriction,* in which case the network is prohibited from making the calling subscriber's identity available to the called party.

Since the called party and the actually connected party are not necessarily identical, the service *Connected Line Identification Presentation* provides the calling party with the connected party's number, as soon as the latter has accepted the incoming call.

A subscribing user may also inhibit the above feature through the *Connected Line Identification Restriction* service, which prevents the network from conveying the connected party's number to the calling party.

Malicious Call Identification, although not completely defined, provides for the recording of certain data such as the number of the calling party and the date and time of the call by the network. This recording can be invoked on a per-call basis by an indication from the subscriber to the network, or on a permanent basis for all incoming calls. This service will also supercede any service requiring the suppression of the calling party's number.

The last service in the category of number identification, *subaddressing,* involves the availability of subaddresses. Its precise meaning and application have not been defined.

10.4.2 Call Offering Services

The second group of supplementary services, known as *Call Offering,* provides the subscribing user the ability to pass on certain incoming or established calls to other parties. This handoff can be invoked unconditionally, or only in certain predefined situations. It can be directed to a specific third party or to any of a set of parties with given specified characteristics.

The *Call Transfer* supplementary service offers a subscribing user A, who can be either the calling or the called party, the ability to transfer a fully established call with user B to a third party C, resulting in a new call that excludes user A, the party invoking the transfer. Three methods of call transfer have been specified. In the normal method, the network, upon an indication from A, puts the established call between A and B on hold. A then establishes a call to C. The network completes the call transfer by establishing a call between B and C, at the same time clearing the calls between A and B and A and C. In the so-called *single-step* call transfer procedure, A indicates to the network the address of C, whereupon the network establishes a call between B and C and disconnects the call between A and B. In the third alternative, known as *Explicit Call Transfer,* user A, after having put the call to B on hold and established a call to C, explicitly requests of the network that the call be transferred to C.

Call Forwarding Busy permits a subscribing user to direct incoming calls encountering a busy condition to another ISDN number. This diversion applies only to a basic telecommunications service and can be restricted to specific telecommunications services or be applicable to all such services. The service can be invoked repeatedly—that is, user A forwards the call to user B, who in turn forwards it to user C. The total number of times a call may be forwarded is, however, limited. An indication that a call was forwarded, as well as information regarding the reason for forwarding and the forwarded party's number, may optionally be provided to each forwarding user.

Call Forwarding No Reply is in many respects similar to Call Forwarding Busy. A user subscribing to this service may direct the network to relay incoming calls, to which the user does not respond within a certain time interval, to another ISDN number. The forwarding can be unconditional or restricted to specified telecommunications services and can be invoked sequentially a limited number of times.

Call Forwarding Unconditional permits a subscribing user to direct the forwarding of all incoming calls, or just those associated with a specific basic telecommunications service, to another number, regardless of the condition of the user. This type of forwarding may also be invoked repeatedly in a sequential manner, again with a limit on the total number of forwardings.

Line Hunting enables a subscriber to direct the distribution of incoming calls over a group of interfaces. The specific interface to which a call is directed is selected in a predefined manner to achieve certain objectives such as uniform or sequential distribution of calls.

10.4.3   Call Completion Services

This category currently includes three services. In the *Call Waiting* service a subscriber, all of whose information channels across the user-to-network interface are involved in connections, is notified by the network of an incoming call and the fact that no information channels are available. This notification is normally conveyed over a D channel, but may optionally be transmitted within the information channels. The called party may then accept the incoming call and disconnect the existing call or place it in the hold state. The called party may also ignore or reject the incoming call, in which case the network will clear the call request after a predetermined period of time.

The *Call Hold* service permits a subscribing user to temporarily suspend an existing call over an information channel and retrieve it at a later time. The call may be placed on hold at either the calling or the called party's user-to-network interface. Once it is interrupted, the associated information channel is then available for other uses. Call retrieval is subject to the availability of an appropriate information channel, which can be guaranteed through a channel reservation option.

The service *Completion of Calls to Busy Subscribers* is currently only identified in name. Its detailed characteristics are scheduled for further study.

10.4.4 Multiparty Services

The services in this category are intended to enable a user to engage in several simultaneous connections with other users. Two specific services have been defined.

Conference Calling provides the user with the ability to communicate with multiple parties at the same time or in a sequential fashion. The parties may also communicate among themselves. The population of users participating in a conference call may be changed by adding or dropping parties at any time during the conference. Participants can also be split from the conference in the sense that they remain connected to and may communicate with the designated conference controller, but are prevented from communicating with any other members of the conference. In addition, a participant may be isolated from the conference and prevented from communicating with any of its members, but not disconnected from it. The splitting or isolation can be reversed by a reattachment feature.

Three-Party Service allows a user A, who is engaged in a call with user B, to place that call on hold and create a connection to a third user C. User A may then alternate between a connection to B and a connection to C, with the network providing the necessary privacy of the call. Alternatively, the service could be implemented as a three-way connection, allowing all parties to communicate with each other in the manner of a conference call.

10.4.5 Community of Interest Services

The supplementary service *Closed User Group* allows the definition of groups of users within which certain communications capabilities exist. Several versions have been defined. Normally, a user belonging to a group may make calls to any member and receive calls from any member of the same group. Calls to and from users outside the group are, however, not allowed. Two restrictions may be imposed on this service. In the first, the user is prevented from calling any member of the group, but is able to receive calls from any of them. In the second, the user may not receive calls from any member of the group, while being able to call any of them. The other versions of the closed user group service affect the user's relationship to nonmembers. Specifically, the service may be configured to allow or disallow calls to nongroup users or may allow or disallow calls from nongroup users.

A second supplementary service in the present category is the *Private Numbering Plan,* which allows groups of users to establish, in cooperation with the network, special network addressing arrangements. Its precise characteristics are currently undefined.

10.4.6 Charging Services

Of the three supplementary services in this category, the characteristics of *Credit Card Calling* and *Reverse Charging* have not yet been specified.

The service *Advice of Charge* offers a user paying for the call information regarding the cost of the call. Three options have been defined. In the first, the charging information is provided at the end of the call and may include the total amount of the charge, the rate at which the call was charged, and the type and number of charging units used. The charge for special features such as supplementary services may also be indicated. The second option is similar to the first, except that intermittent or continuous charging information is provided during the active phase of a call. Charges may be conveyed on either an incremental or cumulative basis, and may be offered periodically, or whenever a certain number of charging units have been accumulated. In the third option, the network provides the user during the call setup phase with information regarding the rate at which a call will be charged. The basis for the charge and the cost of supplementary services are also made available.

10.4.7 Additional Information Transfer Services

Only one service in this category has been defined. *User-to-User Signaling* permits users to exchange a limited amount of information over the network signaling channel in conjunction with a regular connection between them. Three versions of the service exist. In service 1 the user information may be transferred during the setup and clearing phases of the call and is contained in the appropriate call control messages. The call setup does not have to result in a connection, so that it is possible, for example, to transfer a user message in one direction in a call request message and another user message in the other direction in a call reject message. Service 2 allows information transfer only during call establishment and the user information is carried separately from the call establishment messages. Service 3 confines the transfer of user information to the active phase of the call. In all cases the amount of user information that may be conveyed is limited to a maximum of 128 octets.

10.5 Summary and Recommended Reading

Chapter 10 has been devoted to a description of the telecommunications services offered by an ISDN. We divided these services into bearer services, teleservices, and supplementary services and characterized them in terms of a set of attributes. We then defined a number of specific circuit and packet switched bearer services, teleservices, and supplementary services by specifying the values of their attributes.

[KAHL86b] contains a summary of the CCITT service definition concept. A description of the ISDN videotex service can be found in [ROTH84].

APPENDIX A

CCITT Recommendations for ISDN

This appendix contains a listing of the most important CCITT Recommendations of relevance to the ISDN. Their current versions are published in the CCITT *Blue Book,* dated November 1988. The I-Series Recommendations are contained in Volume III, Fascicles III.7, III.8, and III.9. The relevant Q-Series Recommendations are contained in Volume VI, Fascicles VI.6–VI.11. The G-Series Recommendations are contained in Volume III, Fascicles III.4 and III.5.

I-Series Recommendations

Part I—General Structure

I.110	PREAMBLE AND GENERAL STRUCTURE OF THE I-SERIES RECOMMENDATIONS FOR THE INTEGRATED SERVICES DIGITAL NETWORK (ISDN)
I.111	RELATIONSHIP WITH OTHER RECOMMENDATIONS RELEVANT TO ISDN'S
I.112	VOCABULARY OF TERMS FOR ISDN'S
I.113	VOCABULARY OF TERMS FOR BROADBAND ASPECTS OF ISDN
I.120	INTEGRATED SERVICES DIGITAL NETWORKS (ISDN'S)
I.121	BROADBAND ASPECTS OF ISDN
I.122	FRAMEWORK FOR PROVIDING ADDITIONAL PACKET MODE BEARER SERVICES
I.130	METHOD FOR THE CHARACTERIZATION OF TELECOMMUNICATION SERVICES SUPPORTED BY AN ISDN AND NETWORK CAPABILITIES OF AN ISDN

Part II—Service Capabilities

Part III—Overall Network Aspects and Functions

Part IV—ISDN User-Network Interfaces

Part V—Internetwork Interfaces

Q-Series Recommendations

G-Series Recommendations

APPENDIX B

CCITT Specification and Description Language

The procedures by which a pair of communicating telecommunications processes interact can be described in graphic form by a language that has been developed over a number of years by the CCITT. This language, which is known as the *Specification and Description Language (SDL)*, is used extensively in the specification of the ISDN protocols. In the following we briefly summarize and illustrate the pertinent SDL concepts used in this book. For additional information, see CCITT Recommendations Z.100 and Z.110 and the discussion in [BELI89].

SDL is based on a set of constructs or graphic symbols to describe the behavior of a process that can be modelled as a finite state machine. The most important of these symbols for representing telecommunications processes are shown in Figure B.1.

The process exists at any one time in one of a finite number of states. When it receives an input signal it undergoes a transition to either the same state or to another state. During this transition it produces an output signal. Input signals may be received from more and output signals may be delivered to more than one user of the process. State transitions are sometimes governed by variables such as counters or timers and are subject to the outcome of a test on the value of one or more such variables. While in a particular state, the process can undergo a procedure such as the updating of a variable. It may also invoke a call to another entity for carrying out a procedure. The latter may itself be a finite state machine represented by an SDL diagram.

Figure B.2, which is identical to Figure 5.14, illustrates the use of these symbols in a flowchart that describes the layer 2 procedure at the responding side for establishing multiple frame operation. The process is initially in the TEI Assigned state. On receiving the signal SABME from the originating side it performs a test to determine whether or not it is able to establish the multiple frame operation. If not, it transfers the DM signal to the originating side

410

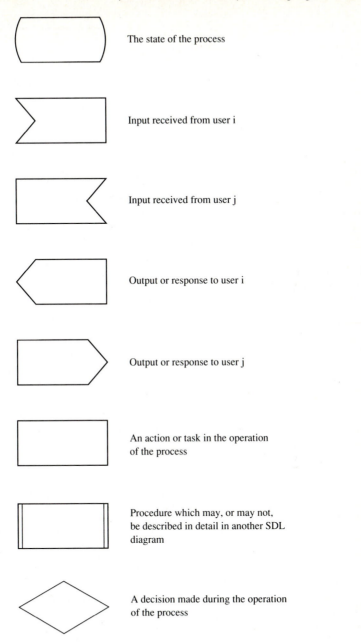

The state of the process

Input received from user i

Input received from user j

Output or response to user i

Output or response to user j

An action or task in the operation
of the process

Procedure which may, or may not,
be described in detail in another SDL
diagram

A decision made during the operation
of the process

Figure B.1 *SDL graphic symbols*

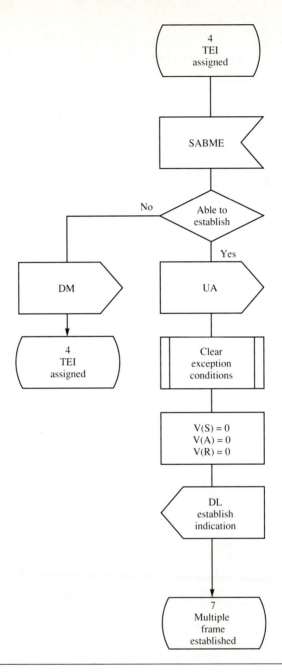

Figure B.2 *Example of SDL diagram*

and returns to the TEI Assigned state. Otherwise it sends the UA signal and makes a procedure call to clear all exception conditions. It then initializes the three variables V(S), V(A), and V(R), conveys the DL-ESTABLISH Indication primitive to its layer 3 entity, and enters the Multiple Frame Established state.

GLOSSARY OF ISDN TERMINOLOGY

Access Attribute. An aspect of a telecommunications service related to accessing the network functions or facilities necessary for the implementation of the service.

Access Protocol. A set of procedures that is adopted at a specified reference point of the user-to-network interface to enable the user to access the services and facilities of the network.

Access Unit. A function logically belonging to a packet switched network that is accessed through an ISDN connection and supports X.25 layer 2 and 3 procedures between itself and an X.25 DTE.

Activation. The restoration of the functions of a terminal equipment or network termination that may have been placed into a mode of low power consumption earlier.

Application Layer. The highest layer of the OSI model. This layer functions as an interface between the system and the user and provides useful application-oriented services.

Asynchronous Transfer Mode. An information transfer mode in which information is structured into short packets or cells. Cells are made available to the source only on demand and in accordance with the required or instantaneous bit rate.

Baseband. The frequency band containing the energy in the time-discrete and amplitude-discrete electrical signal used to represent digital information.

Basic Access. A type of user-to-network interface supporting combined data rates up to 144 kbit/s.

Basic Rate Channel Structure. A composite communications capacity across the user-to-network interface of an ISDN consisting of two B channels and one 16-kbit/s D channel.

B Channel. A portion of the communication capacity across the user-to-network interface with a data rate of 64 kbit/s.

Bearer Service. A type of telecommunication service that provides the capability for the transmission of signals between user-to-network interfaces.

Bellcore. Bell Communications Research; organization established by the Regional Bell Operating Companies following divestiture of AT&T to carry out research and standardization.

Bit Stuffing. The process of inserting zeros into a sequence of 1s in order to prevent the occurrence of too many 1s in sequence.

Bridge Tap. A pair of wires of variable length connected in parallel across a subscriber loop in order to share the loop among several subscribers.

Broadband Channel Structure. A composite communications capacity across the user-to-network interface of a broadband ISDN.

Broadband ISDN. An Integrated Services Digital Network providing a range of data transmission rates up to several hundred Mbit/s.

Broadcast. Simultaneous distribution of information to multiple subscribers to a network.

Call Forwarding. A service whereby a subscriber can direct the network to forward all incoming calls to another number.

Call Waiting. A service whereby a subscriber engaged in an active connection with another subscriber is given an indication that a third subscriber is attempting to obtain a connection.

Calling Line Identification. A service whereby the calling subscriber's number can be identified to the called subscriber prior to answering the call.

Cell. A short block of information usually of fixed length that is identified by a label.

Circuit Switching. An information transfer mode in which switching and transmission functions are accomplished by permanent allocation of channels or bandwidth between the connections.

Closed User Group. A subgroup of subscribers to a communication network with communication restricted to the members of the group.

Common Channel Signaling. A method of signaling in which signaling information relating to a multiplicity of circuits is conveyed over a separate channel by addressed messages. Also used for transfer of network management and operations messages.

Common Channel Signaling Network. A network used to transfer signaling information and consisting of signaling points, signaling transfer points, and interconnecting signaling links.

Common Channel Signaling System. A set of protocols used to convey signaling information over a common channel signaling network.

Completion of Call to Busy Subscriber. A service whereby an incoming call to a busy subscriber is connected when the subscriber becomes free.

Component Channel. A portion of the total transmission capacity across the user-to-network interface.

Conference Calling. A service that allows the simultaneous connection between two or more subscribers.

Connection Element. A part of an ISDN connection defined by a set of connection attributes.

Connection Endpoint Identifier. An address of the data link layer entity involved in a connection, as seen by layer 3 or a layer management entity. It is composed of the Service Access Point Identifier and a Connection Endpoint Suffix.

Connection Endpoint Suffix. The address of a data link layer entity involved in a data link connection, as seen by layer 3 or the layer management entity.

Connection-Oriented Service. A service that allows the transfer of information among service subscribers over established connections.

Connectionless Service. A service that permits the transfer of information among service subscribers without requiring the prior establishment of an end-to-end call connection.

Control Plane. The part of the ISDN protocol reference model that contains the protocols required for the exchange of control information to establish and clear connections, control the use of established connections, and provide supplementary service control.

Control Plane Entity. The conceptual intelligence in a device that controls the operation of connections over an ISDN.

Crosstalk. Undesired energy that is coupled between a pair of circuits in close proximity to each other.

Customer-Premises Equipment. Telecommunications equipment located on the premises of the subscriber to a telecommunications service.

Cyclic Redundancy Check. A scheme used to detect errors that may occur during the transmission of a frame of data. At the sending side a code is generated that is transmitted with the data. The code is compared with another code generated at the receiver.

Data Circuit-Terminating Equipment. Data communications equipment such as a modem that terminates the circuits provided by the network and connects a DTE to the network.

Data Link Connection Identifier. An address consisting of the combination of Service Access Point Identifier and Terminal

Endpoint Identifier and which identifies a data link connection.

Data Link Layer. The second layer of the OSI Reference Model that ensures reliable and efficient transmission of information between adjacent stations in a network.

Data Terminal Equipment. End-user devices such as terminals or computers that convert user information into data signals for transmission, or reconvert received data signals into user information.

Deactivation. The placement of a TE or NT into a mode of low power consumption during a period of inactivity.

Digital Combined Exchange. An exchange which combines both local exchange and transit exchange functions.

Digital Subscriber Signaling System. A set of protocols used for conveying signaling information across the user-to-network interface of an ISDN.

Digital Section. Transmission facility between the network termination on the customer premises and the local exchange.

Digital Transmission. The transmission of digital information through the representation by and transfer of electrical signals that are discrete in time and amplitude.

Digital Transmission System. Physical transmission medium between the network termination on the customer premises and the local exchange.

D Channel. A portion of the transmission capacity across the user-to-network interface. Its capacity is either 16 kbit/s or 64 kbit/s.

D-Channel Access Control. Procedure for the regulation of access to the shared transmission capacity of a D channel in multipoint configurations.

Echo Cancellation. Elimination from the receiving path of a sender of the portion of a transmitted signal that has been reflected back to the sender. Cancellation is accomplished by subtracting a delayed and attenuated portion of the transmitted signal from the total received signal.

Exchange. A network device containing switching stages, the means for controlling connections, and the ability to exchange signals. Its purpose is to enable subscriber lines, telecommunications circuits, and other functional units to be interconnected as required by the subscribers of the network.

Far-End Crosstalk. Unwanted energy coupled from one circuit into another and appearing at the far end of the circuit.

Fast Packet Switching. A method of packet switching that minimizes packet processing delay through the simplification of the packet transfer protocols.

Feature Key Management Protocol. A protocol used over the basic rate access structure for the control of supplementary services in an ISDN.

Flow Control. A mechanism of limiting the amount or rate of data sent by a transmitting entity to avoid congestion in the network or the receiving device.

Frame. A block of consecutive time slots whose positions are identified by reference to a marker indicating the start or end of the frame. Each time slot may contain one unit of data.

Frame Check Sequence. An error-detecting code placed in the transmitted frame that checks for errors when the data are received.

Frame Relaying. A type of packet mode bearer service in which the user information is structured as LAPD frames and transferred in unacknowledged mode under LAPD control. Includes control of the sequence of transmitted frames and the detection of transmission, format, and operational errors.

Frame Switching. A type of packet mode bearer service in which the user information is structured as LAPD frames and transferred in unacknowledged mode under LAPD control. Includes sequence control, flow control, and detection and recovery from lost or duplicated frames.

Frame Synchronization. A procedure whereby the receiver of a frame of bits can determine the beginning and end of the frame.

Functional Group. A set of functions required for carrying out tasks in cooperation with another functional group.

Functional Protocol. A protocol used over the basic- and primary-access structures for the control of supplementary services in an ISDN.

H Channel. A portion of the transmission capacity across the user-to-network interface. Several H channels with different data rates are defined.

High-Level Data Link Control (HDLC). Bit-oriented data link control procedure. The international standard for data link control developed by ISO.

Hybrid Transmission. A method of simultaneous bidirectional transmission over a single channel in which the signals in the two directions are separated by a hybrid circuit.

Information Element. A block of information contained in layer 3 messages conveyed across the user-to-network interface for the control of connections and supplementary services.

Information Transfer Attribute. An aspect of a telecommunications service that characterizes the network's capability for transferring information.

Integrated Services Digital Network. A telecommunications network providing integrated services over digital connections between user-to-network interfaces.

Interface. A physical point of demarcation between two data communications devices. The interface is defined in terms of the connectors, electrical signals, timing, and protocols between the devices.

Intermediate Service Part. A part of the Transaction Capabilities of signaling System No. 7 equivalent to layers 4, 5, and 6 of the OSI Reference Model. Supports TCAP for connection-oriented message transfer.

ISDN User Part. A protocol of Signaling System No. 7 that provides the functions required for the control of basic bearer services and supplementary services in an ISDN.

Keypad Protocol. A protocol used in basic and primary rate access structures to invoke a supplementary service in an ISDN.

Line Code. The representation of digital information in the form of a sequence of electrical pulses.

Line Termination. The physical termination of the subscriber loop on the network side.

Link Access Procedure D Channel (LAPD). A layer 2 protocol used to control the reliability and efficiency of the exchange of messages over the D channel of the user-to-network interface in an ISDN.

Link Status Signal Unit. A signaling unit that contains status information regarding the signaling link on which it is transmitted.

Message Signal Unit (MSU). A signal unit containing a service information octet and a signaling information field that is retransmitted by the signaling link control if it is received in error.

Message Transfer Part. The functional part of a common channel signaling system that transfers signaling messages as required by all the users, and that performs the necessary subsidiary functions—for example error control and signaling security (levels 1, 2, and 3 of Signaling System No. 7).

Multipoint. A communications configuration in which one channel interconnects more than two stations, only two of which can communicate with each other at any one time.

Narrowband ISDN. An Integrated Services Digital Network providing data transmission rates up to 2 Mbit/s.

Near-End Crosstalk. Unwanted energy coupled from one circuit into another and appearing at the near end of the circuit.

Network. A collection of links and nodes that provides connections between two or more defined points to facilitate telecommunication between them.

Network Layer. The third layer of the OSI Reference Model that manages routing, flow control, and sequence numbering of messages that are transferred over a network connection.

Network Service Part. The combination of the Message Transfer Part and the Signaling Connection Control Part in Signaling System No. 7.

Network Termination. A functional group containing functions required for the physical or logical termination of a network on the user-to-network interface.

Node. A network device where one or more transmission circuits terminate or where functional units are connected to transmission circuits.

Open Systems Interconnection. A reference model providing the framework for the development of protocols that enable any OSI-compatible devices to communicate with each other.

Operation, Maintenance, and Administration Part. The application layer entity dedicated to the communications aspects of operations, maintenance, and administration of the Signaling System No. 7.

Packet Handler. A function logically belonging to the ISDN that supports layer 2 and 3 X.25 packet handling procedures between itself and an X.25 DTE.

Packet Switching. A method of transmission in which small blocks of data called packets traverse in a store-and-forward method from source to destination through the

intermediate nodes of the communications network and in which the resources of the network are shared among many users.

Peer Entities. Entities in the same layer but in different systems that must exchange information to achieve a common objective.

Physical Layer. The lowest layer in the OSI Model whose function is to provide a direct connection between neighboring nodes in a network.

Point-to-Point. A transmission circuit that connects two devices directly, without any intermediate devices.

Power Feeding. The provision of electrical power from a power source to a device over an interconnecting medium.

Presentation Layer. The sixth layer in the OSI Reference Model that is responsible for ensuring the proper syntax of the information being exchanged.

Primary Access. A type of user-to-network interface supporting combined data rates up to 2 Mbit/s.

Primary Rate Channel Structure. A composite communications capacity across the user-to-network interface of an ISDN consisting of a combination of B channels, H channels, and one 64-kbit/s D channel.

Private Automatic Branch Exchange. A switching system usually located on the customer premises for establishing connections between subscribers and public transmission facilities. Also used for on-premises switching and for enhanced communications services.

Propagation Delay. The time required for a signal to travel from one point to another over a transmission medium.

Protocol. A formal set of rules adopted by communicating entities to ensure communication between two or more functions within the same layer of the entities.

Protocol Reference Model. A framework for the hierarchical structuring of functions in a system and its interaction with another system.

Pulse Code Modulation. The conversion of an analog signal to digital form where the signal amplitude is sampled periodically, each amplitude is quantized into a finite number of levels, and each level is represented by a pattern of binary digits.

Rate Adaption. The change of the rate at which a device transmits or receives data to or from the rate required for the transmission of the data on the network.

Reference Configuration. An arrangement of functional groups and reference points.

Reference Point. A conceptual point of demarcation between two nonoverlapping groups of functions.

RS232-D. An EIA specification of the physical interface between a DTE and a DCE.

Scrambler. A device that creates a reversible transformation of a string of bits. Normally used to avoid the occurrence of long strings of 0s or 1s.

Service-Access Point. A point at which a layer provides services to its superior layer.

Service-Access-Point Identifier. Used to identify the service-access point.

Service Control Point. A type of signaling point that contains the network database.

Service Primitive. Abstract representation of an interaction between adjacent layers in a protocol reference model.

Service Switching Point. A type of signaling point that permits access to network internal database information.

Session Layer. The fifth layer in the OSI Reference Model that is responsible for managing and controlling the end-to-end dialogue between users.

Signaling. The exchange of information between network nodes or between network nodes and subscribers for the purpose of establishing and controlling connections and for management in a telecommunications network.

Signaling Connection Control Part. Additional functions to the MTP to handle both connectionless as well as connection-oriented network service and to achieve an OSI-compatible network service.

Signaling Link. A transmission circuit consisting of a signaling data link and its transfer control functions. Used for the reliable transfer of signaling messages.

Signaling Link Code. A field of the label in the signaling network management messages; it indicates the particular signaling link to which the message refers among those interconnecting the two involved signaling points.

Signaling Link Set. A set of one or more signaling links directly connecting two signaling points.

Signaling Point. A node in a signaling network that originates or receives signaling messages, transfers signaling messages from one signaling link to another, or performs both functions.

Signaling System. A set of protocols for the exchange of signaling information.

Signaling Transfer Point. A signaling point whose function is to transfer signaling messages from one signaling link to another.

Specification and Description Language. Standard language for the graphical description of the behavior of a process. Developed by the CCITT.

Stimulus Protocol. A mode of signaling in which a small number of simple signals are conveyed between terminal and network, with the meaning of the signals interpreted at the network with reference to a user profile.

Subscriber-Access Network. The total configuration of terminal equipment, subscriber-access

line, and exchange termination between the customer premises and the network.

Subscriber Loop. A transmission channel that connects the equipment on the customer premises to a local exchange of the interexchange network.

Supplementary Service. A telecommunications service that is supplementary to a basic bearer service or teleservice.

Synchronous Digital Hierarchy. A hierarchically structured set of digital transmission rates and multiplexing arrangements for use on broadband communications channels.

Synchronous Optical Network. Standard for a family of interfaces for use in optical networks.

Synchronous Transport Module. Synchronous time division multiplex frame structure for the combining of digital signals in broadband ISDN.

T1 Carrier. A digital transmission facility using time division multiplexing and operating at a transmission rate of 1544 kbit/s.

Teleservice. A type of telecommunications service that provides both bearer capabilities and higher-layer capabilities for communication between users.

Teletex. A worldwide switched message exchange service operating at higher speeds than Telex and that is intended to replace Telex.

Telex. Teleprinter Exchange: a worldwide switched information transmission service for the exchange of Baudot-coded messages.

Terminal Adapter. A conversion device that allows the attachment of non-ISDN-compatible user terminals to an ISDN interface.

Terminal Endpoint Identifier. An identifier used to specify a connection endpoint within a service-access point.

Terminal Equipment. A functional group that includes functions required for protocol handling, maintenance, interfacing, and connection to other equipment.

Time Compression Multiplexing. A method of providing full duplex data transmission over one channel by dividing the transmission time on the channel between the two directions and transferring data at twice its rate when the channel is available.

Transaction Capability. A set of functions that control the transfer of information between the nodes of a network via a signaling network.

Transaction Capabilities Application Part. Functions of the Signaling System No. 7 residing in the application layer that control information transfer between two or more nodes of the signaling network.

Transport Layer. The fourth layer of the OSI model responsible for the reliable transfer of messages between end-users. It provides sequence control, error control, flow control, and multiplexing features.

User Plane. The part of the ISDN protocol reference model that contains the protocols required for the exchange and control of user information.

User-Plane Entity. The conceptual intelligence in a device that controls the transfer of user information flows.

User-to-Network Interface. The point of demarcation between the terminal equipment and the network termination.

V.24/V.28. CCITT recommendations that specify a list of interchange circuits between a DTE and a DCE and the electrical characteristics of the circuits.

Videotex. An interactive data communications system for access to remote databases to retrieve text and graphic information. The information is typically displayed on subscriber video terminals.

Virtual Circuit. A communications path through a network established prior to information transfer, over which the resources are shared by multiple users.

X.21. A CCITT recommendation that specifies the interface between a DTE and a DCE for synchronous operation over public circuit switched data networks.

X.25. A CCITT recommendation that specifies the interface between a DTE and a DCE for operation in virtual circuit mode over a packet switched network.

LIST OF ACRONYMS AND ABBREVIATIONS

2B1Q	Two Binary One Quartenary Code
3PTY	Three-Party Service
ABM	Asynchronous Balanced Mode
ACM	Address Complete
AIS	Alarm Indication Signal
ANM	Answer
ANSI	American National Standards Institute
AOC	Advice of Charge
ASE	Application Service Element
ASP	Assignment Source Point
AT&T	American Telephone and Telegraph
ATM	Asynchronous Transfer Mode
AU	Access Unit
AWG	American Wire Gauge
B8ZS	Bipolar with 8-Zeros Substitution Code
BIB	Backward Indicator Bit
BISDN	Broadband Integrated Services Digital Network
BLA	Blocking Acknowledgment
BLO	Blocking
BSN	Backward Sequence Number
BT	Bridge Tap
CATM	Cell-Based Asynchronous Transfer Mode
CBA	Changeback Acknowledge
CBD	Changeback Declaration
CCBS	Completion of Call to Busy Subscriber
CCE	Connection Control Entity
CCITT	Consultative Committee for International Telephone and Telegraph
CCP	Connection Control Process
CCR	Continuity Check Request

CCSN	Common Channel Signaling Network
CD	Call Deflection
CE	Connection Element
CEI	Connection Endpoint Identifier
CEPT	European Conference of Posts and Telecommunications Administrations
CES	Connection Endpoint Suffix
CFB	Call Forwarding Busy
CFN	Confusion
CFNR	Call Forwarding No Reply
CFU	Call Forwarding Unconditional
CGB	Group Blocking
CGBA	Group Blocking Acknowledgment
CGQ	Circuit Group Query
CGU	Circuit Group Unblocking
CGUA	Circuit Group Unblocking Acknowledgment
CK	Check Bit
CLIP	Calling Line Identification Presentation
CLIR	Calling Line Identification Restriction
CMC	Call Modification Completed
CMR	Call Modification Request
CMRJ	Call Modification Reject
COA	Changeover Acknowledge
COLP	Connected Line Identification Presentation
COLR	Connected Line Identification Restriction
CON	Connect
CONF	Conference Calling
COO	Changeover Order
COT	Continuity
CPE	Customer-Premises Equipment
CPG	Call Progress
CPI	Customer-Premises Installation
CQR	Circuit Group Query Response
CRC	Cyclic Redundancy Check
CRED	Credit Card Calling
CRF	Connection Related Function
CSIEN	Circuit Switched Interexchange Network
CT	Call Transfer
CUG	Closed User Group
CW	Call Waiting
DCE	Data-Circuit Terminating Equipment
DDI	Direct Dialing In
DISC	Disconnect Frame
DL	Digital Link

DLCI	Data Link Connection Identifier
DM	Disconnect Mode
DPC	Destination Point Code
DS	Digital Section
DSS1	Digital Subscriber Signaling System No. 1
DTE	Data Terminal Equipment
DTS	Digital Transmission System
EA	Address Extension
ECMA	European Computer Manufacturers Association
ECSA	Exchange Carriers Standards Association
EOC	Embedded Operations Channel
ERP	External Reference Point
ET	Exchange Termination
ETSI	European Telecommunications Standards Institute
FAA	Facility Accepted
FAR	Facility Request
FATM	Frame-Based Asynchronous Transfer Mode
FCS	Frame Check Sequence
FEXT	Far-End Crosstalk
FIB	Forward Indicator Bit
FISU	Fill-in Signal Unit
FOT	Forward Transfer
FRJ	Facility Reject
FRMR	Frame Reject Frame
FSN	Forward Sequence Number
GFC	Generic Flow Control
GRA	Circuit Group Reset Acknowledgment
GRS	Circuit Group Reset
HD3B	High-Density Bipolar Code of Order 3
HDLC	High-Level Data Link Control
HDTV	High-Definition Television
HEC	Header Error Check
HOLD	Call Hold
IA5	International Alphabet No. 5
IAM	Initial Address
IE	Information Element
IEN	Interexchange Network
INF	Information
INR	Information Request
IRP	Internal Reference Point
ISDN	Integrated Services Digital Network
ISO	International Organization for Standardization
ISP	Intermediate Service Part
ISUP	ISDN User Part

ISW	Inverted Synchronization Word
ITUSA	Information Technology User's Standards Association
LAN	Local-Area Network
LAPD	Link Access Protocol D Channel
LET	Logical Exchange Termination
LH	Line Hunting
LI	Length Indicator
LME	Layer Management Entity
LSSU	Link Status Signal Unit
LT	Line Termination
MAC	Medium-Access Control
MAMI	Modified Alternate Mark Invert
MCI	Malicious Call Identification
MMS43	Modified Monitoring State 4B3T Code
MSN	Multiple Subscriber Number
MSU	Message Signal Unit
MTP	Message Transfer Part
NEXT	Near-End Crosstalk
NIST	National Institute of Standards and Technology
NIUF	North American ISDN Users' Forum
NSDU	Network Service Data Unit
NSP	Network Service Part
NT	Network Termination
OMAP	Operations Maintenance and Administration Part
OPC	Originating Point Code
OSI	Open Systems Interconnection
PABX	Private Automatic Branch Exchange
PAM	Pass-along
PCM	Pulse Code Modulation
PH	Packet Handler
PMF	Plane Management Function
PNP	Private Numbering Plan
PO	Processor Outage
PSIEN	Packet Switched Interexchange Network
PT	Packet Type
RAI	Remote Alarm Indication
RBOC	Regional Bell Operating Company
RC	Retransmission Counter
RDTD	Restricted Differential Time Delay
REJ	Reject
REL	Release
RES	Resume
REV	Reverse Charging
RLC	Release Complete

RNR	Receive Not Ready
RR	Receive Ready
RSC	Reset Circuit
RST	Route Set Test
SABME	Set Asynchronous Balance Mode Extended
SAM	Subsequent Address
SAN	Subscriber-Access Network
SAP	Service-Access Point
SAPI	Service-Access-Point Identifier
SCCP	Signaling Connection Control Part
SCLC	SCCP Connectionless Control
SCMG	SCCP Management Control
SCOC	SCCP Connection-Oriented Control
SCP	Service Control Point
SCRC	SCCP Routing Control
SDH	Synchronous Digital Hierarchy
SDL	Specification and Description Language
SF	Status Field
SI	Signals and Indications
SIF	Signaling Information Field
SIO	Service Information Octet
SLS	Signaling Link Selection
SMAE	System Management Application Entity
SMAP	System Management Application Process
SOH	Section Overhead
SONET	Synchronous Optical Network
SP	Signaling Point
SS#7	Signaling System No. 7
SSN	Subsystem Number
SSP	Service Switching Point
STM	Synchronous Transfer Mode
STM-N	Synchronous Transport Module Level N
STP	Signaling Transfer Point
SU	Signaling Unit
SUB	Subaddressing
SUS	Suspend
SW	Synchronization Word
TA	Terminal Adapter
TC	Transaction Capability
TCAP	Transactions Capabilities Application Part
TCM	Time Compression Multiplexing
TE	Terminal Equipment
TEI	Terminal Endpoint Identifier
TFA	Transfer Allowed

TFC	Transfer Controlled
TFP	Transfer Prohibited
UA	Unnumbered Acknowledgment
UBA	Unblocking Acknowledgment
UBL	Unblocking
UI	Unnumbered Information
UNI	User-to-Network Interface
USE	User-to-User Signaling Entity
USP	User-to-User Signaling Process
USR	User-to-User Information
UTE	User Information Transfer Entity
UTP	User Information Transfer Process
UUS	User-to-User Signaling
VCI	Virtual Channel Identifier
VPI	Virtual Path Identifier
XID	Exchange Identification

REFERENCES

ADAM83   Adams, P. F., and Cox, S. A. "Line Coding and Intersymbol Interference in Local Network Transmission Systems," *Int. J. Electron.*, vol. 55, no. 1, pp. 171–181, 1983.

ADAM84   Adams, P. F., Cox, S. A., and Glen, P. J. "Long Reach Duplex Transmission Systems for ISDN Access," *British Telecom Tech. J.*, vol. 2, no. 2, p. 35, Apr. 1984.

AGAZ82a   Agazzi, O., Hodges, D. A., and Messerschmitt, D. G. "Large-Scale Integration of Hybrid Method Digital Subscriber Loops," *IEEE Trans. Commun.*, vol. COM-30, pp. 2095–2108, Sept. 1982.

AGAZ82b   Agazzi, O., Messerschmitt, D. G., and Hodges, D. A. "Nonlinear Echo Cancellation of Data Signals," *IEEE Trans. Commun.*, vol. COM-30, pp. 2421–2433, Nov. 1982.

AGAZ85   Agazzi, O., Tzeng, C.-P. J., Messerschmitt, D. G., and Hodges, D. A. "Timing Recovery in Digital Subscriber Loops," *IEEE Trans. Commun.*, vol. COM-33, pp. 558–569, June 1985.

AHAM82   Ahamed, S. V. "Simulation and Design Studies of Digital Subscriber Lines," *Bell Syst. Tech. J.*, vol. 61, pp. 1003–1078, July-Aug. 1982.

AHAM81   Ahamed, S. V., Bohn, P. P., and Gottfried, N. L. "A Tutorial on Two-Wire Digital Transmission in the Loop Plant," *IEEE Trans. Commun.*, vol. COM-29, pp. 1554–1564, Nov. 1981.

AIHA83   Aihara, K., Kikuchu, K., and Yamaguchi, H. "Multiple Bit-Rate Synchronous Terminals Towards ISDN," *IEEE Commun. Mag.*, Aug. 1983.

ALLE89   Allen, R. E. "The Effects of Regulatory Policy on the International Telecommunications Market," *IEEE Commun. Mag.*, pp. 26–28, Jan. 1989.

430

AMIN89   Amin-Salehi, B., and Spears, D. R. "Support of Transport Services in BISDN," *Proc. IEEE GLOBECOM,* Nov. 1989.

ANDR80   Andry, J. P., and Sire, A. "A Long Burst Time-Shared Digital Transmission System for Subscriber Loops," *ISSLS '80 Proc.,* pp. 31–35, 1980.

APPE86   Appenzeller, H. R. "Signaling System No. 7 User Part," *IEEE J. Select. Areas in Commun.,* vol. SAC-4, pp. 366–371, May 1986.

ARMB86   Armbruester, H. "Applications of Future Broad-Band Services in the Office and Home," *IEEE J. Select. Areas in Commun.,* vol. SAC-4, pp. 429–437, July 1986.

ARMB87   Armbruester, H., and Arndt, G. "Broadband Communication and Its Realization with Broadband ISDN," *IEEE Commun. Mag.,* pp. 8–19, Nov. 1987.

ARNO82   Arnon, E., Munter, E. A., Patel, S. C., Roddick, P. A., and Willcock, P. W. H. "Customer Access System Design," *IEEE Trans Commun.,* vol. COM-30, pp. 2143–2149, Sept. 1982.

ASHR80   Ashrafi, D. I., Bostelmann, G., and Szechenyi, K. "Results of Experiments with a Digital Hybrid in Two Wire Digital Subscriber Loops," *Proc. ISSLS '80,* pp. 21–25, Sept. 1980.

ASHR82   Ashrafi, D. I., Meschkat, P., and Szechenyi, K. "Field Trial of a Comparison of Time Separation, Echo Cancellation, and Four-Wire Digital Subscriber Loops," *Proc. Int. Symp. Subscriber Loops, Services,* Sept. 1982.

ASAT82   Asatani, K., Watanabe, R., Nosu, K., Matsumoto, T. and Nihei, F. "A Field Trial of Fiber Optic Subscriber Loop Systems Utilizing Wavelength-Division Multiplexers," IEEE Trans. Commun., vol. COM-30, pp. 2172–2184, Sept. 1982.

ATT 84   AT&T. "Requirements for Interfacing Digital Terminal Equipment to Services Employing the Extended Superframe Format," *AT&T Communications Technical Reference,* PUB 54016, Oct. 1984.

ATT 85a   AT&T. "5ESS Switch ISDN Basic Rate Interface Specification," AT&T 5D5-900-301, Sept. 1985.

ATT 85b   AT&T. "5ESS Switch ISDN Primary Rate Interface Specification," AT&T 5D5-900-302, Oct. 1985.

ATT 86   AT&T. "Integrated Services Digital Network Primary Rate Interface Specification," Technical Reference Pub. 41449, Mar. 1986.

BACH85   Bachus, E. J., Braun, R. P., Eutin, W., Foisel, H., Grossmann, E., Heimes, K., and Strebel, B. "Coherent

Optical-Fibre Subscriber Line," *Electron. Lett.*, vol. 21, no. 25/26, pp. 1203–1205, 1985.

BALL89   Ballart, R., and Ching, Y.-C. "SONET: Now It's the Standard Optical Network," *IEEE Commun. Mag.*, pp. 8–15, Mar. 1989.

BECK81   Becker, D., Gasser, L., and Kaderali, F. "Digital Subscriber Loops: Concept, Realization, and Field Experience of Digital Customer Access," *ISS 81*, 1981.

BELF79   Belfiore, C. A., and Park, J. H., Jr. "Decision Feedback Equalization," *Proc. IEEE*, vol. 67, pp. 1143–1156, Aug. 1979.

BELI89   Belina, F., and Hogrefe, D. "The CCITT-Specification and Description Language SDL," *Computer Networks and ISDN Systems*, vol. 16, pp. 311–341, 1988/89.

BELL71   Bell Telephone Laboratories, "Transmission Systems for Communications," Dec. 1971.

BELL82   Bellamy, J. *Digital Telephony*, Wiley, New York, 1982.

BENA85   Benaouda, A., Kells, J. E., and Mettler, F. W. "The Evolution of the AT&T Communications CCS Network to a New STP and the CCITT Signaling System No. 7 Protocol," *GLOBECOM '85 Conf. Rec.*, vol. 1, pp. 307–311.

BHUS83   Bhusri, G. "Optimum Implementation Common Channel Signalling in Local Networks," *Proc. IEEE INFOCOM 83*, 1983.

BHUS84   Bhusri, G. "Considerations for ISDN Planning and Implementation," *IEEE Commun. Mag.*, pp. 18–32, Jan. 1984.

BOCK88   Bocker, P. *ISDN—The Integrated Services Digital Network*, Springer-Verlag, Berlin, 1988.

BOLL83   Bollen, R. E., Prabhu, R. P., and Kopec, S. J. "1982 GTE Outside Plant Survey—An Analysis of the Physical and Transmission Characteristics," TN 83-302.1, GTE Laboratories, Inc., Waltham, MA, Mar. 1983.

BOSI80   Bosik, B. S. "The Case in Favor of Burst-Mode Transmission for Digital Subscriber Loops," *Proc. ISSLS '80*, pp. 26–30, Sept. 1980.

BOSI82   Bosik, B. S., and Kartalopoulos, S. "A Time Compression Multiplexing System for a Circuit Switched Digital Capability," *IEEE Trans. Commun.*, vol. COM-30, pp. 2042–2046, Sept. 1982.

BOSI84   Bosik, B. S. "Time-Compression Multiplexing: Squeezing Digits Through Loops," *Telephony*, May 21, 1984.

BOWM78   Bowman, D. F., and J. Tritton. "Studies for a Subscriber's

Digital Telephone Terminal," *1978 Zurich Sem. Proc.*, Zurich, Switzerland, pp. D3.1–D3.5, 1978.

BRAD85   Brady, P. T. "Performance of LAPD Protocol with Link Errors and Propagation Delay," *Proc. IEEE Int. Conf. Commun.*, Chicago, June 1985.

BROS81   Brosio, A., and others. "A Comparison of Digital Subscriber Line Transmission Systems Employing Different Line Codes," *IEEE Trans. Commun.*, vol. COM-29, pp. 1581–1588, Nov. 1981.

BROS85   Brosio, A., Mogavero, C., and Tofanelli, A. "Echo Canceler Burst Mode: A New Technique for Digital Transmission on Subscriber Lines," *Proc. IEEE Int. Conf. Commun.*, June 1985.

BURM85   Burmeister, W. "Telephone Operating Company Loop and Exchange Network Technology," *Telephony*, Feb. 1985.

BYRN82   Byrne, T. P., Coburn, R., Mazzoni, H. C., Aughenbaugh, G. W., and Duffany, J. L. "Positioning the Subscriber Loop Network for Digital Services," *IEEE Trans. Commun.*, vol. COM-30, pp. 2006–2011, Sept. 1982.

BYRN89   Byrne, W. R., Kilm, T. A., Nelson, B. L., and Soneru, M.D. "Broadband ISDN Technology and Architecture," *IEEE Network*, pp. 23–28, Jan. 1989.

CARE89   Carey, J. "Consumer Adoption of New Communication Technologies," *IEEE Commun. Mag.*, pp. 28–32, Aug. 1989.

CARI74   Cariolaro, G. L., and Tronca, G. P. "Spectra of Block Coded Digital Signals," *IEEE Trans. Commun.*, vol. COM-22, pp. 1535–1563, Oct. 1974.

CARN85   Carney, D. L., Cochrane, J. I., Gitten, L. J., Prell, E. M., and Staehler, R. "The 5ESS Switching System Architectural Overview," *AT&T Tech. J.*, vol. 64, no. 6, part 2, pp. 1339–1356, July-Aug. 1985.

CASO85   Casoria, A. "Interconnections and Services Integration in Public and Private Networks for Office Automation," *Proc. IEEE INFOCOM 85*, 1985.

CATA84   Catania, B. "Integrated Broadband Communication (IBC): A Total Concept for Europe," *PROC. GLOBECOM '84*, Nov. 26–29, 1984, pp. 18.2.1–18.2.5, Nov. 1984.

CERN85   Cerni, D. M. "The United States Organization for the CCITT," *IEEE Commun. Mag.*, pp. 38–42, Jan. 1985.

CHEN89   Chen, K.-J., Ho, K. K. Y., and Saksena, V. R. "Analysis and Design of a Highly Reliable Transport Architecture for ISDN Frame Relay Networks," *IEEE J. Select. Areas in Commun.,* vol. SAC-7, pp. 1231–1242, Oct. 1989.

CHUJ84   Chujo, T., Ueno, N., Takada, A., Hino, Y., and Fukuda, M. "A Line Termination Circuit for Burst-Mode Digital Subscriber Loop Transmission," *Proc. IEEE GLOBECOM,* Nov. 1984.

CLAA81   Claase, T. A. C. M., and Mecklenbrauker, W. F. G. "Comparison of the Convergence of Two Algorithms for Adaptive FIR Digital Filters," *IEEE Trans. Acoust., Speech, and Signal Processing,* vol. ASSP-29, pp. 670–678, June 1981.

COHE81   Cohen, L. G., Mammel, W. L., Stone, J., and Pearson, A. D. "Transmission Studies of A Long Single-Mode Fiber-Measurements and Considerations for Bandwidth Optimization," *Bell Syst. Tech. J.,* vol. 60, pp. 1713–1725, Oct. 1981.

CORN81   Cornell, R. G., and Stelte, D. J. "Progress Towards Digital Subscriber Line Services and Signaling," *IEEE Trans. Commun.,* vol. COM-29, pp. 1589–1594, Nov. 1981.

COX 85   Cox, S. P., and Adams, P. F. "An Analysis of Digital Transmission Techniques for the Local Network," *British Telecom. Tech. J.,* vol. 3, July 1985.

CRAM81   Cramer, B., and Winterbotham, H. "Terminals for New Services," *Electrical Communication,* no. 1, 1981.

CRAW85   Crawford, K. E., Miller, P. R., and Snare, R. C. "The AT&T No. 2 Signal Transfer Point Design and Service Introduction in the AT&T Communications Common Channel Signaling Network," *GLOBECOM '85 Conf. Rec.,* vol. 1, pp. 302–306.

DECI82   Decina, M. "Progress Towards User Access Arrangements in Integrated Services Digital Networks," *IEEE Trans. Commun.,* vol. COM-30, pp. 2117–2130, Sept. 1982.

DOMA88   Domann, G. H. "B-ISDN," *Journal of Lightwave Technology,* vol. 6, no. 11, pp. 1720–1727, Nov. 1988.

DONO86   Donohoe, D. C., Johannessen, G. H., and Stone, R. E. "Realization of a Signaling System No. 7 Network for AT&T," *IEEE J. Select. Areas in Commun.,* vol. SAC-4, pp. 1257–1261, Nov. 1986.

DUC 85   Duc, N. Q., and Chew, E. K. "ISDN Protocol Architecture," *IEEE Comm. Mag.,* pp. 15–22, Mar. 1985.

DUNN89   Dunn, D. A., and Johnson, M. G. "Demand for Data Communications," *IEEE Network,* pp. 8–12, May 1989.

DUTT78   Duttweiler, D. L. "A Twelve-Channel Digital Echo Canceler," *IEEE Trans. Commun.*, vol. COM-26, pp. 647–653, May 1978.

EBER84   Ebert, I. "The Evolution of Integrated Access Towards the ISDN," *IEEE Commun. Mag.*, pp. 6–11, Apr. 1984.

EVEN79   Even, R. K., McDonald, R. A., and Seidel, H. "Digital Transmission Capability of the Loop Plant," *Conf. Rec. 1979 Int. Conf. Commun.*, June 1979.

FALC82   Falconer, D. D. "Adaptive Reference Echo Cancellation," *IEEE Trans. Commun.*, vol. COM-30, pp. 2083–2094, Sept. 1982.

FALC85a   Falconer, D. D. "Timer Jitter Effects on Digital Subscriber Loop Echo Cancelers: Part I—Analysis of the Effect," *IEEE Trans. Commun.*, vol. COM-33, pp. 826–832, Aug. 1985.

FALC85b   Falconer, D. D. "Timing Jitter Effects on Digital Subscriber Loop Echo Cancelers: Part II—Considerations for Squaring Loop Timing Recovery," *IEEE Trans. Commun.*, vol. COM-33, pp. 833–838, Aug. 1985.

FALC79   Falconer, D. D., and Mueller, K. H. "Adaptive Echo Cancellation AGC Structures for Two-Wire, Full Duplex Data Transmission," *Bell Syst. Tech. J.*, vol. 58, pp. 1593–1616, Sept. 1979.

FUKU85   Fukuda, M., Tsuda, T., and Murano, K. "Digital Subscriber Loop Transmission Using Echo Canceler and Balancing Networks," *Proc. IEEE Int. Conf. Commun.*, June 1985.

GASS85   Gasser, L. "Transmission at 144 kbit/s on Digital Subscriber Loops," *Elec. Commun.*, vol. 59, no. 1/2, pp. 127–131, 1985.

GECH89   Gechter, J., and O'Reilly, P. "Conceptual Issues for ATM," *IEEE Network*, pp. 14–16, Jan. 1989.

GEES89   Geeslin, B. M. "Funding the Future Telecommunications Infrastructure," *IEEE Commun. Mag.*, pp. 24–27, Aug. 1989.

GIES84   Giesken, K. "ISDN Features Require New Capabilities in Digital Switching Systems," *J. Telecommun. Networks*, spring 1984.

GIFF86   Gifford, W. S. "ISDN User-Network Interfaces," *IEEE J. Select. Areas in Commun.*, vol. SAC-4, pp. 343–348, May 1986.

GITL75   Gitlin, R. D., and Hayes, J. F. "Timing Recovery and Scramblers in Data Transmission," *Bell Syst. Tech. J.*, vol. 54, pp. 569–593, Mar. 1975.

GITM78   Gitman, I., and others. "Economic Analysis of Integrated

Voice and Data Networks: A Case Study," *IEEE Trans. Commun.*, pp. 1549–1570, Nov. 1978.

GRIF82   Griffiths, J. "ISDN Network Terminating Equipment," *IEEE Trans. Commun.*, vol. COM-30, pp. 2137–2142, Sept. 1982.

GRIT84   Gritton, C. W. K., and Lin, D. W. "Echo Cancellation Algorithms," *IEEE ASSP Mag.*, pp. 30–37, Apr. 1984.

GRUB83   Gruber, J., and Le, N. "Performance Requirements for Integrated Voice/Data Networks," *IEEE J. Select. Areas in Commun.*, vol. SAC-1, pp. 981–1005, Dec. 1983.

HAEN89   Haendel, R. "Evolution of ISDN Towards Broadband ISDN," *IEEE Network*, pp. 7–13, Jan. 1989.

HALS88   Halsall, F. *Data Communications, Computer Networks, and OSI*, Addison-Wesley, Reading, MA, 1988.

HARM89   Harman, W. H., and Newman, C. F. "ISDN Protocols for Connection Control," *IEEE J. Select. Areas in Commun.*, vol. 7, pp. 1034–1042, Sept. 1989.

HEIS87   Heisey, R. E. "Basics of Common Channel Signaling," *Proc. Nat. Commun. Forum*, vol. 41, no. 1, pp. 562–566, Sept. 1987.

HIRS70   Hirsch, D., and Wolf, W. J. "A Simple Adaptive Equalizer for Efficient Data Transmission," *IEEE Trans. Commun.*, vol. COM-18, pp. 5–12, Feb. 1970.

HOLT81   Holte, N., and Stueflotten, S. "A New Digital Echo Canceler for Two-Wire Subscriber Lines," *IEEE Trans. Commun.*, vol. COM-29, pp. 1573–1581, Nov. 1981.

HUI89   Hui, J. Y. "Network, Transport, and Switching Integration for Broadband Communications," *IEEE Network*, pp. 40–51, Mar. 1989.

HUMM85   Hummel, E. "The CCITT," *IEEE Commun. Mag.*, pp. 8–11, Jan. 1985.

IFFL89   Iffland, F. C., Norton, G. D., and Waxman, J. M. "ISDN Applications: Their Identification and Development," *IEEE Network*, pp. 6–11, Sept. 1989.

INOU81   Inoue, N., Komiya, R., and Inoue, Y. "Time-Shared Two-Wire Digital Subscriber Transmission System and Its Application to the Digital Telephone Set," *IEEE Trans. Commun.*, vol. COM-29, pp. 1564–1572, Nov. 1981.

ISHI89a   Ishii, H. "ISDN User-Network Interface Management Protocol," *IEEE Network*, pp. 12–16, Sept. 1989.

ISHI89b   Ishii, H., and Kawarasaki, M. "B-ISDN Signalling Protocol Capabilities," *Proc. IEEE GLOBECOM*, Nov. 1989.

JENS80   Jenssen, B., Justness, B., and Stueflotten, S. "New Line Code for Digital Subscriber Loop," *Electron. Lett.*, vol. 16, pp. 847–849, Oct. 1980.

JULI86   Julio, U. de, and Pellegrini, J. "Layer 1 ISDN Recommendations," *IEEE J. Select. Areas in Commun.*, vol. SAC-4, pp. 349–354, May 1986.

KADE81   Kaderali, F., and Weston, J. "Digital Subscriber Loops," *Electrical Commun.*, no. 1, 1981.

KAHL86a   Kahl, P. *ISDN—The Future Telecommunication Network of the Deutsche Bundespost*, R. v. Decker's Verlag G. Schenck, Heidelberg, 1986.

KAHL86b   Kahl, P. "A Review of CCITT Standardization to Date," *IEEE J. Select. Areas in Commun.*, vol. SAC-4, pp. 326–333, May 1986.

KANE83   Kanemasa, A., and Niwa, K. "An Echo Cancellation Algorithm for Full-Duplex Two-Wire Data Transmission," *Proc. Global Telecommun. Conf.*, San Diego, CA, Dec. 1983.

KANE86   Kanemasa, A., Sugiyama, A., Koike, S., and Koyama, T. "An ISDN Subscriber Loop Transmission System Based on Echo Cancellation," *IEEE J. Select. Areas in Commun.*, vol. SAC-4, pp. 1359–1366, Nov. 1986.

KANO86   Kano, S. "Layers 2 and 3 ISDN Recommendations," *IEEE J. Select. Areas in Commun.*, vol. SAC-4, pp. 355–359, May 1986.

KELL83   Kelly, B. "The ISDN and Divestiture," *Telecommunications*, Dec. 1983.

KIMU80   Kimura, T. "Single-Mode Digital Transmission Technology," *Proc. IEEE*, vol. 68, no. 10, pp. 1263–1268, Oct. 1980.

KOLL73   Koll, V. G., and Weinstein, S. B. "Simultaneous Two-Way Data Transmission over a Two-Wire Circuit," *IEEE Trans. Commun.*, vol. COM-21, pp. 143–147, Feb. 1973.

LASS89   Lassers, H. "ISDN Terminal Portability in the RBOC Networks," *IEEE Network*, pp. 44–48, Sept. 1989.

LECH89   Lechleider, J. W. "Line Codes for Digital Subscriber Lines," *IEEE Comm. Mag.*, pp. 25–32, Sept. 1989.

LEGU80   LeGuillou, J. A., Pernin, J. L., and Schwartz, A. J. "Electronic Systems and Equipment for Evolving Loop Plant," *IEEE Trans. Commun.*, vol. COM-28, pp. 962–975, July 1980.

LIFC85   Lifchus, I. M. "Standards Committee T1—Telecommunications," *IEEE Commun. Mag.*, pp. 34–37, Jan. 1985.

LIN 89   Lin, Y.-K. M., Spears, D. R., and Yin, M. "Fiber-Based Local Access Network Architectures," *IEEE Comm. Mag.*, pp. 64–73, Oct. 1989.

LOHS85 Lohse, E. "The Role of the ISO in Telecommunications and Information Systems Standardization," *IEEE Commun. Mag.*, pp. 18–24, Jan. 1985.

LONG78 Long, N. G. "Loop Plant Modeling: Overview," *Bell Syst. Tech. J.*, Apr. 1978.

LUET86 Luetchford, J. C. "CCITT Recommendations-Network Aspects of the ISDN," *IEEE J. Select. Areas in Commun.*, vol. SAC-4, pp. 334–342, May 1986.

MAIT84 Maitre, X., Levy, M., and Surie, S. "The Multi-Memory Echo Canceller for Two Wire Digital Transmission," *Proc. IEEE GLOBECOM*, Dec. 1984.

MANH78 Manhire, L. M. "Physical and Transmission Characteristics of Customer Loop Plant," *Bell Syst. Tech. J.*, vol. 57, pp. 35–59, Jan. 1978.

MCDO89 McDonald, J. C. "The Regulatory Challenge of Broadband Technologies," *IEEE Commun. Mag.*, pp. 71–74, Jan. 1989.

MELI86 Melindo, F., and Valbonesi, G. "Network and System Architecture: The Integrated Approach to ISDN in the UT Line," *IEEE J. Select. Areas in Commun.*, vol. SAC-4, pp. 1251–1256, Nov. 1986.

MESS84a Messerschmitt, D. G. "Echo Cancellation for Voice and Data Transmission," *IEEE Trans. Commun.*, vol. COM-32, Feb. 1984.

MESS84b Messerschmitt, D. G. "Echo Cancellation in Speech and Data Transmission," *IEEE J. Select. Areas in Commun.*, vol. SAC-2, pp. 283–297, Mar. 1984.

MESS86 Messerschmitt, D. G. "Design Issues in the ISDN U-Interface Transceiver," *IEEE J. Select. Areas in Commun.*, vol. SAC-4, pp. 1281–1293, Nov. 1986.

MINZ89 Minzer, S. E. "Broadband ISDN and Asynchronous Transfer Mode (ATM)," *IEEE Commun. Mag.*, pp. 17–24, Sept. 1989.

MODE86 Modestino, J. W., Massey, C. S., Bollen, R. E., and Prabhu, R. P. "Modeling and Analysis of Error Probability Performance for Digital Transmission over the Two-Wire Loop Plant," *IEEE J. Select. Areas in Commun.*, vol. SAC-4, pp. 1317–1330, Nov. 1986.

MUEL76 Mueller, K. H. "A New Digital Echo Canceler for Two-Wire Full-Duplex Transmission," *IEEE Trans. Commun.*, vol. COM-24, pp. 956–962, Sept. 1976.

OGIW82 Ogiwara, H., and Terada, Y. "Design Philosophy and Hardware Implementation for Digital Subscriber Loops," *IEEE Trans. Commun.*, vol COM-30, pp. 2057–2065, Sept. 1982.

PEAR89   Pearce, A. "The Role of Government Policymakers," *IEEE Commun. Mag.,* pp. 77–80, Jan. 1989.

PHEL86   Phelan, J. "Signaling System 7," *Telecommunications,* Sept. 1986.

POTT85   Potter, R. "ISDN Protocol and Architecture Models," *Computer Networks and ISDN Systems,* vol. 10, 1985.

PUNS87   Punsch, H. "Aspects of CCS 7 Network Configurations," *Telecommunications,* pp. 240–251, Oct. 1987.

RIDE89   Rider, M. J. "Protocols for ATM Access Networks," *IEEE Network,* pp. 17–22, Jan. 1989.

ROBI84   Robin, G. "Customer Installations for the ISDN," *IEEE Commun. Mag.,* pp. 18–23, Apr. 1984.

RONA88   Ronayne, J. *The Integrated Services Digital Network: From Concept to Application,* Pitman/Wiley, London, 1988.

ROTH84   Rothamel, H. J. "Videotex and the Integrated Services Digital Network (ISDN)," *Proc. IEEE Intern. Conf. on Commun.,* vol. 2, 1984.

RUMS86   Rumsey, D. C. "Support of Existing Data Interfaces by the ISDN," *IEEE J. Select. Areas in Commun.,* vol. SAC-4, pp. 372–375, May 1986.

RUTK85   Rutkowski, A. *Integrated Services Digital Networks,* Artech House, Dedham, MA, 1985.

RUTK82   Rutkowski, A., and Marcus, M. "The Integrated Services Digital Network: Developments and Regulatory Issues," *Computer Commun. Rev.,* July/Oct. 1982.

SAIL85   Sailer, H., Schenk, H., and Schmid, E. "A VLSI Transceiver for the ISDN Customer Access," *Proc. IEEE Int. Conf. Commun.,* Chicago, June 1985.

SAST84   Sastry, A. "Performance Objectives for ISDNs," *IEEE Commun. Mag.,* pp. 49–55, Jan. 1984.

SCHL86   Schlanger, G. G. "An Overview of Signaling System No. 7," *IEEE J. Select. Areas in Commun.,* vol. SAC-4, pp. 360–365, May 1986.

SLAT81   Slatter, R., Walsh, W., Kaderali, F., and Schmidt, P. "Customer Access to Integrated Services Digital Networks," *Electrical Commun.,* no. 1, 1981.

SOEJ82   Soejima, T., Tsuda, T., and Ogiwara, H. "Experimental Bidirectional Subscriber Loop Transmission System," *IEEE Trans. Commun.,* vol. COM-30, pp. 2066–2073, Sept. 1982.

STAL89   Stallings, W. *ISDN: An Introduction,* Macmillan, New York, 1985.

STEP89   Stephenson, R. W., and McGaw, S. A. "Southwestern Bell Telephone's ISDN Experience," *IEEE Network,* pp. 25–36, Sept. 1989.

STIN88   Stine, L. L. "Why are ISDN Standards Important?", *IEEE Commun. Mag.*, pp. 13–15, Aug. 1988.

SUZU82   Suzuki, T., Takatori, H., Ogawa, M., and Tomooka, K. "Line Equalizer for a Digital Subscriber Loop Employing Switched Capacitor Technology," *IEEE Trans. Commun.*, vol. COM-30, pp. 2074–2082, Sept. 1982.

SZEC86   Szechenyi, K., Zapf, F., and Sallaerts, D. "Integrated, Full-Digital U-Interface Circuit for ISDN Subscriber Loops," *IEEE J. Select. Areas in Commun.*, vol. SAC-4, pp. 1337–1349, Nov. 1986.

TOUT85   Toutan, M. "CEPT Recommendations," *IEEE Commun. Mag.*, pp. 28–30, Jan. 1985.

TZEN86   Tzeng, C.-P. J., Hodges, D. A., and Messerschmitt, D. G. "Timing Recovery in Digital Subscriber Loops Using Baud Rate Sampling," *IEEE J. Select. Areas in Commun.*, vol. SAC-4, pp. 1302–1311, Nov. 1986.

VANG84   Van Gerwen, P. J., Verhoeckx, N. A. M., and Claasen, T. A. C. M. "Design Considerations for 144 kbit/s Digital Transmission Unit for the Local Telephone Network," *IEEE J. Select. Areas in Commun.*, vol. SAC-2, pp. 314–323, Mar. 1984.

VEA 84   Vea, M. "Moving Toward CCITT No. 7 Common Channel Signaling," *Telephony*, July 9, 1984.

VERH79   Verhoeckx, N. A. M., Van Der Elzen, H. C., Snijders, W. A. M., and Van Gerwen, P. J. "Digital Echo Cancellation for Baseband Data Transmission," *IEEE Trans. Acoust., Speech, and Signal Processing*, vol. ASSP-27, pp. 768–781, Dec. 1979.

VORS88   Vorstermans, J. P., and DeVleeschouwer, A. P. "Layered ATM Systems and Architectural Concepts for Subscribers' Premises Networks," *IEEE J. Select. Areas in Commun.*, vol. SAC-6, Dec. 1988.

WABE82   Waber, K. "Considerations on Customer Access to the ISDN," *IEEE Trans. Commun.*, vol. COM-30, pp. 2131–2136, Sept. 1982.

WALK86   Walker, M. G. "Get Inside CCITT Signaling System No. 7," Telephony, pp. 72–77, Mar. 1986.

WIEN84   Wienski, R. "Evolution to ISDN Within the Bell Operating Companies." *IEEE Commun. Mag.*, pp. 33–41, Jan. 1984.

WILL84   Williams, R., and Gillman, R. "ISDN Access Protocols—Status and Applications," *Proc. National Commun. Forum*, 1984.

WOLF87   Wolfson, J. R. "Computer III: The Beginning or the Beginning of the End for Enhanced Services Competition," *IEEE Commun. Mag.*, pp. 35–40, Aug. 1987.

YAJI85   Yajima, T., and others. "Digital Switching System Software for ISDN," *Proc. IEEE Int. Conf. Commun.*, June 1985.

YOSH85   Yoshida, K., and Tamaki, N. "Subscriber Loop Noise Considerations and the Estimated TCM Application Range," *Proc. IEEE Int. Conf. Commun.*, June 1985.

INDEX